September 2, 2011

D1235734

The Dark Ages of My Youth
and Times More Recent

From his weekly column,
"I Was Just Thinking,"
published in the
Zionsville (IN) Times Sentinel

Ward Degler

For Bob and Marge –
Who knew me long before
all of this.
Enjoy! Ward

iUniverse, Inc.
Bloomington

The Dark Ages of My Youth
and Times More Recent

Cover art and illustrations by the author.

iUniverse books may be ordered through booksellers or by contacting:

iUniverse
1663 Liberty Drive
Bloomington, IN 47403
www.iuniverse.com
1-800-Authors (1-800-288-4677)

ISBN: 978-1-4620-1998-4 (sc)
ISBN: 978-1-4620-2000-3 (hc)
ISBN: 978-1-4620-1999-1 (e)

Printed in the United States of America

iUniverse rev. date: 06/09/2011

This book of selected columns is dedicated to those who inspired them: the people I have met casually, those I've known for a lifetime, and some I have only heard about from someone else. It is also dedicated to every one of you who at one time or another stopped me on the street and told me you enjoyed reading what I had written.

Contents

Foreword xiii

Preface... xv

Acknowledgments xvii

Introduction xix

THE DARK AGES OF MY YOUTH

The Dark Ages of My Youth.. 3

Changes in My Hometown 5

Playing Marbles and Rolling Hoops 8

Saturday Matinees at the Princess Theater.......................10

When the Carnival Came to Town 12

Selling Scrap Metal..14

Neighbors Worth Remembering..17

Banana Nut Bread, Fudge, and Making Taffy.................. 20

Revisiting Big Rock 22

What the Heck Is a Skate Key?.. 25

Breakfast Never Changes... 28

Camping 30

Forest Fires 33

Lilacs—My Favorite Flower... 36

Remembering Charles Kuralt 39

Put the Brakes on Road Rage 41

Decoration Day 44

Firecrackers.. 46

Lawn Mowers 49

Dog Days 51

End of Summer 53

Canning 55

Labor Day—the Last Hurrah 57

Fountain Pens—They Sometimes Leaked 59

Buddy Poppies..61

Mom's Wash Day 63

Spring Cleaning—Grandma Style..................................... 66

Telephones—Yesterday and Today.................................... 68

Trains and the War Effort 70

Working My Way Up at the Greasy Spoon........................ 73

Summer Jobs 75

Libraries Were Like Monasteries.. 78
My Favorite Comic Strips...81
Salting a Bird's Tail and Other Tall Tales 84
That First Bike 86
Litter Bags—Where Have They Gone?................................... 89
Thinking About Cars...91
We Once Had Fans 94
Spring Break—Pioneering the Long Trip 97
I'm a Winner—So Was Mr. Duggan...................................... 99
Gasconade River..102
My Love Affair with Rivers 104
More River Thoughts...107
A Mute Wedding and Another I Survived 110
Once We Wore Galoshes 114
Snow Forts...116
Christmas Marches On 118
A Christmas Story 120
Making Peace with Winter 122
White Christmases I Remember...125
High School—Looking Back Fifty Years............................. 127

THE PROJECT

The Project...129
The Project Begins 131
I Have Created a Monster... 134
The Project Becomes a Teaching Tool 136
Learning by Swinging a Hammer...138
The Project Endures 140
I Learn About Wiring...142
The Roof Leaks 145
It Was Almost Like Escaping from Prison 148
Next Stop, the Sewer 151
The Greatest Invention—Ever..154
The Problem with Time 157
An Anniversary—of Sorts 160
How to Move a Mountain 163
Into the Crawl Space 166
The Shower Gets a Glass Wall...169
What's That Stuff, and What's It For? 172
The Studio Emerges—at Last...174
The Project Is Finished...176

PUPPY DOGS

Puppy Dogs 179
One-Dog Family 181
Another Second Dog 183
Doghouse 186
Raccoons, Dogs, and Cats 188
Trapping Raccoons 191
Trapping the Cat 193
Remembering Moosey 196
Brutie, Like Moosey 198
Choir Practice... 200
Brutie and the Squirrels 202
Checking Things Out with Brutie................................. 205
Jealous Cats 207
The Birds Are Back 210

PEOPLE

People 213
Remembering Sara 215
Grandpa 217
Barbara and Tim Conway 220
Teachers I Have Known 222
A Visit with Polly... 225
Barber Shop from the Past 228
Skinny-Dipping, Mr. Secretary? 231
Dad Saw an Ivorybill 234
Hoboes 236
Dickie Pope 238
Easter 241
Family Reunion.. 243
Charley Barnes Met Stan Musial 245
Gerry Mulligan and His Music 247
Habitat for Humanity—a Good Start 249
Helping Others... 251
Jack Underwood 253
Sometimes Cancer Wins... 256
Kristen's Sandbox 259
Out of Grief, a Book.. 261
John Krouse.. 263
Remembering Jackie.. 265

The Last World War I Pilot 268

Lucius Newsome 270

Lyman Porter 272

Mom 274

Dad at Eighty-Nine 276

Jumper Collins 279

Remembering Mr. Gault 283

Skydiving 285

Small-Town Obit 287

Walt Gelien 290

Lex Cralley's War Souvenir 292

The Unforgettable and Exasperating Bob Heisey 295

My Brother Dies 298

THE BOAT

The Boat 301

The Boat Begins 305

Describing Key West 308

The Boatyard 311

Stock Island 313

Working on the Boat 316

A New Gangplank 318

The Other Side of Key West 320

Key West Chicken Roundup 323

Chicken Roundup, Chapter Two 325

Getting Things Done on the Boat 327

The Bells are Tolling—Hurricane Katrina 330

Wilma! 332

Key West Recovers 334

Garbage Truck at Fort Jefferson 336

Rescue at Sea 339

A Funeral at the Water's Edge 341

One Final Trip to Key West 343

Farewell to Key West 345

THIS AND THAT

This and That 347

My Most Embarrassing Moment 349

Using the Blender 352

Looking for Grodies 355

Moving Pianos...357
Blowtorches and Cows 360
Lawn Mower Racing 363
Farm Sculpture...365
Winter Storms Didn't Bother Stepin Fetchit.................. 367
I Thought I Hated Winter...371
Considering the Horse...374
Lost Soybean Project 376
Beware of Promises Too Good to Be True 379
Cemetery of the Innocent—1995 381
Goodbye to Tavern on the Green 383
Navy Destroyer 387
Patrolling in Taiwan 389
Ditty Boppers at Kunia 392
Newport Revisited... 395
Remembering Pearl Harbor....................................... 398

FINAL THOUGHTS

Final Thoughts..401
Your Columnist Bids Farewell 403

Foreword

I've heard that it's a good idea to have someone famous write the Foreword to your book. It's supposed to help sell the book, I guess. Unfortunately, I don't know any famous people. I have long felt a kinship with Garrison Keillor. I used to listen to his daily radio show when he was a student at the University of Minnesota and I was trying my hand at raising beef cattle on a farm in the Valley of the Jolly Green Giant. A lot of what he talked about happening in Lake Wobegon was happening to me at the same time. I wrote him a letter and told him that. I also asked him if he would write a Foreword to my book. He didn't answer.

It occurred to me that I probably should ask someone who has been involved with my columns over the years, maybe someone I've written about, to write a Foreword. After all, he would be fairly well acquainted with the content of the book and could most likely give a fair accounting of what the reader might expect. He might even steer the reader to a section of the book or a special column that he found particularly redeeming. Plus, if he had a special ax to grind with me, this would be the ideal place to do it.

The more I thought about it, the more sense that made. So I asked My Friend the Boat Owner if he felt up to the task. The following is his response.

A Foreword by Kirk Forbes,
Author of
Love, Kristen

Life is an intriguing journey dotted with ups and downs, interesting people, and indelible memories—memories of things done and places seen in addition to new, exciting experiences. But most importantly, the journey teaches us that the true gift of life is found in the ways we touch the lives of others.

If your life is blessed, the chances are you will have crossed paths on your journey with someone who has had a profound impact on you. When you are around this person, you know there is something very special about him. For me that person is Ward Degler.

Ward has been a friend for several decades. We have shared many of life's experiences together, and that sharing has created a bond of friendship so strong as to be unbreakable. We have worked together, vacationed together, broken bread together, and even buried loved ones together. All of these experiences over the years became the glue that has bonded our friendship.

Ward's impact on my life has invariably left me in awe of the man: his steadfast faith no matter what life has thrown at him, his nautical knowledge, his journalistic talent, and his unwavering friendship. This book of Ward's experiences, his attitudes, and his dreams is not only delightfully entertaining but often profoundly thought-provoking.

If there is wisdom in age, then this book—a collection of his thoughts, written over nearly two decades—is proof of the statement. So, find a good chair and a cool drink because once you start reading Ward's words, you will find it hard to put the book down.

Kirk Forbes
Aboard Winsome
January 2011

Preface

I was always a daydreamer, and when I was about ten years old, a teacher suggested I write down what I was dreaming about. The result was a wildly fanciful tale about an invincible hero who saved the world from some unspecified disaster and then rode off into the sunset. While my teacher applauded my fruitful imagination, she pointed out that my spelling was atrocious and my grammar abysmal. Mercifully, that early essay got lost somewhere between school and home so it never came under the critical eye of either my mother, who insisted on serving up the English language properly, or my father, who thought I should be thinking about more practical matters than saving the world.

A seed had been planted, however, and I continued to write. Over time my grammar and spelling improved, which pleased my mother, and the things I wrote about drifted to more practical subjects, which pleased my father. When I earned my degree in journalism from the University of Missouri, both speculated that I would become a world-famous war correspondent or, at the very least, editor-in-chief of an influential newspaper. I did neither. Instead, I became a columnist, first for a small-town daily in Missouri and more recently for a small-town weekly in Indiana.

Writing columns seemed to suit me. It gave me an opportunity to write about stuff that interested me while avoiding everything that didn't. Plus, as a columnist, people expected me to go off on flights of fancy from time to time, and they usually forgave me for an occasional grammatical impropriety.

This was by no means a seamless journey. My track as a journalist was punctuated by numerous detours starting with two years as a combat medic in the army and four years as a junior officer in the navy. Later side trips included raising beef cattle on a farm in Minnesota and writing video scripts for a paper mill in Mississippi, a diesel engine manufacturer in Central Indiana, a chemical company in Chicago, and a furniture maker in Pennsylvania. I also wrote news releases, marketing plans, and advertising copy for a dozen different venues. Although I didn't know it at the time, each of these endeavors would contribute to the columns I would one day write.

Acknowledgments

Many people have helped me assemble this book, and I owe each of them a sincere word of thanks. A complete list is impossible, but here are the most obvious. To start with, Mary Lee Koppelman, a friend who introduced me to Paula Endress, at that time editor and owner of the *Zionsville (IN) Times Sentinel*. Paula invited me to start writing a weekly column five minutes after we met. Subsequent editors include Greta Sanderson, Scott Slade, Brooke Baker, Jennifer Dawson, Andrea Hirsch Cline, and a quiet, gentle woman whose name I have forgotten but whom I affectionately called "Bogie." They read through more than eight hundred of my columns over the years, quietly straightened a misplaced phrase or two in many of them, caught several hundred misspellings, and corrected factual errors beyond number.

Then there are all the friends and acquaintances who encouraged me to do the book in the first place and who steadfastly promised they would read it once it was published; my publisher, who never complained when the manuscript missed the suggested deadlines; Teresa Mason and Rita Pierce Samols, who undertook the massive task of editing the manuscript; and, most importantly, my wife, Jeanne, who gave up weeks of vacation time and countless weekends and evenings over the past three years to help me get through the arduous task of making something comprehensible from the mountain of paper that was the product of nearly sixteen years of writing. To all of these and all others whom I may have overlooked, I offer my heartfelt thanks.

Introduction

When a friend suggested that I assemble a book of my newspaper columns, I never batted an eye. Sure, I thought, why not? Little did I know what an enormous mouthful I had bitten off. To begin with, my columns began practically in the stone age of publication. The earliest were printed and hand delivered as hard copies to the newspaper office. Someone there had to retype them. Later I delivered my articles on floppy disks and, ultimately, sent them over the Internet. During the first decade of writing "I Was Just Thinking," I replaced my computer and upgraded to new software no fewer than four times. Each software package was light years ahead of and largely incompatible with its predecessor. Assembling a book from this hodgepodge was going to be as delicate and tedious as an archeological dig.

Then there was the matter of sheer volume. Let's face it, you can write a lot of words in sixteen years. At a column a week, I was looking at over eight hundred columns, more than sixteen hundred sheets of paper. Any book that was to be light enough for the average adult to carry without help would have to be limited to no more than a couple hundred columns, presumably of my best efforts.

When at last I sat down with my wife to select the material for the book, the task was staggering. I had written thousands of words on a myriad of subjects. From memories of childhood, to my military years, to what's going on now, the variety was unlimited. There was commentary on political issues foreign and domestic and tongue-in-cheek satire on human foibles including a host of my own. I had written about dogs and cats, birds, raccoons, and gardens; Christmas, Easter, Halloween, and Decoration Day; and people I had known, people I had read about, and some I even made up for the sake of telling a good story.

After flailing away for days against a mountain of paper, we finally decided our first task would be to divide everything into categories. The largest of these would be called "The Dark Ages of My Youth," for the numerous columns I wrote through the prism of nostalgia.

Another category we titled "The Project." It depicts the sometimes painful process of building an addition to our house—an undertaking that stretched from the three months initially estimated for its completion to more than eight years. It was by far the greatest test my sanity and my marriage would ever face.

Next was a group we called "Puppy Dogs" for all the dogs, past and present, that have graced our lives. To be politically correct, this section also includes a few kind words about cats.

The landscape of our lives is often defined by the people who inhabit it, for a short time or a lifetime. For that reason another section of the book is devoted to "People."

At one point a friend bought an aging sailboat, and we tackled the herculean task of restoring it to seaworthy condition. This section—with its surprises, successes, and frustrations—I simply call "The Boat." A final section entitled "This and That" includes an amalgamation of items that didn't quite fit into any of the other categories. Here I parked both the silly and the serious, the commonplace and the unusual.

Writing as a profession is fraught with contradiction. I can think of no pursuit more frustrating and time consuming, and none more satisfying and rewarding when it comes together. Each week, faced with writing a new column, I paced the floor, poured endless cups of coffee, and endorsed every conceivable means of avoiding the task as long as possible. I can honestly say I've probably finished more odd jobs by accident through procrastination than I have by intent. I have organized my bookshelves, cleaned out old files, watered my plants, and even cleaned the bathroom while trying to ignore an approaching deadline.

Assembling this book has followed the same diversionary path I trod while writing the columns in the first place. I have agonized over every page, just as with the columns themselves, and I revel in its completion. If its pages give you cause to ponder or smile, I will consider it a success worth the effort.

Ward Degler
Zionsville, Indiana
December 2010

Some of the columns in this book have been altered from their original form.

The Dark Ages of My Youth

and Times More Recent

The Dark Ages of My Youth

When I was invited to write a weekly column for the *Zionsville (IN) Times Sentinel*, I looked around and decided to write about what I saw in my everyday environment. One of my first pieces was about a headstrong cardinal that had declared war on his own reflection in our bedroom window. The bird attacked the window so ferociously that he left streaks of blood on the glass. It was to be a human interest piece, one that I hoped would invoke sympathy for an insane bird that I appropriately named "Crazy."

Halfway through the column, I wrote the phrase "in the dark ages of my youth," and went on to describe the slate juncos that used to gather around our backdoor in wintertime when I was a kid growing up in Wisconsin. The phrase subsequently crept into many of my columns when something in the present I was writing about would spark a memory. It has become a dominant theme in much of what has appeared under the column title, "I Was Just Thinking."

Once, when I tried to interest a newspaper syndicate in carrying my columns, the editor referred to my work as "nostalgia." Perhaps it is. But for the purposes of this book, they are simply musings from the Dark Ages of My Youth.

Changes in My Hometown

I visited my old hometown recently. It had been years since I'd been back, and I realized that most of my memories of the place were created as far back as grade school.

A lot had changed, of course, but I was amazed how much the town maintained its original footprint. Small towns are like that, unlike their big-city cousins. There seems to be a lingering sense of importance adhering to even the most out-of-date buildings in small towns, whereas big cities seem less nostalgic and more apt to obliterate their pasts and build anew.

Small towns are like antiques—old pieces of furniture, faithfully preserved despite their uselessness. Few cities view themselves that way, except perhaps London and Paris, or maybe San Francisco.

There were a few new roads and streets added as the town expanded into a new city park and a business complex. But all the old streets remained as sort of elder statesmen. The old park in the center of town has a new gazebo for summer band concerts and occasional political speeches, but the old merry-go-round that my sister fell from and broke her arm is still there, still in need of paint.

All the old Main Street buildings are still there, though most have new assignments. Gregory's Grocery is now a real estate office, the dairy has been converted to a tire shop, and Holiday's Drug Store is now a fabric store.

Old Mr. Holiday created quite a spectacle when he sold his drugstore to a man who wanted to open up a Western Auto. Truth was, Mr. Holiday didn't like pennies. Seems his cash register had slots for half-dollars, quarters, nickels, and dimes, but for some reason there was no room for pennies. So, whenever he got pennies in change, he tossed them behind the cabinet next to the soda fountain. After twenty years, he carted two wheelbarrow loads of the copper coins across the street to the bank. When the bank insisted he count them, he rallied all the kids in town to help out. When it was all done, we each got a roll of pennies. Reportedly, the Western Auto guy kept the original cabinet and continued to find pennies for years.

Hemmelman's Hardware stands empty today but the name, once emblazoned on the big window in front, is still visible. Hemmelman's, like its modern counterpart, was the gathering place for every man in town on Saturdays. Unlike today's stores, where everything is arranged on shelves and neatly displayed on racks, the merchandise in Hemmelman's was kept in boxes, bags, and bins in dark recesses throughout the store. There was no inventory except in Mr. Hemmelman's head, and only Mr. Hemmelman knew where things were.

It was a point of pride back then, both for our town and for Mr. Hemmelman, that whatever your hardware need, it could be found at Hemmelman's. In fact, it became sort of a contest to need something that Hemmelman's didn't have.

A neighbor decided to fix up an old stable at the edge of town and came to Hemmelman's for a part to a water trough pump that had been made in the mid-1880s. He announced smugly on entering the store that there was no way Hemmelman's would have this part. Mr. Hemmelman picked up the failed part and, wiping his glasses on his necktie, examined it carefully for several minutes, holding it up to the light and turning it slowly in his fingers. Then he disappeared into the back room, where he began sifting through ranks of obscure boxes. After long, suspenseful moments, Mr. Hemmelman emerged carrying not just one but two replacement parts.

"We don't get much call for these anymore," he said seriously. "If you ever need another, I got a spare."

When the county assessor's office was damaged by fire, Mr. Hemmelman was approached about ordering replacement tiles for the twelve-foot ceiling. The ceiling in the county office, among others in town, was covered with panels of sculptured metal. No one knew exactly when the buildings were constructed, but popular wisdom held that it was sometime around the turn of the century. The county commissioners as a group agreed they would probably have to replace the burned ceiling with something new, but decided to show Mr. Hemmelman the damaged metal anyway, just in case.

Mr. Hemmelman never batted an eye. He stalked off to the back room and emerged moments later with a stack of the sculptured metal panels. Seems it was Hemmelman's who supplied the county with the original materials.

"I figured one of these days somebody would need a replacement," he said, blowing a layer of dust off the panels.

When Mr. Hemmelman died a few years later, the store died with him. There just wasn't anyone who could carry on the tradition. His heirs tried to sell the inventory to a hardware wholesaler, but after a half day of trying to make sense of things, he gave up and left town. Later a few antique dealers rummaged through the place and carted off some treasures. By permission, old-time Hemmelman's customers continued to look through the store for odd items whenever the need arose.

After a year or so, the family gave up trying to empty out the place and just locked it up. Presumably, much of the inventory remains within to this day, which is good to know if I ever need a part for an antique water trough pump.

Dimming memory made it prudent to use some fictious names.

Playing Marbles and Rolling Hoops

Does anyone play marbles anymore? When I was in grade school, not only did we play marbles, it also was a school competition. I had forgotten that until a week ago, when I returned to the small town in southern Missouri where I attended the third grade.

We also rolled hoops, and I had forgotten about that, too. This is not to be confused with shooting hoops, which is, I think, by constitutional amendment required fare in Indiana schools. These were steel hoops between ten and thirteen inches in diameter. We rolled them along in front of us with sticks that had little arms attached to the bottom. The arms formed a V-shaped slot in which the hoop rolled. By twisting the stick, you could turn the hoop to the left or right. Hoop rolling was a competitive activity at my school, too.

I used to comment about hoop rolling to my kids until they flat-out told me that I was making it up. Once they showed me an engraving of a kid in the 1890s. He was rolling a big hoop with a stick.

"Like this, Dad?" they asked with a sneer. I told them the hoops we rolled were much smaller and the stick was different. They looked at me the same way they had when years earlier I had insisted the moon was made of green cheese. Kids have become real cynics.

Back in my third-grade town, I found my way to the small historical society museum. The woman in charge pulled out a dusty folder of old newspapers dated 1943. The war was in full bloom that year, and I wanted to get a little historical perspective to go along with my recollections of multiplication tables and the more advanced adventures of Dick and Jane I remembered learning in the classroom.

In small towns such as this one, the weekly newspaper was a major source of in-depth local and worldwide news. I paged through the yellowed and brittle papers. The War Bond drives told the story of financing the war. One issue explained in exhaustive detail how rationing worked. There was a column each week that gave news of local men and women in uniform.

There was local society news, too, and news from the local schools. The high school football team was having a winning year, and at the grade school, Activity Day featured stiff competition in marbles and hoop rolling. I read the list of winners and gritted my teeth at the mention of my old nemesis, J. D. McGrath. He won in both events. I remember one of the arms breaking on my hoop stick so I couldn't control left turns without slowing down. There was even a photograph, blurry but discernible, of a pack of boys running the course, pushing their hoops. The historical society had no copy machine, but I took copious notes to offer as proof to my children.

As I remember it, the marbles competition was not supposed to be "for keeps," but old J. D. made a command decision to keep my marbles anyway and then dared me to complain. J. D. McGrath was a lot like the character Moe who bullied Calvin and Hobbs.

Despite the Activity Day loss, I recall having a large coffee can filled with marbles all during grade school. My favorite taw, or shooter, was a heavy steely. Of course, steelies weren't allowed in competition. I also had some special "pee-wees" and a handful of "aggies." The aggies, carved out of Lake Superior agates, would be worth several dollars apiece today.

We also played a game called "mumble peg" with jackknives. There didn't seem to be a lot of tight rules about the game. You just had to toss the open knife and stick it in the ground from various positions. Nobody played mumble peg for stakes; you just used the game to accent conversation and to beat the boredom. Girls played jacks and jumped rope for the same reason.

But lest I get maudlin, my granddaughter pointed out the other day that kids still play games to augment their lives. Sometimes they go to the mall. And other times they jump into a new video game.

Saturday Matinees at the Princess Theater

I hadn't seen the place since 1943, and it was still standing. Of course, it had long since been abandoned and had become all but invisible in the way empty and forgotten buildings do.

A faded sign protruding from the front of the building creaked in the soft breeze and testified that sometime in its more recent history it had been the home of Carson's Custom Meats. Above the sign, near the roof line and spread out across the front of the building, however, was the true identity of this place. After more than fifty years, you had to stand just right to see the words, but they were still there showing through multiple coats of faded paint. In 1943 those letters were bright red and proclaimed this building to be none other than the Princess Theater.

In 1943 the Princess Theater was as close to heaven as any ten-year-old boy was likely to get. It was a sanctuary, a safe haven from the brutal realities of school, chores, and, of course, a world war that raged far away but at the same time seemed so close and was so frightening. It was here on Saturday afternoons that we lined up on the sidewalk clutching our dimes in fevered anticipation of imminent immersion into a double feature, three serials, and four cartoons.

In its entire history, the Princess showed nothing but Westerns, although back then we called them cowboy movies. All of our heroes were there: The Lone Ranger with his faithful Indian companion Tonto, Roy Rogers with Dale Evans, the Durango Kid, Red Ryder, Lash LaRue, Gene Autry, Hopalong Cassidy, and—my idol—Tom Mix.

There wasn't an Oscar nomination in the lot back then, and the plot of one movie was predictably similar to the plots of all the others. There were the bad guys, of course, and they almost always wore black hats. The good guy always came out of nowhere, almost always wearing a white hat. Townsfolk or hardworking ranchers being victimized by the gang were sadly powerless to do anything about it. Then the good guy showed up and helped the victims find their own inner strength and defeat the bad guys. Afterward, he always rode off into the sunset, usually after bidding fond farewell to the schoolmarm or the rancher's daughter.

Secretly, we shared the hope of the townsfolk or the rancher that he would stay and take over the ranch and maybe marry the schoolteacher. But we knew he had to leave so he could rescue the next town or the next ranch from the bad guys. That's what good guys did.

Looking back, I realize that I sat there every Saturday, hunkered down in my seat, my feet propped up on the seat in front of me, and I always knew what was going to happen next. As a matter of fact, every kid in the place knew what the bad guys were going to do next and what the good guy was going to do in return. We knew, but we didn't care. The point was that every Saturday these movies proved to us that good outweighed bad ten to one, and—in spite of an unfair war out there—good would always triumph in the end. Moreover, after the last bad guy had bitten the dust, the good guy had ridden off toward the horizon, and the house lights came back on, we were amply fortified to spend the next week carrying that message of faith and hope. For the next seven days I could be Tom Mix, reassuring a frightened world that everything would be all right.

We moved away from that little town and the Princess Theater just before the end of 1943. A couple of years later the war ended, and the country set about the business of building a future. I guess that future didn't include places like the Princess Theater. After all, the war was over, prosperity glowed brightly on everyone's horizon, and we just didn't need to be reminded anymore that good would prevail over evil. I stopped going to Saturday matinees and began looking forward to high school. After awhile they stopped making cowboy movies like that, and all the good guys rode toward the sunset one final time and disappeared.

At some point, the Princess Theater closed down. Folks I talked to said it was a frozen food locker plant for several years. Later, somebody named Carson turned it into a meat market. When Carson closed down, somebody else used the building as a warehouse for a while. After that, the building stood empty. Near as I could find out, no one has used it for anything since.

But I defy anyone who ever scoured up a dime on a Saturday afternoon and sat through a Tom Mix double feature to stand on the sidewalk outside that ruined building today and deny hearing the distant thunder of hoofbeats and feeling deep within that everything is going to be all right.

When the Carnival Came to Town

Every summer when I was a kid the carnival came to town. There was something electrifying in the air from the moment its battered trucks hit the edge of town laden with brightly colored rides and booths and the promise of magic.

We'd jump on our bikes and get to the fairgrounds even before the last truck rolled in, dust billowing. Then we'd settle in on the perimeter and watch as the carnival workers unloaded their priceless treasures. Sometimes one of them, usually dressed in low-slung Levi's and a cool-looking torn T-shirt with a pack of cigarettes rolled into the sleeve, would give us some work. We'd be paid in free ride tickets.

The rides were great, of course—pure fun: the Ferris wheel, the high-energy Tilt-a-Whirl, and the stomach-challenging Loop-the-Loop. But there were other attractions, less well-defined, that were just as exciting: shooting galleries where, if you scored a bull's-eye with every shot, you would win a giant stuffed panda; the baseball throw where you had to knock down wooden milk bottles—that booth had stuffed pandas too; ring-toss booths; darts-and-balloons; and the game where you tried to get bouncy ping-pong balls to land on the five-dollar slot.

The odds were stacked highly in favor of the carnival on these attractions, of course. The five-dollar slot was not as deep as the others; the baseballs were lopsided, and even the rifles in the shooting gallery had faulty sights. They gave away few pandas. But the larceny was minimal, the town's morality generally unchallenged.

Other attractions were less innocent. A freak show subtly confirmed our superiority by allowing us—for the price of a dime—to laugh at a woman with a beard, a man with no arms who ate with his feet, and a woman cursed by obesity who shocked us all by tipping the scales at five hundred pounds.

At the end of the midway was another booth, gaily lighted and charged with the seductive strains of bump-and-grind music. Inside were hoochie-koochie dancers offering the promise of erotic sensations known up till then only by the sultans of old. I don't remember seeing any women lining up for this attraction, and a lot of the men pulled their collars up until they were inside. The guy who sold tickets used to drive us away. Every once in a while we'd slip past him when he wasn't looking.

I always felt uncomfortable for several days after sneaking into see the dancing girls. It wasn't what I saw that bothered me, because the promise far outstripped the delivery every time, but what I had hoped to see, the forbidden fruit that I had anticipated. I suppose the other guys felt the same way, and I suspect a lot of grown men wrestled with their consciences, too.

In time, of course, the town fathers outlawed the dancing girls, along with most freak shows and a lot of lopsided gambling attractions. Carnivals became family fun once more. The rides were still exciting, but there was no longer anything you could do that you would feel guilty about later.

Carnivals are still pretty much like that today. The price of rides has doubled to make up for the money lost on skewed gambling and exotic dancers, but everyone can feel comfortable when their ten-year-old jumps on his bike to go watch the carnival set up.

But for those of you who somehow miss the promise of forbidden fruit, there is a new game in town. Anyone needing a daily allowance of prurient nutrition can visit another kind of carnival with even seedier attractions. Just turn on the television.

It's all there, the excitement, the anticipation, even the turned-up collars. But once again, almost no one wins a stuffed panda.

Selling Scrap Metal

The newest target for thieves is scrap metal. And not just odds and ends, either. These guys are going after manhole covers and sewer grates. Moreover, it seems to be a booming business.

But hold on. What's wrong with this picture? In any community there can be only a limited number of scrap metal dealers. After all, it's not like check-cashing places or magnetic sign shops that can open up overnight in any vacant building. The scrap metal business requires some special knowledge and, of course, lots of room.

Wouldn't you think any local scrap dealer would get a tad suspicious when some guy comes in with a truckload of manhole covers?

"Hey, where'd you get these?"

"Oh, I finally got around to cleaning out my garage."

"Yeah, stuff sure piles up."

"You bet, especially sewer grates. My wife kept nagging me to get rid of them."

Another thing. Collecting manhole covers and sewer grates is not like picking up discarded soda cans along the road. A standard manhole cover can weigh over two hundred pounds, and sewer grates probably come in a close second.

Scrap dealers say they are being robbed, sometimes at gunpoint. I have a tough time imagining any dealer buying back his own scrap metal.

"Hey, those manhole covers look a lot like the ones stolen from me last night."

"These? Nah, I've had these in my basement for the last five years. My wife got tired of walking around them; threw a fit until I promised to get rid of them."

"Hey, you're right. These don't look a thing like my manhole covers."

In any case, these guys are pikers. They don't know what it's like to set your sights on something really big, not like it was back in the dark ages of my youth.

Back then a war was going on, and something every young patriot did was collect newspapers and scrap metal for the war effort. Every Saturday a bunch of us guys would get together, line up our wagons, and go after scrap. We got a few cents a pound for both newspapers and scrap metal. Usually, we made the neighborhood rounds for newspapers in the morning. People saved them for us and sometimes even stacked them on the front porch so we didn't even have to knock on their doors.

In the afternoon we went after scrap metal. It was less organized. A few of the same people who saved newspapers for us also saved their flattened tin cans. But cans didn't accumulate like newspapers, and in any one week we might collect barely a wagonload.

So, to make the scrap metal business pay, we looked for other sources. During the week as we traveled from home to school and back again, we kept a sharp eye out. The biggest plum at first was the railroad tracks. Whenever the railroad gang worked on the tracks, they usually left the old spikes, shims, and rail joints along the right-of-way. In an hour we could load up four wagons with enough metal to net five bucks at the scrap yard. Hey, that was a buck and a quarter apiece, good money in those days.

Another source was local farms. In most small towns, farms crowded right up against the town limit. There were three such farms near my hometown, and we hit each of them weekly. American farmers were never very tidy. If they replaced a broken part on a tractor or cultivator, they invariably left the old one on the ground for us to pick up.

It was inevitable that after a few weeks we had gleaned all the scrap metal available from the farms and the railroad. In fact, those farms never were so neat and clean either before or since. The trouble was, unless we could find another source, we were faced with insolvency.

The solution came to us on a summer day while we were walking back home from swimming in a creek at the edge of one of the neighboring farms. As we crossed a ford in the creek, we suddenly looked up and saw it. A hundred yards or so downstream was an ancient steam tractor, half-submerged in the streambed and streaked with years of dark rust. For four young patriots looking for ways to help the war effort, it was a dream come true.

We quickly realized that moving the giant machine was totally out of the question. We would have to take it apart, piece by piece. It's hard to describe the enthusiasm with which we descended on this relic later that day with hammers, screwdrivers, and several sets of pliers.

I can't tackle a rusted bolt today without reliving the frustration we went through trying to pry parts off that ancient tractor. One of the guys said he had heard that splashing water on a rusted bolt would loosen it. We spent more than an hour throwing handfuls of creek water onto that rusted hulk and then savagely and fruitlessly attacking the bolts.

We spent a total of four days working on that beast, and the only thing we got for it was blisters on our hands and several sets of rust-clogged clothes. Just before we gave up, we sat on the creek bank and played "What if." We imagined pulling the tractor out of the creek and into town, where we would present it to the scrap dealer and pocket our profits.

Our best estimate was that the thing would weigh in at a ton or more. At scrap metal prices at the time, we would have made about a hundred dollars apiece—heady wine for a bunch of young patriots.

It was an impossible dream, of course. But oh, how sweet it was. Sure, we could have checked out the manhole covers back then. But that would have been stealing. And, after all, there was a war going on.

Neighbors Worth Remembering

They don't make neighbors like they used to. One thing I remember about growing up in a small town is that everybody in the neighborhood was different. Everyone lived by his own rules and made allowances for everyone else to do the same. "Live and let live" had special meaning back then.

Old Miss Hansen lived in a small bungalow on the corner. She was very old, and the word was that, until her brother died a few years earlier, she had lived her entire life with him. Apparently neither of them had ever married. Miss Hansen almost never came outside, except occasionally on warm summer evenings when she would emerge from her house and sit in a painted steel chaise on her front porch. We neighborhood kids always made sure we walked past her house on those occasions.

"Good evening, Miss Hansen," we'd croon.

"Evening, boys," she'd cackle in return.

"Going to take the Essex out this Sunday, Miss Hansen?" one of us would ask. Then we'd stop and linger on the sidewalk in front of her house while Miss Hansen considered her answer.

"You know, boys," she'd say at last, "I don't think this Sunday is good. I've got to catch up on my rose bushes. But by and by," she'd add. "By and by."

Truth was, the polished old green automobile in the garage hadn't been driven since her brother died. The two of them used to take drives in the country on Sundays, and she insisted she was going to do so again, "by and by." We kids knew that every time we asked her about it, she'd wait until we left and then she would go to the garage and climb into the front seat behind the steering wheel. We used to peek in the window and catch her sitting there. We weren't being mean. We just figured one day maybe she'd actually get up enough nerve to back out of the garage and go for a drive.

The neighbors next door used to live on a farm outside town. I guess they lost the place during the Depression. Talk was that they had managed to keep one cow, which was pastured at the edge of town. Twice a day the old man put a two-gallon milk can in the basket of his bicycle and rode out to milk the cow. An hour later he'd return, put the bicycle away, and lug the heavy can into the house. He and his wife lived by themselves, and no one could ever figure out what they did with all that milk.

Our neighbors on the other side had a large yard and let us play our rowdy kid games around their house. They were a kindly old couple who got weekly visits from at least five of their six grown children plus dozens of grandchildren. On evenings when they were alone, they would play records. They had an old windup Victrola and dozens of thick black records. I used to listen to the scratchy old songs from my bedroom window. One of their favorites was called "Your Lips Tell Me No-No, But There's Yes-Yes in Your Eyes." Whatever else they played, they always played that song at least two or three times.

Around the corner was the Schaefferkotter place. Mr. Schaefferkotter and his wife had come from Germany before World War I. I guess the anti-German sentiment that swept the country during 1917 and 1918 terrified them to the point that they became hermits. They never spoke to anyone. Their small yard was enclosed by a high wire fence, and they kept chickens in the shed behind the house. In a small garden in one corner of the yard they raised cabbages and pole beans. Each spring the two of them would dig up the garden plot, carefully plant seeds, and water them. Then Mr. Schaefferkotter would set up the tall wooden poles along the rows of beans. They spoke only German and always talked softly. Whenever any of us kids would come around, they would leave their yard and go into the house.

Old Mr. Rausch across the street had been a music teacher before he retired. When I expressed some interest in learning to play the trumpet, the old man brought out his own instrument and taught me the fundamentals. For several weeks I spent an hour or more each day on his front porch practicing. I'm sure the entire neighborhood rejoiced when I decided that, progress notwithstanding, the trumpet was not my instrument.

Mostly Mr. Rausch pulled weeds. He started with his wife's flower beds and then proceeded across the yard, pulling every weed in sight. With each successful tug he would grunt and spit out some special epithet reserved specifically for weeds. Mr. Rausch hated weeds so much that, when his own yard was clear of them, he would migrate to his neighbor's. During one extremely rainy summer, he managed to wipe out every weed within a half-block radius.

Old Doc Willis was a retired dentist who late one summer night chased his wife through the neighborhood with a butcher knife. The town constable came and tried to reason with him, but old Doc just climbed up into Jimmy Porter's pigeon loft and refused to come down. Mrs. Ellis, who was a nurse, took Mrs. Willis, weeping and sobbing, home with her for the night while the constable sat on the hood of his pickup and talked for hours to the doctor above.

Sometime during the night he must have talked Doc down, for by morning the pigeon loft was empty save for pigeons, and Doc had been taken to the county hospital. I guess this sort of thing had happened before. Seems that old-fashioned dentists used to make fillings by mulling the silver and mercury together in their mouths. Everybody said Doc suffered from mercury poisoning.

I remember that old neighborhood sometimes as I drive through today's sanitary suburbs, where all the houses look alike and everybody is too busy to just be themselves.

But now and then I'll notice somebody on his knees digging up weeds with fierce determination. Then I realize there's hope for the old neighborhood yet.

Banana Nut Bread, Fudge, and Making Taffy

I did a little baking over the weekend. Don't get me wrong, I don't fancy myself a baker. I just get bored at times. I think it's an extension of my father's fudge- and taffy-making compulsions from the dark ages of my youth.

It usually happened in the middle of one of those interminably boring Sunday afternoons when the clock languished over each passing minute and there was nothing on the radio except the *Longines Whitnauer Hour* of classical music and *Lux Radio Theatre* was still several hours away. Dad would announce, "Let's make some candy."

Immediately the kitchen became a command post, and everyone joined ranks for a unique form of culinary close-order drill. My job, as oldest squirt, was to measure the sugar carefully into the measuring cup and then into the mixing bowl. When making fudge, Mom was in charge of cocoa and Dad kept a stern eye on the pot once everything was combined and cooking.

Taffy-making had more moving parts and was a lot more fun than making fudge. With fudge, once the ingredients had been combined and the saucepan was a-bubble, it was mostly over. There was little to do but wait for it to cook and cool.

Cooling fudge could be fun, particularly in the north woods of Wisconsin. Dad would pour the candy onto cookie sheets and cover it with metal pie pans. Then the whole shebang got set out on the back porch to cool in the subzero air. In a matter of minutes, dozens of birds would swarm atop the pie pans and hammer away in an attempt to reach the chocolaty treasure below. It was like a convention of snare drummers.

With taffy I not only got to measure the sugar, I also was in charge of filling endless glasses with water to test for "hard crack," the indicator that the taffy was ready to pour out for cooling. I never understood the chemistry of it. Dad just kept dropping spoonfuls of the cooking taffy into water and watching the results. Finally, the stuff would congeal into a ball in the bottom of the glass and Dad would yell "Hard crack!" and whisk the pan from the stove to the table, where the marble slab lay.

It was law in those days that taffy, to be any good at all, had to cool on a marble slab. Nothing else would do. Dad swore he could tell by the taste if the candy had been cooled on any other surface.

The slab also had to be slicked with butter to keep the taffy from sticking. After cooling came the pulling. We all put butter on our hands and grabbed up a handful of the hot, gooey stuff. The object was to pull it into long strands, wad it back into a ball, and stretch it out again. Over and over we'd pull the taffy until it turned white and grew stiff. Once it was pure white and nearly brittle with hardness, Dad would string it out in a long rope on the marble. A few minutes later, he would break the rope into edible pieces and cover them with powdered sugar.

Making taffy and fudge was great for boredom back then. The eating was good, too. And when someone would sneak a piece of taffy to the dog, we could have sold tickets to the performance. The dog would chew until her teeth became immovably imbedded in the stuff. Then she would go into a frantic survival mode, scooting around on her back, all four paws digging away at her immobilized jaws. Finally, tears of merriment rolling down our cheeks, we would come to her rescue.

I haven't made taffy or fudge for years. But this weekend I baked banana nut bread—four gigantic loaves of it. It was something I had threatened to do for a long time. Periodically, the grocery store experiences an exceptionally high tide of rapidly ripening bananas. During the most recent occurrence, I bought a very large bag of bananas for about thirty cents. Then I perused a half-dozen recipes for banana nut bread.

The recipe I selected called for full sticks of butter, cups and cups of sugar, lots of eggs, and mashed bananas. I narrowed my eyes at the pile of bananas and estimated I had enough fruit to make a quadruple batch. I hauled out the mixing bowls to have at it.

"Why don't you just make a double batch at first?" my wife suggested, trying to stay clear of the full grindings of this culinary event. I thought about it and estimated the size mixing bowl I would need if I did otherwise. Smart woman, my wife. I made two double batches.

We didn't have waxed paper to line the bottom of the pans so the bread wouldn't stick. So, we used plastic wrap. Bad idea. The baking process welded this film permanently to the bottom of the bread and had to be sliced off before eating. Take my advice: go get waxed paper.

I wasn't able to eat all of the bread at one sitting, but I confess I made a valiant effort. What bothers me a little is that I used to be able to eat six or eight slices of bread like this without getting a stomachache.

Revisiting Big Rock

Einstein was wrong. You know all that business about the universe expanding? It's a bunch of hooey. Actually, the exact opposite is happening: the universe is shrinking.

I'm not referring to advances in technology either—you know, jet planes that are so fast you can actually get someplace before you leave. Nope, I'm talking about true shrinkage here, the kind you get when you put raw cotton cloth in hot water. The universe is truly un-Sanforized.

Here's the deal. My sister called from Arizona a few weeks ago and suggested a trip back to Missouri, to the town where we lived as kids. The first indication that things had been shrinking came when I picked her up at the airport in St. Louis.

"This airport used to be much bigger," my sister said as we pulled out of the parking lot. "And it was a lot further away from the city."

"Not a chance," I said, shaking my head. "Even the name is bigger. St. Louis International Airport is a yard and a half bigger than Lambert Field." Still, as we drove the short distance to the interstate, I begrudgingly realized she had a point. The airport used to be out in the country, where it covered at least half a county of real estate. Today it's tucked in between shopping malls just a few blocks from downtown.

The trip to Jefferson City in the middle of the state was shorter, too. Of course, that's because of the interstate highway system. Isn't it? Sure, you can drive in two hours on the interstate what used to take half a day to cover. Yeah, that's it.

Next morning we set out for our old hometown. We both wondered about the travel time on that trek.

"Dad always counted on two hours to get to Jeff City," my sister said. I nodded my head in silence. We had made it in about an hour, and there was no interstate here. The highway we traveled was the same two-lane blacktop we had driven dozens of times when we were kids.

"Maybe it's the air-conditioning," I ventured hopefully, remembering the stifling heat of Missouri summers and the agony of traveling any distance in a car without air-conditioning. That would be enough to make any trip seem interminably long.

"Maybe," she said. I could tell she wasn't convinced. Neither was I.

We drove to the house where we had lived and got out of the car. For long moments we stood silently staring at the place. The bay window was still there, and so was the garage with the chipped brick where the coal truck had backed into it. The driveway and the yard: still there, unchanged. And yet ...

"It's smaller," we said simultaneously. "Everything is smaller." There was no denying it. On those warm summer nights when a dozen or more neighborhood kids gathered to play "red rover," we always picked our yard because it was the biggest one in town. You could actually get out of breath running across its breadth. It had dwindled to a postage stamp. Five easy strides took me from one end to the other.

The house was smaller, too. It had been such a monolith when we were kids. Now it was just a medium-size house set on a small yard. Silently, we returned to the car and drove toward downtown. The business district of our hometown used to be at least twenty-four blocks away and took a good half hour to walk. Today it is only nine blocks distant, and we got there so quickly I actually missed the turn onto Main Street.

To get the flavor of the place, we parked the car and walked, just as we did as kids, past the barber shop and the hardware store, the post office, the gas station, the Western Auto, the drugstore, the theater where they showed a new movie every week and a double feature on Saturdays. At the end of the street where you turn right to go to the park or straight ahead into the feed mill, we stopped and looked at each other.

"Shorter," we said. "Definitely shorter." Not only had the street shrunk in length, it had also become narrower. "You really had to run to get across in traffic," I said. Sis nodded agreement as we ambled leisurely from one side to the other, waiting a few respectful seconds for a car to pass.

As disturbing as our visit had been to this point, the crowning blow came when we drove out to the old swimming hole. There was no municipal pool back then, and all of us went swimming in local creeks. The best of these was a place called Big Rock. It was six miles from town on a dusty gravel road, which was a long hour's ride on a bicycle. The place itself was a large pool at the base of a giant outcropping of Missouri limestone. The rock towered a hundred feet into the summer sky, and the pool of water below was a good nine feet deep and stretched at least fifty yards to the sandbar where we piled our clothes. There, on sweltering July days amidst the buzz of cicadas, we doffed our jeans and T-shirts, swam across to the giant rock, then climbed its face to a ledge halfway up, where we took deep breaths and leaped into the air for a few seconds of exhilarating flight before splashing into the cool depths below.

The well-worn path to the place had grown over with weeds and brush, of course, but the hundreds of kids on bikes who had come this way over fifty summers had left indelible scars to mark the way, vestigial reminders that would never entirely disappear—sort of like the chariot wheel ruts that scar the ancient roads leading to Rome.

Last week I stood there gazing at my past and wondering if it was all a lie. Big Rock was no more than thirty feet high, and the pool of water was barely five feet deep. At the most it was twenty feet across. To be fair, I had to admit that annual spring floods can change the landscape of any swimming hole. Yet the rock itself once reached far greater heights than it does today.

And then, on impulse, I decided to check the distance back to town. I set the odometer and drove back along the bicycle route I had taken a thousand times in my youth—six agonizing miles that left me as hot and sweaty on the return trip as I had been on the trip out. When we got back to the gas station on the corner where we always put air in our tires and drank from the station water hose, I checked the odometer. Six miles had shrunk to two and a half.

Putting all of this into perspective, I have to wonder what Einstein would say today if faced with the reality of his mistake.

"Guess what, Albert, the universe is shrinking."

"Oops."

What the Heck Is a Skate Key?

The kids didn't have a clue what I was talking about. "Roller skates," I said, "the kind you clamp onto your shoes."

"Why would you want to do that?" one kid asked, twirling in slow graceful circles on his roller blades. "Besides," he added, pointing to my Reeboks, "how would you attach them?"

Good questions, of course. I still have at least one pair of shoes with heavy sole welts, the kind needed to clamp on a pair of skates. Or maybe I don't. Come to think of it, maybe I tossed them at the same time I got rid of my old bell-bottoms and narrow neckties.

That was the way you used to go skating, I assured them. Lace up the shoes real tight, adjust the skates for length with the bolt in the middle, then slip the shoes in between the clamps and screw 'em down tight. And I mean tight. Those clamps had to cut clear into the sole welt before you could be sure they'd hold.

"How'd you tighten them?" another kid asked, his "blades" rolling silently across the sidewalk.

"Skate key," I said. They mouthed the words like some foreign phrase. "Every kid in the neighborhood had a skate key. Mostly we wore them on strings around our necks, although some guys stuffed them into their jeans pockets. I worried about doing that because if you fell down the wrong way …," I winced in recollection of serious bodily injury.

"My skate key had a chromium handle," I concluded. The kids narrowed their eyes again. Another foreign phrase. They looked interested, but I knew I was dangerously near the edge of ridicule. I remembered the way we laughed at old Mr. Sanders when he reminisced about driving around the country in a (chuckle, chuckle) steam-operated car.

"Did it have a water fountain and a little spigot where you could make a cup of tea?" we would laugh. "Burned kerosene," Mr. Sanders would say, ignoring our jibes. "If we ran out of gas, we'd empty out the headlights. Always had enough in the lights to get us home."

I sat there now and remembered how it felt getting Mr. Sanders revved up about his steam car. I looked at these kids and felt a sudden kinship with the old man.

"You could always tell when the kids were going skating," I continued. "You could hear them coming a block away. Probably like you kids," I said, searching for common ground. They looked at one another and shrugged.

"I mean those old steel wheels really made a racket," I said. That got them. They lined up across the sidewalk like an angry hockey team and cocked their heads to the side.

"Steel wheels?" they asked in unison.

"Yep," I said matter-of-factly, "and if you skated through water you had to be sure and oil them. Otherwise, the bearings rusted."

"Steel wheels?" they said again. "Rusty bearings?" They examined their own skates as though searching for clues to the past. One of them tentatively spun his wheels with his fingers, tough acrylic, nearly indestructible. They shook their heads.

"Why would anyone make skates out of steel?" one of them asked.

"Yeah," said another, "why didn't they make them out of plastic like these?"

"What about your pads?" a third asked. "What were your knee and elbow pads made out of?"

"Didn't have any," I said, "and they didn't have plastic back then." I knew at that moment I had crossed over the edge.

"No pads?" the one kid sneered. "What happened if you fell down?"

"You skinned your knees, maybe broke a bone," I said.

"Sure, then you had to go to the emergency room. Some skating party."

"Nope," I said, "didn't have one of those either. Fixed it up ourselves with liniment and Band-Aids."

"A broken leg?" the kid demanded, making a face. "And what about infection?"

"Well," I said, slowly, seriously, "if it was a compound fracture and infection set in, we'd send for the doctor …"

"Like Dr. Quinn, Medicine Woman," one kid said, sniggering.

"Yep," I mused, "old Doc would ride up in his buckboard and haul in his bag of tonics and nostrums." By now the kids all stood with their mouths agape.

"What happened then?" they asked.

"I remember like it was yesterday. Old Doc just sort of shook his head and Mom and Dad knew they had to make a big decision."

"What decision?" the kid demanded.

"Whether to shoot me or let me die of my own accord."

For several long moments the kids just looked at me. Then, as though on signal, they spun off and skated away. One of the yelled, "Don't fall down, Billy, or we'll have to shoot you." Another whooped and then they all broke up laughing.

"Come back tomorrow," I yelled after them, "and I'll tell you how we used to run around with tin cans on our feet." They were still laughing a block away.

27

Breakfast Never Changes

Breakfast has always been a multiple-choice affair. But it used to be a lot simpler. Our selections were bacon and eggs or cereal. Sometimes we had sausage instead of bacon, and on weekends we had pancakes instead of eggs.

Eggs came sunny side up, over easy, or scrambled. And, if you had the tummy flu, you got poached eggs on toast. For cereal you selected either hot or cold. Hot cereals included oatmeal, Cream of Wheat, and Ralston. Cold cereals offered the immense selection of Wheaties, Post Toasties, Shredded Wheat, and Grape Nuts.

I was always a cereal kind of guy. Our family had hot cereal in the wintertime and cold cereal in the summer. I liked eggs okay; it's just that in our kitchen they tended to be either too runny or a burnt offering.

My favorite hot cereal was Ralston, probably because it was what Tom Mix ate. "Hot Ralston for your breakfast gives you cowboy energy."

Even back in those days cereal manufacturers knew that the way to sell cereal was to capture the kids. Three box tops and twenty-five cents would get you the Green Hornet's Secret Decoder Ring. There were model airplanes you could order: a British Spitfire, a P-40, and a Jap Zero—each for three box tops and a quarter. Walkie-talkies were another favorite, and Jack Armstrong, "All-American Boy," offered every boy in America a chance to get a working model of his own Piper Cub complete with controls.

Before the war, Mother's Oats came with dishes inside. Would you believe it, Depression Glass? We collected a complete set. The sugar bowl was the hardest to find. Sometime during the 1970s, Mom took the pieces that were left and sold them to an antique dealer. She got back every cent she ever spent on the oatmeal, plus a healthy return on her investment.

Nabisco Shredded Wheat used to come in a squatty square box containing three layers of shredded wheat biscuits. Dividing the layers were cardboard inserts with collectible stuff printed on them, everything from geography lessons to games and puzzles. On the outside of the box was a picture of Niagara Falls.

Sometime during the war, I think the cereal makers got bored. Suddenly new products began to emerge. The first version of Kix came packed in wax-coated boxes that looked like what quarts of milk would be put into years later. The cereal was perfectly round pellets, hard as rocks, insoluble in any liquid, and totally indigestible. Later they would puff them full of air so milk would at least make them soggy.

Cheerios came out about the same time. They were pretty good although they weren't called Cheerios at first. They first hit the shelves under the name Cheerioats.

There were some early experiments with hot cereals, too. Malto-Meal and Cocoa-Wheats are two that come to mind. I like chocolate on ice cream. I don't like it on cereal.

These early explorations into breakfast lore seemed to trigger a chain reaction.

Sometime right after the Korean War the cereal industry achieved critical mass. The resulting explosion has made choosing breakfast fare a lot like surfing the Internet. There are virtually an infinite number of choices. Literally every grain on earth has been shredded, puffed, bloated, exploded, and drenched in sugar.

And once the grains ran out, they started with leaves, twigs, and pine cones. There are so many cereals today, I fully expect a new brand of supermarket to open—one that sells nothing but cereal, a sort of PetSmart for humans.

There's also a full lineup of other breakfast goodies, things you prepare in the microwave or in the toaster, about a thousand solid choices here.

Bottom line is these days I'm almost exclusively a hot cereal guy, oatmeal mostly. Big reason is cost. The thing that made cold cereals popular back in the dark ages was that even people with no money—like us, and all our friends and neighbors—could afford to buy them. The average cost per box was about twenty-nine cents. Today some gee-whiz atomic sugar blast concoctions run nearly five bucks a box. Only for the rich and famous, I say, unless I could buy on the installment plan.

Camping

I grew up in a camping family. One of the big reasons back then was that it was an affordable way for us to take a vacation. Plus, Dad was a forester and his work revealed ideal off-the-beaten-path campsites. Many, I swear, had never before received human visitors.

Some of these places would have been tough going for seasoned Green Berets. I remember roads that would have challenged a tank commander. We didn't even have a Jeep, just a car, and a low-slung model at that. Yet Dad was a master at getting us in and getting us out again. Often I was sure the entire underneath side of the car was going to remain behind on a rock or stump, but we got there.

Even when the meager road finally petered out entirely, Dad kept going. He seemed to know where the old logging trail was hiding beneath years of undergrowth. He was like a professional Indian tracker looking for bent blades of grass and worn stones.

Often as not, when we finally came to a halt at the edge of a sheer cliff or raging river, Dad would announce, "We're not there yet." We still had a ways to go before reaching our campsite.

These words always came as a mixed blessing. After hours of bouncing over boulders and struggling through bogs of quicksand, it was a relief to get out of the car, to be reassured we had no broken bones. On the other hand, everything we needed for the camp now had to be carried—possibly for miles—through the wilderness.

On the plus side, Dad was also a master at logistics. He had designed and built a trailer that carried the entire camp and supplies for two weeks. Moreover, everything was divided into luggable parcels.

The biggest and heaviest of these was the tent. It was a family-size model, and in those days all tents were made of heavy, bulky canvas. I have a two-man tent today that is made of lightweight rip-stop poly-something-or-other that weighs exactly nine pounds.

Dad carried the tent, the veins in his forehead bulging as he labored under the load. My sister and I picked up bedrolls in one hand and carried the giant food cooler between us with the other.

I don't recall ever descending rope ladders or swinging on vines across bottomless chasms to get to our campsite, but all lesser challenges were routine. This included wading through waist-deep water, scaling small cliffs, and scooting an inch at a time across fallen trees serving as natural bridges. More than once someone would slip, fall, and get a good dousing and a skinned knee.

Of course, there was always a second or third trip back to the trailer for more supplies. By the time everything was at the campsite, we were too pooped to pitch the tent. By then, however, Mom usually had the kitchen operating. Hot dogs, fresh lemonade, and cookies helped revive us.

As exhausting as getting there was, the campsite itself was invariably a paradise—a mossy clearing, a babbling stream, a gentle breeze, and a panorama of nature's finest laid out before us. Often we never saw another human being during our entire stay. We almost always arrived home tired, sunburned, chigger-bitten, and grubby, but with a sense of inner renewal, something that would last until the following summer when we would load up the trailer and head for some new and equally unexplored section of wilderness.

Camping today is somewhat different. Uninhabited parts of the country are harder to find. Campsites are more like communities, with restrooms and showers. Places where you can pitch your tent are clearly marked, numbered, and assigned. Many are like theme parks with waterslides and concession stands.

Don't get me wrong, these places are wonderful. Camping in today's "wilds" is still relaxing, and I always come away refreshed. It's just different than it once was. Paved roads now lead right up to the front of your tent. Cooking grills are built into the ground, and all trails are clearly marked and safe. There is no risk. Technology and community management have provided an almost totally antiseptic camping experience.

Even an old high school buddy of mine who decided early on to get away from it all has become disillusioned with modern camping. Back in the sixties he became a bush pilot and specialized in flying hunters and fishermen into remote areas of the North Woods.

When I ran into him a few years ago, he shook his head and told me about a new camp he had recently visited. It was one hundred miles from the nearest village and fifty miles from the closest road. It sat isolated on the edge of a meandering lake.

"It was the most remote place I'd been to," he said. "It wasn't even on the map. I had to navigate by guesswork." When he landed on the lake and taxied the plane up to the shore, he knew that something was amiss.

"There was a dock built out into the lake," he said, shaking his head. "And when I approached, uniformed resort employees came out to tie up the plane. The entire place was run off a giant generator. Electric lights were everywhere, and all the rooms were air-conditioned. It was like a Holiday Inn."

Come to think of it, I don't really miss falling off logs and going without a shower for two weeks. Actually, Holiday Inns are pretty nice.

Forest Fires

When it started raining the other day after six weeks of the driest weather I can remember, I felt myself relaxing, even breathing a sigh of relief.

Too much dry weather makes me nervous. I learned to fret about things like that from my dad. He was a forester, and dry weather meant forest fires.

Back at the dawn of time when I was very young and the Great Depression was in its final throes, my dad worked for the US Forest Service as a superintendent at several CCC camps. Every morning he would walk outside and sniff the air. If he didn't smell smoke he would relax. If it was raining, he would let out a deep sigh and have a second cup of coffee.

The Civilian Conservation Corps (CCC) was part of the Works Progress Authority (WPA) that was inaugurated at the height of the Depression to put men back to work. The WPA hired men to do all kinds of stuff: build roads, dams, and schools, write books, paint murals, and even compose music.

Hardly anybody remembers those days and the incredible struggle our nation went through. The CCC offered thousands of men and boys—out of school and out of work—a job to do and a place to live until the country could break the back of the Great Depression. Their jobs were to plant trees in America's national forests, to build a crisscross network of fire breaks through the thousands of acres of trees, and to fight fires round the clock whenever they broke out on federal soil.

For doing these jobs they were paid thirty dollars a month. They were issued army surplus fatigue uniforms and lived in hastily built, board-and-batten barracks in camps at the edge of the forest. Each camp was designed to be a complete community, with a mess hall filled with picnic tables and a full military kitchen at one end and screen wire fly traps just outside the doors. There was a dispatch center, a supply shed, an armory where shovels, mattocks, council rakes, axes, and back pumps were stored, and a recreation hall called a Day Room, where the men could spend off-duty hours playing ping-pong, listening to records, or reading magazines and books from a meager library at one end of the Day Room. Most of the camps had electricity, limited indoor plumbing, and a telephone. The phone was usually in the dispatch office or in the superintendent's office.

The camps were named for whatever landmarks they were close to. Hence, they had names like Great Bend, Cliffton, Birch, Perkinstown, Sheep Ranch, and Ghost Creek. In addition to their pay, the "boys" received room and board, medical care, thirty days' leave a year, plus the privilege of buying soap and untaxed cigarettes from the canteen—which was open for business in the Day Room for one hour every evening after supper. They also were entitled to get their hair cut for fifteen cents at the camp barbershop: a metal folding chair pressed into service in the Day Room from six o'clock to eight o'clock every Wednesday evening. A superintendent was paid one hundred twenty-five dollars a month and, if he had a family, he also got free living quarters. Naturally, he also had barbershop and canteen privileges.

When the Japanese bombed Pearl Harbor, Dad was superintendent at Camp Perkinstown in the middle of the Chequamegon National Forest in north-central Wisconsin. When the order came to deactivate the camp, most of the men had already left. Some had found jobs; most had left to join the military. Enlistments in the CCC had been dropping off for the past couple of years anyway. And now, overnight, the Depression was officially over. When the order came down to close up shop, there were only twenty-five men left. In 1935 there had been more than three hundred.

Everything at Camp Perkinstown that could be used in the War Effort was loaded onto trucks and hauled away, including fatigue uniforms and boots, cots, and blankets. The cookstove and all the kitchen equipment was taken away. Dad guessed it went to an army camp somewhere.

The Forest Service kept the tools—the council rakes, axes, and back pumps. They were kept for the skeleton crew to use in fighting fires after the camp was closed. Dad wondered how the skeleton crew would get to a fire if one broke out since the army also took all the trucks. They left behind one ancient tractor with a two-bottom plow, a bulldozer with a broken track and no radiator, and a Model T Ford four-door sedan. Everything else—the pickups, the three-quarters, and the ton-and-a-half trucks—was driven away to have its Forest Service green painted over with olive drab.

The Rural Electric Authority sent a man out to disconnect the electric transformer at the main feeder line where the CCC road met the state highway three miles from camp. With a flip of the transformer switch, the compound lights went out, and the camp was dark. The electricity would never go on again.

The Perkinstown Telephone Exchange sent a man out on a motorcycle with a sidecar to climb the pole at the edge of the camp and snip the telephone wire.

When all the buildings were empty and the last truck had been driven away, Dad and the couple remaining CCC boys got into the Model T and drove away. They didn't bother to lock any of the buildings except the armory, where the tools were stored. Once the Model T rattled out of sight, the buildings would remain undisturbed until the war ended and the Forest Service would send in men to tear the old camp down. Then they would plant trees where the buildings once stood.

I tried to find the old camp a few years ago, but there was nothing left. Hardly a trace remains of any of the old CCC camps now. Maybe a concrete barracks foundation here or there, but mostly it's just trees. The ones my dad and his CCC boys planted, of course, have long since grown up, and second and third generations are sending their green limbs skyward.

But sometimes I think about those days when my dad had a part in building our nation's forest land. During its lifetime, the CCC planted more than nine billion trees. I don't know how many my dad's boys planted, but I do know he felt responsible for every one of them. And every morning for the rest of his life, he sniffed the air for smoke.

Lilacs—My Favorite Flower

My favorite flower? Lilacs. Definitely lilacs. Partly because of that overwhelming fragrance but mostly because that special perfume and the delicate poetry of lilac blossoms always carry me back in time to a particular summer when life was absolutely perfect.

The recollection always comes as a jolt. The air suddenly fills with the smell of lilacs, and my memory is flooded with the colors of that short but special season.

Everybody's got one of those times tucked away in the recesses of their mind, I think—maybe a special summer or fall, or perhaps a particular school year, sometime when life was so beautiful you wanted to live forever. For me it was the summer of 1941. I was six years old.

To set the stage, the country was not yet embroiled in the global war looming on the horizon, the Great Depression was over, and our nation was happily getting back to work. No one had much money, of course, but there was work. Prosperity was clearly in the offing, and, where we lived in northern Wisconsin, we had just come out of a particularly severe winter.

We had moved into the brick farmhouse in the fall, and, before we could even unpack or explore our new surroundings, the snow came. It buried the house, the yard, and the long, sweeping driveway that connected to the county road at the bottom of the hill. Then it got cold, and the wind blew the snow into huge drifts. For three days we huddled by the stove as the blizzard raged.

On the second day our landlord arrived on a sleigh pulled by a team of giant draft horses. He brought firewood, and his wife had sent a box of food. That night Mom rummaged through our unpacked boxes and found her copy of John Greenleaf Whittier's poems and read "Snowbound" aloud while the drifts accumulated outside.

For the rest of the winter the temperature seldom rose above zero, and Dad struggled every morning to start the car, a cranky Hudson Terraplane. He drained the radiator at night and brought the battery into the house, where it could keep warm. Each morning he filled the radiator with hot water and reconnected the battery. Sometimes the car started; other times it didn't.

Often spring's arrival is hidden beneath the lingering remnants of winter. But in 1941 in northern Wisconsin, we went to bed one night and it was still winter. When we awoke the next morning, it was spring. The sun shone, the temperature rose into the fifties, the snow was melting, and a couple of robins began building a nest in the maple tree outside the kitchen window—all in the space of a single day. I remember Mom opening the doors and windows so fresh air could fill the house. After breakfast Mom and Dad walked through the melting snow to lay out the gardens. Vegetables would go here, and in the middle of the yard, a flower garden.

By April the gardens were in and the landlord walked behind his team and plowed the field at the side of the house. I remember standing at the edge of the field watching as this gentle man coaxed those giant horses back and forth across the field. That was the first time I ever smelled freshly plowed soil, rich and pungent. I remember asking the farmer what made it smell like that.

"Last summer," he said with a wink. "It's been sleeping here all winter, and now we're waking it up." I believed him. I still think it is true.

Later that month a huge lilac bush between the yard and the plowed field burst into bloom. For the next two weeks the house was filled with the pungency and pastels of spring. About the same time, my dad climbed the tree in the backyard and tied a heavy rope to an upper limb. To the bottom he attached a truck tire, and I had my first swing, one that allowed me to fly, to arch outward toward the sun, so high I could almost touch the clouds.

When I tired of swinging, I would follow my dog around the property, inspecting each tiny recess, poking into corners of the barn, and probing the hedgerow along the driveway. Sometimes the dog would scare up a family of field mice and go nuts trying to catch them. Sometimes she did, but mostly they got away.

Once I found a tow chain that our landlord had lost. When it was returned, he picked me up and set me atop one of his magnificent horses and walked me around the yard.

"That tow chain would have cost a lot to replace," he said. "At a nickel a ride, I guess you can ride around on Hennie here all summer long, for free." And I did, clear into fall when the threshing crew showed up for the harvest.

The land in that special part of Wisconsin was perfect for growing things back then. Our vegetable garden thrived in abundance, and I discovered that not everything in God's bounty was necessarily edible. Rutabaga, for example, was never intended for human consumption. Mom's flower garden, on the other hand, was so elegant that people used to drive out to our farmhouse on Sundays to see it. Mom always gave them a bouquet to take home.

There were still a few hoboes on the road in those days, and when they came by the house, Mom always fixed them a sandwich. Sometimes they volunteered to chop some firewood in return before ambling back down the driveway, never to be seen again.

As quickly as the summer came, it vanished, turning cold with the rains of fall. I had turned brown during the summer, and Mom said I looked like an Indian as I started school.

Later, the landlord returned with his plow to turn the earth again before winter. He announced that he was going to plow closer to the house this year so he could plant another couple acres.

"We're gonna be at war," he mused. "Country's gonna need more food." To feed the world, he plowed down the lilac bush. I didn't think much about it at the time, and then we moved away, and the war started.

Many years later I returned to that part of Wisconsin and visited the farmhouse. It looked much the way I remembered it. The tree in the backyard was gone, but there was still a field next to the house. Right at the edge of the field was a lilac bush.

Remembering Charles Kuralt

A salute to Charles Kuralt. To my mind he was our last link with an American institution known as the Sunday Drive.

We always went for Sunday Drives when I was a kid. That was entertainment out of the house. There were no shopping malls then, and all the stores in America were closed on Sunday anyway, except for the drugstore, of course. It was open for those essential notions and nostrums needed to get through the day. And the soda fountain had to be open anyway to serve up ice cream sodas to the matinee crowd from the movie theater.

So, if you'd already seen the movie, most often once Sunday dinner was cleared away and the dishes washed, everybody would pile into the family car and go for a Sunday Drive. The thing that makes Charles Kuralt so important in all of this is that he went in search of the unusual among the plain and ordinary. That's what we did on Sunday Drives.

You'd take the highway out of town, of course, but then you'd refine your choices, seek out the back roads and neglected trails, exploring what was hidden beyond the familiar hills.

"How about this road?" Dad asked on one outing. "Last time we tried it the rains had swollen the creek, and we had to turn back." Everybody cheered, and we turned down the inviting road.

We discovered many fascinating things on our Sunday Drives. We met a set of twins, men in their fifties, who had built identical houses next door to each other on the family farm. Not only were their houses identical, they married twin sisters as well. Probably the most unusual thing about this arrangement was that the men insisted they had never once had an argument.

On another Sunday Drive in southern Missouri, we discovered a fast-moving stream that came to an abrupt end at a stone bluff. The river simply went underground at that point, and no one who lived in the area had a clue where it came out again.

We once found an unusual bridge made of two long wooden troughs a car width apart, spanning the creek. You drove up to the bridge, eased your front tires into the troughs, and then let go the steering wheel and sort of freewheeled across. It was eerie. You couldn't see the bridge from the car, so it was like being suspended in midair.

On another outing we discovered five miles of old corduroy road made of thousands of posts laid side by side. Somebody told us it had been built in the twenties.

We met one farmer who had a three-legged calf, and we would drive out to see it now and then. Folks in town got wind of it later, and the farmer started charging ten cents apiece to see the animal.

There were various pet animals we saw on our travels, everything from skunks to raccoons, squirrels to deer. One guy kept rattlesnakes. I remember his eyes were sort of narrow slits, kind of snakelike. He gave all of us the creeps, and we hastened on our way.

When we lived in Wisconsin, we usually drove by a crossroads gas station where the owner kept a black bear in a cage. It was fun to stop and buy the bear a coke. The owner would punch a hole in the bottle cap, and the bear would upend the bottle and suck the liquid out of it. Later we heard that a couple of guys got drunk one night and decided to see how much the bear would drink. The animal was found dead the next morning.

Sometimes we got lost and went through the agony of coaxing information from locals who probably didn't know exactly where we were either. Occasionally we'd get a flat tire, and we kids would explore the locality while Dad changed the tire. One Sunday I caught a baby crow that had fallen from its nest. I took it home and kept it for the rest of the summer. It would fly to greet me when I came home on my bicycle. One day it disappeared, and I never saw it again.

Sometimes we got stuck in muddy roads or in the middle of streams while driving across. Then everybody pitched in to get us freed and on our way. It's scary being stuck in the middle of a stream. You don't know if it has been raining upstream and the water could rise rapidly.

There are still a few streams to cross out there and, presumably, a few muddy roads to brave. I'm sure somebody still has an unusual pet or odd house to see. But it takes someone like Charles Kuralt to point out to us that all these back-roads oddities are what make up the fabric of America and are worth looking for.

Put the Brakes on Road Rage

The guy behind me on the interstate was plainly upset at my refusal to speed up to 75 mph. To emphasize his disapproval, he rode close behind me, not a foot from my bumper. And when at last he was able to whip around me—putting at least two other drivers at serious risk, he offered me the ubiquitous single-digit salute. Five seconds later, he slammed on his brakes and began the same idiotic ritual on the rear bumper of another driver.

This scenario is played out hundreds of times every day in this and other cities across the country.

Time magazine said recently that the cause of aggressive driving and road rage is "the never-ending stress in people's daily lives." The article went on to say that people are overwhelmed by jobs they don't like and competitive roles they don't want. Road rage is just one of the ways they act out this discomfort.

Yeah, yeah, maybe, but I doubt it. I think the real reason people act like spoiled children on the road and elsewhere is that we allow it. We have created a culture that explains and condones childish behavior instead of dealing with it the way our parents did—with a well-placed smack across the fanny.

Sure, the speed limit on the beltway probably should be increased from its present 55 mph. Few drivers observe that speed anyway, and cars for the most part are much safer than they were twenty or even ten years ago. But speed is not the issue. Anger, defiance, and aggression are the issues. Rage is the issue. Let's face it; everywhere you look, grown-ups are throwing tantrums.

How much have things changed over the years? A lot. For example, when I was a kid during World War II, the speed limit was 30 mph. Today most of us exceed that leaving our driveways, but in the gloomy and uncertain days of 1943, that was the maximum everywhere. Granted, most cars back then felt like they were breaking the sound barrier at 50 mph, and the roads weren't all that great either. But piddling along at 30 mph was still a boring and laborious chore.

But we did it. Why? Because our country asked us to in order to save on precious gas and to make tires last longer, all of which was going to help win the war. Gasoline was rationed, of course, and unless you had the right kind of ration sticker, you were allowed to buy only fifteen gallons of gas a month. That meant most folks' cars spent much of the war in the garage.

During much of 1943 we lived with my grandmother and uncle in Dayton, Ohio. My uncle designed cooling systems for bombers. His job included a ration sticker that allowed him to drive pretty much whenever and wherever he wished. Even then, family outings in the car were pretty much a Sunday afternoon affair. My uncle was a very patriotic guy. We all were. And he always drove 30 mph—except once.

One of the fun things to do back then in Dayton was to drive along the perimeter of Wright and Patterson airfields. After all, this was the very heartbeat of our military machine, and you could almost always spot some exciting airplane on the tarmac. The air bases were totally fenced in, of course, and armed guards stood at close intervals along the road. You were not allowed to drive slower than 30 mph, and under no circumstances were you allowed to take pictures. Violators were stopped and their cameras were confiscated. Obey the rules, and nobody bothered you. Except one rainy Sunday. On that day we finished dinner at the usual time and piled into the Nash for our weekly drive. When we hit the highway leading to the air bases, my uncle settled the speedometer at a steady 30 mph. For several miles we drummed along monotonously, and then—just as the fencing came into view—something unusual happened. A military policeman armed with a carbine stepped into the road and signaled my uncle to stop.

"Speed up to 45, sir, and don't slow down until you have passed the air base," he said in clipped tones. My uncle nodded slightly, gulped, and eased the car ahead. Slowly he increased the speed until the speedometer registered a flagrant 45 mph. We noticed as we zipped by that there were more than the usual number of guards out that day, and they were standing closer to the road. They all frowned and waved us on with the barrel of their rifles.

My uncle kept his gaze glued to the speedometer, which he kept locked at a steady 45 mph. Every time we passed a 30 mph speed limit sign, he cringed. Beads of sweat popped out on the back of his neck. My uncle did not take breaking the law lightly.

After a few minutes, as we approached the vast expanse of land where the main hangars were silhouetted against the drab winter sky, we suddenly understood the reason for the extra guards and the demand for excessive speed. Sticking out from one end of the largest hangar on the base was the giant tail of an airplane, exposed because the plane itself was too big to get totally inside the hangar. It was the first B-29, and it was strictly hush-hush. When it arrived during the darkness of night, flight crews rolled it into the hangar and quickly disguised the exposed tail with a giant but hastily erected tent.

The problem was that sometime after midnight a windstorm rolled through and demolished the disguise. Now America's best-kept secret was sitting there with its tail exposed to public view. As we zipped past, swarms of crewmen were struggling to rebuild the tent.

The unusual speed requirement continued for another mile or so until the road curved away from the air base. My uncle brought the car slowly to a stop and for several minutes he sat as though in a daze. All the way home he kept the speedometer strictly at the 30 mph mark.

What does this have to do with today's impiety on the road? Maybe nothing. I offer it as an example of times that were much worse, more stressful than most we face today. We were engaged in a world war, with no guarantees that we would win. Everything was rationed and in short supply. Luxuries such as bath soap and chewing gum were almost nonexistent.

And if you want to talk about stressful jobs, just imagine working twelve-hour days, six days a week, under fierce personal scrutiny, with no air-conditioning, few safety rules, and no chance of getting a pay raise—ever. If anybody did complain, he would be avoided for unpatriotic behavior until he got the message and apologized. And if any of us kids complained, we got sent to our room without supper at the least, usually after getting a serious whack across the backside.

Maybe instead of issuing tickets for reckless driving today, we simply ought to treat these drivers as the irresponsible children they are imitating, give them a swat to the fanny and send them to their rooms without supper.

Decoration Day

Memorial Day used to be Decoration Day, a day set aside to decorate the graves of those killed in war. Originally, it was the thirtieth of May. Since then, of course, Congress has changed the name and institutionalized the date so it falls on the last Monday of May. And the holiday has gotten a lot more diversified.

Back when it was Decoration Day, life was pretty simple and so was the holiday. Just about every town in the country had a memorial of some kind dedicated to local men who died during World War I. Many of these towns later added the names of those who died during World War II, the Korean War, and in Vietnam.

Decoration Day usually featured a parade made up of local school bands, a few cars with dignitaries, representatives from local VFW and American Legion posts, a color guard, and troops of marching veterans. The parade always ended at the war memorial. Then somebody would make a speech about freedom and the need to sometimes put our lives on the line to defend it, an honor guard would fire a twenty-one-gun salute, and someone from the high school band would play taps on his trumpet.

Then folks would drift away to the ice cream parlor for a sundae before going home to think about supper and listen to the ball game on the radio. Those who lost sons or fathers in the war often spent some time at the cemetery. There were flowers, of course, and flags. Small United States flags decorated the graves of all those killed in war. Most people also had flags flying at their homes as a reminder of why their sons and fathers had died.

Over time, Decoration Day absorbed other national tributes. It heralded the beginning of summer and what has become known in our nation as the cookout season. Nowadays the entire countryside smokes with the pungency of grilled hot dogs and hamburgers on Memorial Day weekend. Aliens from outer space would think the planet was on fire.

It also announced the start of swimming season at city pools. In the northern reaches of the Midwest where I grew up, venturing into the arctic waters of the local pool on the last day in May was not for the faint of heart. I used to watch the local high school football heroes take the plunge and try to act casual in front of their girlfriends as they turned blue. Now, of course, people have pools in their backyards. Many are heated, and pool parties often start right after spring thaw.

Memorial Day still has a lot of the original Decoration Day flavor. Many towns still have parades honoring veterans and paying tribute to those who died in combat. All our National Cemeteries have somber ceremonies, and each white grave marker is adorned with a flag. It's hard to keep a dry eye when confronted with all those flags fluttering in the breeze.

This year in New York, Memorial Day coincided with Fleet Week, a celebration of sea power. Naval vessels from all over the world sailed into New York Harbor to join our nation in a worldwide tribute to the victims of war and the desperate need for world peace.

The sports world takes its place during the weekend, too. The NBA playoffs roll on and big league baseball almost always has a full schedule of games on tap. In Indianapolis, of course, a month of nervous automotive energy beckons upwards of a half-million race fans to the city, where it culminates in a noisy and boisterous afternoon of expensive car racing.

I went to the race a few times as a fan, and then spent the entire month of May one year photographing race activities for a wire service. All month long I stood in the short chute between turns three and four following the blur of race cars in my viewfinder. Most of the pictures I got were static shots of cars on the track. One, however, was a picture of a tire. The car it had been part of had just slammed into the wall, and the rear wheel was launched through space on a trajectory aimed at the precise spot where I was standing. I snapped the shutter and dove for the ground. The tire missed me by inches, and I retired from race photography immediately after.

These days I spend Memorial Day weekend listening to the race on the radio, checking baseball scores, nervously watching the Pacers inch their way toward fame and fortune, and cooking burgers on the grill.

And, oh, yes, I still take a few minutes to remember those I used to know who died in World War II, in Korea, and in Vietnam. And I say a small prayer that one day Memorial Day will be nothing but a history lesson celebrated in the midst of world peace.

Firecrackers

I used to save my money all spring so I could buy fireworks for the Fourth of July. There was a special fireworks catalog that came in the mail in early April. It was chock-full of fireworks assortments. I'm not sure how I got on their mailing list. I suppose they just knew I was twelve years old and eager to buy explosives.

By the time I had enough money to actually order anything, the pages were dog-eared and pulled loose from the staples. My friends and I would spend hours scrutinizing each assortment, counting out every three-inch firecracker, every two-incher, every one-incher, and every cherry bomb in the package.

Each assortment came with a certain number of rockets, so many Roman candles and Mount Vesuvius displays, and so many boxes of sparklers. And then there was the tally of firecrackers. The catalog didn't call them firecrackers, however; it called them "reports." We thought that was stupid, but it did give us a special code to use on the Fourth:

"Hey, Charley. How many reports you got left?"

"Twenty-five big ones, thirty mediums, and two bags of little ones."

Assorted reports. Secret firepower. Fantastic!

After considering the matter carefully, we always ordered the assortment that had the most firecrackers. The cost was $12.50, plus $1.25 for shipping and handling—a lot of money back then. But a couple of us worked part time at the drugstore or the dairy. We saved up and sent our order in and dreamed of one day ordering the $125.00 Master Assortment.

The rockets, Roman candles, and sparklers we divvied up to set off on the night of the Fourth. Family entertainment. The high explosives, on the other hand, were for serious demolition business. We kicked that into high gear right away.

Tin cans were special warm-up targets. Turn one upside down over a three-incher, and the blast would send it sixty feet skyward. We tried bottles once, but some nosy kid got hit by flying glass and we got a serious talking-to. After that it was strictly cans.

Neighborhood sandboxes were pretty neat, too. Pile the sand in a mound, stick a pipe into the middle of it, drop in a two-incher, and pull out the pipe. If things went right, it would blow a geyser of sand four feet into the air. And send the young owner's mother screaming into the yard.

Sometimes we'd take our armaments down to the creek. A mud ball bearing a two-incher, once aloft, could cover a hundred-yard circle with a fine mist of gooey clay. By the time we got home, we looked like we'd bathed in cement. A three-incher weighted down with a rock and dropped into a deep pool could send a glorious pillar of water three feet into the summer air.

There were other targets that deserved attention. Cisterns and septic tanks made wondrous explosions. Empty barrels and downspouts were deeply resonant. The storm sewer on the corner made a burping sound when the firecracker went off deep within its bowels.

One special target we always hit at least once turned out to be the scariest. The flagpole at the post office had a hole in it about eight feet above the ground. If you climbed up and dropped a three-incher into the hole, the firecracker dropped to ground level and went off with magnificent metallic thunder. But the best thing was about a minute later when smoke started streaming out of the hole.

"Hey!" we'd yell. "The flagpole's on fire!" Then we'd run away laughing.

Finally, we got caught. A man we'd never seen before grabbed us by the shoulder and squeezed so hard it hurt. He identified himself as an FBI agent. He wore sunglasses and didn't smile

We'd been caught red-handed destroying government property, he said. They send you to Leavenworth for that. He described the place with a few choice words: cold stone walls, iron bars, concrete floors, bad food, and no ice cream. We got the picture. We meekly surrendered all remaining demolitions and felt lucky to walk away with a stern warning about the wages of terrorism. We turned the corner and stopped to catch our breath.

"Man, that was close."

"Yeah."

"Real close."

"Yeah."

For a few moments we shared a silent communion uncommon among men. We felt tested and purified, clean beyond clean.

"How many reports you got left?" I asked finally.

"About ten big ones," he whispered, fingering his pocket, "and probably a good dozen mediums."

We looked at each other and then down the street.

"The storm sewer," we said together.

"Yeah!"

Lawn Mowers

Lawn mowers have changed a lot since I was a kid. I just bought a new one. My old mower had been threatening to bite the dust since last summer. This year it finally did. I wasn't too surprised. The thing had been too flimsy to handle a yard the size of mine for very long.

I say that while noting at the same time that my neighbor has a mower even smaller than mine. His promises to mow his yard—which is bigger than mine—forever. The difference is that his is twenty years old, built when they still made them to last. Mine, I think, was built to fall apart in five years. It didn't quite make it.

You can still buy mowers that are built to last. Trouble is they cost several thousand dollars. I looked at these machines. You can also buy attachments for them that do thatching, mulching, and rototilling. They cost additional thousands of dollars. It's possible, I realized, to pay more for a new lawn mower than I paid for my first house. You can buy mowers with big engines, some with two and even four cylinders. You can even buy one with a diesel engine. This one is made in Japan. It's expensive, but I'm told it, too, is built to last. Why can't American manufacturers build a small diesel engine?

When I was a kid, the only power mowers around were large reel mowers that had complicated levers on the handles and large rubber tires. They had one at the place where Dad worked. I had never seen such a marvelous machine. Could I try it? Please? Dad said I could mow the office yard if I was careful. Careful? You bet!

He pulled the rope, and the engine roared to life. "This is the clutch," he said, pointing to one of the levers. "Just pull it down, and it will go." I pulled it down, and it went. It went very fast across the yard, cutting a wide swath of grass along the way. I ran to catch up. Once I had hold of the handlebars I felt confident. This was great. I trotted along behind the giant machine.

It was at the end of the yard that I realized I was lacking some important knowledge about the mower—how to turn it around. Dad hadn't said anything about that. As the end of the yard approached, I began experimenting. I pulled on the handlebars, pushed on the levers, twisted with my body weight. Nothing worked. The machine roared straight into the woods behind the office. It stopped only when it ran headlong into a tree. It sat there, drive wheels turning, reel mower whirring, and me wringing my hands in desperation.

Dad finally came to the rescue. He showed me the wheel brake. Then he turned the mower around and threaded it back through the woods to the yard. He complimented me on having wiped out two hazelnut bushes, four young pine trees, and half a bed of petunias. Once back on mow-able turf, he announced that my career as a power-mower pilot was over.

I bought my new mower from a neighbor. It is four years old and has been well cared for. I paid three hundred dollars for it, a lot less than I paid for the one that just died. It has headlights on it. A lot of the expensive ones do, too. I suppose it's possible to mow at night, but I've never known anyone who actually did it.

I used to mow lawns to earn money as a kid. No power mowers then. You had to push the mower to make the blades turn. Most of the people I mowed for had cranky old machines with cast iron wheels and cumbersome wooden handles that gave you splinters. Most of them were at least fifty years old. They never died. I'm sure those old mowers are still cutting grass.

I used to spend a lot of time sharpening the blades and adjusting and oiling the wheels and gears on those old mowers. They worked better as a result, and that made the job easier. Nothing has to be oiled anymore. I still have an oil can, but I can't remember the last time I used it for something.

People had big yards back then, too. It used to take a whole day and sometimes two to mow most of the yards I cut. Once the mowing was done, of course, there was trimming to do. Remember those scissor-type trimmers that you had to squeeze to operate? I had permanent blisters on my hand. Then there were sickles that you used to cut the really tall grass. You had to sharpen those with a file. They gave you blisters, too.

Kids still cut grass to earn money. The difference is now they work for professional mowing services. I used to earn about ten dollars a week, good money back then. Today they make more than that in a single day, I'm sure. And one more thing: if it doesn't have a gasoline engine on it, they don't use it.

Dog Days

Dog Days. The words bring back images painted by the elders of my youth, visions of illnesses that you got only in the desperate heat of late summer.

Dog Days back then was all about some vague malady that came from dogs and found its way into the lakes, ponds, rivers, and streams. Everybody believed it, and after the Fourth of July it was extremely difficult to get permission to go swimming.

"That's how the Thompson boy got sick," somebody whispered. "That's what happened to the Evans twins."

Swimming. That's what did it. Everybody said so. Everybody believed it. Of course, few of us really wanted to swim in the ponds around my hometown late in the summer anyway. Sometime in late July they all developed a thick green crust that floated on top.

I always wondered what dogs had to do with Dog Days. I used to wander around the neighborhood and check out the local dogs for signs of serious illness. I wasn't sure what to look for, but I felt pretty sure I'd recognize it if I saw it. Mostly the dogs I knew spent a lot of time sleeping. And they panted a lot with their tongues hanging out. I wasn't sure that was a sign of anything sinister.

Every once in a while one of them would get up, stretch, yawn, and pad off to find better shade or maybe get a drink of water. But then he'd flop down at the new location and resume sleeping. I may have been questioning hitherto unquestioned wisdom, but the plain fact was the dogs just looked hot, not sick.

It wasn't until years later, when I was studying celestial navigation, that I learned the true meaning of the term Dog Days. It comes from the period in July and August when the star Sirius rises with the sun. Sirius is also known as the Dog Star.

There was one August when the dogs actually were sick. Most of us had never heard much about rabies, but we knew what hydrophobia was. We also knew that hydrophobia, like lockjaw, which you got from stepping on a rusty nail, was incurable. So, when the cry went out one hot Saturday afternoon that there was a dog on the streets that had hydrophobia, the whole town was seized by panic. We went inside and closed our doors.

All afternoon we sat by the living room window looking out through the lace curtains. I don't know what we expected to see out there in that dazzling heat on the dusty street—maybe nothing. Around sunset, when the sky turned a hazy purple and orange, a pickup truck drove through the streets. A sheriff's deputy stood in the back and announced through a megaphone that the danger was over. He didn't say what happened to the sick dog, just that it was safe to go outside again.

That's when we realized that our dog had not been locked in the house with us. She had, in fact, been out in those dangerous streets. We looked frantically around the house hoping she might have just holed up under the porch. No such luck. When she finally came home, it was plain to see that she had been in a fight. There was blood on her feet, and one ear was cut.

For what seemed a long time we all just sat quietly, looking at the dog. Then Dad gently picked her up and walked outside.

"You kids go to bed," he said as we heard the car door slam. The light of a full moon was shining in my bedroom window by the time Dad returned. He and Mom talked quietly for a few minutes. Then they went to bed.

The next day, neighborhood kids were back outside as usual, riding bicycles, skating down the new patch of sidewalk in front of Mr. Berger's house, and sitting on the curb under the elm tree on the corner. Yet in spite of the fact that there was only one week remaining of summer vacation before school started, no one had much enthusiasm for playing. Four of us had given up dogs the night before.

"Mom was pretty sure Skipper was in the shed the whole time," one boy said in carefully measured words. "But we just didn't know for sure. There's no cure for it," he added softly.

We all nodded our heads. Nobody said much after that. Later, when it was time for supper, we all went home.

Dog Days refers to the Dog Star Sirius. It never did have anything to do with dogs.

Except once.

End of Summer

Have you ever noticed that every year in late August there seems to be one specific moment when summer is over? Suddenly, there's a new smell in the air, a haze in the light that wasn't there before, and things we've been hearing all summer suddenly have a different sound. After that, it's fall.

I used to hate that moment when I was a kid. It meant not only that summer was over but also that school was back. I didn't really hate school; I just hated losing summer. It was a tough transition. From barefoot to shoes; from shorts and T-shirts to school clothes; from sleeping in to getting up early; from playing outside evenings to reading books and writing essays.

Of course, there were lots of great things to do in the fall. All summer we used to check out the hazelnut bushes. In September we'd take baskets into the woods and harvest the nuts. Later, after the first frost, we'd go after black walnuts. Both delicacies added a taste to die for to the brownies and oatmeal cookies that Mom baked for Thanksgiving.

That was also the time everybody got ready for winter. Coal trucks arrived in driveways and poured their black burdens into coal bins hidden in cellars. For those of us who burned wood, there was another task—splitting the enormous mountain of firewood dumped in the yard by a delivery truck into stove-size pieces and stacking them in the woodshed.

About the time the leaves began turning bright yellows, ambers, and reds, Dad would devote an entire Saturday to winterizing the house. The screen would be pried out of each window and replaced with a storm window. Each screen was numbered so it could find its way back to the right window again in the spring. Apparently, carpenters had an aversion to uniformity in those days. No two windows were the same size in any house we ever lived in.

Before storing the screens in the garage for the winter, Dad inspected each one, replaced broken screen wire, and painted the wood frames. In the spring

53

he would do the same with the storm windows. He used to say it was better to paint at the end of the season. That way you didn't have the problem of freshly painted windows adhering themselves permanently to the house.

Several houses we lived in during the war years didn't have storm windows. Dad bought rolls of plastic reinforced with a cross pattern of green thread. He cut the plastic to fit each window and tacked it in place with wood batten strips. You could see through the stuff when it was first installed. By spring it was nearly opaque.

In the days before rolls of pink fiberglass insulation, most houses weren't insulated against the winter chill. Another truck would arrive bearing bales of straw. These were shoved tightly against the side of the house. Often, a layer of tar paper was added for additional protection.

Straw, of course, brought another problem: mice. A bale of straw makes a perfect apartment house for nesting field mice. Just about the time their summer food supply ran out, we conveniently set up warm winter quarters for them, with a virtual cornucopia of food to choose from—ours. So, the next winterizing task was setting a battery of mousetraps. We also made sure the cat stayed in at night after that.

Water pipes were protected as much as possible, knowing that in the bleakest cold of winter our only safeguard against frozen or burst pipes would be to keep the faucets running. Even that was no guarantee in the northern reaches of Wisconsin. Some mornings we awoke to find solid icicles drooping down from the faucets.

Winterizing took most September weekends and some in October. But by Thanksgiving, the house was warm, the mice were under control, the cellar was filled with canned goods, the stove was glowing cheerfully, and as we looked out at the first snow dusting across the backyard, we took pleasure in knowing that, because of our efforts, we would survive the coming winter.

I just winterized our house. I opened each window and pulled the storm window down in front of the screen. Then I clicked off the air-conditioning and flipped the thermostat to "Heat," and set the temperature control to a comfortable seventy-five degrees. Then I put new filters in the furnace.

The whole job took fifteen minutes. Afterward I spent a long time staring out at the backyard where the first winter snow would soon dance among the trees.

Next weekend I'll take an hour and winterize my car.

Canning

Okay, maybe I was unfair to the Home Canning Lobby when I made disparaging remarks in my column about the wax beans and tomatoes I had to eat as a kid.

I am not against canning. It was only a few years ago I last spent an entire July weekend joyfully peeling, cooking, seasoning, and canning applesauce—about twenty-four quarts of it—from apples from the gnarled and aging Golden Transparent apple tree in the backyard. The product of those weekends every July was delicious. I have been genuinely disappointed that the tree has yielded no fruit for the past two years.

Also, when we first moved here in 1981, we planted an ambitious vegetable garden of carrots, green beans, tomatoes, and strawberries. For several years we canned tomatoes and froze about a gazillion bags of beans, carrots, and strawberries. Unfortunately, when the owner of the pasture behind us sprayed herbicides to kill off the broadleaf weeds one year, he also killed off our garden.

Putting up part of summer's abundance for winter appetites confirms a sense of purpose. When I was a kid, we kept apples in a barrel in the cellar. By spring we were finding more bad ones than good ones, and even the good ones were wrinkled and leathery by then. But pulling an apple out of that barrel when the snow was flying outside gave me a sense of survival, the kind squirrels probably get when they find a long-lost nut. After all, I was the one who picked them and put them in the barrel in the first place. It was one of my assigned chores.

Another of my chores during the summer was to rid the garden of potato bugs. This job has little to recommend it, trust me. But there was a definite sense of achievement when the mound of freshly dug potatoes grew to shoulder height one mellow day in October.

My dad had a wooden bin in the cellar for the potatoes. The onions were harvested with their stalks on, and these were twisted together and hung from nails.

I have good memories about gardens and canning: steaming kettles of dark red plum juice waiting to be transmuted into sweet, fragrant jelly; light-amber jars of apple jelly; currant preserves; quarts of sugar pears canned with slices of quince and scattered whole cloves; citrus preserves so sweet they made your teeth itch just to think about them; and bread and butter pickles, mellow and tangy. I used to take a personal inventory of these delights on Saturdays in the cellar and calculate how many more slices of bread slathered with blackberry preserves I could look forward to.

I used to inventory other stuff in the cellar, too. Wax beans were at the top of my hate list. It wasn't that they were bad, it was just that we had so many of them. My parents had green thumbs. They could coax a garden to abundance on bedrock. Moreover, they had a special talent for growing things that man was never intended to eat—parsnips, okra, rutabaga, and, of course, wax beans. I remember my mother sitting at the table completely hidden behind a gigantic pile of wax beans harvested in just one pass through the garden.

And, naturally, whatever the garden grew got cooked and steamed and stuffed into quart jars. And then we had to eat it—every day for the rest of our lives. My greatest joy one winter was when something turned the canned beans bad. I eagerly volunteered to help empty the soured jars into the compost pit outside. I could barely contain my joy as I loudly counted all forty-eight jars as I emptied them.

I know now that feeding the family was more difficult that year. It wasn't that we had less than others; nobody had much in those days. Growing a garden and canning the yield was a necessary part of staying alive. Everybody did it.

But I'm also sure that everybody secretly rejoiced a little when the wax beans turned sour.

Labor Day—the Last Hurrah

When Labor Day Monday was over, Tuesday morning was "back to school." I always enjoyed school. Besides, the first day was just a lot of getting books and then cruising the dime store to buy school supplies. It was kind of fun, really. I always bought stuff I didn't need and never used, like pencil boxes and protractors. In eight years of elementary school, I recall only one class requiring a protractor. Yet every year every kid bought a new one. Somewhere there is an enormous glut of unused protractors.

I never could figure out why we needed pencil boxes either. As soon as we got all our stuff to school, it went into our desks where it stayed until we cleared the whole shebang out late the following May. I remember the teacher passing the wastebasket down the row at the end of the school year as we deposited our yearlong collections of scrap paper, pieces of eraser, paper clips, rubber bands, apple cores, bits of forgotten sandwiches, dried paste bottles, blotters with ink squiggles on one side … and broken protractors. We always had to buy notebooks too, with dividers for each subject we would study during the year. Why? I don't know. The teacher always gave us paper for each lesson, and we wound up using our notebooks for drawing pictures of airplanes and writing love notes.

The approach of Labor Day was always traumatic. I remember when school got out in spring, I always sat down with a calendar and planned out the summer. I counted the days, circled the holidays, and wrote notes about things I absolutely planned to do.

Memorial Day was the first holiday, and it happened right at the end of the school year. Back in those dark ages of my youth, we called it Decoration Day. I remember there was always a poster contest and somebody stood up in class and read "In Flanders Fields."

Then a week later we were out. The next target was the Fourth of July. I always tried to get a job as soon as possible to save up money for fireworks. I swept floors in a couple of stores and made deliveries. And most of us mowed lawns, pushing those reluctant cast iron push mowers through acres of tall grass and weeds for three dollars a week.

One or two kids in the neighborhood tried selling Cloverine Brand Salve door to door. Not only did you get to keep the money you made (of course, you had to pay for your two dozen cans of salve up front), but if you sold everything and reordered, you won prizes as well. Even a brand new bike was on the block for some industrious salesman. Every summer I watched dreams of getting rich fade into dull disappointment as the doors the kids knocked on closed without anyone buying. I never sold salve.

There was, all told, a certain minimum amount of swimming, bike riding, picnicking, and tree climbing that had to be done during the summer. There were so many neighborhood games of hide-and-seek and red-light-green-light played late into the evening darkness, and definitely a preordained number of ice cream cones to eat.

By early August, I took stock of the summer. And I always seemed to be behind in some areas. I missed this swimming trip or that bike ride. I was sick that week and couldn't play with the other kids in the vacant lot next door. The summer calendar told the tale.

I tried to catch up, of course, pulling extra shifts on the ball field or at the swimming hole. But when Labor Day arrived, I always felt cheated out of something the summer had promised and had failed to deliver. And so Labor Day arrived with a twinge of regret.

Looking at the list of things I had hoped to accomplish this summer and seeing the ledger out of balance once again, I realized that I faced yet another Labor Day with a touch of disappointment.

Maybe I should go buy a protractor.

Fountain Pens—They Sometimes Leaked

My wife, Jeanne, found her old high school Home Economics textbook the other night, and we spent several hours hooting over some of the items printed between those ancient covers.

Item: "Runs in stockings are caused by a dropped stitch and may be mended at home or taken to a shop where they are mended by machine."

During World War II my mother used to mend her rayon stockings by darning them (a simple weaving technique using thread similar to that of the item). She also darned our socks for more years than I can remember. I think about her back then, sitting in her chair after supper, stretching socks over that magical wooden darning egg, the needle shuttling with lightning speed back and forth. Is there anyone out there who still darns socks? I wonder what happened to the shops that used to mend stockings by machine.

Item: "To remove an ink stain (caused by a leaking fountain pen), soak the article of clothing in milk."

Now I've noticed that the fountain pen has been making a comeback recently, but a few years ago I was hard pressed to find someone who had ever seen one. Technology was the villain, of course. The ballpoint pen showed up about 1949 or so, and the trusty fountain pen joined the ranks of rayon stockings and wooden darning eggs.

I got my first fountain pen in the sixth grade—a shiny black Parker with a 14K gold point. I remember going to Newberry's Five & Dime to buy ink, the pen proudly clipped to my shirt pocket. I considered the selection: an entire display case filled with inks for fountain pens. The big players in the ink business in those days were the same companies that made the fountain pens. Shaeffer offered bottles of Scrip ink. Parker made something called Quink (which was, I believe, a contraction of Quick-Drying Ink). Waterman had its entry, and there were a handful of lesser-known brands. One even had a bottle the exact size of the inkwells in school desks. Desks were made back then with holes in the top to hold bottles of ink.

I was torn between loyalty to the Parker company, which assured me that my pen would perform better if I used nothing but its ink, and Schaeffer, which offered the handy feature of an easy-fill reservoir at the top of its Scrip bottles. The problem with filling pens from ink bottles came when, after many fillings, the ink in the bottle ran low. The nib had to be submerged entirely in order to fill the pen. And when the bottle was mostly empty (presumably after writing thousands of pages), you had to tilt it. And, well, that's when you learned the true value of milk. With Schaeffer's reservoir, you simply turned the closed bottle upside down, and—voila—the reservoir was full, even when the bottle was nearly empty. I chose the Schaeffer.

Color was another tough decision. There were black, blue, blue-black (preferred by nine out of ten teachers), green, brown, red, and purple inks. I favored brown myself, although I had a secret compulsion to use nothing but red. Yielding to authority, however, I bought blue-black. Later, a girl in my eighth-grade class penned her assignments in a flawless hand with purple ink. She always got A's. I went right out and bought a bottle of brown ink for my trusty Schaeffer pen. Lamentably, my penmanship improved but slightly and my grades not at all.

By the time I got to college (after a stint in the military), fountain pens had slipped quietly away and Parker's latest entry was a smooth-writing ballpoint called the T-Ball Jotter. Later came the felt-tip pen, followed by today's marvelous microline fiber tip.

I remember visiting my parents' home sometime later and sorting through several boxes of my stuff. I found nine mostly full bottles of Schaeffer's Scrip ink, blue-black mostly, but there was a bottle of brown and—although I have no idea where it came from—a bottle of purple.

"As technology expands geometrically outward, time compresses inward," I am told, which means that none of us is as old as the changes surrounding us would indicate. Jeanne proved that when she checked the publication date of that "ancient" textbook.

"When was it published?" I asked.

"It's not actually very old," she said.

"No?" I asked.

"Just out of date."

Buddy Poppies

They're back on the street corners. Every year about this time they show up wearing their caps and carrying baskets. They are volunteers from Veterans of Foreign Wars (VFW), and their baskets are filled with Buddy Poppies.

The Buddy Poppy was born out of a poem about World War I. The poem, "In Flanders Fields," was written by Major John McCrae, who fought in Belgium and was impressed by blood-red poppies blooming among the rows of crosses at the military cemetery there.

The VFW got involved shortly after the war ended when it announced a program to provide assistance for the widows and orphans of veterans. The effort grew out of the popularity of McCrae's poem. The newly founded veterans' service organization ordered paper poppies manufactured by florists and sold them on street corners.

Later they hit on the idea of having disabled veterans make the poppies themselves at VA hospitals and veterans' homes—a decision that also provided a source of income for the veterans. Buddy Poppies are still made that way today. A total of 848 million flowers have been sold, and annual sales average $16 million. Proceeds benefit veterans in twelve states, a national home for widows and orphans, and various VFW relief funds.

Buddy Poppies drew a lot of attention over the years. For a long time the first poppy of the year always went to the President of the United States, pinned on his lapel by someone from the national home. Later a movie star was named "Buddy Poppy Girl" each year. Over the years Jane Wyman, Doris Day, and Natalie Wood traveled the country making public appearances for Buddy Poppies.

They don't go to the White House anymore, and movie stars no longer go on tour. But there is still a Buddy Poppy Girl every year, sometimes a resident of the VFW national home.

When I was in grade school, the VFW sponsored a poster contest every year based on the poem "In Flanders Fields." We were supposed to depict what Buddy Poppies meant to us. The local VFW post judged the entries, and the winning poster went on display in a downtown store window. In retrospect, it was tough for a ten-year-old to have much of a feel for war in the first place. And it was a little confusing because Buddy Poppies and the posters commemorated World War I while we were embroiled in the middle of World War II.

For my poster I drew rows of white crosses and put blooming poppies in between. At the bottom I drew a lifelike image of a Buddy Poppy, and then added the words "Buddy Poppies Help Us Remember Flanders Fields." I recall that the lettering got a little crowded toward the end of the line, and it wound up saying "Flanders Fils." I figured since I was the best artist in my class I'd win anyway.

Sadly, I didn't win the contest. A girl in my class won with a poster showing one cross and one poppy. The lettering said "My Grandfather lies in Flanders Fields." The man's name was inscribed on the cross. It was a big disappointment. My grandfather was still alive at the time.

Even then it was a point of pride to buy your Buddy Poppy early and wear it to school all day. I used to insert mine into a buttonhole in my shirt and twist the wire stem around the button. Unfortunately, after a couple of mishaps at the water fountain, the thing usually began to fall apart. But I wore it faithfully until bedtime.

I still buy a poppy every year whenever I find myself on a street corner where they are being sold. VFW volunteers don't get into the country or to all the suburbs, and sometimes I don't get one. Several years ago I got into my car and drove downtown just to buy a Buddy Poppy. I remember twisting it into my buttonhole and wearing it on my shirt all day. And sometime during the day I uttered the first words of McCrae's poem:

"In Flanders fields the poppies blow
Between the crosses, row on row ..."

Mom's Wash Day

I got another blast from the dark ages of my youth the other day when my wife asked me to take some things out of the clothes dryer while she was running errands.

"The dryer is set on 'damp dry' so they won't wrinkle," she said, "so be sure to take them out and hang them up when the dryer beeps. That way they'll be ready to wear."

There were further instructions about putting another load of items in the washing machine and what kind of setting to use for that. "All you have to do is push the button," she said.

As I stood there looking at those two gleaming white appliances and flexing my finger so it would be ready to push the button at the right time, I was struck by the vision of my mother doing laundry when my sister and brother and I were kids. That was the time when doing the laundry could be considered a dangerous sport.

Her washing machine was made by Easy Company and consisted of a tub with an agitator in the middle and a set of roller wringers mounted on one side. On the other side of the wringer was a platform that held two large galvanized tubs. One was filled with hot water that Mom heated on the stove in the kitchen and carried to the basement one teakettle at a time. The other one was filled with cold water. She also carried that water down from the pump in the kitchen a bucket at a time.

Of course, the washing machine was also filled with hot water, and then soap was added along with a cup of strong-smelling bleach. In went the clothes, and on went the machine. There were no dials or buttons on the Easy washing machine; you started it by pulling on a gearshift lever mounted on the side of the machine.

We were actually ahead of the times in our neighborhood. Our washing machine was electric. Neighbors on both sides had washing machines that ran on gasoline engines. Sometimes it could take half a day to coax the heavily used engines to run.

After the clothes had sloshed around in the tub for the right amount of time (only Mom knew how much time was needed), she would pull the gearshift lever to stop the machine so she could start running everything through the wringer.

This part was kind of tricky because, unlike modern machines, the Easy didn't dump the water out; Mom had to dig into the hot water to get the clothes. For this job she had a special stick she called her "wash stick." With it, she dipped into the scalding water and pulled the clothing a piece at a time out of the water and carefully fed it into the wringer.

The wringer was electric also, and you engaged it by flipping the gearshift lever into another slot. With the wash stick, she would fish the corner of a shirt, sheet or pair of work pants out of the washer and feed it into the wringer. The theory was, once it caught, it would feed evenly through the wringer and into the hot rinse in the tub on the other side.

That was the theory. What actually happened more often than not was the article of clothing tried to charge through the wringer in one soggy lump. Naturally, this caused the wringer to bog down and finally grind to a halt.

What you had to do then was smack a release lever on the side of the wringer, which made the whole thing come loose. Mom said the release was actually installed so you could break it loose if you got your hand caught in the wringer. There was only one thing wrong with that. Mom was only five feet tall, and it was a reach for her to even feed clothing into the wringer. It was always debatable whether she would be able to reach over to the side of the wringer and smack the release while the wringer was calmly gobbling up her arm. And, oh yeah, you also had to kick the shift lever into neutral at the same time to keep from burning out the motor.

From the hot rinse, the clothes were picked up again on the stick and fed through the wringer into the cold rinse, and then back through the wringer once more before being dumped into a laundry basket and carted out to the backyard and hung up on the clothesline to dry.

In some cases there was a third rinse in starch solution for Dad's shirts and khaki pants. All in all, it was a full day's labor fraught with danger. It was probably the danger more than anything else that prompted Dad to buy Mom a new Bendix washing machine when they hit the market right after World War II.

The Bendix was the actual forerunner of today's modern washers. It had both a wash cycle and a rinse cycle separated by several vigorous spin cycles. I use the word "vigorous" deliberately. The machine developed such enormous torque while spinning that it actually had to be bolted to the floor.

Dad knew this, of course, and dutifully drilled holes in the concrete floor and set bolts into the holes with mortar. Then he edged the machine into place and bolted it snugly to the floor.

The problem was the instruction manual that came with the machine failed to specify what size bolts were needed to keep the machine in place. Dad simply looked at the holes in the mounting brackets on the machine and guessed.

Apparently he guessed a little too conservatively. The very first time Mom fired up the machine, it roared into a spin cycle, snapped off all four bolts, and proceeded to chase her across the basement floor. By the time Dad got to the outlet and pulled the plug, she was sitting in the corner on the floor staring wide-eyed at the frothing machine.

What happened next was one of those profound moments that mark a family for life. Mom, who never said an unkind word about anything, pointed to the Bendix, and in a clear, unwavering voice said, "If you ever want another clean shirt, you will get rid of this damned thing before sundown."

The Bendix was gone within the hour, and the next day Dad brought home something called an Easy Spin Dryer. It was a regular agitator washing machine with a spinning drum mounted right next to it. Mom loved it and used it uneventfully for many years. Even in later years when she simply pushed a button to wash clothes, she would sometimes talk about the days when the most dangerous thing she ever did was the laundry.

Spring Cleaning—Grandma Style

Does anybody do spring cleaning anymore? I'm talking about the old-fashioned, strip-the-house-and-scrub-everything kind that my grandmother tortured the entire family with back in the thirties and forties.

Grandpa insisted that Grandma got a certain twinkle in her eye just before she announced spring cleaning. That's why on this particular spring morning he woke me very early and said we were going fishing. While I rubbed the sleep from my eyes and struggled into my clothes, I heard Grandma and Grandpa talking in the kitchen. I couldn't hear what they said, but a few minutes later Grandpa came into my bedroom and told me to go back to bed. We'd go fishing next week, he said. A few minutes later Grandma came in and told me to get dressed in a hurry. Today, she said, we're doing spring cleaning.

For those of you who never went through an old-fashioned spring cleaning— or who have mercifully forgotten it— let me describe what that day was like.

It started with the fastest breakfast I ever had. Usually Grandpa would have a second cup of coffee and read the paper at breakfast. On this particular morning Grandma whisked the dishes off the table the second the last spoonful of cereal was in our mouths. Grandpa didn't even get a first cup of coffee and definitely no paper.

Then Grandma began issuing orders. It was like being in the army. The first job was to take all the furniture out of the house and set it in the yard. The kitchen table and chairs went first, followed by everything in the living room. Then we emptied the bedrooms. Some of the heavier pieces of furniture, like china cabinets and dresser drawers, remained in the house but were moved into a corner. At some point during this exodus, my aunt and uncle showed up along with some cousins. Everybody pitched in. The men all shared the same look my Grandpa had. I guess they had planned to go fishing, too.

The living room and bedrooms had full-size rugs on the floors. These got rolled up and hauled into the backyard, where they were unrolled and hung over the clothesline. Then Grandma came out with a carpet beater and handed it to one of the cousins.

"Beat them until no dust comes out," she said to all of us, giving fair notice the job would be too big for any one kid. It occurs to me now that I haven't seen a carpet beater in years. The thing looked like a giant fly swatter except the swatter part was made of twisted steel so it sort of resembled the gate in a wrought iron fence. With each whack a cloud of dust billowed from the rug, choking us and covering us with grime.

While we were beating the rugs, the women were on their hands and knees scrubbing the floors with evil-smelling soap and water. Later they scrubbed the bed frames and all the woodwork in every room. The house smelled like an institution. A clean institution.

When dust finally stopped coming from the giant rugs and Grandma accepted them as clean, she hauled us into the house and issued our next assignment. Each of us received a handful of what looked like pink modeling clay with a sweet, pleasant smell. It was wallpaper cleaner. You shaped the stuff into a ball and then rolled it across the wall. It picked up the grime and left the wallpaper clean. The cleaner itself was jet black by the time we finished.

Windows were next, inside and out with strong ammonia water. Our eyes turned red and stung from the smell. But the windows were crystal clear when we were done. All the wooden furniture got scrubbed with soap and water and then had to be waxed and polished.

By nightfall everything was back in the house, and there was a cleanliness that you could feel. Literally, you could feel it. And that was because back then spring cleaning was not complete until each member of the household had swallowed a spoonful of tonic, artfully dispensed by Grandma. I don't know what the stuff was, but it tasted like the very thing we'd been cleaning off the walls. It did its job quickly, and after several trips to the bathroom, we were as clean as the house.

Spring cleaning has changed since then. The big reason, of course, is that houses don't get as dirty as they did back then. Our stoves and furnaces burned coal or wood in those days, and there were no filters to trap dirt. Today everything is electric or natural gas. Carpets are nailed down now, and modern carpet cleaning is as scientifically dedicated as cancer research. Window cleaners work better and actually smell good.

And best of all, nobody has come at me with a spoon and a bottle of spring tonic in years.

Telephones—Yesterday and Today

I think we've made a giant step backward with the telephone. Pick up the receiver and listen along with me, and you'll see what I mean.

Our first telephone was a big wooden box that hung on the kitchen wall. Our first telephone number was a long and a short. That's right, one long ring and one short ring. Our second telephone number was a distinctly more sophisticated, two shorts and a long.

The way it worked was this—every town had its own phone company with a switchboard and an operator. In the smaller towns, the phone company was often one room in the operator's house. If you wanted to talk to someone, you turned the crank on the side of your telephone several revolutions for one long ring. Then you picked up the receiver and listened. Unless it was the middle of the night and the operator had to find her glasses first, she usually answered right away. Then you could tell her the person you wanted to talk to or give her the phone number.

"Mable, give me Clarence Twittle."

"Right. That's long-short-long." Mable would then plug the appropriate line into her switchboard and twist her crank for the right ring.

Since there were a limited number of phone lines, everyone on the road had to share the same line, which meant that when the phone rang in your house, it rang in everyone else's at the same time. This also meant that anyone on the line could pick up the phone and listen in on your conversation. There was a way of knowing when this was happening, though. The phone system was a low-voltage electrical system designed to power one phone at a time. When someone else picked up and listened in, the power was cut in half. The result was you couldn't hear very well.

Most switchboard operators knew when this was happening. They also knew who was doing it and usually were quick to intervene.

"Clarabell Hanks, you hang up your phone this instant. This is a private phone call, and you got no business listening in!" Naturally, Clarabell never admitted to listening in and quickly hung up, but a series of short clicks on the line was a fair indication she still monitored the caller's progress. Of course, the operator listened in. She had to. How else would she know when the call was over? This meant that sometime during the day, Clarabell would just happen to make some trivial call and just happen to get into a conversation with Mable, the operator. Back then, small-town telephone operators were the most popular people around.

Not everyone had a telephone. Some couldn't afford it, of course, but others were without access. That meant the phone line didn't go by their houses. Even after numbers were assigned to subscribers, automated dialing remained years away. You still had to dial the operator and give her the number. And there was still a shortage of phone lines, so most folks continued to share party lines. And some, I have been told, continued to listen in.

Making a long-distance call meant the operator had to call another operator—usually in the closest big city— and place the call through her. That operator had to wait until a line was available and then place the call. Sometimes it could take an hour or more to make a long-distance call. Your operator would then ring you and tell you your call was ready.

It wasn't until microwave transmission and fiber optics arrived on the scene just a few years ago that the shortage of phone lines was resolved. That's when a strange phenomenon occurred.

Years ago people were clamoring for telephones, and the vision of the future was instant communication with anyone and everyone in the world just by picking up the phone. Then we got what we wished for, and today virtually everyone has two or more phones in the house and many have two or more phone lines.

Now, however, you can't really talk to anyone. No one is answering the phone anymore. Call any business and most residences, and you get voice mail with complicated menus and involved options.

"If you want to leave a message for Suzy, press one. If you want to leave a message for Sam, press two. If you want to send a fax, ..."

Hey, I don't want to leave a message for anyone, I want to talk to someone! And I figure if you call me you want to talk to me, too. So call me anytime. Just ring the operator and tell her you want two longs and a short.

Trains and the War Effort

(The following column was awarded First Place in 1995 by the Hoosier Press Association.)

I was driving across town the other day when traffic suddenly came to a halt. I jockeyed close in behind the car in front of me and peered ahead to see what was causing the delay.

Up in front, the red and white barricade of a railroad crossing had dropped into place, stopping the flow of cars. A red light flashed at the roadside, and a dull bell clanged its monotonous warning while a diesel switch engine lumbered into view, tugging a long procession of boxcars.

As I waited, idly reading the painted names and stenciled numbers on the slatted wooden sides of the railcars, I recalled another wait at another rail crossing.

It was probably 1944, a time when America's primary product was war machinery, lethal hardware moving round the clock through the doors of glowing factories onto an endless procession of waiting railcars. There were ranks of dull green tanks, howitzers, trucks, and jeeps. They were loaded onto flatcars and hastily covered with olive drab tarps while the engines up ahead hooked onto their loads and chuffed away toward the main rail line.

Military freight had priority on the rail lines back then. I remember riding the passenger train from Chicago to Indianapolis and being shunted to a siding while a fast freight loaded with half-tracks and trucks roared by. Most of the tarps had blown away, and the weapons stood proudly at attention, anticipating their destiny.

The train we were riding was filled with soldiers and sailors. Many were new recruits, just out of basic training, fresh and boisterous. There were returning veterans too, sitting quietly with their thoughts, rows of combat

70

ribbons decorating their chests. One of these men gave me his cap and said he had a son about my age that he hadn't seen for three years.

Military personnel boarded trains and buses first and got the seats. Civilians were expected to stand. Mostly we did that with pleasure. But I remember on the train a marine stood up and gave my mother his seat. His arm was in a cast. I noticed later my mother had been crying.

In 1944 we lived with my grandmother and my uncle in Racine, Wisconsin. Both my dad and uncle worked for Young Radiator Company, a firm that produced cooling systems for airplanes. They were part of the War Effort, and because of it, my uncle's car had a "C" ration sticker on the windshield. That meant he could buy more gasoline than people who worked in stores or for insurance companies. Because of this, we could go on Sunday drives.

One Sunday we were returning from a drive along Lake Michigan when traffic in front of us slowed to a halt. We sat for a few minutes, the engine idling. Then we noticed the people in front of us getting out of their cars. My uncle shut down the engine, and we got out and followed the crowd. About a block ahead we came to the rail crossing. The barricade was down, the red light was flashing, and the bell was clanging. In front of the barricade were four military policemen, rifles held at high port. The crowd stopped and waited.

Moments later the train came into view. We felt it first, a throbbing rhythm deep in the earth from the giant wheels. Then the tracks began to clatter, and the lead engine hove into view. Two giant steam engines belched columns of smoke as they labored to pick up speed. American flags were fastened to the front of both engines, soot-stained and frayed along the bottom. As the engines rumbled by, the flaps snapped and cracked against the wind like whips.

The cars that followed stretched for miles. Later no one was able to agree on the exact number. I remember my uncle surveying his pocket watch and saying it took exactly twenty-eight minutes to pass. There were open flatcars, loaded too quickly to cover with tarps, laden with armored personnel carriers, jeeps, and huge dump trucks with their steel beds loaded with extra tires. There were cannons lined up tight against one another, their barrels aimed at the overcast sky. I remember counting fifteen cars loaded with ambulances and predicting that each one would save at least one hundred fifty wounded soldiers. Many of the cars bore hastily written signs saying such things as "To Tojo with Love," "Happy Birthday, Adolf," and "God Bless America." One tank had been signed by every worker who helped put it together.

In addition to the flatcars, there were long ranks of boxcars, their doors double locked with huge iron rods. These cars had red flags flying from the front. Munitions, I guessed, maybe torpedoes for our submarine fleet in the Pacific.

In the middle of the train was a lone passenger car, draped from front to back with American flags. As it passed, the military policemen at the crossing snapped to attention and brought their rifles to a sharp salute. At the end of the train, two more engines pushed mightily and puffed smoke into the winter sky.

By the time we got back to the car and crossed the tracks, the entire train had disappeared. Over time I wondered how many of those proud war machines ended up abandoned on the beaches of Normandy or the sands of Iwo Jima. I also wondered how many more passenger cars had been pulled along the lakeshore, flags streaming from the windows.

There was a harmony of purpose all across America in those days, and it felt good to be part of it, even at the age of eight. We are a different nation today, with a different purpose. But every now and then, when I have to wait for a train to cross the road, I'll remember the day I was part of the War Effort.

Working My Way Up at the Greasy Spoon

It just dawned on me that I'm going to be coming full circle in my career one of these days. I know this because I talked to a man the other day who has just done it.

It was lunchtime, and I stopped into a fast-food restaurant to get a sandwich. The man who stood behind the counter looked about sixty-five.

"Just retired," he said, "and these folks have given me a part-time job."

When I was sixteen and legally able to work, I got a job in a restaurant. It wasn't a fast-food franchise, of course, more like a greasy spoon. I started out washing dishes in the back room. They had a slide-through dishwasher for the glasses, cups, plates, and bowls, but I had to scrub the big pots and pans by hand.

Later they taught me how to peel potatoes and shove them through the screen-like cutter that made french fries. I made enormous amounts of french fries.

After a while they showed me how to fry hamburgers and do set-ups. Set-ups were plates decorated with lettuce, onion, tomato, and pickle, awaiting the finished hamburger.

As my training progressed, I learned how to load up the french fry basket with an order of fries and pop it into the hot grease, and how to pull it out and prop it up to drain before serving. I learned how to make coffee and iced tea. I grasped the delicate art of making ice cream sundaes and milk shakes with scoops of real ice cream.

Finally, I learned how to operate the cash register. I was soon able to tally up somebody's bill for his food and even add a quip about the sales tax.

"Five cents for the governor," I learned to say with a smile.

There was even a special language they spoke at the greasy spoon.

"On one!" the counter man would yell out when someone ordered a hamburger.

"On one!" I'd reply and slap the preformed hamburger patty onto the grill.

"Works!" came the cry for one with everything.

"To go!" was the signal to grab a paper bag to put the finished burger into.

I worked at the greasy spoon for two summers and Fridays and Saturdays during the school year. I learned a lot, and I made enough money to buy my own clothes. Then it was time to go to college, and I quit my job at the greasy spoon. During my sophomore year in college, I worked in the kitchen of another restaurant during the evenings and on weekends. This time I made pizzas. And, of course, I scrubbed pots and pans.

I worked in a drugstore for a while, and one summer I worked for a sign painter. We spent all day in the blazing sun painting the back sides of billboards. In those days the backs of billboards were painted green.

Then I graduated, got a real job, and started that upward career spiral I'd heard so much about in earlier times. The years went by. I got married, had kids, and watched the kids grow up. I continued along the career spiral. I started my own business, made it work, watched it decline and peter out, got another job on the spiral and realized that was the way work went—up and down, round and round, keeping an eye on the horizon.

The other day I looked at the horizon and saw retirement looming there. As I thought about it, I realized I would probably have to find a part-time job. At first I was worried. Then I smiled. Hey, I know how to make french fries, and I can fry a mean hamburger.

And I have a lot of experience scrubbing pots and pans.

Summer Jobs

When I wrote about summer jobs I'd had as a kid, I overlooked a couple of important ones. One was the only job that ever scared me, and the other was the hardest work I ever did.

I got scared hauling water. I had a job this particular summer working for a water and cistern company. The company did two things—it hauled water to homes in the country that had no wells, and it cleaned the cisterns the water was kept in.

Central Missouri is very hilly and very rocky. You'd have to drill halfway to Singapore to put in a well. That explains why so many people in the area have cisterns. Essentially, a cistern is an underground tank, usually concrete, that holds water.

In that part of Missouri, most of the water in cisterns starts out as rainwater. Most folks have elaborate gutters and downspouts that channel the water into the cisterns. At some point, usually just before it enters the cistern, the water goes through a filter, which holds back dirt. Filters are almost always imperfect, of course, so some dirt manages to get into the cistern. In time, the dirt threatens to contaminate the water, and the cistern has to be cleaned.

Cleaning a cistern is hard work and highly unpleasant. First, you pump out as much of the remaining water as possible. Then you climb down into the cistern with a shovel, a bucket, a brush, and a bottle of cleaner. The first task is to scoop sediment off the bottom of the cistern with the shovel, put it into the bucket, and hand it up to the outside guy, who empties it and hands it back to you to fill up again.

The reason the job is unpleasant is because cisterns are sealed. They have little or no air in them. The bacteria and tiny water-based organisms that contaminate the water usually smell bad. Then, of course, there is the cleaner, which is pretty powerful and contains chlorine.

We were supposed to wear air masks when we cleaned a cistern, but they were painfully hot and uncomfortable. They reminded me of World War II gas masks. When you wore one for more than five minutes, condensation inside the mask fogged up the eyepieces so you couldn't see what you were doing. So, most of the time we took the masks off and worked as fast as possible, which left us feeling light-headed and nauseated.

That wasn't what scared me about the job, though. That came after we had finished cleaning a particular cistern and had flushed it with the truckload of water we had brought with us. Then we went back to town and the boss told me to load up another tank of water and go back out and fill the cistern. Sure, piece of cake. I filled the tank and headed out of town.

A by-product of the light-headedness was a kind of euphoria. My mind tended to wander. This is not the best thing to happen when driving in hilly country on top of ten tons of water. I snapped to attention just as I approached a sharp curve. The speedometer said 65 mph. I slammed on the brakes just as I headed into the curve. The truck began to buck like a wild stallion as I forced it into the turn. I'm sure I prayed. I don't remember it, but I'm sure it was short and to the point.

Miraculously, I made it around the turn without leaving the road or tipping over. I stopped the truck and spent a good five minutes getting rid of the shakes before proceeding. I quit the job the next day.

The hardest work I ever did was hauling hay at one of the area farms. The thing about hauling hay is that you have to do it in the sun, usually on the hottest day of the summer. The farmer narrowed his eyes at me and shook his head slightly when I applied for the job.

"Ever haul hay?" he asked. I shook my head.

"Hard work," he said. I nodded.

"You sure?" he asked. I nodded again. He pointed me to a wagon hooked to a tractor, where a half-dozen other kids sat. I climbed aboard. We bumped out to the hay field and climbed down. The field was covered with hundreds of freshly cut bales of hay. It smelled sweet.

The job worked like this: The tractor crawled along at a snail's pace while each kid ran over and picked up a bale of hay, lugged it back to the trailer, and horsed it aboard. You horse a bale of hay by balancing it on one knee and giving it an upward kick. One of the other kids showed me how.

The thing about bales of hay is that they have sharp stems sticking out of them, and these become embedded in your leg when you horse them onto the trailer. Another thing is that they start out weighing about twenty-five or thirty pounds, but gain weight rapidly. By noon on that particular July day, I was horsing three-hundred-pound hay bales upwards a distance of four feet to the bed of the trailer.

One more thing about hay bales: as you stack them on the trailer, you have to horse them higher. By the time the trailer was nearly loaded, I was horsing half-ton bales of hay the height of a seven-story building.

When the farmer drove me home at dusk and gave me my pay— about eight dollars, I think— I got out of the truck, agreed with a nod that I wasn't cut out to be a farmer, and watched him drive away. For several minutes I just stood there watching the truck disappear, not because I was lost in reverie, but because I was so stiff I couldn't move. I removed dozens of hay splinters from my leg and hobbled for a week.

Ever since that day, when I drive by a field where men are hauling hay, I salute in respect. And I drive away as quickly as possible.

Libraries Were Like Monasteries

Libraries used to be like monasteries, heavy with silence and thick with serious intent. I don't recall the libraries of my youth being places we went for the fun of it.

In elementary school we went to the library to learn about books. We learned that America's public library system was established by a man named Andrew Carnegie, that there were literally thousands of books in the library, and that we would be able to read any of them we wanted so long as we took care of them and returned them to the library on time. Failure to do either subjected us to fines and severe looks from the librarian.

Nobody talked in the library either. Even whispers had to be of the softest kind and used sparingly, which ruled out any meaningful discussion about what you were reading. Somehow that seemed to invalidate the purpose of going to the library in the first place.

This was particularly painful during high school when we went to the library to copy paragraphs out of the encyclopedia for our essays on Egypt. After all, I needed to know if any of my classmates were going to include the section on the Casbah and belly dancers, neither of which were in Egypt as it turns out.

Of course, there were some perverse pleasures inquisitive young minds could find at the library if you knew where to look—the Scientific section, which included medical books, for example. For quicker appetites there was always *Webster's Unabridged Dictionary*. Lamentably, this three-thousand-pound volume usually sat on a large wooden stand in full view of the crusty librarian. I had a feeling she knew what words we were looking up.

Books were always classified by the Dewey Decimal System. Every subject on the planet was assigned a three-digit classification followed by a decimal and various subclassifications. Just think that one man assigned himself the task of accomplishing this feat. His contribution defies measure, but I bet when he finished, his brain was totally fried.

Every book in the library was listed on a three-by-five index card. In addition to title, author, and publication history, these cards gave the classification number assigned to that book. The cards collectively were housed in magnificent cabinets of wooden file drawers. I seem to remember that all those early files were made of oak and beautifully varnished.

It wasn't until my college years that I found out how to use the library as a tool for learning. Term papers had the perverse habit of covering obscure topics. Your first hope was that someone had written a magazine article on the subject and that it could be found in the Readers' Guide to Periodical Literature. After that, you searched the index cards and haunted the stacks for pertinent material. You might search through dozens of books before hitting pay dirt.

In my senior year I had to write a term paper for a course in Byzantine History. Most of the material had to come from one book, and there was just one copy. The university library kindly let all twenty-five of us use the book on the premises in two-hour increments. We had to sign up in advance. My two-hour period was from midnight to 2:00 a.m. The book, translated from Polish in 1835, didn't exactly make for light reading. I passed the course, but just barely.

When I started writing for the newspaper, I spent a lot of time in the library looking through old issues of the paper—stuff from one hundred years ago. I learned a lot about who did what to whom in the area and managed to piece together a number of juicy stories.

One of the first improvements the library got was a microfilm system. After that, I looked up old newspaper articles from spools of film that covered a full thirty-five years of newspaper reporting at a whack.

Today the libraries have computers and CD-ROMs. The librarians have smiles and let you talk out loud. And the old card files are fading away. I went to the library the other day to look up a poem for my dad. He remembered scattered lines, but that was about it. I figured on a couple of hours searching through anthologies for the illusive tome.

Not so. The librarian slipped a disk into the CD-ROM, pushed a button, and the screen asked me for a line from the poem. I typed it in and voilà! The entire poem scrolled up in front of me. Seconds later the librarian handed me a printed copy, and I was on my way. Total time elapsed—ten minutes, portal to portal.

Technology is wonderful, of course. And I really appreciated the new, fast, easy way to find what I was looking for. But before I become too enthralled with the new order, I must remind myself that the magic of libraries comes from books. And as wonderful as computers are, they can never take the place of ink on paper, pressed into volumes and stacked on shelves, waiting for fertile minds to seek them out.

Come to think of it, I actually looked forward to spending two hours searching through books for that poem. In a way I feel cheated. Just a little.

My Favorite Comic Strips

There is only one thing wrong with the *New York Times*—no comics. Someone told me the paper's founders vehemently refused to run comics years ago as a move to set the newspaper apart from its rivals, whose publishers used comic strips to voice editorial opinions.

Despite the changing times, apparently the paper decided to stick to its no-comics policy. Too bad. Like most other Americans, I'm a comic strip addict, and I believe that comics, like jazz and movies, are uniquely American and have become major threads in the fabric of our heritage.

Part of that heritage is the pleasure I got as a kid sprawled on my stomach Sunday afternoons reading the comics. Even today, I can easily spend comfortable hours with books of *Pogo*, *Peanuts*, and *Calvin and Hobbs* comic strips.

Literally hundreds of comic strips have come and gone over the years. Most older ones I never saw, and many I never heard of. Among the former was *Buster Brown* and his dog, Tige, who graced the pages of the *New York Herald* during the early 1900s. The latter includes strips such as *Count Screwloose,* drawn by Milt Gross, and *Boob McNutt*, done by the wacky inventor/cartoonist Rube Goldberg. Both strips were popular during the 1930s.

I wouldn't know about these obscure comics today if the Smithsonian hadn't gathered them together in a three-hundred-page book. A few strips—like *Prince Valiant, Blondie, The Phantom,* and *Dick Tracy*—have steadfastly stayed the course across the generations. Characters in some, like *Gasoline Alley,* have aged through the years, and we have watched kids grow up, marry, and become parents and grandparents in their own right. Others, like *Barney Google,* started out as one thing and became another. Barney was a city slicker in the 1920s, constantly extolling the virtues of a knock-kneed racehorse named Spark Plug, until he met the consummate hillbilly, Snuffy Smith. Ever since, the strip has given us Snuffy's view of the world from the hills of Appalachia. Occasionally, however, Barney Google pays a visit, still riding Spark Plug, still looking like he just survived the Great Depression.

There were quite a few strips based on the blue-collar work ethic of the 1920s and '30s. *Bringing up Father* was the story of an immigrant bricklayer who won the Irish Sweepstakes and carried his corned-beef-and-cabbage lifestyle into his new Park Avenue environs, much to the dismay of his socially ambitious and pretentious wife. *Moon Mullins* and *Our Boarding House* exposed the foibles and joys of community living during the Depression.

Some American institutions were actually spawned by comic strips. *Bringing Up Father*, for example, made Dinty Moore's Bar & Grill famous, and Popeye's gluttonous pal Wimpy turned the cheeseburger into an American icon. Some strips reveled in high jinks and goofiness. Mutt and Jeff were always plotting escapades that inevitably backfired, and for the highest level of lunacy, no one could match the antics of Smoky Stover, an improbable fireman who drove a two-wheeled fire truck that routinely self-destructed in bursts of speed. Nuts and bolts flew everywhere, and even Smoky's ears would blow off. Somewhere in each of Smoky's strips would be a sign saying "Notary Sojak." Sorry, I haven't a clue.

Some comic strip artists displayed incredible diversity during their careers. Roy Crane created two strips involving the same characters—*Wash Tubbs* and *Captain Easy*. Both involved worldwide adventure and sometimes gothic heroism. When World War II erupted, Crane launched a new strip called *Buz Sawyer*, a navy pilot who fought in the Pacific. After the war, Buz and his shipboard pal Roscoe Sweeney turned to more domestic pursuits. Soon the strip was more about Roscoe and his pal Orville than it was about Buz.

In the 1930s Milton Caniff created a soldier of fortune named Terry Lee and placed him on the high seas of adventure in the strip *Terry and the Pirates*. When the war started, Terry became a fighter pilot and flew numerous missions based on actual news events of the day. At the same time, another artist named George Wunder created a strip about a private detective named Steve Canyon, who also found himself in the Air Corps. When the war ended and the Air Corps became the United States Air Force, Caniff and Wunder swapped comic strips.

In those early days of the Cold War, Caniff was dedicated to accuracy in his comic strip, a trait that got him in momentary hot water with the Defense Department. In one of his strips, Steve Canyon was given the job of test-flying a new jet fighter—the F86 Super Sabre Jet. The problem was the new plane was still under wraps at the Pentagon and no one on the streets had seen it.

"How did you get these pictures?" the military brass demanded, waving photos stamped "Top Secret" under Caniff's nose.

"I wrote a letter to the Air Force," Caniff replied, "asking for pictures of the newest airplanes. And that's what they sent me." Needless to say, the inquiry ended abruptly and quietly.

Maybe the *New York Times* should rethink its policy. Perhaps, in addition to running current comic strips, they could rerun some of the old ones. That way they truly would be publishing "All the News That's Fit to Print."

Salting a Bird's Tail and Other Tall Tales

I must have been five years old when my grandfather told me it was easy to catch a bird: just sprinkle salt on its tail. Naturally, I raced into the house, grabbed the saltshaker off the stove, and spent the next two hours trying to get close enough to a bird to sprinkle its tail.

After repeated failures, I complained to my grandfather that it wasn't working. "Well," he mused, scratching his chin, "you're probably not being quiet enough." Yep, I spent another two hours creeping silently toward one bird after another.

Of course, Grandpa sat there in his lawn chair thoroughly enjoying the show. Years later it dawned on me that if I could get close enough to a bird to put salt on its tail, I could probably catch it anyway.

Nobody seems to know where the idea came from. Grandpa later confessed he had fallen for it when he was a boy. I saw some reference to the tale in eighteenth-century literature. I think Sir Walter Scott wrote about it.

Come to think of it, kids have been the brunt of a whole bunch of myths over the years. A few of the kids in my old neighborhood believed that sparrows were baby pigeons. A lot of kids, after learning that chickens hatch from eggs, have swiped eggs from the fridge and tried to incubate them under their pillows at night. I think my sister tried this when she was six. The egg broke and got in her hair.

Actually my sister was pretty naive. I used to make up stuff to tell her simply because I knew she would believe it.

There's the whole business about pancakes, for instance. Once, when I was in high school and she was finishing up in elementary school, I was cooking pancakes for breakfast. My sister attentively watched my every move.

"You never want to turn a pancake more than once," I told her. "Otherwise it gets tough."

84

"Really?" she asked, eyes wide with the wonder of my knowledge. What the hell? I thought. "That's right, Sis. In fact, the more your turn them in the pan, the tougher they get."

"Wow," she exclaimed.

"You know that's how they made their moccasins, don't you?"

"The Indians made moccasins ..."

"Out of pancakes," I said matter-of-factly. "You see, they always mixed up a lot of extra batter. Then when breakfast was over, they would start making tough pancakes by continuing to cook them and turning them over and over in the pan." By this time her mouth was agape with awe, and she gazed deeply into my eyes.

"When they were tough enough, they would take them out of the pan and cut them into moccasins," I concluded.

"Can we try it?" she asked expectantly.

"I wish we could, Sis, but sadly, we use the wrong kind of eggs."

"You can't use regular eggs?" she asked, pulling the egg carton from the refrigerator.

"Nope, these are chicken eggs. To make moccasins the Indians had to use eggs from the ninny bird."

"Oh," she said sadly. "Could we find some ninny bird eggs?"

"Afraid not," I said, consolingly. "Ninny birds never come out during the day, and they hide at night. Only full-blooded Indians know how to look for them."

Years later—I think it was at her son's high school graduation—we were sitting together on the patio at her home in Phoenix.

"You know," she said in measured tones, "I've lived in Arizona for more than twenty years and have gotten to know a lot of Indians. Not one of them ever heard of making moccasins from pancakes."

"Well, I guess the old ways are dying out," I said as casually as possible, tiny beads of sweat forming on my brow. "They watch TV now, and no longer listen to the elders."

"You know what else?" she said, her mouth twisted into a sarcastic smile. "There is no such thing as a ninny bird."

"Funny how they became extinct all of a sudden," I muttered just as the phone rang.

"Saved by the bell," she cooed.

Man, oh man, I wish I had told her how to catch birds with a saltshaker.

That First Bike

I came across some snapshots the other day. One of them was a picture of one of our grandchildren taking her first ride on her new bicycle. Her face reflects pure ecstasy.

I remember the day. It was her birthday party. The bike, carefully assembled by a proud father, had pink tires and a matching pink seat. Training wheels on the rear promised that the young rider would pedal expertly and safely from the start.

The snapshot was taken on the first ride. There was no second ride. Halfway around the yard something broke, something inside the rear wheel sprocket. The young father rushed to examine the reluctant machine. He was joined by all the men at the party. They examined the thing, concurred it was broken, and conceded that the only thing to do was return it to the store for replacement. I decided to ride along.

At the store, a gracious clerk cheerfully dragged out a new bike. It was a perfect match for the first. On the floor of the store were rows and rows of bicycles. There were others like ours available in assorted colors. There were bikes with fat, knobby tires, and others with slick, narrow touring tires. Some had fenders, others did not. One group had gearshifts with up to sixteen available speeds. The bicycles were painted in various color schemes and outfitted with a variety of accessories— everything from water bottles to saddlebags.

Most notable were the different sizes. There were bikes to fit the smallest peewee to the lankiest long-legs. I calculated a kid could qualify for a new bike every year until he hit high school just by growing.

In the dark ages of my youth bicycles came in two sizes: twenty-four inch and twenty-eight inch. The smaller size were mostly girls' bikes, which made perfect sense since girls were smaller to begin with. All guys rode full-size twenty-eight-inch men's bicycles. Period.

It didn't matter if you couldn't reach the pedals; you coped. One kid fastened wooden blocks to the pedals. Another rode on the outside and reached his leg under the crossbar to the pedal on the other side. All of us learned to apply the brakes by swinging over the crossbar and balancing on one side.

We didn't have training wheels back then either. You learned to ride by getting on and letting go. Coasting down a gentle hill seemed to be a favorite training ground, probably because once you were in motion, you discovered it was impossible to pedal, keep your balance, and watch where you were going at the same time. By the time we were able to cruise down the street and negotiate turns and stops, we had survived a litany of cuts, scrapes, and bruises. My most valued wounds were a cut lip and a chipped tooth. I still bear the scar on my lip.

There was only one name in bicycles back then—Schwinn. If your parents cared, you rode a Schwinn. If not, you had some lesser machine that came from the Monkey Ward catalog. I had one of these. But so did most of the kids in town. After all, a new Schwinn could cost as much as eighty dollars!

Bikes broke back in those days, too. The difference was we fixed them ourselves. Every kid had a repair kit and knew the intricate workings of his bike by heart. Bicycle repair often was a social event. A half dozen of us would gather in someone's backyard and tear our bikes apart. We would clean and oil the parts and put them back together. Of course you couldn't do this without the required amount of bragging and bravado, mostly about speed and durability.

Things that broke included flat tires, broken spokes, loose seats and handle bars, and broken coaster brakes. It was the coaster brake that came most sharply into focus. There were two schools of preference regarding coaster brakes in those days—New Departure or Morrow. Your bike had one or the other, and each kid swore by the virtues of what propelled him through the streets. The New Departure brake was made up of a series of interlocking metal disks that fit on a central shaft. When it broke, one or more of the disks shattered and had to be replaced. The Morrow brake consisted of a brass cylinder that flexed against an outer drum when the brake was applied. Its weakness was the cylinder, which cracked after a certain number of panic stops. The good news was the Western Auto store carried inexpensive replacement parts for both.

You also carried a tire repair kit, also available at Western Auto for seventy-five cents. It consisted of a series of rubber patches and a tube of rubber cement in a cardboard tube. The lid had holes punched in it so it looked like a cheese grater. You used it to roughen the area around the puncture so the patch would hold. Of course, the most important thing about fixing a flat was to find the nail that caused the flat in the first place. There is no stupid like the kind you feel when you fix a flat only to get a second from the same nail five minutes later.

I probably put a gazillion miles on my bike. I painted it no fewer than ten times. I went through three sets of tires and at least as many inner tubes; bought two sets of shiny chrome fenders for it; replaced the front fork once (they break when you hit a railroad track broadside); added and removed a basket and a luggage rack fully a dozen times; replaced no fewer than twenty-five links in the chain; and installed six new Morrow coaster brakes. I know it was six because I saved all the broken ones; war trophies, I suppose. Sometime after I graduated from high school I discovered them in a box.

I doubt my granddaughter will remember her first bike. She had it for less than an hour. The replacement has long since disappeared as well. Yet there is one thing she will treasure forever: the thrill of that first ride, the ecstasy of motion. That only happens once in a lifetime. The snapshot says it all.

Litter Bags—Where Have They Gone?

Whatever happened to litter bags? You know, those free plastic bags you used to get at gas stations during the sixties and seventies.

They came with holes in the top so you could hang them on one of the knobs on the dashboard or on the window crank. And they always were imprinted with the name and logo of the stations giving them away, sort of the same way church fans used to be.

Church fans were always given away by funeral homes. I guess that was in case somebody died during the sermon, you'd know who to call. We used to have them from Kelly Funeral Home when I was a kid. The inscription on them said "Good Luck and Best Wishes." I always wondered what they meant by that.

Just about every gas station gave away litter bags. Because the things were so plentiful, we'd throw the old ones away and put new ones in every time we stopped to gas up. I used to put four of them in my car, one on every window crank, and they were always full. That amazed me, because the kids always handed their sticky ice cream napkins up to the front so we could put them in our litter bags.

Gas stations used to give away a lot of free stuff, even little orange balls you could stick on your radio antenna. One station gave away little tiger tails so you could let them dangle outside the gas cap and tell everyone you had a tiger in your tank. Stations used to have attendants who would pump your gas, too, and check the oil, clean the windshield, and check the air in your tires. But that was back when gas was cheap and they could afford to do things like that.

Litter bags were the biggest giveaway, however. They were so popular that by the time the 1970s rolled around, some cars even came with litter bags built in. I had a 1975 Chevy Laguna that had detachable litter baskets in the front seat on the panel in front of the doors. They didn't have them in back for some reason. I guess they knew the kids always passed their trash forward.

I liked that car. It had special bucket seats that swiveled to face the open door. That way you looked really cool when you got out.

It also had an eight-track tape player and a huge console to hold tapes. Of course, eight-track tapes were so big there was room for only six of them. Then somebody invented the cassette player, and the eight-tracks vanished overnight. I saw a bunch of eight-track tapes at a garage sale a few weeks ago. Nobody was buying.

Now the cassettes are gone and we have CD players in our cars. A friend of mine has room for one hundred CDs in a console smaller than the one for my six eight-tracks in the Laguna. I understand the next wave of technology will offer a small chip that you simply plug into your radio. You'll be able to buy the chips the way you did cassette tapes. They'll hold up to one hundred songs on each chip.

The litter bags disappeared about the same time the eight-tracks did. One reason, I guess, is that cars no longer have window cranks. They're all electric now. You just push a button. I don't remember the last time I saw a crank-up car window, or a litter bag, for that matter.

One thing bothers me about that. What's happening to all the litter? We get more of it today than ever before. Sandwiches, soft drinks, candy, chips—everything is wrapped in paper or plastic. That's the stuff we used to put in our litter bags.

I seriously wonder about that. The stuff has got to be going somewhere. Of course, I haven't checked the backseat lately either.

Thinking About Cars

Summertime rolls around and I find myself thinking about cars, mostly because of my early training. As kids, most of us guys spent our summers thinking about cars and talking about cars and dreaming of the day we could slide our butts behind the wheel and tool down the road on our own, free as birds, with nothing but the wind, the radio, and the endless pavement stretching out before us. Yeah!

We used to walk along those small-town dusty summer streets, running our hands across the hoods and fenders of cars parked along the sidewalk. And we'd extol the virtues of different engines, gearboxes, and paint jobs. We knew our facts back then. Buicks were big and soft-riding, for instance, but mostly they were driven very slowly by little old ladies. And they were always painted black. Oldsmobiles, on the other hand, had Rocket V8 engines and automatic transmissions, definitely hot and built for speed. Mostly they were painted British racing green or fire engine red. Very few little old ladies drove Oldsmobiles.

The car with the reputation of being fastest on the road was the Hudson. It was built close to the ground to handle high-speed turns better. It was so low to the ground that advertisers claimed you had to step *down* into it. My dad had a 1939 Hudson Terraplane, and I don't remember it being particularly fast. I do remember that a lot of mornings it wouldn't start.

One car was definitely faster than the Hudson, and that was the Tucker. There were only a few prototypes of this amazing car on the road, but everybody I've met claims to have seen at least one of them. One of the more vibrant claims was that Tuckers whipped along the highways and byways at speeds in excess of 100 mph, and when they passed you, a sign on the trunk lit up saying "You've Just Been Passed by a Tucker!" Tucker went out of business before his cars got into production.

Henry J. Kaiser teamed up with a guy named Fraser, and they built Kaisers and Frasers for a couple of years. They were very comfortable and very expensive, and they soon disappeared. Later, Kaiser developed the first economy car in America, a stripped-down little thing called a Henry J. Since Americans still bought gas for twenty cents a gallon, economy wasn't much of an issue. Kaiser took the concept to South America, where the Henry J. became wildly popular for more than two decades.

While we argued and dreamed of one day owning our own highly polished road rockets, we learned how to get our hands dirty on older, less glamorous models. A couple of the high school guys owned Model T's, and every once in a while we younger guys got a chance to help work on one of them. Mostly, we handed the owners different tools as they called for them.

Helping out, of course, entitled us to paint our names on the doors along with everyone else's for the July Fourth parade. That's what you did to Model T's in those days, painted them with crazy slogans. Most of us would have been astonished by the care and pampering lavished on the few remaining Model T's today.

Some of the guys used to buy Model A's and put beefy V8 engines in them. Then the 1933 Model B came along with a V8 already in place. It didn't take long for someone to figure out that if you reversed the leaf springs and removed the fenders, the Model B became the meanest machine on the road. Henry Ford himself would have been stunned to know that this short-lived transitory car would become the quintessential American hot rod.

I never owned a car until I got out of high school, although once I came very close. In 1949, a fun-loving couple from Kilgore, Texas, moved into the upstairs apartment in our house. He was a welder for the pipeline company. She drank Manhattans and played bridge. He drank red-eye whiskey and played poker. One night he won, among other things, a 1935 Lincoln from the local Chevy dealer. Seems some guy brought it by right after the Depression, hocked it for a few dollars, and never came back for it.

The next day was my fourteenth birthday, and the new owner offered his prize as a suitable present. Lamentably, my father nixed the whole idea and refused to relent—a wise decision as I view it today, although I didn't forgive him for years. Needless to say, for several days I tried to ignore my father's refusal and spent every waking moment at the Chevy garage sitting behind the big wooden steering wheel of "my very own car." For a short while, I was the envy of every kid in town.

Another missed opportunity came years later when I heard from a friend who raced stock cars on the local quarter-mile dirt track that his buddy had just bought a 1935 Ford Cabriolet that he was going to chop up and put on the track. I rushed to the scene only to despair at the sight of those big leather seats sitting on the junk pile and those swooping full fenders being cut into scrap.

What was so special about the Cabriolet? For many years, whenever Hollywood needed a romantic car for a particularly moving scene, they used a Ford Cabriolet. Dozens of movie stars kissed their leading ladies goodnight behind the rolled-up windows of the Cabriolet.

The special thing about cars back then was they were fun. They were also affordable, and you could work on them. Many's the Sunday afternoon I've spent in the backyard lowering a rebuilt engine into place or installing a new transmission with nothing but a handful of tools and a six-pack of beer.

Today's cars are not only expensive but also so complex you can't even change spark plugs anymore. Now we just run our cars through the automated car wash and count the payments left at the bank.

We Once Had Fans

The air conditioner in my car died just about the time the weather got hot. I called a guy I knew of who has a thriving business going around town fixing people's air conditioners. I called him twice, three times.

Finally, after two weeks, he returned my call and said he might be in my area in a day or so. Maybe. That was three weeks ago, and I haven't seen him yet.

Meanwhile I drive with the windows open and the blower blasting away on high. Every time I get out of the car, my shirt sticks to my back and trickles of sweat inch down my armpits.

I swear daily that I will stop waiting for this clown and take it to the dealer. A hundred bucks and a two-hour wait would have me driving down the street in refrigerated comfort.

And daily I get too busy.

This really shouldn't bother me. It's not the first hot summer we've had, after all. And looking back, I have to admit that every car I owned up until a few years ago was conspicuously without air-conditioning. In fact, it wasn't until sometime in the mid-1970s that carmakers made air-conditioning standard equipment on new cars.

We drove with the windows open, and on hot days or when we got stuck in traffic, sweat dribbled down our backs. We didn't mind it much. As Confucius says: "Where there are no alternatives, there are no problems." Most of the cars in those days had wing ventilators in the front windows. Swing them all the way open and a channel of fresh air poured into the car.

Some cars back then also had vents located near the floor that you could open for a supply of fresh air. The problem with some of these, however, was they wouldn't close in the winter.

My worst experience driving in the heat was in the summer of 1962. At high noon in the middle of the Nevada desert, a dump truck loaded with gravel overturned on the highway. Traffic came to an abrupt halt and sat immobile for three hours. Three already irritable kids and a pregnant wife in an un-air-conditioned car made for the longest three hours in human history. It is a matter of record that once we got moving again, no one in the car spoke for the next three hundred miles.

Everything is air-conditioned today: cars, trucks, even farm tractors. Those little cabs on the tractors are cool as a frosted watermelon on a scorching July day. A few years ago my wife bought a convertible, air-conditioned. Any day I expect to see a new lawn mower come out with air-conditioning.

And you can't find a building, public or private, that isn't air-conditioned today. The refrigeration works so well that a lot of people wear more clothes to work in the summer than they do in the winter. Otherwise they'd freeze.

When I was a kid, the only building in town that was air-conditioned was Finch's Drugstore. It was great fun to come in off the sizzling street, dripping wet with sweat, and feel the Artic chill sweep across our overheated bodies. It became so much fun that Mr. Finch finally banned us from his establishment unless we wanted to buy something.

Buildings had fans. Casablanca-style ceiling fans churned the hot air around, creating the illusion of comfort. Exhaust fans pulled air through the building and created a pleasant if not actually cool breeze.

We had an exhaust fan in our house, one of those big ones that ran off a drive belt rather than directly off the motor. It was mounted in one end of the house on the top floor. At night we closed all the windows in the house except for one in the basement and one in each bedroom. Then we turned the fan on low. The result was a pleasant breeze that wafted across our brows throughout the night. It was a beautiful and foolproof system. Almost.

One particularly hot night when I was about sixteen, my parents left me home alone while they made a trip out of town. I decided to get the maximum good from our cooling system. I closed every window except the one in the basement and the one in my bedroom. Then I turned the fan on high.

The result was a Force 10 gale that whipped through my window and rattled the pictures on the wall. It was wonderful. Three times I had to retrieve the covers from the floor. About midnight the novelty wore off, and I decided to moderate the blow. Besides, I was getting windburned. I got up to turn the fan down to low. That was when I discovered that the wind had sucked all the sawdust from my father's basement woodworking shop into the house and was blowing it around like a miniature tornado. Every room in the house was filled with an undulating cloud of sawdust.

I spent the rest of the night with the fan turned off, running the vacuum and dusting furniture. I finished the cleanup shortly before dawn, and turned the fan back on low before collapsing in overheated exhaustion in bed. My dreams the rest of the night were tortured with visions of sand dunes made of sawdust, swirls of fine dust blowing across an endless desert.

The next day Dad slapped me on the back.

"Thanks for emptying the sawdust bin," he said, adding something about wonders never ceasing. I curbed the urge to confess and accepted the compliment as an unexpected gift.

Spring Break—Pioneering the Long Trip

It must be getting close to spring break. The drugstores are suddenly out of suntan lotion, and the tanning centers have put on extra shifts. The tanning beds are generating so much heat, all the ice within a block of the place has melted.

Any day now, packs of marvelously tanned college kids will pile eight or ten to a car and drive 1,300 miles without stopping to the shores of Daytona Beach to get a suntan.

"You've already got a tan," I said to one of them. "Why bother?"

"If I get my tan before I go," she responded, "then I can focus on other things." There was little doubt about what the "other things" were.

"Boys," another added with a smile.

Before tanning beds, the kids would emerge from the classrooms looking like bleached parchment and return from Florida looking like boiled lobsters. Tanning beds may not be great for your skin long term, but they do relieve the shock of sudden sunburn.

And that, of course, leaves time for other things, like parties. Although spring break isn't quite the beer bust it used to be, the breweries still add an extra shift around the first of March.

I suppose spring break has been a tradition since colleges began. I've heard that the ancient Greeks held some pretty wild mid-semester toga parties. And young people are not designed to sit endlessly in classrooms pondering the nocturnal habits of eastern wombats. Their engines are set at too high an idle. They've got too much horsepower. They need to break free and peel rubber.

We had spring break back in the dark ages of my youth when I was in college. We just didn't call it that. And we didn't migrate to Florida either. Most of the gang I was in school with had part-time jobs and earned a few extra dollars over Easter. And we goofed off.

I did make one high-velocity trip over spring break. I was a freshman at the Kansas City Art Institute, dreaming, of course, of the fame and glory all young artists dream of. Several of us had been studying the legendary painters of Taos, New Mexico. What a great life, we agreed: high up in the mountains, clean air, beautiful scenery. Why don't we check it out?

At first, six of us were planning the trip. We would be finished with classes the Thursday before Good Friday and didn't have to be back until a week from the following Monday—eight glorious days. We started planning.

Most of us didn't have cars. And any car we did have was lucky to make it back up the driveway after a drive around the block. Except for Bernie. He had a new car. We decided that Bernie would drive and we would buy the gas.

By Wednesday night everyone had dropped out except for Bernie and me. I had twenty-five dollars; Bernie had thirty. We could do it if we spent no more than ten dollars on food. Besides, Bernie had a friend living in Taos. We could stay with him. We packed our watercolors and sketch pads and hit the road. Ignorance is more than bliss; it's essential to survival when you're young.

While we planned our costs carefully, we gave little thought to how long it might take us to drive clean across Kansas, part of Colorado, and into New Mexico. There were no interstate highways back then, so we had to slow down every five miles for another small town. Kansas has a lot of small towns. In addition, Bernie was very proud of his new car. It wasn't even broken in. He insisted we drive no faster than 50 mph. After a full day and half a night of driving, we had made it to the eastern edge of Colorado.

About midnight we checked into a dust-blown motel at the outskirts of some Colorado crossroads to get some sleep. I remember thinking the bed had to be the offspring of some medieval torture device. Pointed springs poked through the threadbare mattress in a dozen places. And just as I dozed off, Bernie announced it was time to get going.

By the time we got to Taos, both of us were so tired we only wanted to sleep. So we spent the first day of our spring vacation unconscious.

We spent the next few days seeing the astonishing beauty that had overwhelmed those early artists who came to Taos. We made firm resolves that we would return and be great just as soon as we finished school.

On the return trip, Bernie decided his car was broken in enough to exceed the 50 mph limit, and he drove like a man possessed. I don't recall exchanging more than five words during the nineteen hours it took to get back to Kansas City. It was nearly dawn when he left me at my rooming house. I dropped my sketching materials on the floor and flopped on the bed. Loose change fell from my pocket. I counted seventeen cents. I remember thinking that was enough for another half gallon of gas

I'm a Winner—So Was Mr. Duggan

I keep winning things, things I never see. At least eight times this year I've gotten urgent notices in the mail proclaiming that I'm a "Winner." At one point my sweepstakes winnings tallied to just under $15 million. Of course, I haven't actually gotten any of the money yet.

One of these sweepstakes—one tied to a consortium of magazine publishers, I believe—has been so sure that I'm a Winner they've sent me no fewer than five different notices, proclaiming my winnings at five different amounts. Now, I'm not sure whether my actually winnings are the cumulative total of these five different figures or if the amount keeps changing, sort of like barometric pressure, and, as a result, I've won only the amount listed in the last urgent notice. I guess I'll find out when the check arrives.

It's possible, I suppose, that these sweepstakes are like Duggan's Dry Goods back in my hometown. After many years of stagnant business, Mr. Duggan decided to hang it up. To speed up the process, he painted some signs announcing a "Giant Going Out of Business Sale" and put them in the store window.

The chronicles report that business at Duggan's Dry Goods was so brisk Mr. Duggan had to hire extra help to take care of the flood of customers. People came from surrounding towns and even from the city seventy-five miles away to capture a bargain at Duggan's Dry Goods Going Out of Business Sale.

As a result of this unexpected windfall, Duggan's Dry Goods remained open for another five years—the most prosperous period in the store's history. Every week or so, Mr. Duggan painted a new batch of signs for the window: "Prices Slashed … Closing Our Doors Forever," "Sacrifice Prices … Below Cost," "Time Is Running Out," and "Lost Our Lease." This latter claim, of course, was abjectly suspect since Mr. Duggan owned the building himself. But no one seemed to notice, or if they did, they didn't seem to mind.

There is no doubt that Mr. Duggan was onto something when he launched his sale, some fundamental marketing verity, no doubt. The fact that the terms of the sale flagrantly contradicted themselves didn't seem to matter. People loved it. Maybe all these sweepstakes are just another form of a Giant Going Out of Business Sale, and as long as they keep reminding me that Time Is Running Out, I'll keep ordering more magazines.

On the other hand, I keep getting other things that I don't want. *Truckers News* is a monthly magazine dedicated primarily to selling used trucks. It's sort of a *Wheels and Deals* for big rigs. Five years ago or so, I bought advertising in a publication for a client who had used trucks to sell. As proof of advertising, the publisher sent me a copy of the magazine each month. After a year my client changed his marketing strategy, and we discontinued the ads. Be that as it may, every month like clockwork I receive my copy of *Truckers News*. Maybe this is likewise due to some special marketing wisdom. Who knows, one day maybe all this subliminal advertising will overpower me and I will yield to the impulse to buy a used Peterbilt and a fifty-five-foot trailer.

I also receive a chiropractic publication for the same apparent reason, likewise one on heavy equipment, another representing the tool-and-die industry, and still another on no-till farming. However, I may be about to lose the grandparent of all these unstoppable publications. *Great Lakes Fruit Growers News* has just advised me that my subscription has expired.

Fifteen years ago I was tinkering with farm life up in Minnesota and came on the idea of putting in a commercial apple orchard. I had only a few acres, but local wisdom held it was enough to support about three hundred apple trees.

Now, I know next to nothing about growing apples, and back then I knew even less. But a successful orchard owner in the area took me under his wing, so to speak, and gave me some pointers. The first thing I needed to do was join the Great Lakes Fruit Growers Association. With my membership came a subscription to *Great Lakes Fruit Growers News*, a thick and pithy publication filled with sage advice about grafting, fighting blights, using pesticides safely, and marketing the fruits of my labor. Had things worked out, it no doubt would have been a bible to help me plot my horticultural success. I might even be taking the third-grade class on tours among the trees these days and offering up my own brand of apple-polishing wisdom.

Alas, my life unexpectedly shifted gears about that time, and I abandoned the orchard, sold the farm, and moved to Zionsville. *Great Lakes Fruit Growers News*, however, dutifully tracked me down and has been arriving in my mailbox faithfully ever since.

The notice I received in the mail cordially invites me to renew my subscription for another three years for the bargain-basement price of only fifteen dollars—about forty-two cents a copy. By my calculations, my last three-year subscription stretched out for an unprecedented fifteen years, putting the per-copy price at just over three cents.

I'm tempted to renew, just as I was staring in the window of Duggan's Dry Goods to Not Miss This Outstanding Opportunity. After all, how many things do you know of that you can really count on for the next fifteen years?

Gasconade River

I'd been there before, gliding silently along the dark green water of the Gasconade River in Central Missouri. I was outdoor editor of the *Jefferson City (MO) News-Tribune* back then and wrote a column called "Outdoors in the Ozarks." That made my float trips official work. I never let on that they were also a source of great personal pleasure.

When I went to work for the newspaper in 1958 and was handed the outdoor column, it was mostly a job that nobody else wanted to do. Correspondents across the state sent in news items. If they had anything to do with hunting or fishing, they were slated for "Outdoors in the Ozarks." Once a week somebody on the news desk pieced the column together from contributed items. I guess the editor figured I'd handle it the same way.

What the editor didn't bargain for was a conservation nut. My dad was a forester who believed trees and the land they sprang from should be nurtured and protected. He sensed that advancing technology would one day threaten our resources. I must have inherited his zeal, for after I had assembled two columns from spare parts, I decided it deserved better.

I started traveling around the state, taking notes. I floated the rivers, walked the fields, fished the waterways, and tried to feel the pulse of outdoor Missouri.

Sometimes what I wrote was well received. Sometimes it wasn't. A piece on the folly of stocking quail to satisfy hunters was picked up and reprinted in no fewer than a dozen publications around the country. Another column condemning the proliferation of billboards around the Lake of the Ozarks provoked blistering attacks from area merchants. I donned a disguise when visiting the Ozark region for several months after that.

When Secretary of the Interior Stuart Udall visited the Current River and declared that the area would be thereafter protected as a National Monument,

I heralded the move as devoid of politics and filled with conscience. When the state government launched a sorely needed boating commission, I lamented the political strings attached to the effort. I said what was needed was a mechanism to protect the state's lakes and rivers and those who enjoyed them from others who would exploit both for their own gain. I urged the commission to focus on preserving our resources and protecting our citizens from reckless boaters.

Regrettably, I left the newspaper and Missouri before the Boating Commission established a track record. My career took me along different paths thereafter, but I often thought about the staggering beauty that I had seen in Missouri and my fears that one day it might all be lost to neglect and greed.

Over the Fourth of July weekend, my wife and I accompanied my daughter and her family on a half-day float trip down the Gasconade River north of Vienna. It was a route I had floated several times before. Old memories flooded back as we slipped the canoes into the current and headed downstream. Old concerns came back, too. Would the river be dirty, polluted? Would the banks be littered with trash? Would building along the stream be out of control?

In less than a mile I knew my fears were groundless. The water was clear and abounded with fish. We stopped at several gravel bars to rest, eat lunch, and swim. In our entire trip we found just one soda can and one beer bottle— no paper, no trash, no junk. Homes built along the river were unobtrusive.

Motorboat traffic was heavy, but even though few bothered to slow down for slow-moving canoes, everybody smiled and waved. There was none of the aggressive high-speed destruction that so often marred holiday water sports three decades ago.

I'm glad I came back to the Outdoors in the Ozarks that I loved so dearly years ago. I know the state faces many new challenges. But everybody needs to know that as far as this conservation nut is concerned, it's doing a darned good job.

My Love Affair with Rivers

I've always had a thing about rivers, mostly because of my incurable wanderlust. Every river is a road to somewhere.

It's impossible to live on a river and not think about where you could go if you just had a raft or a boat. Mark Twain wrote books on the subject.

As a kid I lived on the banks of the Current River in southern Missouri. This crystal blue spring-fed stream wanders through endless crags and gullies along the Missouri-Arkansas border. Bass, goggle eye, and rainbow trout abound in the eddies. Canoes and flat-bottomed Jon boats ripple silently along with the current, lulling their passengers into stuporous contentment.

I used to sit on the riverbank at Doniphan, where I attended the third grade, and watch these sated souls drift by. After a while, I began to eye a pile of scrap lumber stacked at the river's edge, while my mind began equating the size and construction of a raft that would carry me downstream. When I could stand it no longer, I spirited a hammer, saw, and some nails from my father's toolbox and began to fashion the vessel of my dreams.

Some dreams are just too big for one small boy to handle by himself, so I decided to enlist a partner. His name was Cecil Franklin Jones, and he thought we ought to "float clear down to Arkansas, maybe even to the Mississippi River." I allowed as how we should just fool around under the bridge. Finally we reached a compromise and agreed to float down to the sawmill three miles downstream. We figured that would take about half a day, what with stops at various gravel bars along the way to explore for pirate treasure and the like. Cecil insisted his cousin who lived in the vicinity of the mill would tow us back upstream behind his motorboat.

Construction took most of a week. We had the basic raft completed in a couple of days, but we kept thinking up necessary modifications. At one point we decided the raft ought to be equipped with a cabin so we could sleep aboard at night if it ever came to that. And even if we weren't going someplace, we could use it to hold secret meetings.

The whole shebang was about eight feet long from stem to stern and about six feet from side to side. The cabin stood about three feet high and three feet square, with a slanted roof covered with real shingles we had found in a trash can behind the hardware store. We figured every good ship needs a flag, so we attached a cane fishing pole to the rear of the cabin and ran up our own national ensign. It started out to be a hand-painted version of the American flag. Then for good measure we added a picture of a fish. I don't recall why the fish exactly, but we deemed it crucial at the time. We also discussed building some sort of steering device, but we gave up on that when we ran out of nails. A couple of ash poles commandeered at the last moment would have to do.

The Saturday we picked for the maiden voyage dawned clear and sunny. I raced through breakfast and bolted for the door. My mother, always quick to sense portents and omens, cut me off at the porch. Where was I going in such a hurry, she wanted to know. I didn't lie. I told her Cecil Franklin and I had built something and were going to try it out. I prayed she wouldn't ask exactly what it was we had built. She didn't.

The two of us met at the river's edge where our raft waited, tied to a willow sapling. I remember stopping on the bank and scrutinizing our handiwork. I don't remember ever seeing a more beautiful craft. The food we had stowed aboard the night before was still there. We even had a jug filled with drinking water.

After checking everything out at least three times, we untied our vessel, climbed aboard, and pushed away from shore.

What happened next is unclear, but it became immediately apparent that some finer points of marine architecture and boatbuilding had been grievously overlooked. The raft began to float sideways downstream. We tried using the poles to correct the problem but only succeeded in turning it completely around so it was going downstream backward. We also discovered that planks by themselves provide little flotation. The weight of two nine-year-olds, plus the cabin, the food, and sundry odds and ends, put the vessel perilously low in the water. Moreover, when we both stood in the same place on deck, that part of the raft submerged, and our tennis shoes were awash in the icy spring water.

Frantically, we attempted to turn the raft and balance it at the same time. It seems we also had misjudged the current, which propelled us pell-mell in the direction of Arkansas. You need to understand that the Current River is a zigzag series of quiet pools, sharp turns, and white-water rapids. It was a combination of the latter two of these that got us into serious trouble about a quarter mile downstream from our launch point.

As the raft lurched into the rapids, it turned slightly, and one corner rammed hard into a protruding rock. The entire raft shuddered mightily and spun around on its axis. The second corner was now wedged in between two rocks, forcing the entire rear end under water. This sent the two crew members scrambling for the forward section. About this time the current caught the raft broadside and twisted it into an arch. Immediately, planks began breaking loose and nails popped their moorings throughout the length of the craft. Next thing I remember is everything broke apart at once, and I was in the water.

Somehow I managed to grab onto a rock and inch myself toward shore. I had lost track of Cecil Franklin, but after reaching the safety of the riverbank, I discovered he had managed to make the opposite shore. I glanced downriver in time to see the only thing remaining of our raft—the cabin—bobbing along the current like an abandoned box. There wasn't another splinter to be seen.

By the time we had walked back to town, our clothes were fairly dry. We parted company quietly, preferring to grieve in solitude.

I think of that ill-fated adventure sometimes and wonder with brief thanksgiving what forces protect the hides of reckless little boys.

More River Thoughts

More stuff about rivers. There's a state park in Minnesota where you can step across the Mississippi River. It's almost inconceivable that three thousand miles south it takes two hours in a ferryboat to cross the same river. And when it's foggy, you can't see from shore to shore.

It doesn't take Old Man River very long to get big, either. When you consider all the rivers and streams in Minnesota and the fact that they all flow into the Mississippi at some point, it's no surprise that the river is fully navigable by the time it reaches St. Paul. A few miles downstream, the St. Croix flows into the Mississippi, nearly doubling its size again.

I used to take float trips down the upper St. Croix. We'd start from that part of Wisconsin known as the Chippewa Flowage—a stone's throw north of Danbury—and float our canoe down to the dam at Taylors Falls. Below the dam the traffic is mostly motorboats. On the upper St. Croix, however, almost everyone travels by canoe. The water here is stained a golden iodine color by tamarack trees, and it is so clean you can drink directly from the river.

We'd float during the morning, stop on a sandbar for lunch and a swim, and then float on till evening. We always camped on one of the islands in the middle of the river. Why? No mosquitoes. Seems these pesky insects have an aversion to flying over water. That was some years ago, of course. I understand the Park Service has since prohibited camping on the islands. Too many people left too much trash, I guess. Too bad. It was peaceful on those islands, water rippling on all sides of you, the westering stars overhead.

The Gasconade River in Missouri hosts what is known as the US Army's navy: the squadrons of Corps of Engineers workboats that maintain the locks and dams on the Mississippi. The men who work on these boats will tell you the army has more boats than the navy. I've seen them, and I believe it.

The Mississippi is awesome and unforgiving. When the water level dropped during the drought a few years ago, the skeletons of several paddle-wheel riverboats, giant queens of the river, were exposed for the first time above the shoals that sank them a century or more before. In the 1950s, a barge carrying fifty new cars from the Ford plant in St. Louis ran into a submerged piling and sank to the bottom. Amateur divers and salvors by the hundreds flocked onto the river to see if they could salvage a new car. Folks who knew the river never bothered to try. They knew nothing that sank would ever resurface. They were right. The divers worked frantically for a few days, and then drifted away empty-handed.

If the Mississippi is unforgiving, the Missouri is just plain dangerous. I didn't know this at first. When I moved to Jefferson City and saw this powerful river churning past the state capitol, I could think of nothing better than building a houseboat and exploring the lengths of her shores. You'd think that after my homemade raft disintegrated in the rapids of the Current River and dunked my nine-year-old body into the freezing water years earlier, my lust for danger on the high seas would have abated for all time. But memory has a way of softening over time. Besides, as I said, I didn't know about the danger.

Until a month later, that is. I was a general-assignment reporter for the *Jefferson City (MO) News-Tribune* at the time, so when one of the giant towboats that push coal barges back and forth between Kansas City and St. Louis got hung up on a sandbar thirty miles upstream, my editor yelled at me to get out there and get the story.

"And take the movie camera and get some TV footage," he added.

By the time I finally found the obscure river road that would take me to the site, it was completely dark. I inched between the cornfields along the river until I could make out the work lights on the water up ahead. I got as close as possible and parked. Then I got out and walked to the bank of the river.

I could see the shape of the boat against the water. The bow was high in the air, and the stern disappeared at the water's edge. In the lights that glowed against the high cabin, I could read the boat's nameplate in block letters: *St. Charles*. Another boat was alongside. Near as I could tell, it was a dredge, essentially a giant floating vacuum cleaner used by the Corps of Engineers to suck silt out of the river channel. There was no one on shore, and it was too far out to the boats for anyone to hear me. I went back to the car and hunkered down to get some sleep until daylight.

When the first gray mists of dawn crept down the river, I crawled out of the car and walked stiffly over to the river's edge. What I saw astonished me. There was nothing there. The towboat was gone and so was the dredge. I aimed the movie camera at the river and filmed a ten-second panorama of peace and tranquility. Then I drove back to town to call the Corps of Engineers. They must have gotten the towboat freed during the night, I told myself.

"We buried it," the engineer on the phone said matter-of-factly. I was incredulous. Seems the Missouri bottom is mostly silt. When it rains, the silt moves. It can fill up the channel and build new sandbars in a matter of hours. It had been raining for three days.

"When the tow hit the sandbar, the stern went under and the aft compartment filled with water," the engineer explained. "Once a boat is sucked down into that silt, it's impossible to pull it out. The only thing we can do is bury it." I tried to imagine burying a boat more than a hundred feet long.

Back in the newsroom I wrote the story and had the film developed. When I showed it to the editor, he rubbed his eyes as the peaceful, empty river flickered on the screen.

"What the hell is *that*?" he demanded.

"A graveyard," I said. "That's where they buried the *St. Charles*." Later at my desk I came across my sketches of the houseboat I was planning. Quietly, I dropped them into the wastebasket.

A Mute Wedding and Another I Survived

I once wrote a short piece about a deaf-mute wedding. The entire ceremony was conducted in sign language in utter silence, except for a woman standing in the corner at the front of the church translating every sign into spoken English. I remarked that she stood in the same place where another woman stood on Sunday mornings translating spoken church services into sign language.

I didn't attend the reception that day but remember wondering if there was dancing and, if so, what kind of music they danced to. The piece brought in a lot of mail, most of it pointing out that I didn't know very much about the hearing impaired. Of course there was dancing! And the music was the same kind you'd find at any wedding reception. Music, I found out, was not just a hearing experience.

The piece also led to a whole slew of invitations to other weddings. The word got out that I was interested in unusual weddings. One was a wedding on horseback. The minister was thrown off his horse and sprained his ankle. He finished the ceremony while lying on a litter in the back of an ambulance.

Another wedding was for two Olympic swimming team hopefuls and was held in the YMCA pool. Another one was held under water in scuba gear. I missed most of the ceremony since I was standing on the shore, but at one point the best man surfaced and asked for help to find the ring, which had floated away during the vows. Dozens of guests donned flippers and masks to probe the lake floor for lost treasure. After a few minutes, the best man resurfaced and yelled, "Found it!" to the anxious crowd on the shore.

There were a lot of weddings held in caves. In fact, Bridal Cave in southern Missouri still has a constant procession of weddings held before its gaily lighted stalagmites. I heard that during one, the power went off and the entire wedding party had to wait in the dark for more than an hour for rescuers to arrive with flashlights.

There were weddings on riverboats, on trains, on basketball courts, and one unforgettable one in the middle of our city's busiest downtown intersection. This one was a marriage between two traffic cops. Planning went slightly awry, and the resulting traffic jam was the worst on record. It was sheer luck that no one got run over. Both the bride and groom wound up clearing cars from the streets for an hour after the ceremony.

One I heard about but did not witness was conducted during a skydive from five thousand feet. Halfway down, the wind shifted and the groom broke a leg when he was slammed into a barn, while the bride spent the first hour of her honeymoon hanging from the upper limbs of a tall tree.

It's an old joke that newspaper reports of Polish weddings begin with "Among the injured were ...", but my personal experience with a German wedding leads me to believe that anything could happen. This event took place in the small village of Kindsbach, Germany, while I was stationed there in the army. The wedding was for my landlady's daughter, and planning took the better part of a year. The money spent was, without doubt, the savings of a lifetime.

Before dawn on the day of the wedding, villagers turned out to decorate the town's single street. Flowers by the basketful were arranged along the cobblestones. Every one of the village's one hundred fifty residents took part. No fewer than thirty unsmiling and sober *hausfraus* descended on the bride with needles and thread to finish up her gown, while a similar number of totally smashed men assisted the groom with his uniform. Someone prepared a beautiful garland of fresh flowers for the bride, and I recall that several men made it their mission to string together a half-dozen cabbages and hang them around the groom's neck.

A virtual army prepared food in the kitchen while another task force set up chairs and tables in every corner of the house, in the small yard, and into the street. At one point two trucks arrived with deliveries. One was loaded with beer and the other with cases of white and red wines from the local vineyards.

Guests arrived from near and far, including a pair of cousins who managed somehow to get across the border from East Germany to attend the wedding. They spent much of their time looking worried and sitting in dark corners. Everyone brought food and presents.

Weddings in Germany at that time consisted of two separate ceremonies—a short, formal, and precisely official ceremony at the city hall conducted by the Burgermeister and a second immediately following at the church. Once both ceremonies were over, the real festivities began.

The first order of business after the bride and groom paraded back to the house from the church was a round of toasts. A corps of young men and women was enlisted to pass out wineglasses and pour wine for every toast. At this time there were no fewer than two hundred fifty guests and well-wishers in the street surrounding the happy couple. Each one offered and drank a toast, which meant everyone started off the celebration with a minimum of two hundred fifty swallows of wine. Even the bride, who kept her participation to the smallest of sips, was feeling woozy by the time someone signaled for dinner to begin.

Somehow I got seated at the head table next to the mother of the bride, and she took it upon herself to make sure I received a decent serving of everything that came to the table. I leave it to you to imagine what a three-hundred-pound German mother of the bride might consider a decent serving.

The meal started with an incredibly light and tasty soup, followed by fish, and then two or three meat dishes surrounded by vegetable side dishes, noodle dishes, pasta dishes, fowl dishes, and dumpling dishes. Everything was smothered in its own special sauce and accompanied by various pastries. Of course, every mouthful called for a new round of toasts.

I managed to crawl away to my own apartment sometime between a liberal serving of cream-covered strudel and a fiery plum brandy that could have propelled rockets into outer space. For several hours I writhed in agony as the food and drink I had consumed swelled to almost unimaginable proportions.

Sometime around midnight I awoke and staggered back to the party, by now a full-blown street dance. Drinking had shifted from wine to beer but had by no means diminished. Nor did any of the participants show signs of fading. I managed a glass of beer and a couple of slower dances, after which my body gave up entirely and I returned to my apartment.

The dancing continued throughout the night, and as guests splashed cold water on their faces, the village constable, the fire department, the sewer and water company, and the Burgermeister and all his clerks arrived for the official village breakfast with which they welcomed the new couple to the village.

Of course there were more toasts, more food including at least five different kinds of potatoes, and lots and lots of speeches. I managed a piece of toast and a mouthful of potatoes before my stomach rebelled and sent me back to my rooms.

The wedding feast continued for two more days and nights before finally petering out around 3:00 a.m. with a parade of guests snake-dancing through every building in the village—entering and exiting through the windows. At some point during the middle of that final night, someone kidnapped the bride, and the groom fell asleep in a wheelbarrow filled with goat feed.

Somehow the couple managed to get back together in time to catch the train to some unnamed destination for what I suppose was a well-deserved rest. Cleanup at the bride's home and throughout the village took the better part of the week, and for several days people showed up at the local constabulary to claim lost articles and to chip in a few deutsche marks for repair to broken streetlights and missing cobblestones.

I enjoyed the experience, of course, but I was happy to be shipped home soon after. I figured I was lucky enough to survive that first event, but I didn't want to tempt fate. My landlady had one more unmarried daughter.

Once We Wore Galoshes

Anybody out there remember galoshes? You know, those oversize rubber boots that you slipped on over your shoes.

Sometimes we called them overshoes. You pulled them on, tucked your pants legs inside, and then closed them up with four or five big snap-type buckles.

To be honest, I hadn't given galoshes a thought for years, not until Christmas Day, when the previous night's rain turned to a heavy snowfall. It came down for hours, flakes as big as dinner plates flopping onto the soggy ground, building up about four inches of mucky slush.

By the time I made three trips to the car to load up the Christmas haul, my shoes were soaked. That's when I thought about galoshes. As a kid I hated them. For one thing, they were huge—at least six times the size of my shoes, which expanded my feet to something slightly larger than an adult elephant's.

I don't know about you, but I don't ever remember an elephant winning any races. Young boys, on the other hand, live to win races. They are required by law to move at the speed of light, an utterly impossible task while wearing galoshes. It was like running with your feet stuck in buckets of wet cement.

But I wore them anyway. The reason was money was tight back in the dark ages of my youth. Each of us kids got one and only one new pair of shoes a year. We had to wear them not only to school every day but also to church and other stuffy functions that usually involved combing your hair, washing the back of your neck, and putting on "Sunday clothes."

The tricky part of all this was our shoes always had to look good—clean and shiny, with a fresh coat of polish. How could a guy go to school in all kinds of weather, play softball during lunch hour, and still keep his shoes looking good?

Part of the answer was shoe polish, of course. We went through probably a gallon of Dye'n'Shine polish every month. This was a polish made with ten-year-old boys in mind. It was a thick, opaque liquid. It was like giving your shoes a fresh coat of paint three times a week.

The other part of the answer was galoshes. If it was raining or snowing—or looked as though it might—Mom dragged out the galoshes. We groaned, but we wore them. The alternative—wet shoes—was too painful to risk.

If you slogged into the house in the middle of a tempest, soaked to the skin with your shoes oozing water, you had to dry them next to the stove overnight so you could wear them again the next day. The problem with leather is this: if you get it wet and then force it dry next to a hot stove, it takes on all the characteristics of cast iron. Wearing rock-hard shoes almost always guaranteed at least a half-dozen blisters. All in all, it was easier to wear the galoshes.

One other thing about galoshes. It was never a good idea to try to put them on after it started raining and your shoes were already wet. Once your shoes were wet, the galoshes wouldn't go on. You could get them about halfway on when they would suddenly and permanently seize up. You could neither get them the rest of the way on nor get them off. The only solution was to pull your feet out of your shoes and walk home barefooted. Then, of course, both your shoes and your galoshes got dried out next to the stove overnight.

So, as I walked into the house Christmas night with my shoes making squishy wet sounds, I thought about galoshes. And I wondered if anybody still wore them. That's when one of the grandkids showed up sporting a pair of bright pink zip-up rubber things on her feet—dainty and kind of pretty, actually. A fashion statement. "What are those?" I asked. "Galoshes," she said, proudly.

"Not even close," I muttered, "not even close."

Snow Forts

Okay, maybe I do like snow sometimes, a little. I was driving past the elementary school the other day and noticed a small pile of melting snow at one end of the school yard. There's no question what that pile of snow was originally—a Conqueror-of-the-Universe-Invincible-Forever Snow Fort. Yea!

I had a hand in building one of those when I was in the fourth grade. Heavy, wet snow had been falling all night, and when we trudged to school the next morning, it was up to our knees. As we entered the school building, a signal passed from boy to boy in my class. It said, "Recess: Snow Fort." I noticed a similar signal coursing through the fifth-grade population as well. We would be at war before the day was over.

Our first class in the morning was reading, and in the fourth grade we got to read about King Arthur and the Round Table. There were damsels in distress and the castle was under siege. When we stormed out for recess at the end of the period, you could almost hear the clanking of armor and the clattering of horses' hooves in the hall.

The world's greatest engineers are grade-school kids with a mission compressed into a twenty-minute recess. The choreography was quick and precise. While one kid drew out the floor plan with a stick, a dozen others began clearing away snow and rolling it into building blocks.

"Camelot!" we cried, and "All for one and one for all." So, we were confusing our literature. Who cared? The fort was the thing. Camelot. Yea! By the time the bell summoned us back to the dreary halls of learning, our fort stood proudly at the edge of the school yard. It was twenty feet long, four feet high, and had sides that swept back providing a safe enclosure for ammunition. Willie Jenkins, who was the self-appointed leader of the fourth grade on account of missing almost a full year of school because of rheumatic fever, pulled out a bright red engineer's bandanna and tied it to a stick. As we ran back to the school, he thrust the stick into the top of the wall. The fort was commissioned. The castle was safe.

The fifth-graders had managed to complete their fort, too. It stood ominously just beyond our own, a good snowball-throw away. Their banner was black. The battle lines were drawn.

The next hour and a half dragged by at a snail's pace, science followed by history (yawn). It wasn't even good history, with knights and such. When the lunch bell rang, the entire school stampeded out to the school yard in five seconds flat. One of the teachers commented that we had beaten our best fire drill time by a good seven seconds.

Instructions were brief and to the point: "You stand here," Willie Jenkins ordered, grabbing a kid by the arm and shoving him to a spot on the fort wall. "You are here, this is your place; and Joey, you keep the girls working." I should explain about the girls. They were noncombatants, but they were an important part of the war effort. They made snowballs. Ammo! In summer the boys played softball. The guys with the best throwing arms were put at strategic spots on the fort wall.

Within a minute or two the ramparts were manned, and snowballs began to fly. So did the taunts and jeers. Many of these were aimed at Willie Jenkins because he should have been in the fifth grade and on their side. They called him a sissy. That was a mistake. Willie threw snowballs like a man possessed. And he urged us on to throw faster, harder. He ran up and down inside the fort yelling like mad and hurling snowballs with deadly accuracy. It was beautiful.

Then fate stepped in. From the sidelines one of the third-grade girls, who had been playing on the swings, walked into the line of fire. One of Willie's snowballs thrown at nearly the speed of sound hit the girl squarely in the face. For a second or two, she just stood there. Then her legs buckled and she dropped to the ground. A trickle of blood ran down from her nose. Then she screamed.

Exactly two seconds later, Miss Mackinaw, the third-grade teacher, rushed in from the edge of the school yard, gathered up the wounded girl, and screamed at both sides to cease fire. Later the principle visited our classroom with the solemn news that the war was over. We were to dismantle our forts and forge our snowballs into plowshares. Furthermore, we were to live in peace from that day forward.

Just like Camelot. Yea!

Christmas Marches On

The Ghost of Christmas Past would be amazed by the changes we've made to Christmas over the years. Most of what is visibly Christmas came from evolving tradition in the first place, and much was borrowed from different cultures.

The Christmas tree itself didn't show up in America until the early 1800s when German immigrants in Pennsylvania decorated fir trees with fruit, paper flowers, and candles. Use of the fir tree itself probably came from early pagan times because it alone showed promise of surviving the winter.

The first Christmas tree in the White House was decorated by President Franklin Pierce in 1856. Today, millions of Americans watch on television as the President flips a switch lighting the enormous White House tree.

Queen Victoria and her German-born husband, Prince Albert, popularized the Christmas tree in England and introduced the first glass ornaments, all made individually by hand. Commercially made ornaments showed up just before the dawn of the twentieth century.

Lights on the tree started with candles. I read in one Pennsylvania Dutch journal that the writer's job on Christmas Eve was to fill a bucket with water and stand by in case the tree caught fire. Insurance underwriters would shudder at such a practice today. Now everything is festooned with lights, not just the tree, but the windows, the porch, the fence, and even the roof. Some folks' electric meters spin so fast during Christmas you can't read them.

It's hard to imagine making Christmas decorations from scratch. We did that one year. It was 1941; Japan had bombed Pearl Harbor, America was at war, and we had just learned that Dad would not be going into the service after all. We had been waiting for weeks while the doctors reviewed his medical records. He had ulcers, and sometimes they flared up.

We were all sure he would have to go. That's why we packed up a lot of our things and put them into storage, including our Christmas decorations. The minute Dad was called up, we would move.

A week before Christmas he got the news. No active duty for him; the ulcers were just too bad. I remember Dad walking up the path toward the house. It had been snowing all day, and it was piled high on the road and in the yard. We met him at the door, and he shouted the news. Mom ran through the snow to greet him, and they actually danced in circles in the snow. It was wonderful.

Later we talked quietly about the war. Dad wasn't going, but that meant somebody else would have to. I think we said some prayers that night. Later Dad made some eggnog with brandy, and we sang Christmas carols. The next day he found a small fir tree in the woods and brought it home. That's when we realized we had no decorations.

Frantically we looked around for materials. We had popcorn, of course, and a box of cranberries Dad had skimmed from a frozen bog nearby. Mom spilled out the contents of her abundant button jar, and we mixed brightly colored buttons with popcorn and cranberries.

We fashioned ornaments from colored paper and attached ripe quinces to the tree. I still get a twinge whenever I smell the spicy aroma of a quince. At last the tree was done except for a star at the top. It was fine, except that without a star it seemed somehow unfinished. Without a word Dad pulled the pack of cigarettes from his pocket and removed the wrapper. He turned it inside out and exposed the shiny foil interior—instant star.

We had our decorations back for the next Christmas, of course, and after that we added new lights, new balls, and even a new star, one with a blinking light in the center. Over time the old decorations all gave way to new ones, and we forgot about the Christmas of 1941.

But I think about it whenever one of my grandchildren sits down at the kitchen table with blunt-end scissors, construction paper, and a pot of glue. Kids, it seems, aren't fooled by all the fancy lights. For it to really be Christmas, you have to make the decorations yourself.

A Christmas Story

In 1949 a joyous event occurred in a little town in northern South Dakota. A family that had been separated by the ravages of war in Europe was once again united. Two members of the family—a brother and sister—had gotten to America in 1945. They found good jobs, new homes, prosperity.

But it wasn't until four years later that their parents were finally found alive. The old man and woman were living in separate displaced persons camps in Germany. They were quickly united with one another, and a few days before Christmas, they arrived in the United States.

Christmas dinner that year was an unparalleled feast. The brother and sister loaded the table with turkeys, hams, roast geese, and an almost endless variety of prepared delicacies from their native land.

When all was prepared, they sat down. But the old man shook his head sadly and refused to eat.

"Do you children remember the last Christmas we spent together?" he asked. They remembered a cold shack in a labor camp in Poznan, a small, desolate community in the Polish Corridor. It was 1942.

Together they recalled how on Christmas morning their father had left the shack before sunup. There was no food, and their last five sticks of wood burned in the makeshift stove in a feeble attempt to warm their frozen home.

Late in the day the old man returned. He carried with him the branch of a spruce tree and four potatoes—their Christmas tree and their Christmas dinner.

But the fire had long since burned out, and the stove was cold. He gave his wife the potatoes and told her to put them in a pot of water. Then he went to his bed and removed the straw from his mattress. A handful at a time, he fed the straw into the stove while the potatoes slowly began to cook. But when the straw was gone, the potatoes were still raw. So the woman brought the straw from her bed and burned it as well. Even that was not enough, so the two children joyfully dragged their mattresses to the stove and fed the straw into the flame.

When all the straw was gone, the family sat down at their table in front of the spruce branch now decorated with pieces of colored yarn from the woman's sewing basket. The potatoes were only half cooked.

"But we've never had such a meal," the old man sighed. "We sang Christmas carols and felt so good we didn't even mind sleeping on bare wooden bunks."

So, in 1949, this family's holiday feast—a festival of reunion and immense joy—began by sharing four half-cooked potatoes. It became a family tradition, observed each Christmas Day until the old couple died two years apart some twenty-five years later.

Making Peace with Winter

Every winter I think it's going to be different. Every winter I think this time I will see the beauty of snow. This time I won't be cold.

It never works. I am cold from the first frost in autumn until the first subtropical day of summer. And the snow is just a grim reminder that I am cold and that no amount of clothing or blazing fireplace can warm my freezing pelt.

You would think after all these years that I would have become resigned, that I would somehow have gained acceptance and thereby made peace with winter. Never, I tell you, never! Winter is the enemy that prowls the deep recesses of my soul and makes me fearful.

It started when I was a little kid living in northern Wisconsin in houses that had no insulation and no central heating; houses where frost coated the windows and even the ceiling joists; where at night even the shy deer mice would venture out on the cross beam above the table to absorb warmth from the kerosene lamp below. In those houses every member of the family got dressed in the morning while standing around the living room stove.

Later, when we moved to Missouri, I thought it would be better. It wasn't. It still snowed in winter, just not as much. Water still froze, windows still frosted, and we still got dressed next to the stove.

When I was in junior high, I took a paper route. It was June, school was out, and it was warm. I had no problem getting up at five o'clock in the morning and riding my bike across town to deliver newspapers.

Fast-forward to December and January. I still got up at five and pedaled across town with a basketful of papers. But I never left the house with fewer than two sweaters and two coats, a stocking cap pulled down over my eyebrows, and two pairs of gloves. Even so, I took a deep breath when I stepped outside and never let it out until I was back home three hours later.

When I had the chance to take a trip in the spring, I used it as an excuse to quit the newspaper delivery business. I also sold my bicycle so I wouldn't be tempted to ever do it again. After that I made sure all my after-school jobs were inside, preferably in the boiler room.

I actually found a store where I could linger inside pretending to contemplate a purchase while waiting for the bus to arrive. The proprietor never asked why a high school junior was so interested in plumbing fixtures, or why he might come into the store day after day and study faucets and sinks without ever making a purchase. In case he had asked, however, I had an answer rehearsed.

"Hey, kid. What are you doing in here?"

"My dad says I can have a sink in my room if I pick it out and earn the money to pay for it."

"A sink in your room? Why do you want a sink in your room?"

"I like to wash my hands after I do my homework." I actually thought that was a great answer. It's probably a good thing that nobody asked, and after awhile the people who worked there got used to seeing this weird kid agonizing over grease traps and showerheads every afternoon between five and five-thirty.

My most memorable bout with cold weather happened several years later when I was in the army, stationed in Germany. The Soviets had just put down the ill-fated Hungarian revolt, and NATO launched a giant military exercise along the eastern border of Germany.

I was a medical corpsman normally assigned to warm hospitals or heated ambulances, and thus the supply officer felt I had no real need for Arctic clothing. It only seemed natural, therefore, that I would be assigned as a road guard in the middle of a small village at midnight. My job was to stand at the intersection of two roads and wave an endless line of army trucks in the right direction. Did I mention this was in January?

It only took about two hours, but by the time the last truck stopped to pick me up, I was so cold someone had to help me get into the back of the truck. I was shaking so hard someone tossed me an Arctic sleeping bag and told me to get into it. I was so cold I couldn't even say thank you for a half hour. Then I fell asleep for the remaining five hours of the trip. I even offered to buy the sleeping bag when we stopped.

For the remaining year in my tour of duty, I made it my life's work to never be cold again. I planned the shortest routes from the barracks to the mess hall, waited around until I could bum a ride with whoever was going to the other side of the base, always found a reason to work inside when the rest of my company was assigned to some outside task, and never went anywhere without at least two layers of clothing.

I even packed an extra sweater for our battalion picnic on the warmest day of summer. Hey, when the sun went down, it got cold. People started calling me "Frosty." I didn't care as long as I could stay warm.

So, if you see this large mound of clothing gliding across the parking lot at the grocery store, don't be alarmed. It's just me staying warm.

White Christmases I Remember

I hate the cold, but I really treasure a white Christmas. As a child I was fortunate enough—in the White Christmas Department—to have lived in Wisconsin, where snow nearly always blows in sometime around Thanksgiving and covers the ground till the daffodils beg for mercy.

Later, I came by default to live in Minnesota, where nine months of winter and three months of damned cold weather is far more than an idle boast. In those beautiful but frigid regions, they not only patently guarantee a white Christmas each year but often throw in Labor Day and Easter as well. I have even seen snow fall in August.

In between Wisconsin and Minnesota, I lived in Missouri, a more temperate place where snow is wished for but seldom seen at Christmas. My recollection is that Christmas in Missouri was often warm and rainy. On those days children had to find contentment in trying out their new wagons and bicycles, while wistfully leaving their sleds idle and untested.

When snow did come to Missouri, cars that had to get around—taxis, ambulances, police cars—all suited up in clanking tire chains. Where snow is not a factor, neither is snow removal. By comparison, the streets of Minneapolis are quickly cleared even after the heaviest snows. No doubt the budget for snow removal in that city alone could pave half the state of Nevada.

I spent one winter in Washington, D.C. The climate there is even more temperate than here. And when it snowed that winter, people by the thousands abandoned their cars right in the middle of the street—stopped, got out, locked up, and left.

Turns out it all had to do with the way insurance companies wrote their accident policies on automobiles in Virginia and Maryland. Coverage was excluded for imprudent driving. And guess what. Imprudent driving included driving in snow.

I've been in Cleveland, where lake-effect snow can gather at the rate of a foot per hour. Christmases are usually white in Cleveland, likewise Syracuse, New York, where standing snow by the end of December can measure nine feet deep. In upstate New York, I'm told, people attach long poles with red flags to their cars. That's how they can tell if traffic is coming at the intersections.

The scariest snow I know of happens in South Dakota. The winds sweep across the prairie and create what the local residents call "whiteouts" or "ground blizzards." Ten feet up the sky is blue and the air is clear. But on the road, you can't see the front of your car. All you can do is slow down and inch to the right until you feel the shoulder. Then stop and wait and hope no one runs into you.

I was told once that Air Force pilots do much the same thing when their planes are caught in whiteouts in Antarctica. They slowly descend until they feel the ground. How about that for an exciting way to finish the day?

"Hello, Honey, I'm home."

The most un-Christmas-like Christmas I recall was on a navy destroyer in the harbor of Kaohsiung, Taiwan. The ship was dressed in brightly colored lights for the season, and Christmas songs blared nonstop from the ship's public address system.

Lamentably, shipboard sound systems have all the fidelity of tin cans connected by a string. They are designed to convey simple voice messages, such as "Abandon ship!" As a result, even the most familiar Christmas carols sounded like Chinese opera sung by angry tomcats.

We made up for it the day after Christmas. The entire ship's company went to a local orphanage and put on a party for one hundred twenty-five homeless kids. Most of them weren't really sure what Baby Jesus was all about, but they were happy to be invited to his birthday party.

A couple of years later I spent Christmas in Hawaii. Two weeks before the holiday, I was amazed to see cargo planes bring thousands of fresh-cut Christmas trees to the islands. Except for "Mele Kalikimaka" on the radio and fresh-sliced pineapple on the table, I would have thought I was back in the Midwest. Come to think of it, when I looked past the Christmas lights toward the beach, the moon on the sand almost looked like snow. Except it was a balmy seventy-five degrees.

I said I hated the cold, and I do. My body wasn't built with the right kind of thermostat to thrive in winter. I once promised to strap a snow shovel onto the top of my car and head south. When I reached a place where someone asked me what that thing was, there I would settle.

But even if one day I seek out the warm sands of more tropical climes, come this time of year, this overwhelming season of Christmas, I confess: I would look to the north, sniff the air ...

And quietly pray for snow.

High School—Looking Back Fifty Years

A lot has changed in the past fifty years. I really didn't know how much until I traveled to Missouri for my fiftieth high school class reunion.

The first thing I noticed was that everyone had gotten older—except me, of course. I hadn't changed a bit. At least that's what one of my classmates said as he sat down next to his Seeing Eye dog.

We all had name tags, of course, so we could cheat. "Hey, George, I would have recognized you anywhere!"

"I'm Fred." Darn, I knew I should have gotten new glasses.

Actually, some people were easy to recognize—same smile, same height and weight. We recognized others only after we found out who they were. One guy we called Porky had lost fifty pounds, and it wasn't easy recognizing him after a half century.

There were other changes, too. The guy who had a full head of flaming red hair was bald as a bowling ball. Come to think of it, I don't remember ever looking at his face before, just that outrageous head of hair. There was a lot of gray hair I don't remember seeing before. And almost everyone wears glasses now.

But there was another change, too. We used to be pretty protective of our cliques and pretentious about our status. There were borders we honored, lines we didn't cross. At some point all that had melted away. Maybe watching our own kids waste so much energy on the same pursuits had something to do with it. Or maybe by virtue of growing older, we also grew wiser.

There was a lot of achievement to talk about. Some became lawyers, others doctors. We had educators, corporate vice presidents, store owners, politicians, preachers, and farmers. One guy who chose a career in the marines said his greatest achievement in life was leading eighty-five men into combat in Vietnam and, a year later, bring all eighty-five back out alive.

We grew up in homes that survived the Great Depression, and we knew how to have no-money fun. As kids we played with homemade toys, and as teenagers we sacked groceries, delivered newspapers, and set pins at the bowling alley to buy our school supplies and after-school sodas. We were the last generation to completely support a war, and we were the first generation to wonder at the wisdom of calling a war by any other name.

We were by no means perfect. We got into trouble here and there, mostly by being in the wrong place at the wrong time. We used to have a snake dance through downtown on Halloween. We wound through the streets, stopping traffic and making a lot of noise. In our junior year it got out of hand, and a bunch of us wound up paying for the damage. Every now and then one of us would get caught with beer on our breath, and occasionally we'd find ourselves paying speeding tickets and being grounded for several weeks.

There were problems in school, too, and most of us were guilty of at least some of them. The six biggies were talking in class, chewing gum, making noise, running in the halls, breaking into line in the cafeteria, and missing the wastepaper basket with our trash. Come to think of it, considering today's school problems, I guess we weren't so bad after all.

In the final analysis, none of us found the solution to world peace or the cure for cancer, and probably none of us significantly changed anything for either good or bad.

But we did our best to live responsible lives, raise our children, support our communities, and worship the God who created us. Maybe in doing that we have in some small way left the world in better shape than when we found it.

THE PROJECT

Lots of people build additions to their homes, usually after identifying a particular need and undergoing extensive planning. Then, wisely, they hire a contractor to do the job. We didn't do it that way. We did it ourselves. The fact that we didn't have a clue what we were getting into was probably a plus; with no experience to draw on, the job looked easy.

Looks can be deceiving, however, and The Project, as it came to be known, stretched agonizingly from the three months originally estimated for its completion to more than eight years. Costs grew like weeds in summer, and the strain to our marriage sagged at times like an albatross around our necks.

We did have help. An uncommonly generous friend, a professional draftsman and framing carpenter, was with us from the beginning. He not only developed the plans for The Project but also volunteered to help us build it. For uncountable weekends and lax periods between his regular building jobs, My Friend the Carpenter helped lay foundation, construct flooring, erect walls, and assemble a roof over the structure. He also estimated materials needed for various phases of the job and cheerfully served as supervisor on the numerous occasions when other friends, knowing that we had bitten off far too much to chew by ourselves, showed up to help. Moreover, he did it all for minimum pay, sometimes no more than a hot meal.

Today we enjoy the fruits of our labor, and the scars on our budget and marriage are mostly healed. Am I glad we did it? Absolutely. Would I do it again? Not in a million years.

The Project Begins

Let's talk about evolution. I think the process described by Charles Darwin years ago has finally given up waiting for humans to conform to its wacky laws and has shifted its energies to man-made projects instead.

Moreover, the whole process has accelerated, sort of like time-lapse photography or fast-forwarding the VCR. And I think my newest project is its latest victim.

It started a couple of years ago when we shut down a family business and found ourselves with lots of "stuff" we couldn't get rid of but didn't really have room for at home: desks, chairs, filing cabinets, bookshelves, wastebaskets—there must have been a sale on wastebaskets, you know, "Buy One Get 50 Free"—and files, lots and lots of business files.

The simple solution was one of those public warehouses you rent by the month. Hooray! We could rent one for a couple of months, sort through everything, and then move out. Simple, yes? Well, not exactly. We hauled in some thirty truckloads of "stuff" quickly enough, but then we closed the warehouse door and locked it.

That was the problem, you see. It's an ironclad rule that if you want to sort through anything, you should never lock it behind closed doors. Locks have a way of making you forget everything.

It was a year or two later, I suppose, when we were tallying up expenses one day, that we suddenly realized that what we thought was last quarter's national debt was actually our warehouse rent. Whoa! Time Out! Quickly we grabbed a clean sheet of paper and began considering alternatives. That's when I got the idea for The Project.

A pole barn! That's what we needed. Yeah. We had plenty of room in the backyard for such a structure, and it was the perfect solution. We could clean out the expensive warehouse and store the whole shebang-load of "stuff" in our pole barn. Then we could sort through it and get rid of it. My wife and I danced for joy around the kitchen.

Then we discovered a couple of minor flaws in our plan. While it was true that we would eliminate monthly warehouse rent, we would still have to pay for building the pole barn. Pole barns aren't exactly cheap, and if you put in an asphalt floor, the price nearly doubles.

The second flaw had to do with our overall objectives: to sort through and get rid of "stuff." By transferring the "stuff," weren't we just transferring the problem? We visualized some future generation unlocking our pole barn and sorting through the relics of a bygone age—our "stuff." And worse, suppose we actually did sort through and get rid of everything. What would we need a pole barn for then?

Discouraged, we sat back down at the kitchen table and pondered our plans. The Project thus began its evolution. As I watched, the sketch of the pole barn began changing shape. Moments later it had become a garage! Hooray! We had long ago converted our existing garage into office space and had spent several winters lamenting the abuse our cars took every year sitting in the driveway. A garage was perfect! We could store our "stuff" in the garage until we sorted through it, and then we could park our cars indoors.

Then we began adding up what it would cost. Garages need concrete floors, of course, and concrete floors are vastly more expensive than ones made of asphalt. We were stunned to learn that the floor would actually cost more than the building. Plus, there was the question of heat and electricity. Once more we sat down in despair.

"What if," my wife began slowly, "we changed our office area back into the garage it was originally?" I raised one eyebrow. "That way we could park our cars indoors without having to build a new garage." I looked at her squarely in anticipation.

She narrowed her eyes as though scrutinizing some vision in her mind. "Then suppose we were to build an addition onto the back of our house, which would give us new office space. First we could use it to sort our 'stuff,' and then it could be converted into another bedroom." The idea exploded in my mind. Build something that would add value to the house! It was brilliant, and we sat down to sketch out our vision.

"You know," my wife said several hours later, looking up from an array of drawings of walls, rooflines, windows, and doors, "we have always talked about putting in a master bathroom someday." I edged closer and peered at the pile of drawings. A beautiful master bathroom materialized right before our eyes.

"What if," my wife said sometime later, looking up from a stack of remodeling books, "what if we would tie the new addition into the kitchen and add a combination sunroom/dining room?" I peeked over the mound of books and magazines at a picture of the most beautiful sunroom/dining room I had ever seen. "That way we could remodel the kitchen at the same time." I nodded silently in appreciation of the forces at work here. I knew at that moment The Project had taken on a life of its own and I was no longer in control.

Since then we have added yet another room, a deck, a skylight, and another exterior door. Moreover, landscaping plans have mysteriously shown up, and I have spotted drawings of rock walls, hanging gardens, and atriums.

What are we actually building? I don't know. I am told a man with a bulldozer will be here next week to excavate for the foundation. And several new remodeling magazines have appeared on our coffee table. One is entitled *Affordable Castles.*

I Have Created a Monster

Honestly, folks, all I wanted to do was build a simple addition to the back of our house, but it has already taken on proportions I never imagined. According to the blueprints, this structure is not much bigger than a carport and has about as much cubic footage as a U-Haul trailer. My wife and I have already lamented the fact that it will be too small.

But if that is true, why do I now have a hole in my backyard the size of the Gulf of Mexico? And right next to it is a mountain of dirt that looks like the south slope of Mount Everest.

For several weeks we walked around the whole project in the backyard while waiting for someone to dig out the crawl space. We had stakes at the corners and we laid out string to show where the walls would go.

"Not very big," my wife said, shaking her head. I nodded agreement. Maybe we wouldn't even need to bring in heavy equipment to dig out the space under the floor and pour the footings. Maybe a couple of guys with shovels could do it on a weekend.

Right.

I can categorically say it would take the entire population of Buffalo, New York, a month and a half working round the clock to move this much dirt. Did I say it was big? I expect the FAA to come by with orders for a beacon to be mounted on the top as a warning to low-flying aircraft. I couldn't see the top of it this morning because of low clouds. Really.

And it was scary how fast it all happened. The contractor showed up at seven-thirty in the morning and unloaded a machine the size of a locomotive. It had six-foot wheels and giant digging arms attached to each end. While I was walking over to introduce myself, the operator started the engine and began digging. I quickly jumped out of the way and stood there watching with my mouth open. Three hours later he was finished, and I was still standing there with my mouth open.

I guess I expected some sort of ceremony as we peeled the sod from the yard and carefully rolled it up for re-use. Each shovelful of dirt should have been consecrated to good health and happiness in the new structure. I guess I expected the contractor to take enough time for me to visualize our addition taking shape an inch at a time. But it didn't work that way. There were no ceremonies for sod or anything else. There wasn't even any sod, come to think of it. Everything just came up in huge buckets and got dumped in a pile.

By the time the excavator was finished and had loaded his machine back onto the trailer, the cement truck had arrived. Twenty minutes later he was done. I don't think he even saw me standing there. He just pumped out seven yards of concrete, hosed down his equipment, and drove away. Meanwhile, the two men finishing the concrete swished their tools across the surface, steadied their levels, nodded their heads, and then they vanished.

For a long time after that my wife and I just stood there taking it all in, trying to catch our breath.

"Looks awfully big," my wife said. "Are you sure that's the right size?" I shook my head. I wasn't sure of anything except that if it rained before we got our project "under roof," as they say in the construction business, we would have an Olympic-size swimming pool in the backyard, not to mention a mountain of mud right next to it.

At one point the cat ambled by, scolding us for digging holes in her yard without consulting her. Cool it, cat. They didn't consult with me either.

"One thing for sure," I ventured, gazing toward the top of our mountain of dirt, "no one could ever accuse us of thinking small."

The Project Becomes a Teaching Tool

Our new addition—The Project—has become a powerful teaching aid. Some things that I thought I knew—or should have—have been solidly reinforced with the smash of a hammer or the zip of a saw. Other lessons emerge but remain unsolved for later appetites.

One lesson I thought I knew has to do with bricks. In order to attach the floor of the addition to the existing floor, it was necessary to remove the bottom six rows of bricks from the back of the house. Later, of course, we would remove the rest of the bricks and re-use them on the outside of the new addition. But that, we reasoned, we could do at our leisure when we had time to carefully remove each brick, clean it, and stack it on a pallet.

Even as I write these words, this seems like such a sensible plan. But there was something that I had overlooked. It has to do with the nature of bricks. Imagine that a wall of bricks is like a stack of books laid flat one on top of another. Then, count six books up from the bottom and pull that one out. Is it reasonable to expect that all the books above would remain where they are? Of course not. Any schoolchild will tell you that all the other books will fall down.

Now, why did I expect the remainder of my brick wall to stay where it was after I had pulled out the sixth row? All I can say is I honestly never thought the entire wall would crash into the crawl space after that final hammer blow drove out the last brick.

We stood there as the dust settled, eyes wide with astonishment. My Friend the Carpenter finally squinted into the gloom and pursed his lips with that mark of wisdom carpenters are noted for.

"The bricks are down," he said softly.

Hastily, we tossed the fallen bricks into a haphazard pile on the ground. There they will sit until spring. Stupid bricks. On the positive side, the back side of the house is completely clear of bricks and ready for interior construction. I look at it as working ahead.

Another lesson has to do with geometry. It is simply this: If you build onto a crooked wall, the thing you build stands a teeny-weeny chance of being crooked as well. When the excavator measured for the crawl space, he squinted through his amazing electronic transit, shook his head, and said, "Your house is three inches out of square."

Right, I thought. How could he know that? I narrowed an eye and sighted along the back of the house. It looked pretty good to me. "Your addition goes halfway across," the excavator added, "which is going to put you an inch and a half out. You might want to compensate for that before you lay your foundation."

I nodded agreeably and forgot about it. In self-defense, I need to point out that neither My Friend the Carpenter nor I had ever laid a single concrete block in our lives. The fact that we came out "dead-on" on two walls and within a quarter inch on the third was for us reason enough for three days of celebration. Being an inch and a half out on the south wall was a small price to pay.

Besides, as he observed, "The mark of a professional carpenter is his ability to compensate for mistakes. We'll just add an inch and a half over the span of the floor." I think that bit of philosophy has a future in The Project.

Learning by Swinging a Hammer

I have been amazed by how much one can learn swinging a hammer. In fact, building the addition to our house, a.k.a. The Project, has become a substantial post-graduate course in humility.

I have learned, for instance, that most building problems can be solved by common sense. I have also learned that common sense is the first thing to go out the window when my ego is at stake. Plus, I have learned that most important bit of carpentry wisdom: when you cut a board too short the first time, cutting again doesn't help.

Last week it rained, snowed, and turned cold. From this I learned all about work gloves. Work gloves, you see, are designed to keep your hands safe from splinters and blisters. And when it's cold, they will keep your hands warm. This is important because of the nature of hands. When they are cold, they get stiff. Stiff hands tend to drop things like nails, hammers, and other heavy objects, often onto the hands or feet of other workers.

When we started working on The Project a month ago, I took note of the gloves My Friend the Carpenter wore. They were rich leather, soft and supple. I immediately went to the store and bought myself a pair just like them. After all, having the right tools is vital. This is especially true if there is the slightest chance you don't have a clue what you're doing.

For the next few days on the job, I wore my beautiful new leather work gloves whenever I was working. Not only did my hands remain blister- and splinter-free, but also the gloves began to turn a rich brown from use. I was impressed. Moreover, anyone who happened by and saw me perched high on the rafters of The Project flailing away with my hammer would know for certain that here was a man who knew what he was doing. Heady wine indeed.

Fast-forward to last week. As I said, it rained, snowed, and turned cold. Fortified with sweater and coveralls and my rich brown leather work gloves, I strode into the weather, hammer poised. Within five minutes I learned a few things about leather work gloves that I had not known before. First, they are not waterproof. As a matter of fact, they tend to suck up water like a sponge. Second, when they are wet, they cannot keep your hands warm. In mid-swing, I dropped my hammer and suddenly realized I could not flex my fingers enough to pick it up. I also realized that my hands were frozen solid.

"Problem?" My Friend the Carpenter asked. I tried to wiggle my fingers while wincing in pain.

"Ah," he nodded, slightly amused. "You need a pair of these." He showed me his gloves. They were heavy knitted wool. Underneath he wore light nylon liners. "Even if wool gets wet, it can keep you warm," he added, wiggling his own warm and toasty fingers.

I knew that. I even wrote a piece on the insulating qualities of wool some years ago. Hey, I know about wool. Common sense, yeah.

Another lesson had to do with the nature of numbers. For instance, when you read them upside down, they become totally different numbers. The number "32," for example, can be misread as "23." As amusing as this may be in an academic setting, it becomes downright infuriating in the art of carpentry.

Why, you might ask, would anyone read a number upside down in the first place? The answer has to do with the design of tape measures. So far as I know, all tape measures read left to right. This means that if you are measuring a board from right to left, the numbers on the tape are upside down. If you think it isn't easy to read the numbers wrong, just try it. It is especially tricky when you're dealing with fractions. Twice, for instance, I measured a board thirty-six and a half inches long and cut it at thirty-five and a half.

This reinforced the earlier lesson about basic carpentry: when you cut a board too short the first time, cutting it again doesn't help.

The Project Endures

Remember The Project, that teensy little addition to our house that was going to take no more than ninety days to complete? Well, I am happy to report that effective the first of the year, we no longer have to rake leaves off the floor or wear raincoats when working on the inside walls.

The roof is on! And it only took, um, well, one hundred twenty days. Now, let me clarify the word "roof." It is covered with wood and long strips of black roofing felt. And one whole side is actually shingled. We had some shingles on the other side, too, but had to take them off when we skipped a step.

This brings me to the dynamics of things like The Project. You may recall I expressed a suspicion some time ago that the mere act of nailing two boards together could create a life force. Moreover, that life force would grow exponentially with each additional board and nail. Well, I now suspect that this life force also takes on intelligence. And I am convinced it has a sense of humor.

And, in case you hadn't figured it out yet, I have become the brunt of that humor. Why else would carefully measured boards be too short when cut? And even after I cut them a second and third time, why would they still be too short? Why else would trim that is nailed precisely to a straight chalk line wind up crooked?

I'll tell you why. The Project is laughing at me. It has even pulled a joke or two on My Friend the Carpenter, like several weeks ago when we needed a new extension cord to run electric drills, saws, and such. My Friend the Carpenter took care of it, and the next Saturday morning he uncoiled a beautiful new cord—with a female plug at each end.

Let me tell you about the step we skipped, the one that forced us to remove the shingles from one side of the roof. Before you shingle, you must nail onto the edge of the roof a plastic doohickey called a drip rail. This thing causes rain to run down the fascia instead of seeping under the shingles and ultimately leaking onto your head when you're trying to enjoy Sunday dinner.

Normally, according to My Friend the Carpenter, you put on the fascia first and then you put on the drip rail. Normally. But wouldn't you know it, the lumberyard failed to deliver the cedar fascia material with the previous day's shipment.

"No problem," My Friend the Carpenter says, "we'll just nail some three-quarter-inch spacers in place, attach the drip rail over them, and then remove them when the fascia material arrives." Simple.

And so help me, that's what we did. Stacked in one corner of The Project are odd pieces of building materials left over from various construction steps. Included here was a plethora of leftovers from the subfloor—all assembled, I might add, of three-quarter-inch particle board. We selected a few healthy pieces, cut our spacers, and nailed them in place.

Then, of course, we nailed down the drip rail, and after that, the shingles. Fast-forward to the next Saturday, when the tardy fascia material is finally delivered and My Friend the Carpenter and I smugly set about to remove the three-quarter-inch spacers under the drip rail and install the three-quarter-inch fascia.

Ceremoniously we put the ladders in place, ascended with smiles of achievement, and then suddenly My Friend the Carpenter stopped smiling. I stood on my ladder, still smiling, and watched as he cocked his head, closed one eye, and suddenly frowned. Now, if there is anything you don't want to see while doing carpentry work, it's a frown. Frowns are almost always followed by words of discouragement, usually short, four-letter words.

"I know we put in three-quarter-inch spacers," he said in measured tones. I nodded agreement and looked at the spacers above. They looked thinner than they did when we put them up. In fact, they didn't look like three-quarter-inch spacers at all.

"These spacers are half-inch," My Friend the Carpenter snarled. Again I nodded agreement. There was no question we had a firm grip of the obvious that morning. We descended the ladders and picked up several scraps left from cutting our three-quarter-inch spacers. We stared in disbelief at the half-inch material.

"Well, they were three-quarter-inch pieces when we cut them," My Friend the Carpenter said. Once more I nodded agreement. "I guess they just shrank," he added. "Things do that when you skip a step."

We spent the rest of that day tearing off the shingles so we could move the drip rail. This time, of course, we put the three-quarter-inch fascia in place first.

Next week: How to re-shingle.

I Learn About Wiring

There is a vague possibility that the new addition to our house, a.k.a. The Project, may yet one day become a habitable structure. I go out on a limb to say that, I know, but I risk it because a major milestone has passed. The electrical wiring is finished, and—what's more—it has been approved by none less than the Inspector General of the Greater Building Code Permit Scrutinizing Army of Marion County, Volts and Ohms Division.

I haven't felt so relieved since I passed my first Commanding Officer's Inspection as a buck private in another army back in the days of the Korean War. I sweat bullets—literally—over that one and have taken inspections of any kind seriously ever since. For example, when the lawn treatment guy with the green truck stops by in the spring to inspect for weeds, I cringe in utter terror of "dandelion infestation." I usually rush into the bathroom and remain there behind locked doors until my wife assures me there are very few dandelions, only a smidgen of burdock, and no more than a tiny patch of nimble will.

My first thought when it came time to install electrical wiring, junction boxes, switches, and outlets in The Project was to hire an electrical contractor. A couple of cost estimates later, I realized I was going to have to do it myself if it was to be done at all. I called the county building permits office to see what, if anything, I could do.

"You'll have to pass a test," the woman at the permits office said cheerfully. "Then come in, and we'll issue a homeowner's permit allowing you to do your own wiring."

The only thing that scares me more than inspections is tests. The first time I took a written exam for my driver's license I took three days off work and locked myself in a room to study the driver's manual. Actually, I memorized it, every word on every page. In fact, when I did take the exam, I noticed a comma in one of the test questions had been left off. I pointed out the omission to the clerk at the license branch. She was not amused, but she gave me a perfect score anyway. I felt vindicated.

Needless to say, passing a test to install live electrical things in a house seemed a lot more serious than learning the proper way to signal for a left turn. I drove to the library and asked the clerk to help me find the books I would need.

"Are you sure you need all of those?" she asked as I lugged no fewer than sixteen heavy books on electrical subjects to the desk for checkout. I reviewed the titles. There was *The Principles of Electrical Engineering*, one called *A Contractors' Guide to Wiring Warehouses and Store Buildings*, another entitled *Understanding Sensitometry Variances in Electrical Engineering*, and still another called *The Master Electrician's Guide to Electrical Installations*. Several promised that I could pass both the Electrical Contractor's Examination and the Master Electrician's Exam on the first try. And, of course, I had copies of both the 1993 and the 1996 National Electrical Codes—thick books both, printed in very small type.

For the next three weeks I studied. I read, I reviewed, I memorized, and I took notes, pages of notes. When, shortly after midnight at the end of the third week, I was able to accurately calculate the electrical requirements for a seven-story office building and parking garage, I deemed myself ready to take the test. I called and made an appointment with the inspector.

The test was a single photocopied sheet of paper containing ten true-or-false questions. Surprisingly, not one of them had anything to do with the material covered in the books. Moreover, I was uncertain of the answers to half of them. A wave of despair swept over me as I calculated the best guesses. I told the inspector that I had been studying for weeks. I rattled off the books. He just whistled and shook his head.

"Hey, you passed," he beamed a few minutes later, handing my test paper back to me with his written approval to issue me a Homeowners Electrical Permit. "Call me when your wiring is in, and I'll come out to inspect it," he added. I groaned. Another test.

Next day I went down to the government center to get the permit. I have to admit I felt a little out of place, standing there in line at the permit counter in my suit and tie with a dozen other guys all decked out in loaded tool belts.

Back at The Project, I took the plunge. I figured out where I wanted electrical outlets, where the switches should go, and where to hook in ceiling fans. I drilled holes and threaded in a mile or so of white cable. At every step I consulted the book. A week later I tapped the final outlet box in place and realized I was finished. I called the inspector and told him I was done with the wiring.

"Great," he said. "I'll stop by in the morning to check it out." His voice sounded courteous, but I knew there was sinister innuendo behind that warm smile. I braced myself for the worst and headed for the bathroom.

The next morning he arrived ten minutes early and I knew I was in serious trouble. Inspectors don't arrive early unless they are up to no good. I led him through the house to The Project. For the next five minutes, he wandered casually among the sawhorses and boxes of nails, peeking and poking at my wiring while I braced myself between two wall studs and closed my eyes. Then he turned and looked at me.

"Good job," he announced, signing the permit. "Did you use one of your books to help you with this?" I admitted that I had. "Which one?" he asked. Sheepishly I showed him the book. I had picked it up at Kmart. It was entitled *House Wiring for Idiots*.

"That's a good one," he said. "I use it all the time."

The Roof Leaks

Time for another update on The Project. You know, that fifty-thousand-square-foot addition to the back of my house. Actually, it started out being only a little more than seven hundred square feet, but with the spring rains and warm temperatures, I can testify that it has taken root and grown as though demon-possessed.

I'm kidding about the size, of course. Shucks, it's probably no more than twenty thousand square feet by now, twenty-five tops. But rain has played a big part in The Project since my last report. Mostly this has to do with the nature of rain. Rain, you see, travels pretty much in a straight line—down. This means if there is the slight breach in a roof, the teensiest itty-bitty hole or crack, the rain will find it and continue on its natural course toward the center of the earth.

In my case this meant passing through the roof, down the walls, and onto the floor of The Project. This does not mean My Friend the Carpenter and I are bad roofers. At most, it means that maybe we didn't fully understand the Continuity Principle Governing Roofs. The Continuity Principle states that there shall be One and Only One Complete and Uninterrupted Roof covering a structure. Anything more or less violates that principle and will doom you to carrying buckets and mopping up after every rain.

My Friend the Carpenter and I reasoned that if we completely roofed the new addition with honesty, integrity, and the Pledge of Allegiance to the Flag, it wouldn't matter if we left the old roof as it was to replace next summer. To ensure watertightness where old roof met new roof, we spread great sheets of thick plastic that we weighted down with hundreds of pounds of concrete blocks.

For the first couple of weeks, it was perfect. Of course, it didn't rain for the first couple of weeks. When it did rain, we learned the infallibility of the Continuity Principle Governing Roofs. In short, we discovered that the Continuity Principle makes no exceptions and brooks no compromise. In a word, we had leaks.

Although the sheets of plastic covered every possible avenue of leakage, the water nonetheless got under the plastic, roamed at will across both old and new roofs, and poured through every available breach. This, of course, proved another principle governing water and roofs: the Principle of Unlimited Exploration. Water, you see, will violate every law of physics on the books and travel vast distances laterally and even uphill to get to a place where it can leak through and continue its downward passage. On The Project, rain actually traveled eighteen feet under the protective cover of brand new shingles to drip out around the new skylights. As a result, for several weeks we kept a large collection of buckets and bowls distributed strategically around the inside of the place. This, obviously, enacted the Law of Random Selection, which caused the leaks to move to new places not covered by buckets and bowls.

Meanwhile, progress had to continue. I managed to get all the electrical wiring installed, inspected, and approved. Unfortunately, with water cascading around and through switches and outlets whenever it rained, My Friend the Carpenter and I agreed that actually turning on the current probably would be imprudent. As we stood there one rainy Saturday morning, watching water run down the rafters and drip onto the floor a foot from the bucket, we realized there was no solution but to complete the roofing job.

The major troublemaker in all of this, My Friend the Carpenter allowed, was the valley where the new roof met the old roof. We had butted the two together but had failed to intermingle and overlap the shingles so as to produce One and Only One Complete and Uninterrupted Roof. Water from every other part of the roof descended into the valley and proceeded from there to the multitude of openings where it could drip through. Needless to say, we dedicated the next Saturday to compliance with the Continuity Principle Governing Roofs. We put down a layer of black roofing felt and followed this with a wide swath of gooey sheeting called "valley roll." This stuff is like something from a science fiction movie. You can stick a nail through it, pull it out, and it seals itself.

Once this was in place, we laid in our new shingles. Finally, as a contribution to the American tradition of over-engineering, we applied a thick bead of black roofing cement along the bottom of the valley. Archeologists a thousand years from now will uncover the undamaged valley of my roof and marvel at how well they built things back in the latter days of the twentieth century.

When the job was finished, My Friend the Carpenter and I congratulated one another on a job well done. We agreed that this was one roof that would withstand any amount of rain.

"Heck, this roof will stay dry in a hurricane," My Friend the Carpenter said.

"Hurricane, nothing," I volunteered. "This roof is better than Noah's Ark. It would survive another flood."

I did believe those words of trust. But I still left the buckets and bowls in place until The Project had stayed dry through three more days of rain. And I waited for another two downpours before turning on the electricity.

After all, who knows what other principles are lurking out there that I might have overlooked.

It Was Almost Like Escaping from Prison

I have been pondering occupational hazards recently. You know, those infirmities connected in one way or another with the kind of work one does. Tennis players get tennis elbow, for example, and computer programmers get carpal tunnel syndrome. Of course, kids who play video games become brain dead, and anyone who watches television night after night becomes a couch potato.

Well, I have concluded that the primary affliction that comes with being a prison guard is deafness. While I haven't researched this in the medical journals nor consulted with the AMA, I am pretty sure I'm right. The reason has to do with the nature of stone and concrete: when you hit it with a hammer, it makes a loud noise. Despite this verity, our library shelves are filled with books recounting the exploits of those who have hammered their way to freedom from some of the world's most diligent prisons.

All of this came to me as I undertook the next step in The Project, that seemingly endless list of tasks associated with building a small addition to the back of my house. It has been several months now since My Friend the Carpenter completed his portion of The Project and left me to wander the desert alone. Since then, all tasks have quadrupled in size and complexity. The very minute he packed up his tools and drove away, the entire addition grew from 719 square feet to a structure only slightly smaller than a domed stadium. Even the simple job of driving a 16-penny nail into a stud to use for a hook on which to hang my tool belt took the better part of an evening. This has to do, of course, with the nature of 16-penny nails. They bend, and if abused further, they break. It then takes a long period of time to dig out the nail fragment so you can drive in a new nail.

"Why didn't you just hammer it into the stud?" a neighbor who checks on me from time to time to make sure I haven't been swallowed up by two-by-fours and sheetrock wanted to know. I just shrugged. Obviously one of the occupational hazards for those who build house additions is stupidity.

Anyway, the most recent task on The Project is plumbing, and the first job in this department was to provide a path for all the drains and water pipes from the new laundry room and the new bathroom to the existing septic and water lines, which, of course, have been securely tucked in under the old portion of the house since the beginning of time. That meant I had to remove a portion of the concrete foundation separating The Project from the existing house.

The words themselves looked harmless enough. "Remove a portion of the foundation." Simple, not unlike the instructions given to the man in charge of building the Union Pacific Railroad eastward through the Rockies: "Dig a tunnel through the mountain." My Friend the Carpenter, of course, had foreseen this day back when we were rushing to get things under roof before the next snowfall.

"If we don't break through the concrete now, before we put the floor down, you'll have to do it lying down in the crawl space later," he said wistfully. I agreed, but by then it was already starting to snow. "I'll do it later," I muttered.

"Of course, it might be easier to dig a new well and septic just for the new addition," he added, smirking in the way that carpenters sometimes do. "Just kidding," he added.

Now, however, as I squeezed myself into the crawl space under the old portion of the house, armed with a heavy hammer, a chisel, and a can of bug spray, I wondered if maybe that wasn't really a pretty good idea. Flat on my back, I inched forward beneath pipes, wires, festoons of spider webs, and the dangling homes of numerous other bugs. Why do bugs insist on living in dark, damp places? Don't they know that sunshine is healthier? Maybe if bugs lived in the daylight they might not be so ill-tempered.

After what seemed like hours of inching through the muck and mire and spraying for bugs, I reached the designated spot where I was to "remove a portion of the foundation." I snapped on the work light and examined the section of concrete blocks in front of me. They looked a lot bigger and stronger than I remembered. I raised my hammer and tapped the top block. The hammer bounced off without even leaving a mark. I swung it again, this time with all my strength. The noise was deafening and echoed through the crawl space. My ears were ringing. The exertion left me out of breath. I examined the concrete block. There was a small dent in the surface. I had actually made some progress. I swung again. Again the noise was overwhelming. The dent in the concrete was deeper; at least I think it was. Moments later I heard the plaintive voice of my concerned neighbor calling. "Are you okay in there?" he asked. "I heard this loud noise and thought I'd check."

"I'm fine," I assured him, watching a bug crawl up the handle of my hammer and feeling the cool surge of mud and gravel soaking through my shirt.

As I lay there pondering for the gazillionth time my sanity in taking on The Project, I realized that what I was doing was breaking out, hammering through a concrete wall to freedom. I felt like Legionnaire Douglas Fairbanks breaking out of a German prison in the middle of the Sahara. I was one of only a handful of dedicated prisoners to ever escape from Alcatraz. Liberation was closer with each hammer blow.

That was when—lying there with my ears ringing from the percussion and water gurgling between my shoulder blades—I realized that all prison guards must be deaf. If they were not, I can categorically guarantee that no one would ever have escaped from any prison on earth by breaking through concrete walls.

I learned later that my concerned neighbor winced with each slam against the concrete, and all up and down the street people emerged from their houses to see if enemy planes were dropping bombs. Meanwhile, beneath the house I hammered away. When I finally broke through and saw daylight from the other crawl space, I yelled out spontaneously, "Freedom at last!" Fortunately, no one heard me.

Next Stop, the Sewer

Remember the guys who spent six months digging through the wall of an underground sewer to get into a bank vault? When they got caught, the judge tallied the hours they labored against the money they eventually got and figured they'd earned about twenty cents an hour.

I know how these guys must have felt. For the past several weeks I've been lying flat on my back in the "sewer" under my house installing plumbing for The Project. You know, that seemingly never-to-be-finished addition to my house.

Once the electrical service was finished a couple of months ago, I knew the plumbing was next. And since I'd had good luck with installing several miles of wire and hundreds of assorted switches and boxes with little more than a couple of clearly written books and the services of a professional electrician to help me get started, I figured the same process would work for the plumbing.

While waiting for my Plumbing Consultant to drop by and assess the task, I decided to get a jump on the whole shebang by breaking a hole through the concrete foundation separating the new addition and the old part of the house. After all, I would have to tie in the new plumbing to the existing pipes. By working ahead, I would save time later. I spent the next weekend flailing away with hammer and chisel.

The first thing my Plumbing Consultant did when he arrived on the scene was purse his lips and shake his head. I have learned that if there is anything you don't want to see a consultant do, it's shake his head. And you especially don't want to see him shake his head while pursing his lips. My Friend the Carpenter used to do both when we were in the sawing and hammering phase of The Project. In every case, the lip pursing and head shaking were immediately followed by the announcement that something was wrong, usually something I had done while "working ahead." Always, it was something that had to be done over.

"Nice hole," the Plumbing Consultant said, still shaking his head as he surveyed the gap in the foundation. "Of course, you'll need to break another one through about here," he added, tapping a section of foundation six feet away. So much for working ahead. Before the Plumbing Consultant left, he sketched a rough diagram on the back of an envelope and handed it to me.

"Run your drains like this," he said, indicating a series of lines and angles, "and do your water lines like this." The whole thing looked like a fuzzy enlargement of secret wartime plans photographed by candlelight by a nervous spy. I narrowed my eyes to make sense of it.

"Pretty simple, really," he said, getting into his car. "You shouldn't have any problems." I have also learned that you never want to hear a consultant say that a job is simple, especially as he is getting into his car and you know you'll never see him again. As he drove away, I looked again at the sketches. "Simple," I repeated softly.

Working with the sketches, the guy at the plumbing supply place was able to put together a list of materials that we loaded into my old banana van (a retired yellow rental van I bought during another life for a now defunct business venture) and I managed to haul home. To all estimates we added 10 percent.

"That way, you won't have to stop work and run back here for a forty-five-cent elbow in the middle of a project," the clerk said. Good idea, but I have observed such plans to be futile. This has to do, of course, with the dynamics of hardware and plumbing materials. No matter what you buy, you will need something you don't have in the middle of a project and will have to traipse across town to buy it. And, oh, yes, it probably will cost forty-five cents. In the past three weeks while installing the pipes indicated on the envelope sketch, I have had to stop work and go to the store for a missing item no fewer than thirty-two times.

I have learned a lot in the last three weeks. I have learned, for instance, that measurements possible in any plumbing project are always approximate, while measurements needed are always exact. I have also learned that the slightest error in measurement will compound itself instantly. For example, cutting the horizontal main drainpipe a half-inch too short inevitably causes the vertical sub-drainpipe for the sink to careen through the floor at a crazy angle.

I have also learned that once a PVC joint is cemented into place, it cannot be removed. Twice I have had to saw elbows or unions off because—regardless of how exactly I placed them before cementing—once they were cemented, they were in the wrong place. I have also learned that uncemented joints will not hold water no matter how snugly they fit. I learned this lesson two nights ago when I cemented the last fitting in place and attached the new drain system to the main septic system.

"Hooray!" I yelled, surveying three weeks' worth of work. In spite of the endless doubts, fears, and misdirection, the whole thing looked pretty impressive. A network of clean white pipes wove across the crawl space and emptied into the septic line under the house. To celebrate, I poured a bucket of water down the furthest drain and then scooted below to make sure there were no leaks.

At first everything looked perfect. Then my heart sank as I watched water drip in a steady stream from two joints. I imagined the agony of sawing fixtures loose, cutting new ones, and cementing them into place. I gave the whole thing a tug and discovered that I had simply neglected to cement them together. A quick cement job, another test, and—voilà!—no leaks.

Oh, I did learn one more thing. There is no such thing as a simple plumbing job, even at twenty cents an hour.

The Greatest Invention—Ever

There has been a lot of talk lately about what is the greatest invention of the twentieth century. Some say it's television, others opt for the computer, while still others say it's the interstate highway system. One person I talked with insisted it's the electric ice cream scoop.

My vote goes to the drywall lift. Yep, I am convinced that the greatest invention in the past one hundred years has been the mechanical doohickey that enables a guy to install four-by-eight sheets of drywall on ceilings without killing himself, wrecking the drywall, or needing an army of assistants.

Return with me to the golden days of yesteryear when I stood before a century-old farmhouse, hammer in hand, poised to remodel the whole shebang, one room at a time. The biggest task by far was repairing the walls and ceilings, which had been ruined over time by a leaking roof.

These ancient walls were plaster, built up on a network of lath. Great chunks of plaster had rotted in the wetness and now crumbled to the touch. My first thought was to cut away the bad plaster, give myself a speed course in the art of plastering, and replace the old with new.

In retrospect, I have to think that plastering must have been one of the original medieval guilds, and the last person who knew how to do it died during the Crusades. At the library I managed to unearth an antique volume devoted to this neglected art. It was published several years before the invention of the electric light and consisted of some five hundred pages of type so small as to be unreadable.

The first hundred pages were devoted to manufacturing plaster. Everything from grinding gypsum to adding horsehair and other obscure ingredients was covered in intricate detail. I couldn't believe it. Where on earth was I going to get horsehair? The kindly proprietor of the local lumberyard pointed out that he had ready-mixed plaster available in forty-pound bags, no horsehair needed. Just add water and apply.

Carefully, I chipped away the old plaster, cleaned the exposed lath, and mixed up a batch of new plaster. This was going to be easy, and with great artistry and finesse I spread the new plaster and feathered it into the old work.

It must have been about fifteen minutes after I finished that I noticed the plaster wasn't staying where I put it. In fact, it was slowly inching down the wall and gathering into a grotesque bulge. Frantic, I raced back to the lumberyard.

For the next few minutes I stood by as the proprietor narrowed his eyes, pursed his lips, and consulted with every customer who walked into the store. Nobody had ever done any plastering. There used to be a man named Borgman who did a lot of plastering, someone said. But he died ten years ago.

"If I was you," the proprietor said, "I'd tear out the old plaster and install drywall. It'll be a whole lot easier." An hour later I arrived home with a full load of four-by-eight sheets of drywall, a heavy bucket of wallboard compound, a roll of paper tape to cover the cracks between the sheets, and a large box of drywall nails.

I never thought to ask at the time what "a whole lot easier" actually meant. But my doubts began to grow when I stood in the middle of the floor and stared up at the bare ceiling overhead. How was I going to get heavy sheets of drywall up there? Another phone call to the lumberyard provided the answer.

"You make yourself a tee on the end of a two-by-four," the proprietor said. "Then just prop the drywall in place while you put in your nails." Hastily, I fashioned the required tool from scrap lumber, leaned the first piece of drywall onto the end of it, and hoisted away.

In the next thirty seconds or so I learned several basic lessons in physics. First, I learned that a seventy-five-pound piece of drywall on the end of a stick is impossible to control unless you happen to be a professional juggler and have appeared on *The Ed Sullivan Show*. That first piece careened into the wall and broke in half.

Second, I learned that a seventy-five-pound piece of drywall on the end of a stick will sag at both ends and, if not supported within five seconds, will break in half. Third, I learned that the most difficult task for a human being to accomplish is to balance on the top of a stepladder, support the sagging end of a seventy-five-pound piece of drywall, and accurately drive nails into every square inch of it in order to secure it to the ceiling.

Finally, I learned that the probability of getting such a sheet of drywall squarely positioned where it is needed by such gyrations is slim to none. When I finally had my first piece in place, I stood back and tallied up the losses. Three broken sheets of drywall were stacked against the wall, and the single one that was actually installed was a good three inches away from where it needed to be. It also had several hammer holes where I had swung at nails and missed.

Two weeks later when I finally finished the job, I vowed I would never touch a sheet of drywall again. To get the job done, I finally had to build no fewer than three two-by-four tees and hire a neighbor and his son to help me. Every sheet raised aloft required all three of us to support the drywall with our sticks while we slowly maneuvered it into position and nailed it in place.

Needless to say, when I was faced recently with installing about a thousand sheets of drywall in The Project, that never-to-be-completed addition to my house, I was ready to slip away in the middle of the night and never return. I figured I could get a job on a tramp steamer out of Singapore and just melt into obscurity. That's when My Friend the Carpenter told me about the drywall lift.

"Real simple," he said. "It rolls around on wheels so you can move it into position with one hand. Crank it up and fasten it in place." This was too good to be true. I called the rental place to see if I was dreaming. Sure, they had a drywall lift. Would I like to reserve it? Five minutes later I was loading the machine into my truck.

The bottom line to all this is that in a single weekend, working alone, I managed to install drywall ceilings in three rooms. Moreover, every piece fit exactly where it was supposed to, and nothing got broken. When the job was finished, I returned the drywall lift to the rental agency.

"Any problems?" the clerk asked.

"Yeah," I mused, "where was this thing twenty years ago?"

The Problem with Time

I should have known better. I was slightly suspicious when My Friend the Carpenter suggested we take "a couple of hours" and open up the entry from the new addition (a.k.a. The Project) into the existing house.

"All we gotta do," he mused with narrowed professional eyes, "is remove the door frame from the old exterior door, widen the opening, cut out the existing bathroom wall, and then build a new wall four feet further in."

Don't get me wrong. I trust My Friend the Carpenter absolutely. He is a truly professional carpenter who frames houses for a living. After all, he was the one who designed The Project in the first place. It was he who gave unselfishly of his time over endless Saturdays patiently instructing us in the proper use of saw, hammer, and tape measure to get the basic structure built.

Perhaps My Friend the Carpenter's greatest virtue, however, is an almost perfect inability to deceive. This trait emerged only seconds after the initial suggestion that we "take a couple of hours." To that he added, almost in a whisper, "Of course, I really don't have much experience with bathrooms."

Having only recently emerged from the subterranean caverns beneath The Project, where I agonizingly installed miles of four-inch and two-inch plastic drain, two-inch vent pipe, and three-quarter and half-inch copper water lines—all for the new bathroom portion of The Project—I can assure you, of all the rooms in any house, clearly the most diabolical is the bathroom. And the older the bathroom, the more sinister its intent against Those Who Would Remodel.

So, last Saturday morning we assembled, My Friend the Carpenter and I, to "take a couple of hours." Out came the exterior door frame and out came the bathroom wall. So far, so good. The only complication at this point was an assembly of electrical wires that had been installed when the house was built to fuel the bathroom and back-porch lights. The wall gone, they now hung limply from the ceiling like dying vines. Carefully, I applied electrician's tape to the exposed ends and pushed them out of the way. I would deal with them later. Hey, in addition to the plumbing in The Project, I had also installed all of the electrical wiring, outlets, and switches. A handful of old wires was no big deal, even if I didn't know which were hot and which were not.

The wall was down, and the next step was to move the toilet one foot to the north. A mere foot. How much trouble could this be? In theory, none. However, I think My Friend the Carpenter and I both knew that this was where we would meet the dragons. Old bathrooms don't like to be messed with, and old toilets are like dungeons, long forgotten, deep in the bowels of the earth beneath the castle. Once broached, whatever lurks within is loosed like the plagues in Pandora's box.

Toilets are installed in a simple, straightforward manner. Always have been. The fixture is bolted to a flange attached to a piece of curved pipe known as a closet bend. This is then attached to the main soil pipe which goes to the sewer. Today, closet bends, toilet flanges, and soil pipes are all made of lightweight plastic and fitted together with PVC cement. Yesterday, all of these devices were made of cast iron and held together with gallons of molten lead. The result was a ponderous assembly of iron the size and weight of a small locomotive.

This particular toilet was installed some forty years ago, so it definitely fit the locomotive genre. The first task was to shut off the water supply and flush. The theory is that this reduces the amount of water we will ultimately spill on the floor to just under a hundred gallons.

Next, we had to remove the bolts holding the toilet to the flange. I fitted a wrench and gave a tentative tug. Nothing budged. I tried again. Still nothing. Then My Friend the Carpenter gave a try. Still nothing. We got down on our knees to take a closer look. What we saw was a series of bolts that looked as if they had spent the last century attached to the bulwarks of a sunken ship. My Friend the Carpenter agreed and got the Sawzall from its case. This powerful reciprocal saw uses durable bimetal blades that will quite literally cut through anything. I swear, if anyone ever saws the world in two, he will do it with a Sawzall.

Once the toilet was off the flange, the next job was to remove the flange and the old closet bend. A quick look told us what tool was needed. We went to the toolbox and pulled out the biggest hammer we could find. We rolled up our sleeves and began swinging. Forty-five minutes later we were both dripping with sweat and the old closet bend had been reduced to shards of broken metal. We surveyed our handiwork.

"Looks like London during the Blitz," My Friend the Carpenter said. He was right. Debris and twisted metal were everywhere, and the dust rolled in heavy clouds through the bathroom and into the adjoining kitchen. You could almost hear the air raid sirens wailing in the distance.

By the time we had cleaned up the mess and laid out the new wall for the bathroom, it was pitch dark. Our "couple of hours" had parlayed themselves into a full day. Even so, we felt good. Sure, we still had to install the new closet bend, finish the wall, and deal with the dangling electrical wires, but we had challenged the dark powers of old bathrooms and had won. The dungeon was laid to waste. The dragons were dead. St. George would have been proud of us that day.

Future generations that decide to change the bathroom again will have to deal only with plastic. Even so, I plan to put a copy of this column in a waterproof packet and attach it to the bottom of the toilet. That way they will know that once upon a time there were dragons that lived in dungeons.

An Anniversary—of Sorts

Well, it's that time again, time for an accounting of what has and has not been accomplished. Normally, these agonizing scrutinies cover just the summer, so I have only one season to feel guilty about. Besides, summer offers a lot of natural excuses: three days of rain, two weeks of no rain, a bad week of mosquitoes, and, of course, there are always storms. A good summer thunderstorm can delay almost any project by at least two weeks.

This year, however, we also have the anniversary of The Project to consider. It was, in fact, exactly one year ago that we began construction on the simple little addition to our house that has since soaked up every waking moment of my time and every tarnished dime in my overstressed bank account.

I will never forget that fateful Saturday when the man with the backhoe pulled into our backyard and began removing a large portion of it, clawing huge scoops of earth away from the back door. Later, my wife and I stood there looking first at the gaping hole in the ground before us, and then at the mountain of dirt next to it. I remember wondering if we couldn't just put it all back.

The following Saturday, My Friend the Carpenter began his lengthy odyssey of professional energy and charity by leading me and an equally charitable team of friends through the arduous task of "framing in" the addition.

Our first task was laying the concrete-block foundation. When I learned that neither of us had ever laid concrete blocks before, I panicked once more and spent a lot of time gazing wistfully at the pile of dirt and calculating how much effort it would be to put it all back.

Since we didn't know what we were doing, of course, we were extra careful in doing it. As a result, when the foundation was finished, it was only a quarter inch off, unheard-of results even for professionals! Heady wine, indeed.

The next week the first of several truckloads of lumber arrived, and we were ready to start building. Over the next few weeks, troops of very generous friends came early and stayed late each Saturday to help frame out The Project. During the week I prepared window and door headers and accumulated more materials. There were Saturdays when we raised walls. On other Saturdays we installed rafters and ceiling joists. Then there were several Saturdays devoted to installing windows and doors. The final series of Saturdays found dedicated friends joining me up top as we nailed down shingles and buttoned the whole place up for winter.

During this process, time was taken to insulate the crawl space walls, dig a drainage and sump system in the crawl space, spread at least a thousand tons of pea gravel on the ground in the crawl space, and somehow overlook the fact that we needed to break a hole through the old foundation to tie in the plumbing and heating. This last task I wound up doing after everything was built, lying flat on my back, flailing away like a prisoner escaping from a dungeon.

There was time, too, devoted to shoveling a foot of snow off the subfloor and out the open window spaces before the roof was in place. There were other times we worked in the rain, soggy and muddy (you can't build anything without spending at least some time wading through ankle-deep mud), and still others when we huddled beneath fifty layers of coats and sweaters to fend off subzero windchill. That was when I learned it is impossible to hold a hammer while wearing frozen mittens.

Once My Friend the Carpenter had given time and talent beyond measure and The Project was sealed up and "under roof," I began the solo portion of the job. To do the electrical wiring, I first had to study and pass a test. I passed, but I'm still amazed that the work that followed was approved with no discrepancies noted by the building inspector.

Next came insulation in the walls and ceilings. Over the past thirty years the insulation industry has made remarkable product improvements. One they have grievously overlooked, however, is taking the itch out of fiberglass. After an evening of dose after dose of the pink stuff, I was coated with a thin, fuzzy layer of tiny glass shards. I looked like a velveteen rabbit and felt like a leper.

At present, I am finishing the plumbing part of the job. There are now seemingly miles of plastic and copper pipe strung back and forth beneath the floor in the crawl space, like the convoluted web of a giant industrial spider. When I finally hook into the main water lines and turn the whole shebang on, will it leak? The jury is still out on that issue, and I live with a certain dread over the impending verdict. I'll have to get back to you.

Of course, all this time while plodding forward with The Project, I have also mowed my lawn several hundred times, pruned a dozen trees, put in and prayed over several flower beds, sprayed Roundup weed killer on my entire driveway, and moved everything from a warehouse to our patio, where it will remain until we can "sort it out."

So much for the positive side of the ledger. On the other side (sigh) are all the things I didn't get done. The aging roof on the rest of the house was supposed to be replaced this summer, but it will have to struggle through at least one more winter. The gutters and downspouts leak and need to be replaced, but hey, I need to hold off on that until I'm ready to install the gutters on The Project.

And then, of course, there remains the giant mountain of dirt behind the house. That was going to be gone before summer this year. But you know, it does offer certain landscaping possibilities, like putting in a miniature ski slope. I may just call it "Degler's Mountain." Who knows, they may decide to do a television show about this place and the wonderful family that lives here. After all, it worked for the Waltons.

How to Move a Mountain

From the time I was four years old, I knew I was called to be a heavy-equipment operator. I used to sit in my sandbox for endless hours carefully maneuvering bulldozers, steam shovels, and dump trucks from one side to the other, dreaming of one day changing the shape of the world, building some great place for the betterment of humanity.

Alas, somewhere between my fifth birthday and my senior year in high school that dream got set aside in favor of a career in journalism. I left my visions of dozers and dump trucks behind and went to college to learn the proper uses of syntax and simile.

Although years went by and I matured, I never completely forgot the image of giant machines moving tons of earth from one place to another. Whenever these behemoths would converge upon a plot of land and begin excavation to build some brave new world, I would usually find reason to stop by and watch in dreamy anticipation.

I love all of those beautiful machines, from the huge steam shovels to the giant dump trucks, so large they are prohibited from driving on highways. Then there are the hungry earthmovers, those enormous scooping machines so big they are hinged in the middle, bouncing across the landscape, peeling county-size bites from the earth. Too, there are delicate road graders with intricate blade settings to smooth and heal the wounds caused by reckless bulldozers. Tucked in the middle of all these magical machines is one called a Bobcat. Small by heavy-equipment standards, the Bobcat is designed for light earthmoving.

The guy at the equipment rental place agreed the Bobcat was what I needed to move Degler's Mountain. You know, that mound of dirt behind my house created a year ago when we launched The Project, that never-to-be-finished addition to our house. I signed the paperwork, and we walked out to the lot where my machine was parked. I had never seen anything so beautiful.

"It's pretty simple," he said, starting the throaty diesel engine. "You push on these hand levers to move forward, and pull on them to back up. One forward, one back is how you turn." Then he showed me how to manipulate the bucket with the foot pedals. "Now you try it," he said.

I got in and gave the levers a gentle push. The machine inched forward. I pulled back, and it stopped and inched into reverse. I pressed on the foot pedals and watched the bucket rise and lower, tip and tilt. My heart was pounding. My dream of heavy-equipment operation was at last coming true. No power on earth could have removed the smile from my face.

There is a fine line between joy and anxiety, though, and the quick shift from dream to reality is a surefire way to cross that line. My euphoria melted like a Hershey bar in the summer sun within minutes of bringing my prize home. This has to do with the nature of Bobcats and the fact that the guy at the rental place didn't tell me everything I needed to know about the machine.

He failed to tell me, for instance, that Bobcats have all their weight in the rear, where the engine is. This is so you can pick up a bucketful of dirt without pitchpoling forward. Bobcats have four wheels, and they are perfectly balanced over the rear set. Because of this, the machine will often rear up like a stallion on its hind legs, raising the front wheels completely off the ground.

I didn't know any of this when I proceeded to back the machine down the ramp and off the trailer. Instantly, it reared back on its hinds, and my life flashed before my eyes. I panicked and shoved the controls forward. This was exactly the wrong thing to do, of course, and it reared back even farther. Totally paralyzed by this time, I was unable to do anything except let go, which was exactly what I should have done. The machine righted itself and slowly bumped off the trailer. I had been a heavy-equipment operator for less than a minute, and I knew the dream was over. For the next five minutes I sat and shook.

Once I regained my composure, I drove the Bobcat over to the work area and set the blade. I moved forward to pick up a bucket of dirt and watched in frustration as the shovel skimmed merrily along the top and came up empty. I adjusted the angle of attack and tried again. Once more, nothing. A different angle. More power. Nothing. Nothing. Nothing. It was, of course, at this precise moment that my wife popped out the door. Now I not only looked stupid but also had an appreciative audience.

It is quite possibly true that men are, indeed, from Mars and women are from Venus. Wives, it seems, are endowed—perhaps at birth—with the ability to see what should be done in tricky situations. Mercifully, my wife is also endowed with considerable compassion and a lively sense of humor.

"Maybe if you explained how packed the dirt is, the man at the rental place could offer suggestions for digging it up," she said warmly, with that special twinkle in her eye that only comes when she is working hard to keep from laughing out loud. After a deeply desperate moment that only you guys who have faced the inevitable need to stop and ask directions will understand, I conceded and made the call.

The rental guy was matter-of-fact. I swear he read from a script. "Place-the-machine-at-the-entry-point-for-your-dig-and-then-raise-the-bucket to-one-third-stance-and-tilt-the-blade-to-forty-five-degree-down-angle-and-then-lower-the-bucket-to-contact-and-move-forward-while-scooping-upward," he said in a single breath. "That should do it."

I repeated his instructions to myself and returned to the Bobcat. "Scooping," I said. "Of course, you have to scoop." For the next hour I worked on adjusting the angle of attack and practiced moving forward while scooping. I saw progress and actually was beginning to get the hang of it when my stepson arrived. He watched my efforts for a few minutes, and then asked if he could try it.

"Sure," I said, happy to have a few minutes of respite from the bouncing machine. I opened my mouth to repeat the instructions about angles of attack and scooping, when he cocked his head to one side and smiled.

"I guess you need to adjust the angle of attack and scoop as you move forward," he said. He moved the machine forward while adjusting bucket height and blade angle. Seconds later he came up with a full bucket. "How's this?" he asked. I nodded with envious approval. For the next several hours I watched in fascination as this young man attacked the mountain of dirt, moving it bucket after bucket to its new location.

As I watched from the sidelines, I realized that we sometimes learn essential things late in life. I had just learned, for example, that what I really wanted to be as I sat in my sandbox at age four was not a heavy-equipment operator, but a supervisor.

Into the Crawl Space

It's called a crawl space for a reason. Crawling is the only way you can get around when you are down there. You move on your hands and knees at best, more often on your stomach or your back, propelled along by digging your elbows into the ground.

I spent pretty much all day in the crawl space under The Project last weekend. You remember The Project, that never-to-be-finished addition to my house that I started some six years ago, which has been 90 percent complete for the last two years.

The reason I was down in my crawl space last weekend is this: the sump pump I installed when we laid the foundation had stopped working. My guess is it stopped working because it developed a leak, took on water, and shorted out. Or maybe it stopped working because I mistakenly tied it into the ground fault (GFI) outlet in the bathroom, and the start-up surge tripped the GFI.

I'm not exactly sure when the pump stopped working, but judging from the marine growth encrusted on it when I removed it from the sump, I'm guessing it must have been about two weeks after it was installed. I'm kidding. I distinctly remember hearing the pump work for at least three weeks.

The reason I had to put in a sump pump in the first place is that we have a very high water table in our neighborhood. I have been told this is because we are sitting on aquifers, which are sort of underground rivers. Like any river, when we get a lot of rain, the aquifers overflow their banks and we get three inches of water in the crawl space.

When we excavated, I buried a loop of four-inch plastic pipe in a trench that encircled the inside of the crawl space. It's a special type of pipe that has slits in it so that water can seep in. Both ends of the pipe emptied into the sump, a plastic can about two feet deep buried in the ground.

The pump itself was submersible and was dropped into the bottom of the sump. A discharge hose ran from the pump, across the crawl space, and to the outside through a hole I had cut through the foundation wall. A perfect setup. Yea!

What with a high water table and lots and lots of rain, you can imagine how much water had accumulated in the crawl space when I entered—crawling, of course—to install a new pump. Something else you need to know about crawl spaces and ground water. Crawl spaces are like caves. While they never freeze during the winter, they also never warm up in the spring. I'd estimate the temperature in my crawl space at slightly above freezing. The ground water is like spring water that comes from the bowels of the earth. Its temperature is only slightly above zero. It doesn't freeze because it's always moving, I guess.

There is another dynamic you need to understand. This one concerns any kind of work done in difficult-to-get-into-and-out-of places, places like crawl spaces. The dynamic is this: you will not remember one of the tools you need for the job until you have inched your way through freezing water for about a hundred yards.

And bear in mind, jobs like installing new sump pumps have many different phases, each phase requiring special tools that you will remember only when you are already at the job site.

Once I got the new pump installed, plumbing-wise, I still had to hook it up electricity-wise. Naturally, I had to tear out the old hookup from the GFI and tie in a new set of wires to a convenient source—in this case, an existing wall outlet—in the room above.

I use the word "convenient" in a relative sense, of course, since any new electrical installation requires accurate measuring, precise hole-drilling, and then feeding a long, impossibly whippy length of wire through the hole to the outlet above.

Naturally, each of these steps requires multiple trips into and out of the crawl space. And don't forget that dynamic about tools. It also requires reasonable assurance that the electricity in question has been turned off at the breaker box in the garage. Actually, "reasonable" is not the appropriate word here. It really has to be a lead-pipe certainty. Trust me, when you are lying on your back in three inches of water, you don't want the teensiest little nagging question about whether the current is shut off or not.

I made sure of the electrical question by plugging in a light and switching breakers until the light went off. At that point I felt safe. Unfortunately, my work light in the crawl space was also off, a fact I didn't discover until I had crawled halfway in, so I had to retreat and reroute the extension cord.

The new pump was bigger and more powerful than the original one, so naturally, it required a bigger discharge line. Whereas the first one was happy using a flexible hose to carry the water into the yard, the new one insisted on solid two-inch PVC pipe.

And try as I might, I could not get the two-inch pipe to go through the one-and-a-half-inch hole I had chopped through the foundation wall for the flexible hose connected to the old pump.

Finally, the job was done, and I crawled out of the gloom below and stood blinking in the sunlight. Then I crossed my fingers and flipped the breaker.

I have been told that, when a mother gives birth, she forgets the pain immediately upon seeing her child. I can assure you it is likewise true when a newly installed sump pump roars to life and hundreds of gallons of water begin spewing beautifully into the yard. For a moment I even forgot I was dripping wet and shaking with cold.

Actually, there is yet another reason they call it a crawl space. Once you've spent the day there, crawling is about the only way you can get around for several hours.

The Shower Gets a Glass Wall

I did a little more plumbing down in the crawl space the other day. You may recall that last week I installed a new sump pump to get rid of ground water when it rains. This time I worked on the water pipes so I can begin the final assault on the new bathroom in The Project (a.k.a. the never-to-be-finished addition to my home).

The problem with the pipes was this: when I extended the plumbing into The Project, it was to provide water and drainage for both the new bathroom and a new laundry room. The laundry room part works fine; there are only so many ways you can hook up a washer and drier. The bathroom is another story.

The issue is not with the sinks or the toilet. Again, there are only so many options to consider. Ditto with the tub, although there are several places you can put the faucets. Nope, the big deal here is the shower. The shower stall itself is permanently in place, but the location for the faucets and showerhead has changed.

This all has to do with the bay window. Since we were putting in a Jacuzzi-style tub, we thought, gee, wouldn't it be nice to have a big bay window next to the tub so we could lounge around in the tub, relaxing after a long, hard day, and look out the window at a Grecian garden. (The garden is still in the planning stages and will doubtless cause its own series of earth tremors and cardiac incidents as it proceeds.)

But the thing about bay windows is, they let in an awful lot of light. So, here we were with a light and airy bathroom and a very dark shower stall. It was dark because I walled in three sides of the shower stall with concrete tile backer and planned to install an overhead light in a false ceiling above the showerhead. That way I could find the soap I dropped without having to use a flashlight.

However, the shower stall also blocked the daylight into the adjoining bedroom.

"Wouldn't it be nice," my wife cooed one day (it is an established fact that most of the changes in the world over the past millennium have begun with that phrase), "if we had a glass panel in the side of the shower stall facing the bay window?"

I had to agree it would be nice. "But we don't," I said. "We have a nice solid wall all covered with Durock cement board and ready to tile."

"But just think how nice it would be to have a glass panel there instead," she said. I narrowed my eyes thoughtfully and looked at the solid Durock wall. Some people are impressed with thoughtful looks and narrowed eyes. Alas, my wife is not one of them. "The problem is," I began slowly, "the pipes are on that wall, along with the faucets and the showerhead." This was my trump card, and I waited to see if it would turn the game in my favor.

"Move them," she said. So much for trump cards.

Now, about that plumbing—sure, I can move the pipes, but where to? The back wall would be the easiest, but then the spray from the showerhead would hit the door and in all probability leak onto the floor of the bathroom.

The opposing side wall would be the best since the spray would then hit the nice glass panel and keep it clean. But to get there I would have to run the water pipes under the shower floor and up through the sill in the opposing wall. The problem with that was the opposing wall used to be the outside wall of the house before I started building The Project. That meant the sill sits on the concrete foundation, and before pipes can go through it I would have to knock a hole in the foundation. I did that once six years ago, to bring in both plumbing and heating, and I knew better than to think it would be a quick and easy task. To be honest, there hasn't been a quick and easy task in the whole shebang. Not once in six years. But I digress.

Wisely, I had installed cutoff valves on both water pipes where they enter The Project. Unwisely, I didn't install drain faucets in the pipes so I could drain them before soldering new pipes for the bathroom. Yeah, you can't solder copper pipes that have water in them; you can't get them hot enough to melt the solder. Even a thermonuclear explosion wouldn't do it, I think.

So, I turned off the valves, cut the pipes, drained the water (most of it all over myself), and installed drain faucets. Then I crawled over to the area under the shower and cut those pipes. Now I can remove the pipes from the shower wall and install a nice panel of glass.

However, since it was obviously going to take more than an afternoon to whack through the foundation and install new pipes, I now had another problem brewing. The pipes were cut, so I couldn't turn the water back on. This meant we couldn't use the laundry.

Again, I narrowed my eyes thoughtfully and stared at the open pipes. Sure, no one was looking, but it still made me feel in control. Besides, when you're soaking wet and lying in a cold crawl space with your pants full of pea gravel, narrowing your eyes just comes naturally.

For long moments I pondered the situation, and then I said, "Aha!" Not because of any intellectual breakthrough but because I'd finally figured out that the reason my butt hurt was because my pants had gotten full of pea gravel from the crawl space.

I also decided to install another set of cutoff valves to the pipes under the shower. That way I could turn the water back on for the laundry and not be rushed getting the pipes installed in the shower wall. Problem solved. Hooray!

So now I've got a series of copper pipes with cutoff valves at each end and a set of faucets in the middle.

"Sounds like a Rube Goldberg invention," a friend remarked. I agree, and Rube would definitely be pleased.

The Grecian garden landscaping planned for outside the bay window ultimately became a pond with a waterfall and a deck. It was completed several years later.

What's That Stuff, and What's It For?

Once again, it's back to the crawl space. Several weeks ago we finally ordered all the plumbing hardware necessary to finish installing the new bathroom in The Project, that never-to-be-finished addition to my house. And three boxes of stuff arrived the other day.

The problem with all this is The Project started about a hundred years ago, went like wildfire for a while, and has been slowing down ever since, until it has now reached the imperceptible crawl stage. As a result, there are boxes of stuff in the bathroom area that have been sitting there since at least the Crimean War.

I'm talking important stuff, stuff I put there because it was essential to the completion of The Project. What that means is I haven't a clue what it is.

And now there is a bunch of new stuff. This stuff includes a valve for the Jacuzzi bathtub, which has been sitting there long enough that I am considering advertising it as an antique. There is also an overflow drain and drain stopper for the tub.

These two things have to work together using a network of pipes that closely resembles the plumbing schematic for the Pentagon. And, of course, these pipes have to somehow fit into the main hot- and cold-water lines in the crawl space.

Besides the tub, there is a shower, which also has to tie into the tub pipes as well as those same hot and cold pipes down below. My biggest fear is hooking the whole thing up wrong so you can fill the tub only if you also have the shower going full blast at the same time. Naturally, if you wanted to take a shower, you'd also have to fill up the tub. Yeah, I worry about things like that. Anyone who has read this column over the past few years knows that I am utterly capable of doing exactly that. Hey, this is the same guy who spent three days chopping a hole in the old foundation for the new plumbing pipes—in the wrong place—and the same guy who wired one entire room without attaching either end of the wiring to the electrical power. For a week I vainly tried to figure out what was wrong with the electricity. I finally found an unattached cable in the attic.

To complicate matters more, the bathroom was originally designed with an enclosed shower. That happened so long ago that we are actually remodeling it before it is ever built. In the remodeled version, we are encasing it in glass. The problem with that is I don't know how many boxes of that old stuff are supposed to go with the old enclosed shower.

I feel like the shade tree mechanic who tore his motorcycle apart and when he put it back together had enough parts left over to make a sidecar.

Some parts of The Project haven't changed in the past millennium. One dust-covered box in the bathroom space is a ceiling vent, light, and blower. This has to be installed into a square hole in the ceiling and then a vent pipe has to be pushed out through the roof.

The problem with that is that my wife and I have more stuff than we have storage space. As a result, any space that goes unoccupied for more than thirty minutes gets filled up. To install the ceiling vent, I am going to have to pull about ten thousand boxes out of the attic. Naturally, we haven't a clue what they contain either, but I'm sure they are very important; otherwise, we wouldn't have stored them there in the first place.

The difficulty that presents is where to put the boxes. The only space I've got is the bathroom area. And, of course, I'd have to move all the stuff that's already in there out in order to make room. Naturally, I don't know where I would put that.

There are other tasks to be performed, too. A toilet has to be installed. Actually, the plumbing is already in for that. At least I think it is. I also think the water lines and drains are in place for the vanity sinks. But then I haven't seen that part of the bathroom area for so long I can't honestly say for sure.

Actually, I'm not even sure if I installed the floor tile. I'll have to move a few things and see what's down there. Come to think of it, maybe that's one part of The Project that is actually finished.

The Studio Emerges—at Last

In the final advance toward finishing the new bathroom in The Project (that never-to-be-finished addition to my house), I got a couple of extra bonuses. For one, my studio got cleaned out. For the very first time, it stands available for creative pursuits.

I should explain that I have a studio because before I became a writer, I was a painter. You probably didn't know that I was an obscure but crushingly talented artist. Yep, I even thought at one time that I could make my living doing artwork.

Reality, however, quickly verified that there is a substantial reason for the phrase "starving artist." Honestly, the chance of my making a living as an artist turned out to be about as good as my finding a cure for growing old. You may have noticed that I am growing older every day.

But even though my heartbreaking talent is doubtless doomed to the back shelves of obscurity, I never lost the desire to slap paint on canvas. So when The Project was in the planning stages, I suggested to my wife that it could include a studio—a room with a lot of wide-open space and skylights facing north.

North light has always been a big deal for painters. I'm not exactly sure why, but it is supposed to provide the perfect light for painting. That is probably why so many artists paint only during the day and party at night. That's the way I did it anyway. I usually got up at noon and seldom had more than a couple of hours of daylight left to work by the time I picked up my brushes, which might explain why my painting career never got off the ground.

Naturally, my wife was very supportive. "Make a studio if you want," she said, "as long as it can also be used for other things." By "other things," she was talking about sewing, addressing birthday cards, wrapping Christmas presents, and, of course, storing things.

I know what you're thinking. Yes, I did say a week or so ago that I was working exclusively on the new bathroom. I am, and that's exactly why the studio had to be cleared out. Otherwise where would I store all the stuff that has been stacked in the bathroom area since The Project began?

The second bonus I got was rediscovering my books. For some reason I have an enormous collection of books. I must have started collecting them when I was in the sixth or seventh grade. And, I must admit, I have been unable to part with any of them.

I am not sure why. Only a few have I ever read a second time. Others I haven't read at all. I've read pretty much all of the paperback novels and doubt I'll read any of them again. And I can't envision ever needing to read *The Fundamentals of Psychology* again. And while I loved my course in Shakespeare, the last time I opened my ponderous collection of his work was the night before finals. Today I have a tough time remembering who Hamlet and Falstaff were.

Then there are all those workshop and seminar books. I must have gone to a thousand seminars over the years, and I bought a book at each one of them. I even bought one book entitled *How to Make It Big in Seminars*. The first chapter in that one says, "Write a book."

Some of these seminars and workshops dealt with managing projects. *Keeping on Track with Your Project* was the title of one of them. Considering that my home addition project is now in its seventh year, I'd have to say I wasted my money on that one.

Others were concerned with money and asset management. Obviously these were written before 9/11, and the stock market crash turned my 401(K) into a 201(K).

I did throw away some books. There was a stack of 1980s-vintage phone books, for example. And the *1985 Agricultural Supplier Directory* from the Indiana Farm Bureau Cooperative Association was another I was willing to part with.

Several books were damaged by water and had to go. The biggest loss was *Financial Growth in the Philippines Since World War II*. By biggest, I mean it was over a thousand pages long. Another book assessing the real estate market in the late 1970s was lost, too. I'll probably never be able to replace that one.

Still, sixteen storage boxes of surviving books went over to the warehouse, where they will await further processing. What that means, for the most part, is "out of sight, out of mind."

Tomorrow I plan to move everything out of the bathroom area so I can start the grand finale of that part of The Project. My guess is that the stuff I move will fill up the studio again, but I'll figure out how to deal with that later. I think I may even have a book on the subject.

The Project Is Finished

You need to sit down for this. The Project, a.k.a. the never-to-be-finished addition to my house, is about to be finished.

Yep, after a couple of years, well, three or so (okay, make it seven) of sitting steadfastly at 90 percent complete, the lone holdout—the master bathroom—is on the road to completion.

The Jacuzzi tub is installed, the unfinished drywall is in, the ceiling vent and heater are installed, and the shower enclosure is alive with shiny white tiles. Moreover, by the time this issue goes to press, the glass shower walls will have been ordered.

In addition, we have picked out the vanity cabinets and countertop, and they will be arriving at the store in about three weeks. Hooray!

What happened all of a sudden, you might ask. I was afraid you'd get around to that. What happened is we (long pause for mumbling, muttering, and shuffling of feet) brought in a contractor to finish the job. You know, that last measly 10 percent.

When the job hit 90 percent done, it sorta slowed down and didn't move forward as quickly as it had been going. Actually, it was more like it came to a complete state of stuck. To tell the truth, it came smack up against limbo, inertia, and a solid brick wall.

Anyway, one day my wife and I were standing there taking a good look at the dust and cobwebs that had accumulated in the bath area, and we decided, hey, let's just bring in a contractor to finish the job. Okay, I admit it, my *wife* decided to bring in a contractor.

But that's okay. I'm totally cool about it. After all, as Dirty Harry said, "A man's gotta know his limitations." And like it or not, when it comes to that last tiny bit of The Project, I have to admit my limitations were about as obvious as a cement truck in the living room.

To be fair, I must point out that before things started slowing down, I did get The Project and the entire rest of the house plumbed with new three-quarter-inch copper pipe; all sewer lines installed; all electrical circuits, switches, outlets, and GFIs put in, inspected, and approved. All the walls are painted, the flooring is finished (except for the grout in the bathroom, of course), and I even made and installed custom window sills and baseboards throughout.

And hey, if all of this important work hadn't already been done, we couldn't have brought in a contractor to finish that pitiful little 10 percent. I don't ask for much here, just a little credit for work well done. Yeah, yeah, I know that work was "well done" almost seven years ago.

But look on the bright side. In those seven years some of the work has aged and now needs a touch-up with paint here and there, a screw or two has come loose, a hinge needs tightening, and a couple of floor tiles need to be reglued.

When you look at it that way, The Project will still be only about 99 percent finished. And trust me, that 1 percent is right at the top of my list of things to get done.

Construction on The Project started with the excavation in September 1997; the final part, the master bathroom, was completed in the spring of 2006.

Puppy Dogs

It seems as if we have always had a dog. Even when I was a kid back in the dark ages of my youth, I don't remember a time when we didn't have a dog. This was quite a feat, too, considering that Dad worked for the US Forest Service and we were packing up and moving to new horizons sometimes two or three times a year. Our dogs have come in all sizes, shapes, colors, and temperaments. We've even had a couple of dogs with pedigrees, but I can't honestly say that they were any smarter or better looking than the lineup of mutts that have graced our thresholds over the years. The following articles chronicle our adventures with a few of them.

One-Dog Family

We're a one-dog family again. Sandy, the latest in a series of Second Dogs, hit the bricks last week when the windstorm blew the gate open. She hasn't been heard from since.

I have no idea what happened to her, but since she was one of the most affable and joy-filled dogs I've ever known, she probably latched onto the first person to scratch her ears. After that, she probably stole their heart through pure lovability and now is the center of attention in someone else's house. At least I hope that's what happened. The alternative is unthinkable.

Sandy actually belonged to a grandchild who moved away to a place where dogs were not allowed. She had been rescued from the animal shelter as a puppy and spent every day thereafter showing her gratitude by giving everyone in her path a healthy dose of tongue-slathering canine affection. I will miss her. I only hope that whoever has her now will accept the full measure of love this animal has to give.

Sandy wasn't the first Second Dog to come and go. Her predecessor was a pedigreed collie named Lad. He was a son-to-mother present to my wife, who had said for years she'd like to have a collie. Lad was beautiful, tan and white with a touch of black in just the right places. A full mane below his long, tapered nose gave him an air of unmistakable importance.

Although Lad had the breeding and the looks of a true aristocrat, he had the tragic personality of a mental patient. He was paranoid about everything and expressed it vocally at all times of the day and night. A leaf could fall from a tree and Lad would go ballistic. Certain opera singers have shattered wineglasses with their high C; Lad could crumble the plaster off the walls with his high-pitched bark.

Lad also was terrified of thunderstorms. Because of his size—he weighed over a hundred pounds—he was an outside dog. But at the first rumble of thunder, he wanted in, and he wanted in *now*. To prove it, he once bolted through a glass door. If that wasn't enough, he also suffered from severe epilepsy. Virtually any storm would put him into a grand mal seizure. When Lad ran away, it was truly a study in ambivalence. We were saddened, but somewhat relieved. When he failed to show up, we consoled ourselves with the thought that he had been adopted by someone who had nothing else to do but dote on a dog—just what Lad needed.

A few years before Lad, there was a black and white mongrel whose brains were in her feet. Lass loved to run, much to the consternation of neighbors with flower gardens. These folks took a dim view of a brainless mutt galumphing pell-mell through their begonias. Lass couldn't care less. Nor did she exhibit any particular respect for cars. It was this latter tendency that led to her demise. She wound up dead on the street one morning after one of her illicit late-night romps around the neighborhood.

Through all of these come-and-go canines, First Dog Moosey has been steadfast and reticent. Moosey was a crotchety old lady as a puppy, I think, and the years have done nothing to improve her disposition. While Lass, Lad, and Sandy loved everyone, especially children, Moosey tolerates adults grudgingly and children not at all. She is as intelligent and cunning as the Second Dogs were brainless and predictable.

When we got Moosey, it was with the understanding that she would have a place to run. We fenced in the backyard, but Moosey had other plans. She quickly proved herself unbelievably capable at burrowing under fences. It was only old age that finally made her stop.

And now Moosey is in charge again. For some reason, she always took a backseat to the Second Dogs. While they bounced all over the place in appreciation of my appearance, Moosey would skulk off to a far corner of the yard and pout. It was as if she knew that the job of Second Dog was a temporary position. Sooner or later they would go away.

And now that the latest one is gone, Moosey is back to one of her favorite pastimes—stealing the cat's food. Our cat makes her headquarters on the screened-in patio at the back of the house. I used to marvel at how much the cat ate until I discovered Moosey wolfing it down just moments after I dished it out. Thereafter, to protect the feline domain from canine thieves, I put her food dish on the patio and propped the door open with a three-inch block of wood, just enough space for her to slink through but small enough to keep Moosey out. Or so I thought.

Daily, I find Moosey snoozing on the patio, the cat's dish empty. How she forces her sixty-pound body through that narrow space I'll never know. I've even taken to spying through the patio door to catch her in the act. But Moosey's not talking. And when I confront her with admonitions of "Bad dog!" she just gives me a certain look, a look that tells me not to get too comfortable with the status quo.

Another Second Dog

I think the role of Second Dog around our place is jinxed. The third Second Dog in two years just came and went.

First, of course, there is First Dog Moosey, who has been number one hound for ten years or more. Moosey is an unchanging constant in our lives, except that in the past year she has gotten older—much older. She is mostly blind, nearly deaf, and severely crippled by what I suppose is the canine version of a hitch in the gitalong, probably arthritis. Sometimes when she tries to stand up, her rear end fails to communicate with her front end and she winds up starting to walk before all the gears are engaged. As a result, she takes the first three or four steps with her front end while the rear end remains at parade rest, and the whole shebang sort of scoots along the ground. Eventually things get sorted out and she commences walking around the yard in a jerky stiff-legged gait that makes her look like a windup toy with rusty parts. Ka-chunk ka-chunk ka-chunk.

But back to Second Dog. You may recall that an earlier Second Dog was Lad, a knock-out-gorgeous collie with a big heart, a loud bark, and an irrational fear of thunderstorms that sent him through two plate glass windows and victimized him with epileptic seizures. Lad got out of the yard one day and vanished. We never found him and have since hoped that he found a new home with a family that would treat him with the gentle and royal kindness he needed.

Shortly after Lad disappeared, Sandy arrived. Sandy was half golden retriever and half golden chow. She had the best and warmest qualities of both breeds and literally walked around with a perpetual smile on her muzzle. Sandy loved every living thing, including our hapless cat, Minky, whom she would periodically corner and give long, vigorous baths to.

Sandy spent much of each day trying to get Moosey to play. But the old moose hound paid as much heed to Sandy's manic gyrations as she did to Lad's insistent, ear-splitting barks—which is to say, none. Moosey had her rounds, and presumably her daily ablutions, from which she refused to deviate and which she steadfastly refused to share. If there was ever a canine curmudgeon, Moosey is it.

One night after a fierce wind blew open the gate, Sandy disappeared. We never found her and since have prayed that she somehow found her way to a family of ten kids and six other loving dogs and cats.

Two weeks ago Jordan arrived. Jordan was a six-year-old mix of black Lab and sheltie. She had been adopted from the Humane Society when she was a puppy by a loving couple of newlyweds who promptly made her the center of their lives. It was a great life for the dog until the baby arrived. The couple truly thought dog and baby would coexist until one day the dog nipped the child. That was when Jordan came to our house.

She had the loving nature of her Labrador father and the manic, nervous predilection of her sheltie mother. She was intelligent, well trained about etiquette in the house, and immediately took over the job of chief of security. So far so good.

Then we introduced her to Moosey. At the time, Moosey was en route around the yard. Ka-chunk ka-chunk ka-chunk. Jordan aimed at the place where she calculated Moosey would be three seconds hence and erupted with a burst of speed I have not seen since the last time trials at the Indianapolis Speedway. I swear this dog could go from zero to sixty in two seconds flat.

She zoomed in front of Moosey, just flicking the tip of First Dog's nose as she streaked by. Then she stopped to wait for the reaction. There was none. Moosey kept going. Ka-chunk ka-chunk ka-chunk. So she aimed and fired again, closer this time. Ka-chunk ka-chunk ka-chunk.

Her next tactic was to swoop in from behind and give Moosey a perfunctory nip in the rear axle. Ka-chunk ka-chunk ka-chunk. Exasperated, Jordan confronted Moosey face-to-face. Surely a good shot of strange doggy breath in the muzzle would get some recognition. Moosey just turned ever so slightly to the left and kept on going. Ka-chunk ka-chunk ka-chunk.

At that moment I think something snapped in Jordan. She lunged at Moosey, hitting her in the side and knocking her flat. Then she savagely attacked the disabled dog with what I conservatively identified as intent to kill. What I did next was strictly knee-jerk reaction—I waded into the fray and grabbed Jordan by the collar, yanking her free of a completely confused Moosey. The dog then turned her rage on me and managed to bite me twice before reason returned and she realized that she had just committed an unpardonable felony.

Dogs are like people, I guess. Sometimes they can't get over old hurts and thus continue creating new ones. Most people—and dogs, too, I'm sure—can be loved out of their pain. Regrettably for Jordan, I sent her back to her previous owners with the solemn wish that they would find someone who could help this dog.

Moosey recovered from the encounter as she always has, by ignoring the whole thing and focusing on her small, circuitous world. Ka-chunk ka-chunk ka-chunk.

Doghouse

My dog, Moosey, is getting old. She is mostly blind and nearly deaf. She has aches and pains including a "misery" in her hindquarters that makes climbing stairs and even getting up painful.

Yet she remains 100 percent dog. Given a crack in the gate for a few untended seconds, she is gone, intent on roaming the neighborhood. On such forays she is in search, I'm sure, of all that is new and worthwhile. I doubt she has any hidden agendas—beyond getting out in the first place, that is.

Time was, her clever canine wiles and amazing speed made catching her impossible. Age has turned against her, however, and these days I can usually overtake her no more than a house or two away. Gently I stop her and guide her back home.

In deference to her years, I have tried to bring her indoors during the winter months. Unfortunately, she has now spent so many years outdoors, the poor dog can't adapt. Five minutes after coming in, she begs to go back out. I stand at the open door, snow blowing in, and watch her hobble painfully off the step and across the yard toward the bushes where she sleeps.

It has always bothered me that my dog sleeps beneath a yew hedge next to the house. Yet rain, shine, or blizzard, it's where she prefers to be. I noticed long ago that her sled dog heritage served her well. Like her Husky mother, old Moosey digs a burrow in the ground or the snow and snuggles in.

My conscience still tweaks me, however, and this fall when someone offered me an unused doghouse, I accepted. Just the thing, I thought. Now Moosey can have the best of both worlds—remain outdoors but enjoy the shelter of a roof over her head.

I brought in the doghouse and set it up on bricks right next to her bush hideaway. I put an old blanket on the floor and called the dog. Dutifully she came. Dutifully she sniffed the new convenience. And then dutifully she turned and walked away. I called her again and showed her how luxurious these fine new quarters were. She gave me a pained look and ambled back to her burrow.

I got a handful of dog biscuits.

"Here, Moosey," I coaxed, tossing one of the biscuits into the house. The dog gave me another look and inched far enough into the house to retrieve the treat. I tossed in another, farther back. This time she had to go all the way in and turn around.

"Sit," I commanded. Moosey sat. I petted her encouragingly and gave her another treat. "See what a nice house you have," I cooed. Moosey chewed her dog biscuit, and then got up, squeezing past me to return to her bushes. Twice more I tossed biscuits into the house. Twice more Moosey retrieved them and left.

So much for the dog. Minky the cat, on the other hand, would love to work inside, to sleep in the window and watch the outside world from a warm, dry, comfortable perch. Alas, my wife is fiercely allergic to those microscopic hairs that all cats shed and leave floating in the air. Whenever Minky sneaks in and hides beneath a sofa for the day, my wife's face swells and her eyes itch.

Minky, of course, becomes more insistent as the weather deteriorates. By the first snow, she will try anything to get in. So, the other day whilst encouraging the dog to come in and at the same time blockading the cat, I got a great idea: Moosey doesn't want the house; why not give it to the cat? Yippee, I thought, brilliance strikes! I grabbed the cat and headed toward the doghouse. Heck, this might even change Moosey's mind. She and the cat have become friends over time and more than once have snuggled up to sleep in each other's warmth.

At the doghouse entrance I dropped to my knees and, cooing to Minky about how superbly intelligent her master was, placed the cat inside on the blanket. About two seconds later I realized the magnitude of my mistake.

Minky is by any standard a gentle cat. She would rather purr than growl and sleep than fight. I was quite surprised, therefore, when she arched her back, puffed up her tail, and, with a ferocious growl, clawed her way past me to the open air.

Of course Moosey and Minky notwithstanding, cats and dogs are mostly enemies. And here I was, smugly inviting a cat to make herself comfortable in a wooden box that had over time housed perhaps a dozen dogs—all of whom had probably hated cats and left their scent indelibly behind.

I have since decided that the old way of things was not so bad. Moosey probably is happier doing what her ancestors have done—sleeping outside. And I have solved one problem, at least temporarily: Minky no longer tries to get in. As a matter of fact, she has been giving me a wide berth lately. She probably thinks sleeping outside isn't so bad after all.

Raccoons, Dogs, and Cats

I've noticed that my cat has been eating more than usual again. No matter how much food I give her, in a matter of minutes her dish is licked clean.

The last time this happened, our dog Moosey was the culprit. She had figured out how to get onto the enclosed patio and then pigged out on cat chow. I solved that problem by putting the cat dish on the table, out of dog reach.

This time I was puzzled. On a couple of occasions the cat food had been raided by marauding neighborhood cats. But Minky always fought them off, and the ruckus was violent enough to bring me out of a sound sleep. Why can't cats argue during daylight hours?

This time there were no fights. In fact, my cat seemed to want me to pick her up, to console her more than usual—a definite sign that something was amiss. Two nights ago I discovered what it was.

When I got home, her food dish was empty again, in spite of the healthy helping I had given her that morning. I filled her dish and settled in for the evening. Suddenly a loud crash on the patio brought me out of my chair. I turned on the patio light. There on the table in front of the overturned cat dish was the largest raccoon I'd ever seen. The cat was nowhere to be seen.

I whipped open the door and yelled loudly. A good scare should send the most seasoned raccoon packing, right? Not this one. He just sat there eating. If anything, he seemed irritated that I had interrupted his meal. When I got closer, he growled and showed me a row of needle-sharp teeth. I backed off.

It was then I remembered Moosey. Dogs and raccoons are natural enemies. I called the dog. Then I called the dog again. Finally, remembering that Moosey has either lost much of her hearing to old age or has asserted her independence to a new level, I went to look for her.

I found her in her favorite sleeping spot under the yew hedge at the side of the house. I called. She ignored me. I called louder. By this time Moosey sensed my excitement and was certain she was about to be punished for something. I got down on all fours and coaxed her, an inch at a time, from her hiding place.

Meanwhile, the raccoon continued its feast. By the time I got Moosey to the patio, assuring her every step of the way that she was not going to be punished, the raccoon had finished eating and was lazily cleaning its paws. I brought Moosey to the base of the table and pointed her failing nose in the direction of the invader. She sniffed and looked puzzled. Then the raccoon growled at the dog.

Moosey may be nearly in her dotage. She may be almost blind, deaf, and crippled by arthritis. But there is one thing she is not. She is not for even one nanosecond tolerant of growling raccoons.

Now, what did I think would happen when I brought the dog face-to-face with a raccoon in the close confines of a small screened-in patio? A fair question. Honestly, I really thought the dog would smell the raccoon, growl harshly, and then pursue the fleeing bandit out the door and across the yard. The dog would then return for praise and honors. Moreover, I thought the raccoon would be so terror stricken he would never darken our cat's food dish again.

None of this happened. Instead of growling, Moosey frantically clawed her way to the top of the table and attacked the raccoon. And instead of running for the door, the raccoon leaped in the opposite direction and began running in a zigzag pattern across the patio floor, knocking everything over as it went. When it hit the corner—a half second before the dog caught up—it leaped again, this time climbing the screen and leaving behind great rips in the wire fabric.

Within seconds, the patio was a shambles. The raccoon was hugging the screen and trying with all its might to push its way through the steel roof. The dog, meanwhile, was trying to climb the screen, and I was trying to figure out how to undo all that I had created. With the raccoon growling and the dog yelping, I retreated to the house to think things over.

It was then I remembered something that might work. A veterinarian once told me of a cure for dogs that chase cars: ammonia in water. You drive by slowly, let the dog come even with the car window, and then zap! You spray the dog in the face with the ammonia. It stings, it stinks, and, according to the vet, it cures them of chasing cars. Why wouldn't it work on a raccoon?

I prepared my weapon at the sink. Then I returned to the patio. By this time the dog was exhausted and reduced to whimpering, and the raccoon was glaring at the world from its elevated corner. I inched closer and pointed my spray bottle. The raccoon growled. The dog whined. I sprayed.

The veterinarian was right. Ammonia and water not only cures dogs of chasing cars, it also cures them of chasing raccoons. One sniff and Moosey abandoned the chase and left the scene. This left me alone with the raccoon. I sprayed again. The raccoon blinked its eyes and erupted into a sneezing fit. After five or six sneezes, the animal edged down off the screen and, still sneezing, ambled away from the patio, never to be seen again.

My cat still needs to be consoled even though she has plenty of food to eat. And Moosey is giving me a wide berth. I plan to start repairs to the patio next week.

Trapping Raccoons

Someone once projected that when Man perished, the ants would take over the earth. I'm not so sure it won't be raccoons. They may already have gained a powerful foothold.

I've been mindful of the abundance of these cute, clever, and playful creatures for some time. But it wasn't until I felt obligated to draw a line between my world and theirs recently that I understood the magnitude of their position.

I've mentioned on several occasions in this space that raccoons were regular visitors to our house and seemed right at home with my dog and cat, upon whose hospitality they depended. I already knew that whatever food the cat and dog left behind at the end of the day would be polished off by raccoons during the night.

So what? Big deal. Then we decided to leave town for a long weekend.

Prior to the raccoon invasion, we simply put out extra food and water with assurances no one would go hungry until we returned. I decided to double our bets to make sure both Moosey the dog and Minky the cat were properly fed during our absence even with daily handouts to our ringtailed guests. I bought automatic feeders for both, a small one for the cat and a large one for the dog. I brought them home and loaded up the food—ten pounds of cat food and twenty-five pounds of dog food. After all, I reasoned, even the hungriest raccoons couldn't put a dent in this much food.

I am constantly amazed at how wrong I can be in any given situation. The next morning both hoppers were empty; not a crumb remained. I stared in disbelief and looked around expecting to see a couple of very sick raccoons sleeping off their gluttony.

That's when I realized I would have to get rid of the raccoons. After all, if they could eat thirty-five pounds of food in one night, I shuddered to think what they might do if the larder was left empty. I had visions of raccoons tearing down the doors and eating the inside of my house.

I checked with the Department of Natural Resources. "Traps," they said. The local sporting goods store had them. I went trap shopping. I bought a large version of the Havahart live trap, a steel cage with a spring-loaded trapdoor in one end. I read the instructions, put dog food inside for bait, and placed it on the back porch.

Shortly after dark I heard the trap snap shut. I turned on the light and looked into the coal black eyes of one very surprised raccoon. Aha, I thought. This will be a cinch. I loaded the trap into my car and drove my captive deep into the countryside for release. Back home I reset the trap, hoping I might catch another one before morning.

Next morning I smiled into the perturbed face of another captive raccoon. Another trip to the country. That night I set the trap again—just in case there were any more. The next morning there was another raccoon. And the next morning, another. Over the next ten days I captured and released eight raccoons. My fifty-dollar trap investment was certainly paying dividends.

Then two nights of no raccoons. Success! I loaded up the feeders again, confident that the ordeal was over. The next morning the feeders were empty, and the dog and cat looked worried and hungry.

A little research into raccoon behavior informed me that these animals are territorial and generally confine their activities to small areas. This led me to the conclusion that raccoons are already poised and ready to take over the world.

Look at it this way. My rural block has ten residents. The other nine residents on my block probably have their own populations of furry bandits. I trapped eight of the little buggers (and probably have more), which accounts for one-tenth of the block. Assuming even eight raccoons per territory and ten territories per block in a community of more than three thousand blocks, I'd say we have reason for concern. Multiply this number times the number of communities in the state, and it may be time to call out the National Guard.

Trapping the Cat

It's time to talk about raccoons again, and right now my motto is "Never sell a raccoon short." That motto is coupled with another which says "Never give too much credit to a cat."

Let's start with the cat. We got this kitten twelve years ago. We named her Minky, and for a while we let her sleep and eat inside. Then my wife discovered that she was allergic to Minky—watery eyes, puffy lips, you know, typical cat allergy. So, we put Minky outside and provided a sheltered place for her to sleep and a spot for her food where it would be protected from the weather.

The next thing that happened was other cats in the neighborhood heard about the free food and started dropping by for lunch. Some of these had homes and would go away after eating. Two others, probably abandoned or born in the wild, showed up, liked what they saw, and decided to stay on permanently.

These two are a pain because they don't like each other and are constantly fighting. Minky doesn't like them either and she is now in a permanent bad mood. Believe me, cats can sulk worse than kids. I know what you're thinking, but there are only two ways to get rid of stray cats. Being a natural-born softy, I am reluctant to exercise either. I guess I'm still hoping they might one day thank us for our hospitality and head for New York to audition for an all-animal production of the show *Cats*.

Now, about the raccoons. Free food for cats is definitely free food for raccoons. Put food out for a cat and you might as well put up a lighted sign saying "Welcome, Raccoons." And there is no greater opportunist on the planet than a raccoon. If food is there, the animal will find a way to get to it. Lock it up in a safe, and I would expect to get up in the middle of the night to see a raccoon scrunched down in front of it, slowly turning the dial with its paws.

A year ago the raccoon population at our home reached epidemic proportions. They squabbled among themselves, played "romp around the yard" throughout the night, and knocked over flower pots, tools, and anything else lying around. Meanwhile, the cats huddled in astonished dismay at the invasion.

Since the nightly commotion was disturbing our sleep as well, something had to be done. I bought a live trap at a local sporting goods store (don't ask me when trapping raccoons became a sport) and set out to reduce the raccoon population.

In two weeks I managed to trap seventeen of the little beggars. One by one I transported them into the deep woods and released them. Then, suddenly, there were no more raccoons. Problem solved.

Fast-forward to spring 1999. Out of the corner of my eye one day, I saw a blur of what looked like raccoon fur going into the utility shed at the side of our house. I investigated, found nothing, and wondered if I had imagined it. Then the cat food began disappearing from the feeder at an accelerated rate, and suddenly there were noises in the night once again, noises that smacked of raccoon parties. Last week I looked out the window in time to see a mother and four youngsters waddle into the utility shed and vanish among the lumber and tools. I dusted off the trap.

The first night I trapped the mother. The rest will be easy, I assured my wife, setting the trap again. In less than a half hour I heard the trap spring.

"See, we've got one already," I said. We walked to the window to take a look at our prize. There, looking miserable, was our neighbor's cat, hunkered down inside the trap. I released the animal, rebaited the trap, and returned to the house to watch through the window. Moments later, one of our resident cats showed up and began sniffing the trap.

"Go away!" I yelled, rapping on the window. The cat ignored me and walked into the trap to eat. Again, I released the cat, rebaited the trap, stamped my foot at the indignant animal, and returned to the house. Five minutes later we were rewarded by the arrival of one of the young raccoons. Then we watched as it methodically reached its tiny forepaws through the trap and removed the food, one piece at a time. I returned to the trap and moved the bait away from the end as the fearless raccoon waited expectantly just a few feet away.

Astonished, I watched as the raccoon returned to the trap, sized up the situation, and proceeded to dig a tunnel under the trap and again reach in with its paws to remove the food. This time I put the bait on a larger plate and centered it in the trap. After searching the tunnel it had dug and exploring all sides of the trap, it finally went inside, where it managed to eat virtually every morsel of food without springing the trap. It wasn't until the cat showed up again that the raccoon forgot its situation and got caught.

"Thanks a lot," I told the cat as I loaded the trap into the car. "One down, three to go." Later I reset the trap and caught another of the youngsters by morning. Since then a curious thing has happened. I have baited the trap and caught nothing. The food inside disappears, but the trap remains unsprung. How can they do this? I reach in and touch the trigger. The trap snaps shut. A feather could spring it.

So I am left with two very smart raccoons at large, a trap that serves merely as a handy feeding station for them, and an assemblage of cats more than willing to get caught for the sake of a bite to eat. I am working now on a new trap design, one that repels cats and invites raccoons. Maybe, if the raccoon won't spring the trap, I can put it on an automatic timer that will spring the trap after the raccoon has entered and spent a certain number of minutes inside. Or maybe I can rig the trigger to the weight of the bait. Once it loses enough food, it springs. Yeah, that's the ticket. I think I'll write a letter to the engineering department at the university. Maybe they can take it on as a student project, sort of a Rube Goldberg contest.

Remembering Moosey

I had to put Moosey to sleep last week. I hated to do it, but the old dog was no longer able to take care of herself. The recent surge of winter vengeance did the final damage. At the end she was unable to eat or even stand up.

I keep telling myself it was the kind thing to do. I'm sure it was. But I don't feel very kind. The day before, I gave her a bath and petted her a lot. It didn't help.

I think we humans have a tough time showing love to one another, so we rely on dogs and cats to accept our unbridled gooeyness. Most dogs, I think, know more about unconditional love than the most saintly of people. And cats are masters of acceptance about the meanest of life's conditions, while we spend most of our years fighting denial.

My wife and I were silly about Moosey, although I'm not sure why. She wasn't exactly the most lovable or friendly or well-trained or obedient animal on earth. In fact, she was probably the most independent, self-contained, single-focused dog I've ever known. She spent most of her years with us conspiring to get out of the backyard that was her home. No matter how cleverly I designed the fence, she found a way to get out.

She was also unfriendly. She was the canine equivalent of a curmudgeon. Most dogs will bound across the yard, tail awag, to greet you when you come home. Moosey might condescend to arch one eyebrow in recognition of my existence. She had little patience with most adults and none at all with children. Given the number of kids in my wife's family and their natural propensity to roughhouse with every available dog, it was totally inconsistent to have such a dog as Moosey. We were constantly wiping tears from little ones who had wrapped their arms lovingly around Moosey's neck and gotten nipped for their trouble.

Moosey didn't play either. I threw thousands of sticks, balls, and other objects in an effort to get her to fetch. She made it very clear that she considered the whole exercise silly: if she brought the stick back to me, I'd just throw it away again. Maybe she thought I meant to throw it away and didn't want it back. She was nothing if not obliging on that score.

She didn't even walk like a normal dog. You know, laid back, cool. Moosey had a stiff-legged stuck-up strut. It had arrogance written all over it.

Early on, we tried to find a reason for the dog's unapproachable veneer. We knew that deep down she had to be a normal, compassionate mutt. We finally decided that in a previous life she had been a famous and highly temperamental movie star. We watched her one afternoon, nose in the air, strutting indignantly around the yard, and came up with a number of movies she might have starred in. Among the more memorable was *I Remember Moosey*, the story of an immigrant family held together by the strong, loving dog. Then there was *To Kill a Mooseybird*, the story of a lawyer in a small southern town during the Depression. Later she did a spaghetti western entitled *The Good, the Bad and the Moosey*. There were others, of course: *The Moosey Always Rings Twice*, *Moosey Come Home*, and *Citizen Moosey*, the story of a tyrannical newspaper publisher.

Did she have no good traits? Well, whenever she ran away, she always returned home, even offering us a slight touch of remorse. Sometimes she would let us scratch her ears. Then, of course, she had those big brown eyes. Just when she needed it most—usually after doing something infuriating— she could roll them toward you and look pathetic. More than once that soulful look milked the last ounce of compassion from me and assured total forgiveness.

Yeah. She was worthless, hostile even. But I loved her, and I will miss her.

Brutie, Like Moosey

My old dog Moosey used to get a gleam in her eye when she had outfoxed me, which was often. She was determined that I would not keep her in the fenced-in backyard. She was right.

I tried everything. I even buried the bottom of the wire fence a foot beneath the ground. Moosey dug under it. In flights of fancy I even considered razor wire and armed guard towers with searchlights and sirens. I'm convinced it wouldn't have made any difference; Moosey would have found a way out.

This war of wills went on for several years. Only the infirmities of old age finally called a truce. Moosey just got old and feeble and gave up. It was a sad day when I had to put her down.

I had almost forgotten those contentious and frustrating days. Then, over the weekend I happened to glance outside and saw my dog Brutie wandering around in the front yard. Since we were in the middle of a family birthday party with kids everywhere, I assumed one of them had simply let the dog out the front door.

But Monday morning I let the dog out the back door only to have him emerge at the front door moments later. Oops! I guess someone opened the gate and forgot to shut it. Tsk, tsk.

A quick inspection of the gate proved that was not the way Brutie had gotten out. Suddenly, it was Moosey's Great Escape all over again. My heart turned to ice. Moosey was indifferent to everyone, but Brutie tends to be aggressive. He figures that our yard, the neighbors' yards, and even the street in front of our houses are his to protect, and he will challenge anyone who trespasses. I shudder to think what would happen if someone disputed Brutie's claim.

Quickly, I slipped on my coat and whistled up the dog for a backyard romp. I figured sooner or later he would betray his secret and show me how he was getting out. For five full minutes we played tag. Then, just as I yelled "You're it," he was gone. A moment later he appeared on the other side of the fence. How did he do that?

Desperately, I called him. Hey, if he got out that easily, maybe he'll come back in the same way. Something else I learned from Moosey, though: dogs may look dumb, but challenged, they usually prove to be a whole lot smarter than we are. Then they get that gleam in their eye. I hate it when they do that.

Okay, quick trip into the house, open the front door, let Brutie in, and return to the backyard one more time. Show me that again, dog. And he did. And again I didn't see it. For the next twenty minutes I patrolled the perimeter, checking every inch of the fence to see where he might have climbed over or gone under. Nothing.

One of the problems was that as long as Brutie knew I was watching him, he stayed put. For the next half hour we would play tag and then I would pretend to lose interest while keeping a furtive eye peeled on his every move. Nada.

Finally, I decided it was time to launch a new strategy. If he wants to play, how about I go into the front yard and leave him in the back? Heh heh heh. This was going to be fun. So long, Brutie, I've got work to do in the front yard.

For several minutes I puttered around in front close to the fence while Brutie bounced and galumphed around in back. I never took my eyes off him. Still nothing.

Then, suddenly, inspiration struck. Actually, it was more like belaboring the obvious. Call him, stupid; call the dog. When I did—oh, I love this part—good old smug Brutie gave himself away. In one corner of the yard behind a clump of tall pampas grass, the fence wire had come loose from the post. It was like a flapping doggie door. Zoom—Brutie roared through it and bounced up to where I was waiting. Good dog!

I got the hammer and a couple of staples, and the problem was solved. Brutie's freedom was a thing of the past. I won.

Still, when I looked old Brutie in the face and gloated for a moment over my victory, I noticed he had that gleam in his eye that told me the war was not yet over.

Choir Practice

Every Friday at eleven o'clock we have choir practice at our house. The choir is composed of my dog, Brutie, our son's dog, Hurri, and the emergency sirens located a few blocks away. When the sirens begin to wail, the dogs begin to howl.

What makes dogs do that? What do they hear when a siren wails? Is it a pack of wild dogs barreling through the neighborhood once a week, calling out to join the chorus? Or is it some traveling dog act howling its way across the country from town to town, working for Milkbone and dreaming of steak?

Do dogs dream of running away and joining the circus? Do they heed some primal urge harking back to a time when wolves roamed the steppes?

The truth is the sound probably just hurts their ears. Hey, sirens bug me too. An emergency vehicle wailing in the distance always stops me cold. I drop whatever I'm doing and just wait until the sound has faded into the distance.

In the final analysis, howling might be a pure form of protest.

I know for a fact that dogs hear things we don't. And they sometimes react to sounds in strange ways. My old dog Moosey used to growl at the vacuum cleaner as if it were an invading alien. Of course, she also used to attack the lawn sprinkler, so admittedly, she wasn't the sharpest knife in the drawer.

Another dog we had for a short time cringed and whimpered whenever it thundered. Actually, he was so terrified of storms he once plowed through a plate glass window to get away.

A friend of ours has a dog that hates helicopters and barks savagely every time one flies over the house. Of course, he comes back grinning smugly after successfully chasing it away. He also hates UPS trucks. FedEx vehicles are okay for some strange reason, but a UPS truck will send him into a full-blown dither. Hey, everybody has the right to prefer one small-package-delivery company over another, I guess.

Years ago I had a dog that hated the mail truck. How she could distinguish that vehicle from all others on the road remains a mystery, but she started barking when the truck was a half mile away and never let up until it vanished over the next hill.

In the dark ages of my youth, our family dog used to go nuts at the sound of certain birds. Robins and chickadees chirping outside the kitchen door would send her into a frenzy of barking. If we let her out, she would bolt from the house, barking and howling in pursuit of the birds. Naturally, the birds knew what was coming and always made it to safety.

Maybe it was a game the dog played with the birds. Unfortunately, one day it wasn't a robin or a chickadee outside, but a mockingbird imitating one or the other. The dog didn't know this, of course, and went roaring into the yard making "I'll kill you!" sounds at the startled bird.

Anyone who knows anything about mockingbirds will tell you they don't scare easily. Presumably, they also don't enjoy playing games with mouthy dogs either. As the dog charged, the bird flew up to a low-hanging branch and then immediately went on the offensive.

From that day forward, the mockingbird attacked the dog at every opportunity. It would wait quietly in one of the trees in our yard until the dog showed herself. Then it would dive-bomb the poor animal savagely until she retreated to the safety of the house.

By the end of the summer, the dog was so paranoid she would go out only at night. And even then she whimpered fearfully until she could return to safety behind the kitchen door. Later, my dad made the observation that the dog never again barked at a bird. In fact, when we got a parakeet several years later, the dog steadfastly refused to enter the room where the bird was caged.

As for the Friday choir practice, I'm going with the theory that the dogs are protesting. As a matter of fact, I think I'll join them and howl along. Who knows what might happen.

Brutie and the Squirrels

Just when I was beginning to think my dog Brutie had at least a level ounce of brains between his shaggy ears, he goes and falls for the oldest trick in the book—The Lure of the Squirrels.

Because we have oak trees in our backyard, we just naturally have squirrels. And I hate to admit it, but squirrels are smarter than dogs. Truth be told, I think they may even be smarter than people.

I think that because back in the dark ages of my youth I used to go squirrel hunting every fall. No matter how quietly I approached the "squirrel tree," a large hickory loaded with nuts, they always knew I was coming long before I got there. Then, of course, they managed to stay on the opposite side of the tree.

I remember standing there and looking up at a completely empty tree, one that just moments before had been filled with happy, party-crazed squirrels. But I could still hear them—on the opposite side of the tree, laughing.

I would move slowly around the tree hoping to catch them unaware, but they always stayed ahead of me. Actually, the only times I ever managed to shoot a squirrel was when I got to the "squirrel tree" before they did and waited quietly for them under the tree. Even then, I seldom got more than one or two.

Once and once only did I get several of the little rascals at one time. A storm had broken the main limb off of one of the trees adjoining the "squirrel tree," and when the squirrels arrived, expecting to use that limb as a highway to breakfast, they suddenly had no place to go and couldn't hide from me.

We had squirrel for dinner that night, but when I went back a week later they had found a new route and were as invisible as they had ever been.

Okay, a note of explanation for those of who wonder why anyone would shoot innocent, adorable squirrels. In those days my pitiful paycheck was heavily assaulted by living expenses. And sometimes, when there was an unexpected car repair or medical expense, I literally had to go hunting or fishing in order to feed the family. Saying that now makes me feel ancient indeed, like maybe I should have spent more time talking to Abe Lincoln before he went off to Washington.

Come to think of it, my paycheck is still pitiful and heavily assaulted, but now I've got McDonald's, where a Quarter Pounder with Cheese costs about the same as a box of rifle bullets, so I no longer have to hunt for food.

But squirrels are just as smart as they ever were. And they love nothing better than finding a dumb dog to torment.

As I said, Brutie shows definite signs of having some smarts. He's got "down" and "sit" down pat, and when we go for a walk, he stays at my side and even ignores other dogs along the route. And he's a good listener. When I want to talk about something, he sits, cocks his head, and hangs on my every word. Occasionally he will nod slightly or whine in agreement. Yeah, a real smart puppy.

That is, until a squirrel ventures down the oak tree to the backyard, where last season's acorns lie in a heavy blanket on the ground. Then Brutie loses it completely. He reminds me of Wile E. Coyote, foiled again by the Road Runner. He literally bounces up and down on all four feet as if they were loaded with springs. And he yelps and slobbers and lolls his eyes around in his head. "Lemme out! Lemme out! Lemme out!" he yelps. So I let him out.

Of course I know what's going to happen, and lord knows I have tried to explain it to Brutie when he is in a listening mode. "They are making a fool of you," I tell him. "They are laughing at you. And you are never, never going to catch them."

Once again, it's Wile E. Coyote roaring out past the edge of the cliff and then realizing that once again he has been duped. The squirrels sit tantalizingly on the ground and watch him charging out the door like an enraged rhinoceros. Just as he closes in, they take one short leap to the tree and yahoo! They win again.

Brutie, of course, does a fast reverse and starts running pell-mell around the base of the tree. Naturally, the squirrels easily stay ahead of him. Sometimes one squirrel will leap to another tree, and then Brutie is totally frazzled and doesn't know which one to pursue.

After a few minutes of frenzy, Brutie gives up and comes back to the house. The minute he's inside the door, the squirrels quite naturally return to their feast on the ground. Yeah, then it's showtime all over again.

Don't get me wrong; I haven't given up on Brutie. I think he really is a pretty smart dog. Maybe he just doesn't quite understand me when I talk to him about the folly of his actions. I've decided that what I really need are some visual aids to help him get the message.

I've put together some comparative diagrams showing the distance between him and the squirrels and between the squirrels and the tree. I've even developed a table showing how much speed he would need to attain in order to catch one of them. Dogs can't run that fast. I've underlined that part.

To reinforce the whole message, I plan to show Road Runner cartoons. And if that fails, I have a bunch of pictures of my returning empty-handed from squirrel hunting.

Checking Things Out with Brutie

Every morning we "check things out," my dog, Brutie, and I. We have a routine that got started last spring about the time the winter tundra had thawed and the great deluge of spring had subsided.

For weeks we waited, drumming our fingers (since Brutie doesn't have fingers, he just chewed on the furniture) as the snow and ice slowly melted. And just when that first sprig of green popped up in the perennial bed, announcing the advent of spring, the skies opened up and washed everything (including the green sprig) away. Naturally, I went back to drumming my fingers, and Brutie started eating all my ballpoint pens.

Finally, with no more fear of freezing solid or drowning in the backyard, I threw open the back door and announced, "Let's check things out." Now, I have no idea what those words translate into in dog language, but I'm guessing it's something like "Run for your life—your tail is on fire!"

Each morning, Brutie launches himself from the back porch and roars into the yard. When I say launch, I mean it in the purest sense of rocket science. Never has there been a dog so eager to slip the surly bonds of confinement. He has actually left paw imprints in the concrete.

As I amble forth and begin a leisurely walk across the yard, Brutie reaches the speed of something better than Mach 2. Within microseconds he is a blur. By the time I reach the flower bed, he has circled the entire yard five times, inspected every tree for recent squirrel activity, nosed through the woodpile for hints of chipmunks, and peed on every shrub in the yard.

What I am looking for, on the other hand, are signs of new life in the flower beds and signs of moles in the yard. After I get marigold and zinnia seeds in the ground, I check for life signs two or three times a day. And I have always been especially vigilant in keeping a sharp eye open for moles. Their crisscross tunnels not only destroy the yard but can also put a quick end to all signs of life, new or otherwise, in flower beds.

The good news in the mole department is that ever since Brutie and I started "checking things out," there aren't any. Apparently, in his supersonic tour of the yard, he also sniffs out the little beasts. Then, later, when I return to the house to pick up chewed pieces of ballpoint pens, Brutie digs in and roots them out. I have personally seen him catch several and have disposed of the remains of others.

The bad news about this is that Brutie gets the moles by digging holes. A couple of these are big enough that I could plant a half-grown tree in them. When it rains and they fill with water, I think about giving them names, something like "Lake Mole Hole."

More good news is that at least I know where these holes are, unlike mole tunnels, which can appear like crop circles in the night. It is especially disturbing to be mowing the grass and suddenly lose the mower in an unannounced tunnel.

After Brutie has finished "checking things out," has scouted out any new mole activity, and has barked at a couple of imaginary squirrels, he lies down on the patio and catches carpenter ants. He doesn't eat them; he just catches them, plays with them, and leaves the bodies for me to sweep up.

Watching him do that has given me an idea for a new program for my dog. I call it "catching Japanese beetles." These nasty bugs have invaded by the thousands and are making fast work of my zinnias, my marigolds, my cosmos, and my rose of Sharon. Hoo boy, do they love the rose of Sharon.

The way I figure it, since Brutie seems to enjoy more of everything, the Japanese beetles should be a treat beyond his wildest dreams. I think I'll catch him on one of his orbits the next time we "check things out," and show him some of the beetles.

"Sic 'em, boy. Go get 'em!"

Jealous Cats

I didn't know cats could be jealous. I always thought jealousy was one of those sentiments pretty much reserved for humans. Like when I have spent a tad too much time working on The Project (that humongous addition to our house) and my wife walks by the latest stack of two-by-fours and kicks it, saying something like "I don't know what you see in these things." That's jealousy.

But cats? I know tomcats will challenge one another for milady's affections, and mothers will protect their kittens from marauding males. But I wasn't aware that felines are capable of routine, garden-variety, day-to-day, hissing-and-spitting-in-your-face jealousy.

Until Trigger showed up last fall, that is. Trigger is the second of two feral strays that in the past year have stopped by to ask directions and wound up moving in and staying on.

Let me explain. We are a one-cat family. And our one cat has for twelve years been a lightweight disinterested female calico by the name of Minky. She has become known throughout the neighborhood as a creature of sweet and even disposition, eager for affection and tolerant of human foibles. She also shares with all cats that certain inscrutable mien that allows her to sit unmoving for hours on window sills and car hoods in deep consideration of life's eternal verities.

She is, in short, a likable cat.

Even when the first stray showed up, she remained unruffled. That was Spike, a gray tiger-striped male tabby with a smudge of gray fur on his face that made it look dirty. When I first spotted him at the feeder on the front porch, he reminded me of a Dead End Kid or one of the Bowery Boys, a warmhearted ruffian with dirt on his face and a frog in his pocket. I immediately named him Spike.

Minky wasted no time explaining the rules of the manor to this newcomer. The house was hers. The people were hers. The food was hers. Don't forget it, and we'll get along just fine. An occasional throaty growl was the only reminder I ever heard after that. As long as Spike minded his p's and q's, there was peace in the valley.

Then came Trigger. This feral stray showed up in late summer, making brief appearances at the edge of the yard. He was very young and obviously high-spirited. He was also drop-dead gorgeous, with a full body of long, fluffy jet-black fur with a silver tip on the end of each hair. He wanted to join the party but obviously had no experience with humans. For several weeks I talked to him from a distance. Each day he came a little closer, carefully watching me, wanting to be touched yet fearing the consequences.

When he finally came close enough for me to touch him with the tip of my finger, he hauled off and swatted me with open claws. "Quick on the trigger there, aren't you, cat?" I wheezed, nursing my bloody hand. The name stuck, and he's been Trigger ever since.

For the next few weeks I practiced being patient and Trigger practiced being brave. What I didn't notice was Minky drifting into a bad mood, growing cantankerous and ill tempered. Once I finally made friends with Trigger, I was keenly aware that he and Spike were mortal enemies. The minute Spike sensed that Trigger was around, he'd rush in madly and chase him off the premises. Minky, meanwhile, developed a habit of sitting by, seething and uttering deep, throaty growls, as if alerting Spike to the enemy's presence and egging him on. "Go get him, Spike; go get him!"

I admit I took little notice except for the daily chase when Spike roared in to drive Trigger away.

Then, late in the fall, things began to change. Trigger reached adulthood, full tomcat status, and realized that he, not Spike, was the dominant one, the alpha male. It took several knock-down, drag-out, fur-in-your-face fights in the middle of the night (Why, oh, why do cats fight only at night?) before Spike became convinced. For several weeks Trigger did his best to drive Spike away permanently.

The great leveler between Spike and Trigger seemed to be the feeder. Cats are nothing if not utterly practical where food is concerned. After a while they managed to put together a basic cease-fire agreement and now live in an atmosphere of hostile indifference, except for Minky. She spits at me now in the morning when I come bearing food and milk. "Not a good idea to hiss at the hand that feeds you," I remind her. She hisses again and growls, as if I was responsible for all of life's tribulations. I pet Trigger, of course, because he has become a very affectionate cat. This just makes it worse, and for the past two weeks if I pet him before I feed her, she stalks away and refuses to let me pet her or even to eat. Minutes later, she'll appear at the edge of the porch, glaring at me.

I try to talk her out of it. I reassure her that she is still Number One Cat. She just growls. I reach down and scratch her behind the ears. "Get over it," I tell her. She hisses and stomps away. I'm surprised and disappointed. This is human behavior. People act like this. Somehow I expected more from a cat.

The Birds Are Back

The birds are back. All winter the feeder outside the kitchen door has had only a few visitors, sparrows mostly, an occasional chickadee, and now and then a finch dressed in winter gray.

But the very minute the tulips poked through the early spring mud, everything with feathers that has been keeping out of sight suddenly returned, demanding top billing at the feeder. Juncos, English sparrows, and tufted titmice abound. Goldfinches, which have lived humbly through the winter in muted attire, are back with a vengeance in arrogant gold and black.

Purple finches have returned and picked up the quarrel among themselves that they left unsettled last fall. They chatter indignantly outside the back door. Flocks of squawking starlings swoop in black ribbons across the sky and settle for a few minutes in the backyard, where they busily glean seeds from the awakening grass. Then, as though by a prearranged signal, the entire chattering colony lifts into the sky and swoops away.

Even Crazy, the cardinal, sings a few special melodies from the spruce branches. Crazy, you may recall, was the cardinal that picked a fight with his reflection in our bedroom window a few years ago and damn near killed himself before giving up to resume more peaceful domestic pursuits. I don't know if it's the same bird or not. I call him Crazy just the same.

The robins are here, of course, doing their usual hop-hop-hop across the yard, finding morsels here and there. None of their number has made moves to build a nest on our window sill again, as they did a couple of years ago.

In a few weeks we'll hang a new potted plant from the sill on the front porch and watch to see if finches build a nest in it again. For the past two years they have waited patiently until we put up a new plant and then moved in.

I've even seen a couple of mockingbirds this spring. They are rare in our neighborhood. Of course, a single mockingbird can seem like a hundred when it decides to take up arms against our cat. Mockingbirds are actually frustrated fighter pilots, I think, and like to make up for their inadequacies by dive-bombing any cat in the neighborhood that walks across the yard.

Years ago the cat we had was a little on the insecure side anyway. No matter how hard he tried, he just couldn't master normal cat things. He would miscalculate while climbing a tree and fall with a thud to the ground. He would fall asleep on a window sill and topple off. We called him Rookie and shook our heads a lot. That summer a mockingbird moved into the neighborhood and assumed the responsibility of terrorizing the hapless cat. After a couple of near misses and a direct hit or so, Rookie took up refuge under the shrubs by the porch. For the rest of the summer he came out only to eat.

Redwings have a similar devilish spirit, but they don't limit their attacks to cats. I have seen dogs run desperately for cover under strafing attack by a fast-moving redwing. Even people aren't safe. I once unwittingly walked too close to a redwing nest and came under immediate attack. Not only do redwings charge in and rake you with their beaks, but they also have the unnerving ability to hover like miniature helicopters just overhead. I moved quickly to safer ground while the redwing flew like an armed escort overhead.

I look for other birds. Having lived long in Missouri, I keep an eye out for Eastern bluebirds. For some reason there are none. We had brown thrushes one year. They never returned. Another year we had a Baltimore oriole couple nesting in our backyard, their long, drooping nest swaying lightly in the breeze. Once I found a dead indigo bunting in the yard, and I've seen several scarlet tanagers.

Mostly I have finches and sparrows for company. I appreciate their tolerance. I think I know why so many birds come and go. Considering the treatment humanity has given the environment over the years, most birds probably are holding out for better neighbors.

PEOPLE

Someone once said that everyone has a story. It might have been Ernie Pyle writing about the soldiers he interviewed on the battlegrounds of World War II. I was never a war correspondent, but over the years and under varying circumstances I have met some notable people. Because of who they were or what they did or maybe how they did it, I felt compelled to write about them.

Some of them were members of my own family. Others I knew during my military service or later in my civilian work environment. Still others were celebrities who had touched my life and the lives of others in a special way. Yet others were totally unsung heroes who worked in factories or stores, or who taught school in a day when teachers were among the most underpaid members of our society.

I wrote about some people because of their unflagging principles or uncommon valor. Others lived or died tragically. A few I wrote about simply because they were there at the same time I was. Some were famous, others nameless. All had a story.

Remembering Sara

Our granddaughter died tragically on April 13, 1992. She was ten years old.

There was something about Sara's feet. And that something was they were always dancing. There in the kitchen while Mom whipped up good things to eat, Sara talked about the usual things girls of ten find worth talking about, and while she talked, she danced, her tall, thin torso balanced like a two-by-four above those ever-dancing feet.

Left, right, hoppity hop.

Left, right, hoppity hop.

Those feet, they never rested. There they were, dressed in funny shoes and socks so bright they looked like traffic lights blowing in the wind.

Left, right, left, right.

Hoppity hop.

Later at the table munching french fries and still talking, her feet maintained the cadence down below. Even while doing homework, with a pencil in her teeth, a frown across her brow, the books spread out before her, her shoeless feet tapped out the seconds on the clock, measuring time with her toes until she went to bed.

And when she read a book or lounged in that amorphous way that only kids can do in front of a television set, Sara's feet were always hard at work, flipping rhythms back and forth, keeping time to some mysterious march within, some inner rhapsody that only she could hear.

Did I mention that Sara talked? She did. A steady stream of words and phrases, sentences and sometimes full-blown paragraphs formed an up-to-date critical review of the world around her and the one within her heart. She seldom stopped, it seemed to me, with that soft, deep, dulcet voice and those nimble, dancing feet.

And if you sat and watched and listened, as I did from time to time, you'd discover soon enough that Sara's dance and Sara's words were two parts of the same theme—in fact were orchestrated, choreographed symphonic poems from life, expressed quite simply by the unfettered heart and grand imagination of a little girl in Reeboks and a gaudy painted shirt.

"I talked to my teacher after school today ..."

(Hoppity hop)

"And she said my grades were getting better every day."

(Hoppity hoppity hop)

"She said the other kids ..."

(Hoppity hop)

"Should do the same as me ..."

(Hoppity hop)

"Except for you-know-who ... and she's a genius."

(Hoppity hop, stomp, stomp, stomp)

So, while she hopped and chattered through the adventures of her life, another thing that Sara did most of us never saw at all.

Because of the special way she was put together, she could look at you and tell if you had some hidden hurt. Then, once she'd seen the thing that burdened you, she'd take it for her own. She'd put it in her tiny heart and carry it away.

Oh, I don't think she wanted to, or even knew she did. She just seemed to have an instinct for consolation, a reflex for nursing the worries of the world.

And whenever she did, for a little while Sara walked alone and felt the chill of winter in her bones. But soon enough, her feet grew tired of moping about and shuffling here and there and danced up a little lick. And then, with a quizzical smile—as though she knew something special that no one else could see—she gave her feet free rein and broke into a hop, a jump, a pitty pat, and kick ... and talked again, of course, of school and clothes and other brightly colored things.

So, over time, I think the things she gave us will outlast the grief we feel, though not for a while. And certainly not for me whenever I stand amidst the silence in the kitchen in the empty space where the dancing used to be.

Originally written as a eulogy, "Remembering Sara" was published for Sara's October 4, 1994, birthday.

Grandpa

Recently I've been pondering the verities of grandfatherdom. Oh, I've qualified for the role for quite a few years now; I just never thought much about what a grandfather should be. Grandmothers are easy. Everybody knows they smile a lot, bake cookies, and look like Mrs. Wilson next door to Dennis the Menace. But grandfathers seem less distinct.

I remember my grandfather fondly, although I doubt he would make the perfect role model. In retrospect, I think he was cast from a mold long since destroyed. Grandpa believed that life was for the pursuit of pleasure, and that pleasure was strictly a male province.

During World War II he was a foreman in a defense plant. Before and after the war, the company built stoves. During the war it built life rafts. What with overtime and higher quotas to meet, Grandpa spent a lot of time at work. He also made a lot of money, most of which he spent on pleasure.

Pleasure for Grandpa came in the form of fishing trips and beer. Two or three times a year, he'd gather a bunch of his cronies together and head for Canada. There they would fish and drink beer throughout the day and play poker and drink beer throughout the night. At the end of each trip, they would pack up the legal limit of fish and head for home. Grandpa paid most of the expenses on these trips, and he always arrived home flat broke. My grandmother quietly paid all the household expenses out of her earnings as a seamstress.

In the winter, when it was too cold to go fishing, Grandpa spent his off-hours at the Elks Club. There he sat with his cronies, buying rounds of drinks and telling stories about the most recent fishing trip. Sometimes he and his cronies would gather at the house for a fish fry. Late into the night they would eat fried fish sandwiches, drink beer, and spin yarns.

Grandpa was an excellent craftsman, although the quality of the job at hand depended solely on whether it was something he wanted to do or something Grandma wanted him to do. He patiently crafted superb wooden jewelry chests with inlaid woods and fine carving. At the same time, in a fit of impatience, he would fix a broken door with three different kinds of hinges. Or when asked to paint something, he would paint just one side—the side that Grandma saw.

During the war he also fashioned magnificent hunting knives during his spare time at the factory. He must have made several hundred of these fine weapons. He gave them all away to servicemen headed overseas. After the war he got several of them back with notches carved into the handles.

When the plant returned to peacetime production, Grandpa retired. They gave him a glass-encased Anniversary Clock with a brass plate attached to the bottom. After a few years, the clock stopped running. Grandpa tried to fix it, but it never ran again.

For a few years after retiring, he worked part time painting water towers. Standing on a scaffold seventy-five feet in the air is not something I would have attempted even as a young man. But for Grandpa it was just a job to do. I think he must have had a bad scare at one time, however. After one particularly long day, he told the foreman he was quitting for good. He cleaned up his brushes and left, never to return.

When I was in the navy en route to an assignment at Pearl Harbor, I stopped off to visit my grandparents. For much of that summer, Grandpa had spent his days fashioning bird feeders from white pine, painting them, and selling them to the local lawn and garden store. It was a few dollars and something to do. His real passion, however, was homemade wine, which he brewed in five-gallon glass carboys stowed in his workshop behind the house. After supper, when Grandma had retired to the television, Grandpa cracked open a gallon of his finest vintage. I quickly got the idea the old man was starved for someone to talk to. His cronies didn't come around anymore, and he was lonely. He poured the wine and started to talk.

When Grandpa was twelve years old, he ran away from home, lied about his age, and joined the navy as a cook's assistant. During his four years at sea, his ship made one port of call at Pearl Harbor on the island of Oahu in what was then the US Protectorate of Hawaii. For the next four hours, he described that visit in uncanny detail.

"You can catch a rickshaw just outside the Pearl Harbor main gate," he said wistfully. "Tell the coolie to take you down to Wye-kee-kee." He described the narrow dirt road that followed the shoreline toward Diamond Head. "Just before you get there, the road gets swampy," he cautioned. "Just make sure the coolie takes you through to the other side so you don't get your dress whites dirty."

He paused to pour more wine and described what I could expect to find at Wye-kee-kee.

"The Hawaiians live in these grass shacks on the beach down there," he said. "You can get the best rum at Mama Liu's place. It's right at the water's edge sitting up on stilts. Just go in and ask for Mama." Further delights included a number of local girls that, according to Grandpa, danced the hula wearing grass skirts and little else.

It was apparent that Grandpa had lost touch with the passing of time. I had been to Hawaii the previous year. I didn't have the heart to tell him that the dirt road was now a four-lane highway and the grass shacks had given way to high-rise hotels.

I was able to report a few years later, just before he died, that there indeed was a place on Waikiki Beach named Mama Liu's. And the rum was still quite good.

Barbara and Tim Conway

My wife's sister has made it to the big time, sort of. At the very least, she has received the fifteen minutes of fame that pop artist Andy Warhol predicted everyone on earth would get sometime during his lifetime.

To set the stage for Barbara's fifteen minutes, you first must recognize that she has an enormous heart and a spirit of community to go with it. In other words, if there is something she can do for people that will enrich their lives, she will do it. Past recipients of this generosity have included family members, neighbors, friends, total strangers, and, of course, the hundreds of children she helped mold during her years as a teacher.

Early on, Barbara discovered that one good way to enrich the lives of others is to volunteer for organizations that enrich the lives of others. In our city one such life-enriching organization was Starlight Musicals, a not-for-profit group that brought Broadway musicals to town. The volunteers who took tickets, sold T-shirts, and handled publicity were called Starlighters. Barbara was a Starlighter.

Over the years a lot of big names came to town to put on shows such as *Annie, Show Boat, Man of La Mancha*, and so on. Sometime before or after the show would be the inevitable reception for the cast. It was there that the Starlighters got to rub elbows, however briefly, with stars such as Robert Goulet, Danny Kaye, Red Buttons, and Tim Conway. Season after season, Barbara rubbed elbows with them all.

Fast-forward to a few weeks ago. Barbara and her husband joined a group of teachers on a trip to Rome. There were the usual tours, of course, including the Coliseum, the Trevi Fountain, and, of course, St. Peter's Basilica. It was at St. Peter's that fame caught up with my wife's sister.

There is always a crowd at St. Peter's. Visiting priests, religious brothers and sisters, and pilgrims from all over the world come to worship and pay homage at the birthplace of Christianity. Add to this devotional throng an endless tide of tourists.

As Barbara moved with her group silently among the magnificent stone columns, she spotted him. There, standing with another group, was Tim Conway, the man who had enriched the lives of so many on *The Carol Burnett Show*; the man who had come to our city to sing and dance in a Starlight Musical; and the man Barbara had once rubbed elbows with.

It was like seeing an old friend. Barbara sidled up to the star and introduced herself. Yes, he remembered being in our city, remembered the show, and graciously testified to enjoying the experience. What Barbara did next testifies to the true goodness of her heart and the childlike joy she gets from other people.

"I leaned over and asked him if he would do something for me," she recalls. "I asked him if he would do his famous little old man shuffle."

What Tim Conway did then testifies to the true goodness of *his* heart. He brought his elbows to his side and, with a smile, shuffled across the worn stone floor of St. Peter's Basilica.

"I was horrified that I had asked such a thing in this most hallowed place," Barbara admitted later. "But he was very gracious about it."

The truth is, probably no one at St. Peter's even noticed the event, and Barbara's moment of fame might have passed into obscurity had Tim Conway not been a guest the next week on the *Regis and Kathy Lee* television show.

The hosts asked Conway about his trip to Rome.

"I was standing in St. Peter's Basilica," he said, "when this woman came up and asked me to shuffle like a little old man. And I did," he added with a twinkle.

Teachers I Have Known

My sister just retired after thirty years of teaching. She sits across the table from me, looking tired.

"I just couldn't do it anymore," she says. "I've been an administrator, a mediator, a janitor, a politician, and a policeman. But I haven't really been a teacher in years."

Sis says she'll survive as a retiree, what with some retirement investments she put together over time and Social Security down the road.

She admits that whatever evil the system has become heir to since the 1940s and '50s, it has at least improved the financial lot of teachers. It needed improving.

In the dark ages of my youth when I was in grade school, teachers rented small apartments or lived in boardinghouse rooms. They had few possessions; any one of them could have packed everything he owned into a couple of small boxes.

Mr. Jackson was my science teacher when I was in the eighth grade. He was a short, balding, dough-faced man whose shirts were too small around the neck. As a result, he wore his tie loosened and his collar unbuttoned, a practice that constantly rankled our principal, Mr. Tapmeyer. Often Mr. Jackson would come wheezing and red-faced into the classroom, set down his books, and unbutton his collar with a great sigh. We all knew he had just had another run-in with Mr. Tapmeyer.

While "the system" expected my sister to be many things besides a teacher, it expected Mr. Jackson only to teach. And teach he did.

He made science come alive in that shabby laboratory classroom. The first day of school he introduced General Science with a series of delightful surprises that left all of us wide-eyed with wonder and eager to come back the next day. He changed clear liquids into bright colors, filled the room with the brightness of the sun by burning a piece of magnesium, and raised a ten-pound anvil two feet into the air with an electromagnet. This final demonstration, of course, would not have been complete without dropping the anvil from that height onto a dozen walnuts that Mr. Jackson had placed on the table.

"Science can be helpful when you're hungry," he said, popping a handful of nutmeats into his mouth.

Over the course of that school year, Mr. Jackson helped us build an electric motor, showed us how to turn white daisies blue by putting dye in the water, demonstrated the dangers of mixing acid and water, built a miniature ecosphere in a glass aquarium which regularly treated us to actual rain showers, and taught us the patience and consistency of nature by germinating corn in a cigar box of dirt.

I don't know how much Mr. Jackson was paid; enough, I guess, to allow him to live in the basement of someone else's house and occasionally drive his ancient Chevrolet on weekends. Mostly his car sat in the driveway. Even with gasoline only twenty cents a gallon, it was a luxury Mr. Jackson could ill afford.

When winter came that year, with days of blowing snow and bitter wind, Mr. Jackson came to school wearing the strangest-looking overcoat I'd ever seen. He had bought an army surplus coat and then tried to camouflage its origin by soaking it in a tub of All-Purpose Rit—a popular fabric dye the manufacturers claimed could make anything look like new. Army overcoats apparently were exempt from these claims.

Mr. Jackson said the fabric had been treated with waterproofing before the coat was made. Some of it remained, and when he tried to dye it, the waterproofing resisted the dye. The result was a coat that looked as if it had been splattered with dark mud—blotches of navy blue mingled with faded areas of olive drab.

Never one to miss an opportunity to teach us something, Mr. Jackson proudly displayed his coat as an outstanding example of an experiment gone awry. He snipped small, affordable pieces of fabric from the lining of the coat and demonstrated how certain chemicals dissolved the waterproofing so the fabric would accept the dye. He never redyed his coat, however. He couldn't afford the chemicals.

On Saturdays and during the summer months, Mr. Jackson worked part time at Carp's Department Store. I didn't know this until one Saturday when my mother angrily sent me to the store to return a pair of my brother's pants that had shrunk the first time they were washed.

"The clerk said they wouldn't shrink," she said, admonishing me to not leave the store until I had received a full refund. I marched into Carp's filled with resolve. And there behind the counter, his tie loosened and his collar unbuttoned, was Mr. Jackson.

My anguish at that moment was indescribable. Here was a man I revered only slightly less than God—forced to be a mere clerk in a department store. I mumbled something about shrinking pants and held the package out with trembling hands.

"Aha!" he exclaimed cheerfully, examining the ruined pants. "Do you know why cotton shrinks when it gets wet?" For the next ten minutes he explained the properties of natural fibers in terms that made me want to go into the textile business.

"Always buy Sanforized," he concluded with a smile, handing me the refund.

I moved away from that town the next year. Many years later when I returned for a visit, I learned that Mr. Jackson had taught for several more years, and, when forced to retire, had lived out the final years of his life in the County Home—the equivalent of what my grandparents used to call "the poor house." I heard he used to teach the nurses what he knew about antiseptics and how they killed germs.

His possessions were few. Even his battered Chevrolet was sold to help pay for his care. Somebody said it brought fifty dollars.

A Visit with Polly

Let me tell you about Polly. I never knew her last name. I met her when I was ten years old and we lived in a very small farm town in central Missouri. Our house was one of a grand total of fifteen in the entire town. Virtually every house was separated from the others by farm fields.

Polly lived in a small shack at the edge of one of these fields about a quarter mile down the road from our house. Her home consisted of a single room no more than ten feet square, and a smaller lean-to which served as her bedroom. There was no electricity, no running water.

I met Polly by accident. One of the farm kids I went to school with—after months of indifference—suddenly took a liking to me. His name was Howard Jenkins, but everybody called him Cracker. He was shaggy-maned and wore the same bib overalls, clodhopper boots, and faded flannel shirt year-round.

After school this particular day, Cracker elected to show me his favorite fishing hole. The most direct route was a straight line across three fields. When we reached the fence of the second one, Cracker paused and shook his head.

"Bull's out," he muttered. "We'll hafta go 'round." I narrowed my eyes against the drooping sun. Sure enough, at the far edge of the field a massive black bull grazed. With each mouthful of grass he pawed the ground impatiently with a front hoof.

"Meanest bull around," said Cracker. I agreed. When we skirted the field, our new route took us directly behind Polly's shack. As we passed, a voice crackled from the dark interior.

"That you, Cody?"

"No, Ma'am," Cracker replied.

"Who, then, come t' see Polly?" the voice demanded. The shack's door opened and out stepped a small, wrinkled woman. She stood on the stone stoop and squinted toward us. She wore a soiled and threadbare housedress and held a frayed shawl over her shoulders. A faded kerchief was tied around her head.

"Young Jenkins, that you?" she inquired. "C'mon in here now and visit," she added, not waiting for an answer. Cracker nodded assent and headed toward the shack. I followed doubtfully, waiting for a signal from Cracker. There was none.

Inside, Polly motioned for us to sit. "Who's that with ye?" she asked.

"This here's Polly," Cracker mumbled in my direction. I introduced myself since it seemed apparent Cracker wasn't going to. The old woman studied me for a moment through rheumy eyes.

"Now, you'uns sit," she said. "I'm going to get out some cookies." With that she shuffled to a shelf and fiddled with some jars sitting in a row amidst some unidentified objects. I brightened at the idea of cookies.

"No thank you, Ma'am," Cracker said almost formally. "We done et."

"Well, then, you'uns sit," she said, abandoning the jars. Dutifully, we sat. There was only one chair, an ancient rocker with a piece of linoleum tacked across the seat where the upholstery used to be. That was obviously Polly's. She maneuvered back to it, sat, and commenced rocking. Cracker plopped his lanky frame on a short three-legged stool. I perched tentatively on a open box filled with empty fruit jars.

For the next half hour or so we sat. Polly rocked and talked. She talked about everything—the weather, people I'd never heard of including the person she had earlier referred to as Cody, and things that had happened presumably long before. Most of the time she seemed to forget she had an audience. Twice more she offered cookies. Twice more Cracker solidly declined. Once she got up and rummaged through boxes stacked against the wall, emerging with a battered cigar box. It was filled with ancient paper dolls.

Time ticked away slowly. Then Cracker stood abruptly and announced, "We's got to git on." Without another word he headed for the door. I followed.

"You'uns come back again," Polly croaked from her rocker, still absorbed in her reverie with the paper dolls.

"She ain't got no cookies," Cracker said as we crossed the field leading to the creek, hurrying to make up for lost time. "She ain't got nothin'. She just says that to get you to stay."

I never saw Polly again. Years later I returned to the town to show my wife where I had lived during my tenth year. I showed her the one-room school, since abandoned. The general store was still there, and so was our house. I drove down the road to the place where Polly's shack had stood. It was gone. Not a trace remained, and soybeans grew where it once had been.

The man at the general store had never heard of anyone named Polly; neither had the woman who ran the feed store down the road. She did recall, however, that her father used to talk about someone by that name who lived in a shanty over on the Kramer place.

Sometimes I think about Polly. I think of her sitting alone, desperately offering courtesies she can't afford for a few minutes of company with a couple of boys in a hurry to be someplace else.

Barber Shop from the Past

It was like stepping into the past, back about fifty years or so. It had been so long since I had been inside an old-fashioned barbershop, it took my breath away.

Barbershops don't really exist anymore. Nowadays they're called hair salons, and it's mostly women sitting in the chairs or under the driers. And when you go in for a haircut, they always start you out with a shampoo, a rinse, and what the operators call a "comb-out." I never could figure out why they needed to shampoo my hair since I had already scrubbed it in the shower just hours earlier. At first I tried to tell them that, but they insisted on shampooing anyway.

Generally, I get a haircut about every four to six weeks. I'd probably go longer, but by that time it's sticking out over the tops of my ears and I'm beginning to look like an unweeded garden. The only time I ever got it cut more frequently was during the two years I was in the army. The sergeant insisted on weekly haircuts, and he had an uncanny knack of knowing when it had been longer.

"Private, did you get a haircut this week?"

"Yes, sergeant."

"My eyes tell me otherwise, private. Why don't you come into my office this Saturday and write a full report on the haircut you got this week."

If there was anything I developed an aversion to in the army, it was spending Saturdays writing reports. To avoid this administrative exercise, I got in the habit of getting shorn weekly. Of course, I also polished my boots daily, pressed my shirts nightly, and knotted my tie tightly. The sergeant also liked to read reports on loosely knotted ties, wrinkled shirts, and scruffy shoes.

That was then, of course, and I seem to recall that when I got discharged, I deliberately went an entire month without getting a haircut. I also grew a beard, wore baggy clothing, and said things like "Cool, daddy-o, cool."

Naturally, reality stepped in shortly thereafter, and I shaved, got a clip, and even shined my shoes—all so I could get a job and pursue the American dream, which, by the way, I still haven't caught. That was also when I got into the habit of getting haircuts only when my ears vanished.

Fast-forward to last week. I really needed a haircut, but the hair salon I normally go to was booked up. My wife and I were in Missouri helping our granddaughter celebrate her twelfth birthday.

Saturday morning we arose and slouched around the kitchen table catching up on family news and eating cornflakes and donuts.

"You need a haircut," my wife said. I shrugged agreement.

"You do look a little shaggy," my daughter chimed in. I shrugged again.

"There's a barbershop right downtown," she added. "I think it's open on Saturday." I looked at both of them, quickly reading between the lines. "I'll be back in an hour," I said. If there is anything I have learned over the years, it's how to read between the lines of a woman's conversation. In this case it was easy to see that my wife and daughter were not merely passing on information.

Larry's Barbershop sits right off the main drag in downtown Jefferson City. It is pressed so tightly between two other buildings, it would be easy to miss if it weren't for the red and white striped barber pole turning lazily next to the door.

The minute I walked into Larry's shop, I felt like a kid again. There were hair clippings on the floor at the base of the big old-fashioned white ceramic barber chair. The linoleum floor had visibly worn paths around the chair and between the chair and the television set mounted on the back wall. In the waiting area just inside the door by the window, a distinctly 1950s chrome and plastic kitchen chair sat amid an assortment of year-old magazines. The air smelled of bay rum, and Larry stood smiling and knowing next to the chair, comb and scissors protruding from the pocket of his white barber's jacket.

I slid into the chair and opened the conversation. In old-fashioned barbershops it was always up to the customer to open the conversation. Any opening was acceptable including the well-worn "How about those Cardinals?" I opened with the fact that I hadn't been in a barbershop in years.

"You do look a little ragged," Larry said.

"I meant an old-fashioned barbershop," I said.

"I know what you meant," he said with a twinkle. "I hear that a lot."

"You don't shampoo before you cut, either," I added.

"I figure you did that in the shower this morning." What a guy. I settled back in the big chair while he snipped hair around my ears and along the back of my neck. This was the way it was supposed to be.

"How long have you been here?" I asked.

"Forty-five years last Thursday," he said.

"Seen a lot of changes, I'll bet." He nodded.

"Hair's the same, but the people are different. Always cut the governor's hair. And all seven justices of the state Supreme Court used to come in after their weekly judicial committee meeting. These guys always wore dark suits, and they didn't joke very much. Today, if one of them comes in, he most likely is dressed as though he's got the day off. Seems like we've lost something," he said soberly. I agreed and closed my eyes as he raced his clippers along the sides of my head.

"What about retirement?" I asked.

"I figure I'll work another twenty years," he said, pausing and narrowing his eyes as though trying to visualize it in his mind. "I'll be ninety by then, and I figure I can coast for the next ten years." I looked at him in the mirror. He was smiling.

With that, he splashed the back of my neck with bay rum, dusted me off with his soft brush, spun the chair, and whipped off the cover. "You should be able to hear a little better," he added with a grin.

I paid Larry and walked out of his little shop. It occurred to me as I drove back to my daughter's house that this was the first time in years I had seen someone who was truly happy in his work.

Larry was still cutting hair at age 86.

Skinny-Dipping, Mr. Secretary?

When I was outdoor editor of the *Jefferson City (MO) News-Tribune*, I accepted an assignment to spend two days on a river with a bunch of politicians. Little did I know that I was about to witness history in the making.

It was late in the summer of 1961, and Rep. Richard Ichord of Missouri had just introduced a bill in Congress that would turn almost two hundred miles of a southern Missouri river system into a National Monument. Secretary of the Interior Stuart Udall announced that he wanted to come to Missouri and take a look.

Udall had just been appointed to the cabinet position by President Kennedy, and this was his first big assignment. The three rivers named in Ichord's legislation, the Current, the Jacks Fork, and the Eleven Points, were acknowledged pretty much everywhere as an area of unequalled, even staggering, beauty. It was heady wine indeed.

As an official member of the press corps covering the event, I managed to hitch a ride in one of the state government's airplanes. The first stop was the Kansas City airport, where I interviewed Ichord about his bill. Government intervention was necessary, he said, because the area was all privately owned land and in danger of being exploited by any number of outside interests—everything from resorts and amusement parks to high-density home construction. The state had earlier staved off an effort to build a dam on the Current River, and Ichord was determined to keep similar threats from surfacing in the future.

Actually, I had something of a vested interest in the Current River myself since I had lived on its banks as a kid and had spent every spare moment at the water's edge. A buddy of mine and I even built a raft and launched it from the riverbank with lofty dreams of sailing clear to Arkansas. Fortunately, we piled up on some rocks on the first turn. The raft broke apart and dumped us into the water. I hate to think what would have happened if we had made it further downstream to the really dangerous rapids.

The river is fed by several springs, and rainbow trout abound in the icy waters, making it a popular float-fishing paradise as early as the 1930s. Jim and Marian Jordan, known to radio fans in the thirties and forties as Fibber McGee and Molly, were among the dignitaries who often came to Missouri to float down the Current River.

After the Ichord interview, we headed back out to the plane to fly down to the river. Unfortunately, the plane had a problem and couldn't fly, so I wound up waiting for another plane to take reporters down and return for a second trip. By the time I got to the river it was early evening, and the camp was a bustle of activity.

There was every kind of government functionary you could think of milling around the place, along with reporters from major newspapers across the nation, local dignitaries from towns along the river, numerous conservation-minded citizens, dozens of vendors who hoped to get a piece of the action when the government takes over, plus more law enforcement people than you might see at a police convention. There was even a State Patrol helicopter.

As I was arriving, somebody tossed about fifty T-bone steaks onto a gigantic charcoal grill, while another person dumped a bucket of ice over a tub of soft drinks and beer. Meanwhile, a truck loaded with flat-bottom Jon boats was slowly backing up to the bank. Jon boats are long, wide, flare-sided fishing boats favored for river passage because of their shallow draft and remarkable stability. Early settlers fashioned the original boats from green lumber and caulked the seams with pitch. These boats were made of aluminum.

Secretary Udall sat on a picnic table, beer in hand, surrounded by several state legislators, the heads of at least three state government departments, a sizable bevy of dedicated conservationists, and at least a dozen reporters. I sidled up to the crowd and took out my pad. Udall was expounding on the future of the area.

"I predict that if this becomes a National Monument, as many as eight hundred thousand visitors will come every year to float down this beautiful riverway," he said. He was wrong, of course. Last year more than 1.5 million visitors floated the Current River.

Suddenly, Udall stood up from the table and announced that he was going to go for a swim. "Who's with me?" he yelled, whipping off his shirt. Nobody budged. After all, the Current River is spring fed and glacier cold even on the hottest summer day. Besides, nobody had even thought about bringing a suit. This was, after all, a dignified affair with a member of the President's cabinet.

Then, as the Secretary of the Interior stripped to his bare pelt, one of the local sheriff's deputies stepped forward.

"Hell, yes," he said, dropping his gun belt and unbuttoning his shirt. Several others did the same, and with a rush of bravado I kicked off my shoes and joined the party. With a whoop consistent with boys in the summertime, the gang of us—naked as jaybirds—bounded down the bank and into the Arctic water. For the next five minutes we kicked, splashed, and laughed in the rushing current. Then, as though on signal, we all waded out and, shivering with the cold, rushed into our clothes.

The next day a parade of about twenty boats floated for about five hours down those milky blue waters and then pulled into shore at a second camp that had been set up as we floated. Somebody asked Udall if he had caught any fish. "Nope," he said with a laugh, "I didn't want to get arrested for not having a license." Later, in a more serious tone, the Secretary of the Interior announced that he would fully endorse making this river system a National Monument for all citizens to enjoy for all time.

It didn't happen without a fight. Local residents wanted nothing to do with it. After all, it was their land that the government was going to take. Conservationists supported it in fear of losing the river altogether if it wasn't protected. In addition, the measure was supported by both senators from Missouri and the governor. The opposition was eventually defeated.

In the end, the Eleven Points River was eliminated from the proposal, and the number of miles on the Current and Jack's Fork was reduced to 134. President Johnson signed the bill into law in 1964 creating the Ozark National Scenic Riverways.

Some people in the area—mostly landowners and developers—are still bitter about what they call government interference, but the good news is this: today you can float down the Current River in Missouri, and it is just as clean, pristine, and astonishingly beautiful as it was on that summer day forty-three years ago. And the chances are good it will stay that way as long as the river flows.

Stuart Udall long ago retired from public service, of course, and returned to his home state of Arizona. I don't know if he ever returned to that beautiful river. I hope he did, for he is responsible for preserving some of the most beautiful country on earth.

I get back there occasionally and float along its undulating curves, alongside sheer bluffs and overhanging trees. And when I am there—the sun on my face and the slap of water against the side of my boat—I always think about the time I went skinny-dipping with the Secretary of the Interior.

Dad Saw an Ivorybill

Recent news from Bayou DeView, Arkansas, would have had my dad dancing in the street. The news had nothing to do with the town itself. Actually, the place is so small that apparently both Rand and McNally decided it wasn't worth putting on the map.

What happened in Bayou DeView is that it's the place scientists recently confirmed the sighting of an ivory-billed woodpecker—a bird long thought to be extinct. The reason Dad would be overjoyed is that he reported seeing an ivorybill in the late 1940s in the boot heel of Missouri, about fifty miles to the northeast.

At the time, Dad was a forester working for the Missouri Conservation Commission. On that day he was surveying an area of dense timber in the swampy land along the Arkansas border. When he got home that night, his eyes were glowing as though he had been abducted by aliens. He was more excited than I ever saw him either before or after.

"I was sitting on a fallen log eating my lunch when the bird flew up and landed on a tree just a few feet away from me," I remember him saying. Dad added that he watched the bird for several minutes before it flew away.

To show us what he had seen, he pulled out the encyclopedia and turned to the picture and description of the bird. The text confirmed that the ivory-billed woodpecker was thought to be extinct. That same evening Dad drew a picture of the bird he had seen and colored it with a set of colored pencils he used for making maps.

The next day he sent the drawing with a letter describing the sighting in detail to the state ornithologist at the university. A couple of weeks later he got a reply saying that he was mistaken and that what he had actually seen had to have been a pileated woodpecker—a bird that resembles the ivorybill. The ornithologist added that, sadly, the ivory-billed woodpecker was extinct.

Dad was crestfallen. He was also more than a little angry. He was a scientist himself—a trained observer—and although he was not an ornithologist, he was used to doing fieldwork and making highly detailed observations. What he saw was not a pileated woodpecker, but an ivory-billed woodpecker. All of this he put down in another letter that he fired off to the university.

I remember the letter he got in response. It was a single, handwritten line that simply said, "The ivory-billed woodpecker is extinct!" It wasn't even signed. I remember Dad reading it slowly several times, shaking his head, and then returning the letter to its envelope and filing it away in his desk. He never mentioned it again.

Dad died several years ago after a long battle with Parkinson's disease. He had lived in a nursing home for some years, and pretty much all that he did in his professional life had long been forgotten. Sadly, the drawing he made and the letters from the university have also vanished.

But now—more than five decades after that day when he sat eating his lunch on a log in the woods—comes documented proof that the ivory-billed woodpecker has indeed survived. And so, it seems, has the validity of my dad's claim. Way to go, Dad!

Hoboes

We were talking about hoboes, the lady who cuts my hair and I. She said that when she was a girl, a hobo came to their house on Main Street and her mother gave him something to eat.

"She made him stay outside," she said. "She wouldn't let him into the house. But she gave him something to eat."

The thought of it struck me. Back in the thirties and forties, when those tattered and unshaven men roamed across America—victims at first of a Depression that emasculated the country, and then of the habit they had acquired of always looking, but somehow never finding—that's what you did. You fed them.

I remember, as a small boy living in a farmhouse in Wisconsin, the hoboes walking up the long drive to the house. They came one at a time, as if they knew that if they came in groups they would be feared. So, one at a time they came, and my mother would tell them they could wash up at the pump while she fixed them a sandwich.

Then they would eat sitting by the pump and make small talk across the yard to where my mother stood with me. They might say where they'd come from and where they were going. They usually asked if we knew of any work in the area. Afterward they would get up, nod their thanks, walk back down the drive, and continue along the road.

Every once in a while, one of these nameless men would offer to split some firewood in payment for the food. Sometimes my mother thought that would be a good idea, and then she supervised as they filled the wood box beside the kitchen door.

We never talked about the hoboes. They were just there, a moving part of the landscape. Only later did I learn that they rode freight trains, had their own network of campsites, and even managed a sort of broad-based society with elected officials, rules, and codes of honor.

Then the war came along. The Depression was suddenly and irretrievably gone—and with it the hoboes. I don't think I ever saw another hobo after Pearl Harbor.

After the war ended, I remember there was a period of time when gypsies came through town with their trucks and trailers. They camped at the edge of town and played strange and exciting music into the night. I wasn't brave enough to sneak out those nights, but I'd sit in my bed with the window open, propped up on the window sill, listening with all my heart.

I don't know what happened to the hoboes or the gypsies. They just went away and never came back.

Later, when I was a teenager, Jack Kerouac bummed back and forth across the country and wrote a book about it. There were tales of motorcycle gangs riding through the night along dark highways. But they weren't hoboes, and they weren't gypsies.

Then in the sixties, young people by the thousands dropped out and swarmed across the country to hold love-ins in the unheated doorways of distant cities. They ground their own flour for healthy bread and got stoned on bad drugs.

I remember once getting stuck in a road-building project in Nevada. Hundreds of cars crawled through the dust and the heat. Ahead of me, a Volkswagen Microbus painted with bright psychedelic designs was filled with half-naked teens. They were headed west. As we inched along, a boy crawled through the open roof of the van and stood on top. In his hand was a violin. He bowed to his audience of crawling automobiles and began to play. Someone said it was Chopin, a violin concerto. To my ears, it was played flawlessly. And I remembered thinking that somewhere a mother who had spent a lot of money on music lessons was wringing her hands in anguish.

The beatniks and the hippies weren't hoboes or gypsies either. Wherever they were going, they seemed to sense that one day they would be coming back.

But, I guess the hoboes and the gypsies never looked back. They just kept going down the road until they were gone.

Dickie Pope

We were going to talk about the river, Dickie Pope and I. We planned it a year ago when we ran out of time at the annual family reunion and realized we had just touched the surface. Dickie Pope had spent fifty years on the Ohio and Mississippi rivers, most of them as the captain of a towboat. He had a lot to tell, and, as a writer, I wanted to hear it all.

But the family reunion was Dickie's time to socialize. Everyone wanted to spend time with him because Dickie Pope was one of those remarkable people who literally loved everyone. I was only one member of the family. It wouldn't be fair to take up all his time.

"Next year," he said, accepting a gratuitous hug from a passing kid, "we'll sit down at that picnic table over there and we'll talk about the river. I'll tell you stories you won't believe," he added with a twinkle.

Dickie Pope died unexpectedly last weekend. He was sixty-five and had been a member of my wife's family since he married my wife's cousin Alice several years ago.

Much about the river and Dickie will remain untold now, of course. But I'll tell you some of what he did share with me, and I'll pass along a few observations that might help you understand how much we miss him.

First and foremost, Dickie was a character, a self-made man. He was tough as an ox, stubborn as a mule, and gentle as a lamb. Life on the river was responsible for all these traits, I suppose, that and the fact that he started life at the tag end of the Great Depression. Life was tough and uncompromising everywhere in the early 1930s. It was even tougher on the river.

His real name was Angelo, but he was called Dickie from earliest memory. He had three brothers and four sisters. When Dickie was fourteen, his mother got a job as a cook on a towboat. From that moment on—according to his older brother Parker—Dickie never went ashore again, and all of his brothers and sisters spent at least part of their working lives riding riverboats up and down the country between Cincinnati and New Orleans.

Dickie loved the river from the first moment he saw it. He soon realized he had a natural knack for reading the fast-moving and often deceptive currents. Most work on the early riverboats was backbreaking, greasy-handed, sweat-in-your-face labor. Dickie hauled halyards and stern lines with the best of them. He hopped from barge to barge, fended off half-sunken logs, and worked with dangerous steel cable—all the time reading the river and keeping his eye on the pilothouse. That was where he wanted to be.

He was seventeen when he got his captain's papers, the youngest certified captain on the river. But for a long time no one knew that; regulations said you had to be twenty-one to be a captain. Dickie lied about his age, and it almost got him in serious trouble a year later when he was called up for the draft at age eighteen.

"Dickie swaggered into the draft board with a cocky smile on his face," his brother Parker remembers. "He pulled out his captain's papers and slapped them on the desk. 'I'm a riverboat captain,' he boasted. 'That means I get a deferment.'" According to Parker, the head of the draft board picked up the license, looked it over carefully attesting to its authenticity, and then slammed it back down on the desk.

"What it means," he roared at young Pope, "is you're going to jail because you lied when you got your license. You're only eighteen, and you're illegal as hell."

That was when young Dickie Pope discovered that the Lord granted occasional favors to reckless riverboat captains. He also discovered that his hard work and determination had already made a definite impression on his employer.

"The boss came down and bailed him out," Parker remembers. "Then he got him a deferment so he could keep working on the river." Even then it was obvious to everyone that Dickie Pope did nothing halfway. Although virtually all the towboats on the river by then were diesel powered, Dickie insisted on becoming certified to operate steam-powered vessels as well. He was the last person to ever do so.

I saw Captain Dickie Pope in action years before I ever met him. At the time, I lived in Hastings, Minnesota, a small town situated on a bend in the Mississippi just south of St. Paul. Boats picked up barges loaded with grain in St. Paul and then headed south to markets downriver. Just north of Hastings, it was necessary to maneuver through a lock and dam. Dickie knew that, when the lock opened, it was prudent to hold back a few minutes and let the surge of water get downstream ahead of your boat.

"Otherwise you'd wind up crosswise at Hastings, and you'd never be able to make the turn," Dickie told me. On this particular summer night, Dickie moved out of the lock only to discover that the tow in front of him—a boat and several barges—had ignored this counsel. The tow was, indeed, hung up on the turn. I stood on the shore watching as the frustrated and inexperienced captain tried to maneuver the turn. Again and again he slammed into the shore. Meanwhile, Dickie edged his tow against the riverbank behind him and waited.

After an hour of no progress, the radio crackled in the pilothouse of the errant towboat. "Listen carefully," the voice said in measured tones. "Move into shore because I'm going to come down there and show you what it is that you're doing wrong." Five minutes later the stocky and plainly agitated frame of Captain Angelo Pope jumped aboard the immovable boat and strode up to the pilothouse. Moments later the engines roared, and the tow twisted and backed up the river. A few minutes later, it slipped around the turn and disappeared into the darkness of night. Before long, a motor launch came into view, heading back upstream with Captain Pope standing in the bow.

It wasn't hard to get Dickie to talk about the river. He'd tell you about floods and groundings, about heroic rescues by boat crews, and about river pirates. "They knew better than to mess with me," he said with a smile.

Between pushing barges up and down the river, Dickie married and raised a family. When he met and married Alice, he became a fixture at the annual family reunion. He played guitar, sang songs no one ever heard of, and called all the girls "Darlin'" and all the men "Old Buddy." He retired from the river a couple of years ago and devoted his time to his flowers, his kitchen, and his wife, whom he called "Old Alice, Little Darlin'."

Dickie loved to eat and felt that everyone deserved a good breakfast. To make his point, he would often don an apron and whip up sausage and eggs with fried potatoes and homemade biscuits for a dozen or more friends and relations who happened to drop by.

Sometimes at night, Dickie would grow quiet and shake his head. "It's not the same now," he'd say softly. "College kids are running the river now, and they don't have the love for it. It's just a job."

That may be true, but for years to come everyone on the river has got to feel a certain vacant space where Dickie Pope used to be.

Easter

When you're part of a family like my wife's, holidays take on a tone that transcends their traditional intent. Easter is no exception.

Call me stodgy, but when I was a kid (back in the dark ages of my youth), Easter was a day of two separate values. You went to church; then you went home and polished off a big dinner followed by chomping down on all the Easter eggs and chocolate bunnies you could handle. It was a sort of harmonious dichotomy, a mixture of feeding the soul and stuffing the body.

Historically, I guess, there is a precedent for this. Easter is, after all, the apex of the Church year—the holiest of days. It is also the end of Lent. As such, it's the day you can officially come in from the desert and resume doing whatever you gave up for the Lenten season. Assuming I'd given up chocolate bunnies for Lent, I could probably feel pretty good about stuffing myself with them on Easter Sunday.

I gave up coffee this year—tough choice for an old seagoing sailor. I was accustomed to six or more cups a day. Needless to say, I missed it every minute of every hour of every agonizing day. Funny thing, though, when I poured that first steaming cup on Sunday morning, it didn't taste as good as I thought it would.

When my wife and I first married, she announced that we would be having some people over for Easter Sunday. "Just family," she added. I had visions of polite visits by a handful of close relatives—a half hour of cordial howdy-dos followed by quick goodbyes. But my wife is Irish, for crying out loud. I should have known better.

She was up at dawn preparing food—enough to feed the entire US Army. The centerpiece was the biggest turkey I'd ever seen. There were hams—two of them—plus assorted vegetable dishes, breads, cakes, and other desserts, plus candy of every conceivable kind.

The first group to arrive were relatives from Southern Indiana, so many of them they had to come in two cars. And they brought food, tons of food. They just opened the trunks of those wonderful cars, and out it came—pans, bowls, bags, and dishes of incredible goodies including one to-kill-for dessert called Death by Chocolate.

As I stood there in amazement at this growing tableau, other relatives began drifting in. They arrived, on average, one car per minute for the next hour or so. I expected the National Guard to show up and direct traffic. By that time every room was crammed with people, our entire acre-plus yard was filled with kids of all ages, and food covered every square inch of flat surface in the house—literally. Just walking from one room to another was an experience in overeating.

After we all had suitably gorged ourselves, a silent committee took a huge steel bowl filled with Easter eggs outside and began hiding them. Each egg had someone's name written on it. The assignment was to mill around long enough to find your own egg. Most were successful, I recall. The dog got one or two, of course, and somebody's egg—we never learned whose—wound up in the crotch of a tree some twenty feet off the ground. I remember it was still up there the following year. The years have proven that neither rain nor sleet nor dark of night can keep my wife's family from its Easter egg hunt.

Another family Easter tradition I was exposed to that day was gifts. Trinkets, really. There were bubble pipes, water guns, toy cars, ball games, and the like—five-and-dime stuff. It was as though my wife had secretly been agonizing over a lack of generosity at Christmas and used Easter to make up for it.

One of the most amazing features of the Easter migration to our house every year is that it happens virtually without planning or invitation. A couple of phone calls, perhaps, but nothing engraved, no RSVPs, and no finely tuned schedules. It just happens, like swallows returning to Capistrano. Everybody comes; everybody visits, eats, plays, talks, and shares the uncomplicated joy of being family.

And I get the feeling that this—perhaps more than anything else—truly expresses the spirit of Easter.

Family Reunion

We attend a family reunion every August. It's a big, rambling, largely unfocused affair where members of my wife's family come together for the weekend to relax, play volleyball, eat too much, sing songs, and talk through the night catching up on important family matters.

Photo albums from various families are passed around to document weddings, births, christenings, vacation trips, and—sometimes—funerals.

New boyfriends and girlfriends get introduced around, solemnly warned about what they are getting into, and then welcomed and accepted as though they were already members of the family.

The largest contingents come from Indiana—mainly the Indianapolis and Jeffersonville areas—and from the Louisville, Kentucky, area. Smaller groups come from Tennessee, Texas, Louisiana, Illinois, Minnesota, and Wisconsin. To be fair, it must be stated that both the Louisiana and Minnesota contingents—as well as those from Tennessee—are actually "moved-away" parts of the Indianapolis contingent.

Not everybody makes it every year. But the roster of those attending in any given year seldom slips below one hundred.

One of the topics of conversation this year was babies. That's because there seemed to be more of them this year than anyone ever remembered before. Infants and toddlers were literally everywhere. I personally counted sixteen at one time in the dining hall, and most I don't recall ever seeing before.

One of the Jeffersonville group allowed as how a few years ago only two families brought any kids to the reunion. Someone else remembered that about the same time a significant wave of boyfriends and girlfriends began showing up for the first time. Everyone agreed there was probably a connection.

For the past few years, the reunion has been held at one of the family camps at McCormick's Creek State Park. The camp consists of a dining hall with kitchen, freezer, and walk-in cooler, a couple of small cabins, and large dormitories with military-style double-deck bunks. Admittedly, the bunks aren't so comfortable, but since sleep isn't high on anyone's list of priorities, it probably doesn't much matter.

Everybody brings a good supply of food and drink. As a result, the family could feed half the park at any meal and still have leftovers when the reunion breaks up on Sunday.

There seems to be a natural ebb and flow to the reunion. During the day some strike out to explore the miles of hiking trails, the pool, the recreation hall, or the nature center. Others stay in camp to make sure anyone who wanders by gets something to eat and a chance to look at the latest photo albums. Periodically, there is an unofficial changing of the guard. Some who have been out on the trail, so to speak, settle in to mind the camp and watch kids, while the erstwhile sentries head for the volleyball court or the pool.

In the evening, there's usually a campfire in the clearing by the dormitories. Someone breaks out a guitar and those assembled sing at least once every song they ever knew. Meanwhile, those in the dining hall deal out the euchre hands, and the tone of the evening is set. Noise from the kids begins to wane sometime before midnight, and the adults tend to call it a day sometime before dawn.

There are subtle changes from year to year. For the past year or so, euchre has been the game of choice. A few years ago it was Trivial Pursuit. One year at least a dozen family members brought radio-controlled toy cars. You risked your life to venture across the parking lot or go into the kitchen for a cup of coffee.

A member of the Indianapolis contingent is a musician and once played in a rock band. One year, the band was invited along and put on an extended concert. Other visitors to the park, hearing the music, thought it was a scheduled function put on by the Parks Department and gathered round. Midway through the evening, fully a dozen non–family members had settled in with sandwiches and drinks and were asking for the dates of next year's concert.

Family members come from all walks of life. Some are retired, while others are just starting out. There are pharmacists, teachers, computer programmers, restaurant owners, engineers, and even a riverboat captain. It was the latter who ventured the opinion that "everyone should have a family this big."

"Why?" someone asked.

"So they could have a family reunion like this one," he said matter-of-factly. Everyone agreed.

Charley Barnes Met Stan Musial

I've never been a true baseball fan even though I grew up in a small Missouri town where we played ball every waking moment and huddled around the radio whenever the Cardinals played.

The greats back then were Stan Musial and Joe Garagiola. "Stan the Man" was at the peak of his career and was voted National League batting champion seven times while I was in grade school and high school. Every one of us, every time we picked up a bat and walked to plate, thought, "Musial steps up to the plate…He waits for the ball…He swings…It's long and high… Holy Cow, it's a home run!"

It was also when Harry Carey announced Cardinal games, long before he moved his Holy Cow enthusiasm to Chicago.

I worked as night sports editor for a small-town daily a few years later. I laid out the sports page, wrote headlines, edited copy, and covered local ball games. Still, I've never considered myself a true fan.

So it was a complete surprise to me when I heard Bobby Richards talk at a prayer breakfast the other morning and felt the thrill of 1950s baseball again. Richards played for the Yankees at a time when they almost owned the World Series. Starting in 1947, they won eleven times over the next fifteen years; Richards played in seven of those games.

He described being a kid in high school and seeing the movie *Pride of the Yankees*. "It was enough to make a nun want to go into baseball," he said. A short time later, he was invited to try out for the Yankees.

"I was seventeen," Richards said, "and I showed up just in time to run into Mickey Mantle and Roger Maris—the greatest players for the greatest team that ever was. I could have died happy at that moment even if I'd never made the team."

A kid from my hometown in Missouri felt the same way about Stan Musial. Charley Barnes (not his real name) loved baseball. And he was good. Despite being a big guy, he was the fastest kid in school. If he dove for a line drive, he caught it. When he connected at bat, at least half of the time the ball was over the fence.

Every summer in those days, the Cardinal ball club held a two-week baseball camp to give promising kids a chance to show their stuff. We all knew Charley would be invited. It was inevitable.

We were right, of course. The letter came during the last week of school. "I've been called up to the majors," Charley crooned, waving the letter. He left two weeks later, and the rest of us fully expected Charley Barnes to be signed with the Cardinals. After his bus disappeared down the highway, we talked about what it would be like to know somebody who knew Stan Musial. Yeah!

It didn't happen. Turns out Charley had a bad heart. Doctors found it during the required physical before checking in for camp. He never even picked up a bat, and he came home two days later. We gathered around Charley down at the gas station, which was also the bus depot. We didn't say much, of course; we just kicked the ground with our scuffed shoes and shrugged our shoulders a lot. Tough break.

"Guess what?" Charley interjected, breaking the somber mood. "They took us all to lunch, and I sat right next to 'Stan the Man'! No kidding. I shook his hand, and he talked to me and everything."

"Wow!" we all said in unison. I remember the smile on Charley's face. Meeting Stan Musial had been almost as important as playing for the Cardinals. Certainly, it had been the most important event in his life.

I moved away later that summer. I heard several years later that Charley had died. I remember thinking that it was terrible to die so young. But to have met Stan Musial. Yeah!

Bobby Richards went on to play some serious baseball with the Yankees. He retired at thirty but never lost touch with Mantel, Maris, and other members of his team. In fact, he was with Mickey the day he died.

"Mickey told me that as great as it was to be named to the Baseball Hall of Fame, it was better to be named to God's Hall of Fame."

Maybe I'm more of a fan than I thought.

Gerry Mulligan and His Music

Gerry Mulligan is dead. For those of us who got caught up in this man's music back in the 1950s, it's pretty clear an era has passed.

World War II was over, and America was in a high-speed chase to make up for lost time. The great swing orchestras that had woven the fabric of the 1930s and 1940s were in decline. Oh, people still liked the sounds of groups like Tommy Dorsey, Woody Herman, and Buddy Morrow, but high costs were making it tough to move full-size orchestras around the country. Instead, small groups with a handful of improvising musicians were developing. Mulligan was part of that.

Gerry Mulligan (he pronounced it "Gary") played the baritone sax—a deep, throaty brass contrivance that made the air resound for hours after the music stopped. He usually brought in a couple of other instruments—a trumpet or tenor sax—along with a bass and percussion. He invented a sort of counterpoint which added an exotic harmony to otherwise simple tunes. Anyone who has heard his version of "Moonlight in Vermont" knows what I mean.

Mulligan wasn't alone. He was part of a whole new concept in American music. Others included George Shearing, Dave Brubeck, Stan Getz (who sometimes played with Mulligan), Pete Rugelo, Thelonious Monk, Charlie "Bird" Parker, and literally hundreds of lesser-known composers and musicians who shared the need to break away from conventional sounds and blow a little fresh air through their horns.

I was in Kansas City in the early 1950s—young, impressionable, and definitely tuned in to this new music. It was possible in those days to squeeze into a table where a group was playing, absorb the official music until 2:00 a.m. when the joint closed, and then get invited to the after-hours session in the back room. That's where the real music happened. In Kansas City these

247

jam sessions spilled into the dark corners of the Muehlebach Hotel or into the basements of remote clubs out on Blue Ridge Road in what was known as The County.

Musicians have always jammed, of course, and this extemporaneous overflowing of musical goodwill was literally a page borrowed from Dixieland artists in New Orleans, St. Louis, and Chicago during an earlier time.

What seems remarkable about that time is the absence of drugs. There was a little Benzedrine, of course, to keep things running in high gear, and booze to maintain the flow, but most of the musicians I knew back then didn't even smoke pot. Everyone knew what they wanted to say and they put all their energy into saying it.

The same was true with another type of music developing at the same time—folk music. Pete Seeger took the socialist protest songs of the 1920s and reissued them through a melodious group called The Weavers. After that came the rare voices of Joan Baez; Peter, Paul and Mary; The Seekers; and The Womenfolk. It was possible to spend the entire night absorbed in the plaintive melodies of these musicians. I remember stopping for a drink at a small cantina in Taos, New Mexico. A random group of musicians was warming up. One guy played a pocket-size trumpet that he called a "folk coronet." Another, whom I recognized as a character actor from the television series *Have Gun Will Travel*, played a Mexican troubadour's harp.

I finished my drink and was about to leave when they played their first song. I couldn't believe my ears. I ordered another drink and sat down. These musicians, who just happened to be in town, must have played every song they ever knew. They finally quit their unpaid, unplanned gig at 5:00 a.m. Afterward, all of us—about ten listeners and six musicians—invaded the truck stop at the edge of town and ate breakfast together.

That night in Taos—like other nights at the Muehlebach and out on Blue Ridge Road—were studies in artistic sharing at its best. The musicians' jobs were to make music. Mine was to listen with all my heart and soul. With guys like Gerry Mulligan making the sounds, it was easy.

Rock and roll long ago took over where Mulligan and his kind left off. I'm not sure, but I don't think all-night jam sessions happen with today's musicians like they did back then. I think they'd like to have them, but they're too famous. They can't do anything without massive security. Besides, it's a different world today. Too many contracts, too many managers have made real music—the kind that happens at four in the morning—all but impossible.

I'm sure that would make Gerry Mulligan sad.

Habitat for Humanity—a Good Start

A young friend of mine recently spent three weeks with a group from her church working on the Pine Ridge Sioux Reservation in western South Dakota. They went there to help, to do what they could where they could.

I know it wasn't easy for these young, inexperienced missionaries. There is no more impoverished place in the country than Pine Ridge. And that kind of poverty can't be fixed by repairing screen doors and broken windows. Poverty at its best is desperate; at its worst it's hard, resentful, and mean-spirited.

No busload of eager middle-class kids is going to rebuild the broken spirit of the Sioux people. But it's a start.

Sometime ago I talked with a staff member at St. Joseph's Indian School in Chamberlain, South Dakota. He told me most of the Indian children on the reservation literally give up hope by the time they are twelve years old. The school helps. It takes the kids out of the poverty of the reservation for a few years and gives them a chance to develop a sense of self-worth. It doesn't work for everybody, and the school can take only so many. But it's a start.

Leo Tolstoy was mortified by the plight of Moscow's poor, who were living and dying on the streets of the city. They clutched at his clothing as he walked among them.

"What can I do?" he lamented. "There are so many, and I am just one." In desperation he turned to Scripture. In the third chapter of Luke he found the only answer available: "If you meet a man who has no coat, give him one of yours."

Thus Tolstoy was able to help a few, those put in his path. It wasn't much. But it was a start.

When I was a young newspaper writer back in the late 1950s, a small-town high school shop class got an idea: if they spent the school year building a house in the community, the students could learn a valuable trade. Then, if they could sell the completed house for no more than the cost of materials, they could help someone buy a home who otherwise could not afford it. The money could then be used to buy materials for the next year's housing project.

The idea caught on. Local banks offered to help the home buyers finance their mortgages. The last I heard, the home building project in this small town was still going on. Students had built and sold thirty-eight homes. I'm told schools in other towns are building homes for the poor. Each class builds but one house a year. Not much, but it's a start.

Habitat for Humanity has taken the same idea and applied it on a global scale. In cities all across the United States, corporate sponsors put up the money and the volunteer labor to build houses for those who need them but cannot afford them. Sponsors in Indianapolis built seven such houses in Indianapolis last month. Volunteers by the hundreds measured, sawed, nailed, assembled, polished, and cleaned up for seven solid days. At the end of the week the houses were finished.

Since its inception nearly twenty years ago, Habitat for Humanity has built some forty thousand houses around the world, small potatoes on a grand scale. But it's a start.

I know that my young friend saw more than she expected and accomplished less than she hoped during her visit to the dust-blown prairie of South Dakota. I know that during the bus ride west, she and the other youngsters vowed to make a real difference in the lives of those they would meet on the reservation.

I also know that when their three-week mission was over and they climbed back aboard the bus to return to their homes, they were left with the nagging feeling that they should have done more.

Like Tolstoy, they recognized the blunt fact that the needs were many and they were few. They could do little in the time allotted.

But it was a start.

Helping Others

A bunch of the guys got together last weekend and raked leaves for a friend recovering from surgery. It took about an hour and a half.

After a recent windstorm, I noticed a neighbor walking the entire length of the street picking up trash cans that had blown into the road. He retrieved them from where they had blown and returned each to its rightful owner's property, about a fifteen-minute job. On several occasions, another neighbor has walked from his house to mine to deliver a piece of my mail inadvertently left in his box—at least once in the rain.

In Amish farm country the entire community traditionally turns out to plant, harvest, or build for a neighbor. And in the rural reaches of Minnesota, neighbors are constantly checking up on you to see if everything's okay. More than once when everything wasn't okay, these same neighbors pitched in to cook, clean, fix, and do whatever needed doing.

I once found myself a member of such a work team when a farm owner broke his leg in the middle of soybean harvest. He didn't ask for help; it just showed up. About fifty neighbors hit the man's place at dawn, and by four that afternoon the harvest was in, the equipment put away, and supper was on the table. To my recollection, nobody even worked up a sweat. The kindnesses of many always seem to exceed the sum total of their parts.

Another neighbor in Minnesota, a cranky old German—who had, over time, alienated just about everyone in the community—collapsed with a massive coronary while putting a new roof on his house. He was dead by the time they got him to the hospital. Only his widow remained, utterly alone after years of living in the shadow of her defiant husband. Yet while she and a handful of mourners attended the funeral, someone finished putting the roof on the house. No one ever found out who.

Being kind can also backfire. I know a man who found a woman's purse along the road. He stopped his car and picked it up, thinking the owner might have accidentally placed it on the roof of her car while unlocking it and then drove away without retrieving it. The purse contained the usual things: receipts, a couple of postage stamps, a packet of tissues, nail file, compact, and a wallet. The wallet contained identification and a telephone number. He called the woman and reported finding her purse. She wept bitterly as she recounted cashing her Social Security check and then setting her purse on the counter for "just a minute." In that minute the purse was gone. It was all the money she had in the world, she wailed.

The man was deeply moved by her plight and took a twenty-dollar bill from his own wallet and tucked it into the woman's purse before returning it to her. He was probably feeling pretty good about his kindness. It was short-lived, however, for when he reached the woman's home, she accused him of being the thief. A crowd of grim-faced neighbors assembled as she railed against the man. He finally set her purse down on the ground and retreated amidst curses and fist shaking. For days afterward, the Good Samaritan was in a daze of disbelief.

Then there was a woman named Mary. Life had conspired against her over time until her autumn years found her alone, penniless, and living in a one-room, unheated apartment. Toward the end of each month before her Social Security check arrived, she ate whatever she could find. Sometimes these meals came from garbage cans that lined the alley behind her apartment house. She had no family, no friends. She died without anyone knowing she needed help.

The contrast of kindness and neglect used to confound me until a friend pointed out that they are simply two sides of the same coin.

"If you or anyone else had known about the starving woman, you would have helped," he said. "The fact that you didn't frees you of responsibility." He added that each of us is responsible only for those in our path, those we meet who "have no coat," to paraphrase Luke 3:10.

Somebody figured out that through the wizardry of mathematical proximity, we are no more than six feet away from every person on earth—which should make it pretty easy to see who's in front of us.

Jack Underwood

Maybe there is someone like Jack Underwood in your past. I didn't actually know Jack, but I knew his younger brother Bobby, who was a year older than I. He was in the eighth grade, I was in the seventh. It was 1947.

Jack died in the war. He was drafted in 1943, shipped out to the Pacific, and caught a sniper's bullet during the battle for Saipan. He was buried where he died along with other Americans killed in the late hours of the war with Japan. He would have been astonished when, a few months later, American forces moved onto the nearby island of Tinian and built a huge air base. It was from this base that our B-29s launched the final raids against Japan, including the ones which carried atomic bombs to Hiroshima and Nagasaki.

When I got to know Bobby Underwood, Jack had been dead nearly two years. He didn't talk about his brother except to say he died in the war, but his mother still kept the Gold Star banner hanging in the living room window. Then, in 1947, the army contacted the Underwoods to inform them that their son's body was coming home.

I suppose it was as if time had been compressed into a bottle at the news of Jack's death and then suddenly released two years later. I remember Bobby saying that it felt like Jack had died just the day before. The local American Legion post worked with the army on funeral arrangements. Since it was already the middle of May, they scheduled the funeral so it would be included in regular Decoration Day services the last Sunday of the month.

Jack Underwood was not the only one from our small community to die in the war, of course. Tommy Crawford's father was killed at Normandy, and the twin Lester sisters, who lived on a farm outside town and came to school on the bus, lost their older brother in Germany. But they died while the fighting was still going on, and their funerals were held soon after. Jack was the only one to be returned so long after the war had ended. It was almost as though, in our haste to build a new postwar world, we had forgotten about the war and Jack Underwood.

The body of Jack Underwood was flown to the United States from Japan aboard a military transport. Then the casket was loaded onto a train and carried to St. Louis. The hearse from our town's only funeral home met the plane and brought Jack Underwood the rest of the way home. The casket was covered throughout the entire trip with the United States flag. By the time the trip was over, the flag was torn at one corner and stained in several places.

The return of Jack's body had a profound effect on nearly everyone who had known him. The high school principal, who was also the basketball coach and who had helped Jack Underwood grow into a serious and talented player, pulled the team picture from the trophy case next to the first-floor lockers and tacked it up on the bulletin board at the entrance to the school along with a large sign that said "Remembering Jack Underwood."

Two days before the funeral services, Mrs. Underwood took all of Jack's clothes out of his bedroom closet, where they had been since he had gone into the service, and hung them on the clothesline in the backyard. Later she brought them back into the house, ironed all the shirts, and brushed the pants and jackets before hanging them back in the neglected closet.

Mr. Underwood watched her for a while and then disappeared into the garage, where he went to work on the old Ford. When the war broke out, Jack had helped him put the car up on blocks. After all, his insurance office was only six blocks away from their house, and by not driving, he was saving gas for the war effort. When Jack came home on leave before going overseas, he and his dad went out and looked the car over. Mr. Underwood remembered telling Jack that the day he came home they would put the car back in service.

Mr. Underwood worked most of the night cleaning the carburetor and pumping air into the tires. Shortly before 6:00 a.m. he started the car and backed it out of the garage for the first time in four years. By breakfast time, he had washed it and cleaned the upholstery.

I had been to only one funeral in my life, but all the kids in town were invited to attend Jack Underwood's. The casket arrived in the same hearse that had transported it from St. Louis. From there to the grave, it was carried by six soldiers sent from Fort Leonard Wood. An honor guard marched in, carrying flags and rifles. The minister spoke about life, death, and resurrection, about bravery and honor. Then the honor guard fired their rifles, and Jimmy Fife from the high school band played taps on his trumpet. The six soldiers folded the flag that had accompanied Jack Underwood's casket all the way from the other side of the world and handed it to Mrs. Underwood. She clutched it to her breast for a long moment, and then handed it to her husband. Later that day, Jack Underwood's flag was raised to the top of the county courthouse flagpole, where it flew proudly until nightfall. I remember riding down to the courthouse on my bike and looking up at it, trying to imagine all the places it had been, trying somehow to discern—in the flickering red, white, and blue—the real significance of this special flag.

We moved away from Jack Underwood's hometown a year later, and I pretty much forgot the place. I heard later that the Underwood flag was flown at the courthouse every Decoration Day after that until Mr. Underwood died. I heard that Bobby Underwood was killed in Vietnam, but by then I barely remembered him. I never heard if they held a special funeral for him the way they did for his brother.

Decoration Day went on to become Memorial Day, and now it's mostly a three-day weekend filled with barbecues, swimming pool openings, car racing, and NBA basketball. I confess, I don't think often about the wars we've fought and those who perished in them. But when I raise the flag on the front of my house at the beginning of Memorial Day weekend, I silently salute Jack Underwood, a man I never met, one of thousands who died for his country.

I never met him, but I'll never forget him.

The following three columns document the desperate and tragic battle of one young woman and her family against terminal cancer. It was a year of shock, anguish, hope, fear, and—ultimately—resignation. Yet out of despair born of loss came the bright light of hope as the girl's father painfully put it all into the pages of a book in the hope that those who read it will join the fight to eradicate cervical cancer from the earth. The book is Love, Kristen. *You can find an excerpt of it at www.kristeneve.org.*

Sometimes Cancer Wins

My best friend buried his daughter a few days ago. Kristen was twenty-three years old and had been fighting a losing battle with cancer for ten months.

It started last July with pains in her thigh. An MRI showed a blood clot. It also showed a tumor on her cervix.

After consulting with the doctors, the first step was surgery. Everyone had high hopes that the tumor would be operable. Unfortunately, it proved to be intricately connected to muscle tissue and blood vessels. Any attempt to remove it would likely be life-threatening.

Again, Kristen and her parents sat down with the doctors and agreed upon a chemotherapy-radiation combination that had proven to be effective against cervical cancer.

After several weeks of treatment, another MRI showed inconclusive results. While the tumor didn't show signs of shrinking, it appeared to have stopped growing. Still, the doctors had hoped for more positive results.

The plan then was to let Kristen rest for a short time before continuing with the second phase of treatment. The idea was that if, after completing the full course of chemo and radiation, results were still iffy, Kristen might qualify for a clinical trial of a new drug that looked promising.

Meanwhile, Kristen was wracked with pain, possibly from the tumor or the blood clot. She was also exhausted by the chemo and radiation along with the massive painkillers the doctors had prescribed.

By this time, it was apparent that she would not soon return to her new job as assistant manager at Walgreen's, nor would she be able to continue living alone in her apartment. Reluctantly, she gave up both and returned to her parents' home in Noblesville.

Over the following weeks, Kristen had some good days and some bad ones. Some days she would feel good enough to go shopping with her friends or sit up late into the night working on her scrapbook. She spent many evenings playing with her two kittens and watching movies with friends.

She also spent agonizing days and nights convulsed with pain and vomiting, followed by endless hours of bedridden sleep. For weeks she seesawed back and forth, emerging again pain-free and ready to resume the fight.

Through it all her faith never wavered, and she never lost hope. She looked forward to resuming her treatment. Unfortunately, before she could continue chemo and radiation, she suffered another setback. The tumor was still growing and had now invaded her intestine. The doctors performed a colostomy and put her on a liquid diet. After it became clear that she was unable to get the nourishment she needed that way, she returned to the hospital, where the medical team inserted a port in her shoulder. Through it, she could receive special nutrition to help her regain strength for the next session of cancer treatment. The port also allowed the doctors to check her sensitive blood chemistry.

Two weeks ago, Kristen said she was ready to resume chemo and radiation treatments. She managed the first sessions with no ill effects and even announced that she wanted to go shopping with her friends. She was feeling pretty good.

Then the other night she cried out for help. She was weak and hemorrhaging. Her parents rushed her to the hospital. After several frantic hours the doctors told my friend that the transfusions could not keep pace with the bleeding. Quietly, they agreed to discontinue efforts to save Kristen's life and she died at 1:40 the next afternoon. Her family was with her.

Throughout these months, her dad and mom were with her constantly. You probably know her dad as My Friend the Boat Owner. He and I have spent many years sharing life's ups and downs.

When he was working at his job as a pilot for NetJets airline, Kristen's mom stayed with her, often sleeping all night in a chair in the hospital room. Every minute her dad wasn't working, he was at Kristen's side. He brought movies and games and—remembering her childhood passion—coloring books to her hospital room. At Easter he brought an egg-coloring kit, and everyone including the hospital staff took part in coloring Easter eggs.

On each of the numerous times she returned to the hospital, her room was decorated with mementos from friends and family. She was surrounded with things from people who loved her, as well as some who had never met her but who had heard of her brave fight.

Her dad accompanied her everywhere she went—to the hospital for chemo and radiation treatments and to the emergency room in the middle of the night. At home, he helped her get in and out of bed; he held her hand as she drifted off to sleep.

And he accompanied her the other day when she made her final trip from the church to the cemetery. That had to be the hardest part for him, knowing that he and everyone else assembled there that warm and windy afternoon would turn and go back home while Kristen, now free from pain, would stay behind in that quiet place.

Kristen's Sandbox

Kristen's legacy continues. In the two weeks since my friend's daughter died of cancer at the age of twenty-three, the impact of her struggle has reached hundreds. Many of them never even knew her but have nonetheless been affected by her.

For example, the five-year-old son of one of Kristen's friends now has a brand new sandbox to play in.

It happened this way. Kristen's illness was progressive, and throughout the ten months of her affliction, her ability to do the normal day-to-day things eroded from week to week.

At first she could no longer work, and then she had to give up her apartment and her car. Later, as the cancer progressed, she underwent a colostomy and could no longer eat. Finally, the pain and swelling in her legs became so severe she could no longer walk.

That's when her dad built the wheelchair ramp at the house. With the ramp, on good days Kristen could leave the house to spend a few hours with her friends. On bad days, it afforded quick access to the car for another emergency trip to the hospital.

After the funeral was over, Kristen's parents began the arduous task of closing the books on their daughter's life. It wasn't easy. There were medical bills and insurance papers, credit card statements, funeral expenses, and, of course, her numerous possessions—the myriad of things she had collected throughout her short life.

After two weeks, the list of things that had to be done was mostly completed. But there was still the wheelchair ramp attached to the front door and leading to the driveway, a grim reminder of Kristen's final days.

As her father said, "It had to go. Neither of us could stand to look at it. But what to do with it?" Then he had an idea. One of Kristen's friends has a young son. Why not use the lumber to build a sandbox? Sand was one of Kristen's favorite things, whether at the local beach on Morse Reservoir or along the coastline of Florida.

A couple of friends were invited over to help; together they turned a wheelchair ramp into a large sandbox. Then they delivered it and filled it with a half ton of sand.

As an afterthought, Kristen's mom took a small brush and painted across one of the seats built into the corner two words that will forever tie this young boy to a woman who died tragically when he was only five. She wrote the words "Love, Kristen."

Kristen had available to her all the latest advances in the fight against cancer. Sadly, none was sufficient to save her. Yet even as the impact of her struggle continues to spread, newer and more exciting breakthroughs are happening.

In England, for example, a man with metastasized skin cancer that had already invaded his lymph glands and lungs was recently cured with massive injections of his own white blood cells. To treat the man, doctors extracted white cells from his body, cloned them by the millions, and re-injected them into his body. They call the process immunotherapy. It is well known, of course, that white cells attack disease, but in the case of cancer, the number of cells available to do the job naturally are too few in number.

To be clear, this is not a guaranteed cure any more than is the Kanzius Noninvasive Radio Wave Cancer Treatment—the breakthrough using radio waves to kill cancer cells treated with metallic nanoparticles. But both are exciting and promising.

Doctors have known for years that given the proper motivation and weapons, the body can heal itself of just about any ailment. In my own case, a topical ointment called Aldara kicked my immune system into high gear to attack dozens of basal cell skin cancers I had accumulated through years of exposure to the sun. In a matter of months, my skin cancers were completely gone.

Today, we are increasingly confident that a true and final cure for cancer is on the horizon. In this we can rejoice.

Kristen would have wanted it that way.

Out of Grief, a Book

My Friend the Boat Owner has written a book. I wish I could tell you it was a frothy tale about sailing his beloved sailboat *Winsome* to far distant and exotic shores. I wish I could regale you with images of sandy beaches and palm trees and warm breezes blowing through the night.

This book is not about such pleasant things. This book is about his daughter who spent a year in a lopsided battle against cervical cancer. When she died this past June at the age of twenty-three, he was overwhelmed with grief, numb, and—by his own account—about as empty as a man can get.

How do you process such a thing? How can anyone look back at ten months of radiation treatments, chemotherapy, bedside vigils, late-night runs to the emergency room, and small glimmers of hope followed by crushing blows of defeat, and then set it aside and get on with your life?

For my friend, the answer was to write it all down. It helped, of course, that his daughter kept journals. Since she was a young girl, she had written down the things she thought about—the hopes, dreams, and disappointments that coursed through her life.

At the time of her death, she had filled seventeen books with such things. Two of them documented her illness. A couple of others were filled with poetry that flowed from her young heart over the years.

During her illness, her dad wrote literally hundreds of e-mail updates documenting diagnoses, treatments, setbacks, small miracles, and the prayerful support that poured in from friends, relatives, and total strangers across the country.

He saved them all, and when he returned to his job as an airline pilot, he used his time on the ground between flying assignments to assemble everything into a book. His e-mails are there, along with her journal entries, her poetry. He included statements from doctors, nurses, and numerous others

261

who came in contact with this remarkable young woman during her months of illness and treatment.

He researched cervical cancer and put a statement in his book from the scientist who developed Gardasil, a vaccine that can prevent the disease. He received comments and endorsements from numerous persons around the globe, both famous and unknown.

And when he had spent his grief and anguish, had taken his indescribable pain—and that of his wife and other two children—and poured it out, through countless hours, into the pages of the manuscript, when he was assured in his heart that his daughter's story was complete and ready to be told, he packaged it up and sent it to the publisher.

The title, *Love, Kristen,* comes from the sandbox built for the young son of a friend after Kristen's death, from the wood of her wheelchair ramp. Painted onto the seat in the corner of the box is the inscription "Love, Kristen."

My friend's hope is that his daughter's story will increase awareness of the proliferation of cervical cancer and the very real opportunity to prevent it through inoculation. His greatest hope is to see this cancer blotted off the face of the earth.

While it is true that my friend lost a daughter almost before her life really began and that he will miss the laughter of grandchildren who might have been and the years of celebrating birthdays and holidays with her and her family, he has documented her story and offered it as a legacy that will hopefully live long into the future and become a measurable benefit to mankind.

When I said the book was not about sandy beaches and palm trees, that was not totally accurate. As it turns out, his daughter's favorite things included sand, sun, and palm trees, and there is a picture of them on the cover of the book. She would no doubt approve.

Love, Kristen *was published in February 2009 and is gaining wide acclaim as a testimonial to the ravages of cervical cancer and an intensifying resolve to eradicate it. In 2010, the author established the Kristen Forbes EVE Foundation. EVE stands for Educate, Vaccinate, and Eradicate.*

John Krouse

To many who live in our village, the corner of Oak and Main Streets may already be thought of as the domain of John Krouse. Truth is, John Krouse was a fixture there most days, sitting on that white bench. He was always there or somewhere nearby, perhaps walking slowly down the street toward lunch or some as-yet-unthought-of destination. Sometimes he simply stood on the corner and smiled at people as they passed by.

John always smiled. And I mean *always*. No matter who they were, John had a smile for them. And if they tarried more than a minute, he would inevitably grace them with an almost unbelievably corny joke, usually with himself as the brunt.

"My mother used to call me her golden boy. Then I found out I was just tarnished brass."

Trust me, they never got any better than that. John wasn't just a fixture; he was a character. And, near as I could tell, one totally without guile.

John Krouse was not a great scientist or an inventor. He studied neither medicine nor law. He made no great contributions to the world of business or finance. He left no legacy other than his childlike humor and broad, trusting nature. John never married and had no family. When he died of a heart attack at the age of seventy-two, he was survived by one cousin.

John didn't drive and depended on others to get him where he was going. In spite of this, he attended church regularly, sometimes several times a week. His persona was felt even there, for John had what you might call a slight problem with timing. When prayers were offered, John's "Amen" usually came in slightly behind everyone else's. And since he also had a problem with volume, it also came in several decibels louder than everyone else's.

He regularly sang in the choir, and although he sometimes wandered slightly away from the preferred key, no one could deny his contribution. He even sang a solo once—the first verse of "Amazing Grace." It was beautiful. Somebody said it was his favorite hymn.

John owned very little in this world, but I am convinced he has a great stake in the next. He left us a ton of gentle memories and a sadly empty bench at the corner of Oak and Main. It is my quiet hope that whoever in our village is responsible for that bench might consider having a small plaque engraved and attached to it. A suitable inscription might be:

> "This bench is dedicated to the memory of John Krouse
> who spent many hours sitting here
> improving the lives of all who passed by."

A short time after this column appeared in the paper, a plaque with those words was attached to the bench.

Remembering Jackie

Jackie Kennedy Onassis' funeral brought back sharp images of the early '60s in Washington, D.C., and the small but indelible mark this woman made on my life.

I was in Washington in 1963, fortunate enough to be a junior officer assigned to the Naval Photographic Center.

It was magical being a young naval officer in Washington during those days, darting around town wearing the same blue and gold our Commander in Chief had worn just a few years earlier and emulating that JFK smile, that charm—basically riding on those charismatic *PT-109* coattails.

Mostly, the Photographic Center helped keep up the US Navy's public image. It produced films, newsreels, and public service announcements for television. There was a portrait studio where the top brass from all branches of the military had their official portraits taken.

The Still Department ground out thousands of black and white and color glossies for distribution by navy recruiting offices and public relations offices around the globe. These were mostly pictures of ships, with lots of aircraft carriers. Of course, we had photographers that went everywhere shooting the US Navy in action.

The Center also was the navy's official testing laboratory for photo equipment. An endless chain of designers and manufacturers brought a potpourri of experimental equipment for the navy to test—everything from sinks to cameras, film processors to waterproof photographic print paper.

During World War II, planes landed on the runway in front of the Center and film exposed by cameras mounted in their noses was processed, printed, and examined by experts. When I was there, the runway was strictly a roosting place for seagulls, and most of the hush-hush stuff was done by the navy's Photo Interpretation Center in another part of town.

We still operated a small aerial department, and occasionally we saw some interesting stuff. The original flyover shots showing missiles on Cuba were first laid out on our tables. Moments later the entire second floor was posted "Off Limits," and no one without a top secret clearance could get in. We also developed the first tragic photos of the wreckage of the nuclear submarine *Thresher* after she collapsed and sank, killing all aboard.

There was a special photo lab on the third floor. No one talked about it. It was just called the Special Projects Lab. You had to know the four-button combination to a security lock to get in. The combination was changed every day.

When I became department head of the Still Department, I learned about the purpose of the Special Projects Lab. Officially, Special Projects was the White House. Unofficially, it was Mrs. Kennedy. In addition to being an excellent writer and editor, Jackie was an accomplished photographer, a skill she carried with her to the White House.

The chief photographer's mate who ran the lab was a wizened veteran of nearly thirty years in the navy. Despite his lowly enlisted status, this brilliant man was a graduate of Rochester Institute of Technology—the physics and chemistry proving grounds for Eastman Kodak Company's photographic wizardry. He also had a natural eye for color correction. He could usually look at a color negative and come within a point or two of guessing the right correction.

The chief claimed Jackie was even better.

"She never misses," he used to muse after processing a roll of the First Lady's film. "She'll clip out the shots she wants printed and write the color correction for each one of them on a sheet of paper. I'll check them on the densitometer, and she'll be right every time."

Jackie would call the chief on the phone when she had film to process. Once she got him out of bed at three in the morning. She wanted the negatives back by six o'clock and corrected prints by eight. When I got to the lab at seven, the chief had the final product of this important mission laid out on the retouching table.

They were pictures of John John's birthday party the day before. She wanted the prints on the President's desk when he reported to the Oval Office that morning. Top-priority stuff.

In spite of this close connection, I never met the First Lady, nor did I ever meet the President. I stood on Massachusetts Avenue in November of that year and shot pictures of her husband's funeral procession. One shot shows a dark and tragic Jackie behind a gray veil in the backseat of the limousine.

I think about this photograph sometimes. It was the end of an era. Now another era has ended and everything is different. When I think about those days, mostly I remember a perfectly composed, exposed, and corrected photograph of President John F. Kennedy horsing around with his son on his birthday ... and the remarkable photographer who took it.

Jacqueline Kennedy Onassis died May 19, 1994.

The Last World War I Pilot

Nobody knows if Henry Botterell ever came in contact with the Red Baron or if he knew Arthur Roy Brown, the pilot credited with shooting the baron down in 1918. But he could have because Mr. Botterell flew a Sopwith Camel in combat during the last two years of World War I.

During his career in the skies over France, he shot down two German planes and several observation balloons. One of the latter victories was captured by aviation artist Robert Taylor in a painting called *"Balloon Busters."* It hangs in the Air Force Museum in Dayton, Ohio. It shows Botterell rendering a salute to the German balloon pilot as he parachutes to safety.

When Mr. Botterell died a couple of weeks ago at the age of 106, he took with him the last personal memories of those famous air battles. Most of the other pilots who survived The Great War had long since departed this life. Mr. Botterell was the last.

He was a bank clerk in Canada when the war broke out. He enlisted in the Royal Navy Flying Service and after flight training was shipped to France. There his flying career almost ended before it began. During his second take-off, his engine failed and his plane crashed, breaking several bones and earning him a medical discharge.

He refused to quit, re-enlisted, and was soon airborne over France. He flew missions right up to the end of the war, when he was wounded during a flight and lost consciousness. He came to just in time to land his plane.

After the war, Mr. Botterell returned to his bank job, which he held until he retired in 1961. At the time of his death he was living in a nursing home in Toronto.

There aren't any Sopwith Camels around anymore and precious few vintage airplanes of any kind. Thousands were built, including the fabled Curtis Jenny, America's entry into the air war. Many of the Jennys that survived the war continued flying during the barnstorming era of the 1920s, but virtually all of these planes are gone as well. Some crashed, of course, but most simply faded and fell apart. Airplanes in those days were made of wood and cloth, like giant box kites. What the weather didn't get, the mice and insects did. A number of World War I planes are at the Air Force Museum, but most are replicas.

Although Sopwith, Jenny, Spad, and Baron Von Richthofen's notorious tri-wing Fokker are the best-known names, there were many others that I never heard of, including Albatross, Nieuport, Hanover, Breguet, and Rumpler.

Not only were most of these planes frail structures, they were unstable and difficult to fly as well. If you put enough power in the plane to make it a threat in dogfights, it was prone to ground-looping during landings and take-offs. Every air base in France was littered with the broken remains of airplanes that had flown successful missions only to buy the farm the minute they touched down.

All of this made Mr. Botterell a staunch hero. Not only did he shoot down the enemy, but also he figured out how to survive a multitude of dangerous landings.

As for the Red Baron, he shot down seventy-seven Allied planes before he was brought down. Did Mr. Botterell ever see him? Possibly. After all, the men who flew planes during World War I were a small and very tight community. They really did salute a downed enemy after a fight. Legend has it that Von Richthofen even landed at an enemy base to pay his respects at the funeral of one of the pilots he had shot down.

The Sopwith Camel, of course, has been memorialized more by Snoopy and his flying doghouse than by all the for-real World War I flying aces put together. And last week, I'm sure, Snoopy would have taken off into the blue sky and flown a low pass over the field—white scarf blowing in the wind—as he rendered a final salute to Henry Botterell, the last pilot of World War I.

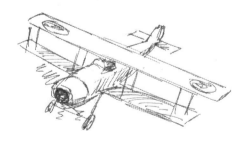

Lucius Newsome

I don't know where he sleeps. Every month, for two or three days, he sleeps in his own bed in his home near Chattanooga, Tennessee. That's when he rests and spends time with his wife and family. The rest of the time he is on the road, begging for food and delivering it to the hungry.

His name is Lucius Newsome, and up until eight years ago he was a Baptist preacher, ministering to the congregation of a black church in Tennessee. Then he retired. After all, he had been in the pulpit for thirty-five years, and he was approaching seventy. It was a good time to relax and go fishing.

Then he received an unexpected invitation to preach and help serve an annual Thanksgiving dinner for seniors in Indianapolis.

"These people were hungry," he said. "Many had no money and no food of their own. I enjoyed serving them dinner so much, I volunteered to serve breakfast the next day."

The group didn't serve breakfast, he was told, only Thanksgiving dinner once a year. Lucius was incredulous. "Hunger doesn't take a holiday. It isn't right to feed these people on Thursday and let them go hungry again on Friday. Besides, every child has the right to smell cooking in his own kitchen every day." He insists that what he did next was not his idea but the Lord's.

"My church had given me a new car when I retired," he said. "I took the backseat out of it and started begging for food. Then I went door-to-door and gave it away." Lucius made the rounds of grocery stores and local churches, asking for donations of food and clothing. The response was so good that today he collects an average of four thousand pounds of food daily. Five area Catholic churches regularly collect food for Lucius' ministry.

He wore out his car, managed to get another one, and wore that one out. "I realized I needed a truck," he said. He got a used one from Ameritech, and a local car dealer contributed a new truck when the used one wore out. The sign on the door of the truck says "The Lord's Pantry."

"God provides everything," Lucius says. This includes a steady stream of volunteers from the ranks of those he has helped. "They're always there to help me load the truck and distribute food," he adds.

He works seven days a week and admits to getting tired, but "hunger never takes a day off," he says. While Lucius spends much of his time feeding the hungry in Indianapolis, his ministry goes wherever there is need. He delivered truckloads of food and clothing to North Dakota when that state was devastated by floods a couple of years ago. When tornadoes wiped out much of Birmingham, Alabama, Lucius Newsome was there.

Lucius is also attentive to other needs of the poor. He pays rent and utility bills and helps out in other ways. At night he collects homeless adults and abandoned children and puts them up in a motel. Sometimes he doesn't have the money to pay the motel bill.

"But I promise the motel manager I will pay, and God always provides. The money is always there when it's needed," he says. His personal income consists of a $287 Social Security check each month. "I am the Lord's biggest beggar," he says with a smile.

A year ago Lucius became a Catholic. "I knew I was called on to serve the Lord by feeding the poor," he says, "but I really needed to feed my own hunger at the Lord's table."

Lucius Newsome is seventy-six years old now, but he doesn't think about slowing down. He'll be at the grocery stores again tomorrow and at the churches the day after that. Every day he will find hungry people to feed, and every night there will be someone needing protection or shelter. "I know I'll have to quit someday," he admits, "but if the Lord wants this ministry carried on, He will provide. The Lord always provides," he adds almost prayerfully.

"Then maybe I'll go fishing."

Lucius Newsome died in 2009 after a long battle with cancer. After a full life of serving the poor and the marginalized, he may have lost the battle but he definitely won the war.

Lyman Porter

If you knew Lyman Porter, you would agree he never did anything halfway. When he set his sights on a target, he never stopped until he'd hit it smack in the middle.

That's how he learned to fly an airplane. He told me the story late one night in a deserted hotel coffee shop in a small town in southern Mississippi. We were there to photograph a new paper mill built by the Weyerheuser company.

Once he'd decided he was going to become a pilot, flying became an all-consuming passion. He wrangled a few lessons at the local airport. Then one day someone asked if he would ferry a plane over to a neighboring airport. Lyman never hesitated. He climbed into the plane and took off. A few minutes later he landed safely at the other airport.

"Weren't you scared?" I asked.

"Sure," he said matter-of-factly. "But I already knew how to take off. The only thing I still had to learn was how to land. Since I didn't have any acceptable options, I was highly motivated," he added with a smile.

As Confucius said, "Where there are no alternatives, there are no problems."

Lyman built his business the same way. He learned early on that he had a special talent for telling stories visually. This was particularly true of the type of stories that make sales meetings successful—human-interest stories, stories of promise and fulfillment. He would photograph a company's business activities, and then combine the pictures—35mm slides—on the screen with appropriate narrative and music. The results were always successful, sometimes astonishing.

As a result of this success, a lot of companies wanted Lyman Porter to produce their meetings. Over the years, he helped Eli Lilly define its heritage and Cummins Engine Company restructure for the future. He dignified the quiet nobility of farming—first for the Indiana Farm Bureau Co-op with a show that proclaimed the farmer as "a pretty good thing to be" and then for a number of firms in the agricultural industry which felt the farmer deserved a voice in the world that he was feeding. Through Lyman's unique efforts, America's farmers got a voice, one that spoke eloquently.

Many were the companies that profited from Lyman Porter's special magic. He gave voices to them all—voices that put form and shape to other people's efforts and dreams. He was there to help International Harvester convince stockholders the company could bounce back from the brink of bankruptcy. He was there to redefine the sanctity of motherhood for Gerber baby products. He was there to help Sears explain a new concept in store management and merchandise arrangement.

Endless were his devices and varied were his methods. He photographed people on a train and called it "The Success Express." He visualized salesmen soaring to new heights by telling their stories with colorful hot-air balloons. He once demonstrated the toughness of a door lock by driving a fire truck over it. Other stories were told by children and by clowns or told silently through the graceful movements of ballet dancers.

Lyman saw the human equation in everything he did. Regrettably, telling stories for others meant he sometimes neglected his own. His was a business of deadlines. More than once he was out of town or working through the night when he would rather have been at home with his family. Lyman Porter did nothing halfway.

And when last fall he learned he had cancer, he vowed that he would fight. After surgery, he accepted the best that local medicine had to offer, and then he made the rounds of specialists. Two weeks ago his fight took him to the Mayo Clinic, but the doctors there could do no more. He died on the twenty-fourth of January.

In the eighteen years I knew Lyman Porter, I know I received more than I gave. He enriched my life in unexpected ways. There is no more time to talk about the things he didn't do, of course. We can only speak now of what he did and what he was to each of us. And if you knew him as I did, you would agree that being Lyman Porter was "a pretty good thing to be."

Mom

Let me tell you about my mom. She was eighty-five years old last Monday. She died peacefully in her sleep five days later, her tired body unable to recover from cancer surgery.

We debated the wisdom of surgery at such an age and ultimately agreed with the doctor that the advanced stage of her cancer, left to grow, would bring her unspeakable pain.

After the funeral arrangements were complete and Dad had been made comfortable (he is eighty-six and suffers from Parkinson's disease), my sister, brother, and I sat around on Sis's patio and reminisced about Mom.

The fundamentals were pretty simple, really. She was married to Dad for sixty-six years. She was a devoted mother to us kids, of course, but—first, last, and always—she was wife to our father. It was almost as though she stepped out of the Old Testament and proclaimed to my dad, "Whither thou go, I will go; thy people shall be my people." So it was with Mom.

Like Old Testament wives, she lived a subservient role with total acceptance. She cooked, cleaned, did the laundry and ironing, dressed us kids for school, and was the family nurse. For her personal pleasure, she played piano and sang. Her mother was fond of reminding us from time to time that Mom could have had a career in music had Dad not come along, but she never regretted her choice. During one severe winter in Wisconsin when we lived in a cabin without running water or electricity and she had no piano, she sang anyway, carrying the accompanying melody in her heart. I remember walking up the long driveway through the frozen woods and hearing her melodious voice piercing the subzero silence.

She was an utterly virtuous and faithful woman, but she took sly pleasure in belonging to a crocheting club called "The Happy Hookers." She enjoyed reminding Dad of Milton's adage that "Every man should be deemed capable of mischief."

Her family lineage harkened back to Colonial days, claiming, among others, Sir John Hawkins as a direct ancestor. She shrugged off invitations to join the Daughters of the American Revolution, preferring to spend her energies on improving her recipe for bread-and-butter pickles. And should Dad occasionally mention the long and famous family tree, Mom cut the conversation short by reminding everyone that Sir John was hanged for piracy from the yardarm of his own ship, by order of the Queen of England.

Her faith ran deep and began in the arms of her Quaker father. She practiced his teachings of brotherly love, acceptance, and nonviolence throughout her life. Occasionally, when assailed by the pangs of anger, she would walk briskly from room to room and slam every door in the house as hard as possible. Then she would peel potatoes for supper.

Once, when an unthinking neighbor made hurtful remarks about a family member, Mom quietly got up, thanked the woman for tea, and returned to her own home, where she loudly announced to us:

"My father always told me if I could not say something kind about someone, I should say nothing at all." For a few moments she paused as the rest of the family stood, mouths agape, at the forcefulness of her voice. Then she added, "And about that woman I have absolutely nothing to say."

Nor was Mom given to gossip, but she relished passing along stories from her father—mostly from his Quaker background. One such tale involved a devout Quaker farmer who became exasperated with his recalcitrant cow and informed her: "Bossy, thee knowest that my Quaker faith binds me from punishing thee. But know thee also that this afternoon I shall sell thee to a Methodist, and he will beat the hell out of thee."

As we remembered, we grieved. We shed tears for our loss. And now we go through the transition from knowing her to remembering her.

Mom died June 28, 1997.

Dad at Eighty-Nine

My dad will be eighty-nine this December. For the last twenty years he has experienced the progressive debilitation of Parkinson's disease. Ten years ago he and Mom made the difficult decision to sell their personal home in Mesa, Arizona, and move into an assisted-care facility. He needed help getting dressed, he said, and Mom—weakened in her own right by arthritis, heart disease, and the early stages of Alzheimer's—was unable to provide the help he needed.

Mom died two years ago from complications following her second mastectomy, and in the time since then, his disease has progressed severely. In no more than five or six years, he went from having full mobility (when I accompanied him to the grocery store, I had a hard time keeping up with him as he wheeled the cart up and down the aisles) to being a virtual invalid unable to feed himself.

When he and Mom moved into Chris Ridge in Phoenix a decade ago, they had a lot of misgivings about giving up their personal lives. Actually, it was a step up for them because they immediately found themselves surrounded by others in similar circumstances. They had their own apartment in a beautiful facility that sported a swimming pool, exercise spa, game rooms, its own post office, and a sumptuous dining room with linen tablecloths and crystal glasses along with a truly appetizing menu. Plus, there was an array of energetic activities from which they could pick and choose. They went on day trips to various places in the Phoenix area, and Dad offered his lifelong experience as a gardener/horticulturist/forester to soon become chairman of the Chris Ridge grounds committee. Mom, meanwhile, parlayed her love of crocheting into full flower as a member of the crocheting club.

Things were great for a while. But Dad began having more difficulty doing normal day-to-day things. He fell repeatedly and had to call for assistance.

Several times these falls resulted in late-night trips to the emergency room for stitches. My sister, who lives in Phoenix and has assumed the role of primary caregiver, began getting phone calls at all hours: Dad had fallen again. Dad was unconscious. Dad was being rushed to the hospital.

It was obvious to both the staff and to Dad, as well as to Sis, that the time had come to step up to more closely supervised care. The problem was, while Mom and Dad were able to afford unassisted living at Chris Ridge, the cost of adding twenty-four-hour assistance made the facility unaffordable. Sis spent the next several weeks visiting extended-care facilities in the Phoenix area. She had to consider not only the level of care needed at that moment but also the inevitability of total care as Dad's Parkinson's and Mom's Alzheimer's progressed.

They settled on, and moved into, one place only to discover within a month that the owner was skimping on resident services while taking expensive vacations. Twice when my sister visited, Dad complained of being hungry. A little probing disclosed a kitchen bereft of food. Quickly, she sought better quarters.

A few weeks after moving into a new facility, which provided a single room sparsely furnished with a bed, dresser, and closet for each of them, plus a shared bath and a place to put their television set, Mom was diagnosed with breast cancer. Three years earlier she had undergone a mastectomy of her other breast and had come through the surgery with flying colors. Everyone had high hopes for the same outcome for the second breast. Lamentably, she developed pneumonia after surgery and never recovered.

Dad, meanwhile, continued to worsen. His voice, which had started to fail with the first symptoms of Parkinson's, disappeared almost completely. A short time later he was unable to get into and out of his favorite chair, a recliner he had stubbornly held onto for years. The chair was moved out and a wheelchair moved in. Yet another lifelong passion—reading—was taken from him as his eyes clouded with cataracts. The disease and the medication treating it combined to weaken him further. He developed difficulty swallowing, and today he can eat only pureed foods. Because his hands tremble constantly, a nursing assistant must come in for each meal and feed him.

Tragically, while his body fails, his mind remains sharp. He knows who he is and can vividly trace the path of his life, along with the friends he has had, the places he has worked, and the joys he shared with his wife. Memories he can now share with no one. I can only guess at the anguish this spawns in his heart. Sis visits him several times a week. She sits on the edge of his bed and talks about her day, about taking her dog to the vet and her constant fight against the persistent weeds in her yard. He responds with nods and hoarse whispers. They both have become too sad to do much else.

I write letters occasionally and fax them to the nursing home. Sometime during the day, a nursing aide will come by and read them to him. I should write more often, but I don't know what to say. It's easier to talk about the insignificant things, tiny threads from a tapestry rich in love and experience, than it is to plumb the depths of the entire fabric. I'd like to tell him that the angry issues between us for so many years have vanished. I'd like to tell him that the love we never openly shared in the past is throbbing gravely in my heart.

I know that diminishing life and ultimate death form the culmination of life on this earth. I know that very well in my head. I just haven't learned it in my heart.

Dad died a few months later, February 21, 2000. My sister was with him at his bedside.

Jumper Collins

Somebody asked me the other day if I believed in guardian angels, and that got me thinking about Jumper Collins. If you asked Jumper the same question, he would probably shrug and mutter something unintelligible before shuffling away.

Jumper is self-conscious about stuff like that, you see. But the truth is he believes. Admittedly, he didn't used to. As a matter of fact, Jumper will tell you he didn't really believe in much of anything.

"Nuthin' I couldn't see, touch, taste, or feel," he says with a slight echo of Cockney left over from his youth in London.

But that was before the storm.

I didn't know anything about the storm when I met Jumper three years ago. He was just another worker in the boatyard in Key West who helped me with a number of projects on The Boat (The Other Project—that never-to-be-finished boat restoration courtesy of My Friend the Boat Owner).

Actually, Jumper was incredibly knowledgeable about all things related to boats, so I relied on him a lot. A few years earlier he had sailed his own thirty-two-foot sailboat across the Atlantic from England, puttered around the east coast of the United States for a while, and eventually washed up on the shores of Key West. I guess he liked what he saw because he anchored his boat just offshore, and there it has remained ever since. He lives aboard and putts ashore in his dinghy every morning to go to work at the yard.

After a particularly tedious day trying to get a balky autopilot to work, I invited Jumper to stay aboard for dinner. "Snow crab and steaks," I told him. He said he'd be happy to if he could bring his daughter who was visiting from England. "Bring her along," I said. I looked forward to meeting her.

Cynthia Collins was a quiet, attractive thirty-year-old who had her dad's naturally curly blond hair as well as his penchant for being quiet—until I poured the wine. After several glasses of wine and a plate of snow crab claws, the girl got Jumper reminiscing.

"Tell that story, Dad," she would say. And when he did, it always reminded her of another. "Oh, tell that one too," she would add.

By his own admission, Jumper didn't fit the traditional English boarding school image when he was a kid. "I was a rebel," he said, "always pulling pranks." The long and short of it is, his pranks got him expelled and into trouble in the streets. The courts got him into sea school.

In America you've got reform school. In England they send you to sea school. It was there Jumper learned how to sail. He mastered the skills of an ordinary seaman and learned to love and respect the sea. As soon as he graduated, he bought his first boat, shoved off, and never lived ashore again.

I served the steaks and steaming baked potatoes and, after we had eaten, poured the coffee. "You haven't told about the storm, Dad," Cynthia said quietly. "You've got to tell about the storm." Jumper shook his head and muttered something. "You've got to, Dad," she said.

"I know you believe in God," he said softly, "so maybe you can understand what happened." He paused for a long moment and then told me about the storm.

He had spent the year sailing in the Mediterranean and was passing Portugal on his way back to England when he was hit by a storm. "Storms in that area can last a week or more," he said, "and this one didn't show signs of stopping."

Storms happen, of course, and the usual course of action is to douse all sails, secure all loose gear, go below, and ride it out. Unfortunately the storm hit just as Jumper was passing close to a fifty-mile stretch of sheer cliffs that drop straight down into the sea.

"There's not a port or anchorage anywhere along those cliffs," he said, "and I was no more than a half mile offshore. The waves were enormous, and it was all I could do to keep the boat from spilling sideways." The worst part of it was he had not slept for more than twenty-four hours, and his entire body was cramped from endless hours of steering and fighting the sea.

Through the night, all the next day, and into the following night he steered his boat through the pounding waves. His boat crept forward, but there were many dangerous miles to go. "The cliffs went on forever," he said. "I was totally exhausted."

Shortly after midnight, Jumper squinted his eyes to see through the blinding rain and saltwater and was astounded to see a man standing in the bow of the boat. "I thought I'd gone crackers," he said. "I shook my head, looked away, and then looked back. He was still there. And he was smiling.

'Who the hell are you?' I roared, 'and what the bloody hell are you doing on my boat?' He just kept smiling."

Not only did the stranger smile peacefully at Jumper, but he also began pointing toward the cliffs. "It was like he was telling me to turn toward shore. One thing I knew was if I turned toward those cliffs, I'd be dead."

Jumper said for the next hour the man kept pointing urgently toward the cliffs. "I was sure he didn't exist," he said. "He was just a hallucination caused by being so tired. I kept shaking my head to make him disappear. But he just kept pointing toward shore."

Finally Jumper glanced in the direction his phantom passenger pointed and was amazed to see lights. "Red and green channel markers, like there was some kind of major port over there in the cliffs. Trouble is, I knew there was nothing there. I had studied the charts, and there was nothing but miles of sheer cliffs. But that night, in the middle of a storm, there was a lighted channel."

Jumper said he knew at that moment he could go no further. His body was spent. Slowly, he turned his boat toward the lights. The waves that previously had battered the side of his boat now rushed him headlong toward the cliffs, toward what he believed would be certain death.

What unfolded after that has haunted Jumper every day of his life since. "I passed by the lights," he said. "They were real. Then I headed toward a second set of lights, and they were also real. Finally, I passed through an opening in the cliffs and the storm was suddenly behind me. It became eerie and still. Not only that, but laid out in front of me and all around me was a huge city. There were lights everywhere, and I could hear music playing in the distance."

Jumper said the man in the bow of his boat guided him gently toward a pier sticking out from the shore. "When I got there, he took a bit of rope I had tied to the pulpit and secured the boat to the pier. Then the bloke smiles at me one more time, climbs onto the pier, and walks away."

Jumper wasn't sure after that how long he stood in the cockpit of his boat just staring in utter disbelief. "I kept looking around thinking it was all going to disappear," he said, "but after a while I realized it was for real. I went below and flopped onto my bunk without even getting undressed."

Jumper said he woke up late afternoon the next day. At first he thought the whole thing had been a dream. But then he went out into the cockpit and received the shock of his life. "I was tied to a tree branch," he said. "There was no pier. And there was no city. I was sitting in a small cove inside the cliff walls. And when I got under way again and headed back out to sea, where the storm had finally blown itself out, there were no channel markers either."

Jumper recorded the coordinates of the cove, but he said when he went back to the Mediterranean two years later, he couldn't find it. "It was as though it had vanished." He says that didn't surprise him because he had already realized what had actually happened. "The man had to be my guardian angel, and he had to be sent by God," Jumper said solemnly.

Jumper never mentioned the storm again. But if I ever go sailing in dangerous waters, I hope a man with a smile suddenly shows up on the bow of my boat.

Remembering Mr. Gault

I never knew Charles M. Gault Sr., but I know what kind of man he was. He was a man who loved life deeply—all life. This included, apparently, the lives of his enemies.

Mr. Gault died last month. Had he lived another three months, he would have been seventy-nine years old. The family talked about a heart condition that he never mentioned and seldom thought about. His son, Charles Jr., assured me his dad accepted life as it came to him and refused to become a burden to anyone.

For the past few years, Mr. Gault lived in upstate New York, where he managed the state's emergency disaster program. His job was to help people who fell victim to the ravages of nature. Those who knew him say he did it well.

But there was another Charles Gault Sr. that most of the people he worked with in these later years never knew. This was Charles Gault the World War II fighter pilot.

Lieutenant Gault fought against the Japanese in the Pacific. He flew the incredibly powerful P38 Lightning, the only fighter ever designed with two engines. He flew fast; he lived fast; he enjoyed life to the fullest.

Lieutenant Gault became Captain Gault, and, after the war was over, he stayed on as a member of the fledgling US Air Force. He rose to the rank of lieutenant colonel and retired to start a new career dispensing emergency funds for the citizens of New York State.

At the funeral last month, I listened as his son talked about a few things he knew about his father.

"He was a private man," Charles Jr. said. "There were things he did—beautiful Christian things—that none of us knew about." It was the same with the war. Once it was over, Charles Sr. said little about it. But Charles

Jr. remembers a moment when his father let him see a little of Charles Gault the man who loved life.

"I had asked him about the war," Charles Jr. said. "He didn't say much, but he took me out to his garage and began rummaging through boxes of things that he had saved. He pulled out a small piece of metal and handed it to me.

"'Do you know what that is?' he asked. 'It's all that's left of a human life.'" His son explained that during a Japanese raid on the American base, one of the enemy planes was shot down and crashed on the air base.

"Dad went over and picked up this piece of metal and saved it. He said he knew it could just as easily have been him. He didn't want to ever forget that this had been a human life." Apparently, the man's sensitivity to the value of life was bred into him from childhood. Charles Jr. told me that his dad's family used to pray for him while he was fighting in the war.

"But they didn't pray for his safety," Charles Jr. said. "They left that to God's will and simply prayed that he wouldn't have to kill too many of the enemy."

Even if Mr. Gault didn't talk about these things in later years, the kind of man he was rubbed off on others. A friend living in a retirement home in New York felt something needed to be done when he heard that Mr. Gault had died. He got up, walked outside to the flagpole, and lowered the flag to half-mast.

"This man was a hero," the man reportedly said.

Skydiving

It was probably a typical night in the bar. People come, people go. Then some guy comes in with a peculiar glint in his eye. The bartender notices. He edges in to check him out.

Turns out the guy runs a skydiving club up in Anderson. They talk about the growing popularity of the sport, how with the new controllable chutes it's a lot safer, and how you can go through a half day of training in the morning and then jump that afternoon. They talk prices. They talk causes. Later they will talk times and dates.

Another night. This time there are four bartenders. They are friends and they talk among themselves. They talk about their personal desires to give back something to institutions that have been important to them.

Bob Hodge wants to give back to Holy Cross Central School to help pay tuition for kids whose families can't afford it. Tom Schwab's father died of cancer, and Tom wants to give to the American Cancer Society to help others beat the disease. Steve Olson's little brother was stricken with cystic fibrosis at age four. His payback is to help fight this disease. T. David McCaslin wants to give something to support abused children—kids who have no control over what happens to them.

After a few more planning sessions, it's all set: the four bartenders will skydive for their charities. To make money, they offer (for a minimum contribution of fifteen dollars) a specially designed T-shirt commemorating the occasion. It's a good-looking shirt, bold skydivers displayed on the back, on the front an emblem with the words "Jump Back—Give Back—'Cause U Can."

Pretty neat, huh?

Did I mention that none of these idiots has ever jumped before? Not to worry, croons the guy from Anderson. Anybody can do it. Perfectly safe.

Oh, sure. You bet. From an airplane at three thousand feet? Yeah, that sounds safe enough.

I guess some guys will do anything to help a good cause. I suppose the least I can do is make a contribution and wear one of their T-shirts. Plus I can go watch them jump and try to keep my eyes open.

Though skydiving is pretty safe these days, I still wonder why anyone would want to jump out of a perfectly good airplane. To be fair, however, the new chutes are like gliders. You can turn and swoop and touch down with the lightness of a feather (so the guy from Anderson says).

I almost went skydiving once.

Years ago the Missouri National Guard invited me to do a story on their Jump Team, a group of Airborne-trained soldiers who toured the state doing skydiving demonstrations for county fair crowds. I had to sign a waiver, of course: in case I fell out of the helicopter, I wouldn't sue them.

They suited me up in a harness with big clips.

"These fasten to the door," the sergeant said. "That way you can lean out and shoot pictures as the guys jump."

Up we went, leaving an expectant crowd below. At ten thousand feet we circled the jump zone. I eased into place at the edge of the open door, camera at the ready.

Out they went, one after another. I leaned out and began shooting.

Click-click-click.

The helicopter rapidly followed the gliding men back toward earth. I leaned out farther and framed the men in the viewfinder. They were in a circle now, holding hands.

Click-click-click.

As we descended, the air warmed. The humidity condensed in my camera, fogging the lens. I eased back into the helicopter and looked around. That's when I noticed the sergeant had not fastened the clips to the door. At no time had I been attached to the helicopter.

After I stopped shaking, I wrote the story. I got some good pictures. But when I was invited back for another jump, I graciously declined.

The "Jump Back for Charity" event raised $4000, enabling each bartender to contribute $1000 to his charity.

Small-Town Obit

I was driving across southern Missouri the other day and stopped in a small town to get a sandwich at one of the local fast-food places. After I got my burger, fries, and medium soft drink, I carried my little tray over to one of the plastic-coated tables. As I sat down, I realized I could easily be in Lubbock, Texas, or Bangor, Maine, for all the differences I'd see in the restaurants. Then I noticed a small square of paper on my table. Probably some special menu item, I thought, picking it up.

It said: "Harley Putnam, age 84, died today at his home, 204 West Elm Street. Funeral services will be held at Wiggins Funeral Home two o'clock Sunday afternoon. Friends may call at the funeral home Saturday between noon and six o'clock."

Remarkable. Harley Putnam must have been a mover and shaker in town. Or maybe he had been the owner of this fast-food franchise. I asked one of the uniformed teenagers behind the counter.

"I think maybe my dad knew him years ago," she said. She asked some of the other employees. They frowned and shook their heads.

"If you don't know him," I said, "why is this on all of your tables?" I waggled the slip of paper at her.

"Oh, that's Wiggins Funeral Home," one of the youngsters said. "They print these up anytime someone dies. Mr. Wiggins pays some of the kids to put them in every store in town."

"But why?" I asked. "Don't you have a newspaper?"

"Sure," they said. "But it only comes out once a week. Mr. Wiggins says people have a right to know about these things right away. He's funny like that," one of them added. I glanced at the paper again. Sure enough, Mr. Putnam had died that very day.

"Mr. Wiggins says that everybody who passes on is part of the community and should be told goodbye to by everybody in the community one way or another," one of them added.

"But he also writes up stuff about everybody that gets married and the babies that are born," the first one said. They all agreed. "Yeah, he's kind of weird." To prove their point, one of them fished around under the counter and brought up a handful of papers. I took them and read:

"Charles Elliott and Marsha Danner were married yesterday at the United Methodist Church. They are going to St. Louis for their honeymoon and will set up housekeeping on the old Judson place south on Hwy 19."

Another said:

"A baby girl was born Tuesday at noon to Mr. and Mrs. Ted Wulke at County Memorial. The baby weighed seven-pound-six-ounces and looks like her mother. They named her Karen Elizabeth."

Across the road from the restaurant was a gas station. I pulled in to fill up the tank. An older man was working behind the counter. One of the notices about Mr. Putnam was taped to the cash register.

"I see you've heard about Harley Putnam," I said, paying for my gas.

"Did you know Harley?" he asked.

"No, I'm just passing through," I said. "Saw the notices from the funeral home."

"Yes, Mr. Wiggins keeps us well informed," he said. "Here's the one he wrote for my Edna." He pointed to a small glass frame on the wall. A yellowing sheet of paper announced that Edna Weatherly had died on Saturday. "That was nine years ago now," he added. "Everybody in town came to the funeral. Wiggins saw to it."

I asked him if he knew Mr. Putnam.

"Knew him when he worked for the bank," he said. "Then he retired and moved away. Came back after his wife passed on. Saw him now and then. But I guess we weren't close or anything. I'll go by on Saturday to pay my respects."

On a whim, I stopped at a local supermarket. I bought a fruit drink from the dairy case, and when I paid for it the clerk put a notice about Mr. Putnam in the sack. I asked if she would be going to the funeral.

"I doubt it," she said. "My kids don't give me much chance to do things like that. I'll probably just stop by for a minute on Saturday." I asked her if she knew Mr. Putnam.

"My mother and his wife used to work on quilts and the like at the church years back. She was real nice, always singing," she said with a smile.

As I left that small town, I was struck by the simplicity of it. There was nothing remarkable about the town. No landmarks, no famous battles were fought there. I don't suppose anybody famous came from there or even passed through and made a speech from the back of a train.

The buildings are plain, the houses ordinary. Even Wiggins Funeral Home on Oak Street looks just like a hundred other small-town funeral homes across the country. But there was something in that little town that was far from ordinary.

One of these days I'm going to talk to Mr. Wiggins. I'm going to learn his secret. And then I'm going to make photocopies of it and send a copy to every town on the planet. I think it's supposed to be that way.

Walt Gelien

The last time I saw Walt Gelien he was hurriedly packing his sea bag, determined to catch a 6:00 p.m. flight out of Providence to the West Coast. It was already 3:30, and he still faced a long cab ride from the naval station at Newport to the airport.

I was battalion commander of our Officer Candidate School class and had been advised that morning that Walt was dropping out. I stopped by his barracks to wish him smooth sailing.

Walt was different from the rest of us at Officer Candidate School (OCS) in 1962. Most of us were fresh out of college, green kids, inexperienced in the world and life. He was already a successful career military man—a chief hospital corpsman with at least a dozen years of active duty neatly recorded in his service record.

It was probably his flawless service record that got him the shot at OCS in the first place. It was not uncommon for the military to find some of its best officer material among the enlisted ranks, and Walt Gelien was unquestionably among the navy's finest. Not only was he a good sailor and a sensitive, professional medic, but he was also a devoted family man. On top of all that, he was blessed with uncommon good looks and a natural charm that made you feel like an old friend the moment you met him. These latter traits he shared with his younger brother, movie actor Tab Hunter.

There was never any question about Walt's ability to do the course work at OCS. He knew it, and the navy knew it. The flaw in the equation was that Walt didn't really want to be an officer. He liked being a medic, and his principles dictated that he remain a medic. He didn't say much about it at the time. He just smiled and muttered something about being tired of the Rhode Island winter.

So, after a month in Newport he resigned from OCS and requested reassignment. When I shook his hand and watched him get into a cab that day in March, he had orders to a US Marines detachment out of Pearl Harbor in the Pacific Fleet.

Fast-forward to 1965. For the previous year, I had been assigned to Pacific Fleet Headquarters (CincPacFleet). Our adviser status in Vietnam was rapidly deteriorating into active combat. Americans were beginning to lose their lives in a civil war that had already been raging for more than two decades. The French had long since given up resolving the conflict and had abandoned the battlefield.

I had called Walt's home several times since arriving in Hawaii. He was always either at sea or on special duty with the marines somewhere in the Pacific. The last time I called, his wife told me he had been assigned to a marine detachment at Tan Son Nhut Air Base outside Saigon. He hoped to be home for Thanksgiving about a month away. I promised I'd call then.

Three days later, as I was reading the daily dispatches from Saigon, I saw Walt's name on the casualty list. He had been sleeping in a helicopter at the base. About midnight a band of Vietcong infiltrated the airstrip and blew up some planes with hand grenades. Walt's helicopter was one of them.

The funeral was held in Oakland, California, just before Thanksgiving. His widow and five children were there along with his parents and his brother. Walt had grown up in Oakland. He and his brother had roamed the beaches and cruised the streets there. Then his brother got into movies, and Walt joined the navy.

Just before Veterans Day this year, I was in Washington, D.C. It was the first time I'd been back since just after President Kennedy's assassination. I visited some of the old haunts. Then I walked over to the Vietnam Veterans Memorial. I gave the US Park Service attendant Walt's name. She handed me a slip of paper with all the pertinent data: Walter John Gelien, HMC, US Navy, born 18 August 1930; died 28 October 1965; Panel: 03E, Line Number: 001. On his left was the name of Frank David Garrett, PFC, US Army. To the right was Edward Elliott Graboswsky, PFC, US Marine Corps. Both died the same day as Walt.

I didn't really know Walt Gelien very well. I never met his wife or saw his children. Yet standing there in the strange hush of this black marble monument, I felt freshly saddened by his loss more than thirty years ago. And I can't help wishing he'd been a little less true to his principles and had finished OCS.

Lex Cralley's War Souvenir

There's just gotta be a lot of World War II veterans sweating it out right now. You know, about those souvenirs they brought home from the war. This is especially true if they happened to be in the navy during the war and failed to turn in some navy property—like maybe one of those dark blue wool watch caps or perhaps a bosun's pipe.

Apparently, the navy doesn't like to give up anything it ever owned. We learned this last week when the navy decided to sue a guy who'd hauled a wrecked navy plane out of the swamp where it had lain half submerged, a home for crawfish and snakes, since 1944.

The airplane was a Brewster F3A-1 Corsair, an early version of the successful Vought F4-U Corsair—the dark blue carrier fighter with the inverted gull wings. This, of course, was the fighter plane preferred by four out of five movie stars like John Wayne and Spencer Tracy, so we know it was a good one.

Vought built a whopping 12,000 of its Corsairs, while the Brewster company made only 735 of its version The probable reason for that was Brewster had previously made another airplane called the Buffalo. The Buffalo was, according to everyone who ever flew one, a bad airplane. It flew, well, like the buffalo it was named for. During the attack on Midway Island, Japanese pilots said it looked like a watermelon with wings.

Anyway, sixty years after it crashed, this particular plane was hauled out of the swamp in North Carolina by a World War II aviation history buff and airplane mechanic by the name of Lex Cralley. He then began the painstaking and expensive process of restoring it.

If you know anything about restoring old airplanes, you know it usually costs about six times as much to restore them than it cost to build them in the first place. Without guys like Mr. Cralley, much of our war bird history would have long ago vanished.

But within just a few months, the navy decided it wanted the plane back and got the Justice Department to sue Cralley. Not only do they want the plane, but they also demand that Cralley pay shipping costs, plus damage he may have caused by extracting it from its soggy grave. Like, it wasn't already damaged or anything.

Why the navy suddenly decided it wanted the plane back is anyone's guess. After all, this plane never saw combat and was sidelined almost from the day it was built. It was sitting in North Carolina instead of fighting in Okinawa because it was airworthy only for training missions. It was on a training mission, by the way, when it crashed. Who knows, maybe it contained some exciting new technology, like two-way radios or something. Yeah, World War II vintage two-ways would be really valuable to today's defense efforts.

Whatever judge hears the case, I hope he asks the navy why they abandoned the plane in the first place if it was so valuable. And in the unlikely event that Mr. Cralley should lose the suit, I hope he will pack up the airplane and return it to the swamp where he found it. If the navy wants it, let them come and get it the same way he did.

I sincerely hope he doesn't lose, of course. It would set a dangerous precedent indeed. Another war plane enthusiast spent about a gazillion dollars of his own money a few years ago to dig a brand new Lockheed P-38 fighter out of the ice floe near Greenland where it and three others were forced to land during a storm while ferrying the new planes to England in the early war years. You may recall the story. The ice had built up around the planes over the years and was more than fifty feet deep when the salvage operation started. I suppose the Pentagon could decide they want that plane and her sister ships as well.

And what about the *Lady Be Good*, the B-24 Liberator found in near perfect condition in the Libyan Desert a quarter century after the crew bailed out?

A friend of mine was forced to bail out of a B-17 over Belgium during the war. He was the only survivor, and the plane was lost until a couple of years ago, when one wing of the craft was discovered in a Belgian farmer's barn, after my stepson took a side trip to Belgium while in Europe to look for the graves of the crew. He had been engaged to the surviving airman's granddaughter. A nonprofit group paid to have the wing brought to the United States, where it is proudly displayed in the Eighth Air Force museum in South Carolina. I suppose our military brass could decide that wing was important to our national defense, too, and order its return—plus damages and shipping, of course.

Scattered among the islands in the Pacific are literally thousands of American war planes. Some crashed, others were simply abandoned. Today, virtually all are considered common-law property of the local residents and communities by virtue of abandonment. Can we expect our military to start suing to retrieve them all, one by one?

And think of all the DC-3s and C-54s by the hundreds that were sold to individuals, companies, and countries for the sum of one dollar apiece after the war. Maybe the Pentagon will come to the conclusion that it never meant for the planes to be sold for that sum at all and demand their return.

All we can do is hope for the best for Mr. Cralley. Maybe his congressman could meet with the Secretary of the Navy and let him know that World War II is over.

In the meantime, I plan to keep a low profile myself and leave my old navy foul-weather coat hanging in the closet. After all, it was property of the ship I was on, and I never gave it back.

Lex Cralley was eventually awarded ownership of the aircraft by the US Navy.

The Unforgettable and Exasperating Bob Heisey

If you ever wanted a friend you could love and be furious with at the same time, you needed to know Bob Heisey. For seven years Bob lived on his forty-two-foot sailboat next door to My Friend the Boat Owner's boat in Key West.

I counted Bob as a friend from the moment I met him. I had just arrived at the boatyard to spend a couple of weeks working on our sailboat. As I began unloading my car, Bob ambled down the gangplank from his boat wearing a torn T-shirt, a floppy bush hat, and a pair of shorts that looked as if they had been used to soak up engine oil and bilge water. They were kept in place by a length of electrical wire instead of a belt. He held a cat under his arm and had several thick slices of bread in his other hand.

"This is the most delicious bread I've tasted in years," he said, offering me a slice. "I found it at this new Bosnian bakery down on Elizabeth Street. A couple of refugees from the Czech Republic opened it last week."

I took the bread and bit into it. He was right. It was ripe with the aromas and flavors of the Old Country, rich and yeasty. We never formerly introduced ourselves, but from that moment on, Bob Heisey was my friend.

Bob was a native son of Oakland, California. He seemed to have been born with the genes of an adventurer. When he was sixteen, he and a buddy bought a dilapidated cabin cruiser that had been sitting in someone's garage for an interminable period of time. Without checking for watertight integrity or even if the engine had oil in it, they launched it in the bay and roared out toward open water.

Halfway across San Francisco Bay the engine died. When Bob opened the engine compartment he found it was full of water. The boat was sinking. He and his buddy starting bailing like mad. Meanwhile, the tide was going out and they were being pulled out to sea. When they tried calling for help, they discovered that the batteries in their two-way radio were dead.

Fortunately, a fishing boat came by, threw them a line, and towed them back to Oakland, where they promptly hauled the boat onto dry land to check for leaks.

"In retrospect, we probably should have done that first," he said with a sheepish grin. "The boat was so full of dry rot that I'm amazed it didn't disintegrate when we put it in the water."

Bob told that story as though it had happened just the day before and he had only just that moment realized that buying the boat was a mistake. The fact is, Bob Heisey was a man of a thousand stories, maybe more. And in the course of seven years in Key West and two more up the coast in Titusville, I heard them all.

Every time I saw him, I encouraged him to write things down, put them on paper, and send them to a publisher. I can't imagine anyone not being enthralled by the tales of Bob Heisey.

The December following Bob's ill-fated boat episode, the Japanese attacked Pearl Harbor and America went to war. Panic seized the west coast of the United States as rumors of Japanese submarines floated up and down the streets of Oakland.

"I really believed the Japs were going to come ashore within the hour," he said. "I got out my dad's rifle and as much ammunition as I could find, and spent the entire night sitting on the roof of my parents' house. I figured they might get me, but I'd take as many of them with me as I could."

"Write that stuff down!" I would yell, and he would nod graciously and launch into another story. It was infuriating. His words were pure gold, capturing the ear of anyone who happened by. But once spoken, they evaporated into thin air.

Later, Bob became a reporter for the *Oakland Tribune* and covered a myriad of fascinating events in and around the Bay Area, everything from practical jokes to heinous crimes—stories perfectly recorded in Bob Heisey's memory.

After leaving the *Tribune*, he went to work for a major construction company that had a government contract to build airbases, roads, and other infrastructure in Vietnam. More stories.

When his job in Vietnam was done, the company sent him to Kinshasa in Zaire—a city and country freshly born of what had been Leopoldville in the Belgian Congo. Bob arrived shortly after the bloody 1966 revolution led by Mobutu Sese Seko during which the entire country was Africanized and all hints of Belgian influence were swept away.

He was there to witness the fabled "Rumble in the Jungle" prizefight between Muhammad Ali and George Foreman.

Among the friends he and his wife Kathy made while there was a couple who claimed to have benign jobs in some vague and boring area of agricultural development in the emerging country. From time to time, Bob and Kathy would spend the night as guests in their home. On one such occasion, they awoke in the morning to find the couple gone, along with all of their possessions. A terse one-line note asked if Bob would drop the apartment key off at a specified address.

"I had no clue, but in retrospect, I think they worked for the CIA," Bob said. "I never heard from them again."

Later, Bob bought his sailboat *Liebchen* and began a life at sea. At first he sailed frequently around Florida, back and forth to Cuba and in the Gulf of Mexico. He gathered more stories—people, places, and events, all rich, warm, and humanly rewarding.

As the years advanced, Bob stopped sailing. He parked his boat at first one marina and then another, one boatyard and then another, finally winding up on Stock Island next door to Key West.

There he enjoyed the passing scenery, bought used equipment for his boat on eBay that he would never use, tried endless new recipes for exotic dishes, and doted on his two pets: Mazola, the African gray parrot that he bought before leaving Zaire, and a tailless cat named Bob that showed up one day on his gangplank.

Bob Heisey died last week after a two-year battle with cancer. He was eighty-four. He never recorded his stories. It's almost as if a library burned down.

Bob Heisey died March 20, 2010.

My Brother Dies

My brother Jerry died last week. He was seventy-two and had been institutionalized since the age of twelve. By then it was apparent to all of us that the brain damage he received when our mother fell when she was seven months pregnant could not be reversed.

Jerry was a sweet and likable kid when he was a little boy, mostly smiling and generally happy. He never learned to talk, though, and sometimes this frustrated him. He often wanted to say something but couldn't figure out how to do it. Those were the times he cried.

At age twelve he had reached the mental age of a three-year-old. This became a problem at home because despite strict orders to stay in our yard, he would run off and show up at some neighbor's house where there were little kids. He just wanted to play with them, but mostly he frightened them, and sometimes he would take away their toys. Predictably and justifiably, the parents complained.

There were other problems, too. Big kids and even grown men would tease and torment him. More than once I came home with a bloody nose after blindly wading in and taking on three or more guys calling him "retard" and pushing him around.

Mom and Dad made the tough decision to have him committed. I think the day they drove him to St. Louis and left him at the Missouri State Training School was the worst day of their lives. No one said a word on the three-hour drive home, and Mom thereafter carried an almost unbearable weight of grief.

At first we brought him home for weekends. But after one weekend, the superintendent of the school told us the trips home were causing serious depression. Jerry wouldn't eat or even get dressed for days afterward.

"Don't take him home. Don't come to see him anymore," he told us.

The years rolled by. My sister Shelley and I grew up, went to college, left home, and got married. A younger brother, Roger, born just after Jerry was institutionalized, grew up pretty much as an only child, sixteen years younger than I and eleven years younger than my sister. He never knew Jerry, but I know he did much to ease our parents' pain.

Jerry, meanwhile, settled into a life of his own within the confines of the state's welfare system. At first he lived in bare, antiseptic lockdown dormitories with fifty or more others. Sadly, there was little for them to do in those days. He made his bed and picked up his clothes. After that he was simply expected to be quiet.

Years later, however, when the concept of group homes and sheltered workshops took hold across the country, things changed for Jerry. At the time of his death he had lived in group homes outside Bolivar, Missouri, for more than thirty years. He had his own room, a place for his possessions, and was considered the father figure by the four other residents.

For twenty-nine years he had held the same job at the local workshop, where he packed basketballs and footballs into cartons for shipment to sporting goods stores across the country. He had a checking account and a savings account. He was limited by law to the amount of money he could have at any given time, so periodically one of the caregivers would take him shopping.

He bought his own clothes and on several occasions even purchased furniture for the house. He also bought magazines and toy cars, two things he had loved from the time he was a small child. As a matter of fact, in thirty years he built what is arguably one of the largest collections of Hot Wheels and other collectable model cars on the planet. They not only filled multiple shelves in his room but also were stored by the hundreds in large plastic bins in the garage.

I suppose it was natural for me to assume that my brother had no real friends and that, to the caregivers responsible for him, he was little more than a number. I couldn't have been more wrong.

Mary, the house supervisor, met us at the hospital and stayed with us during Jerry's last hours of life. She wept openly when he died. Patty, a caregiver at the home, shared hours of stories about our brother. He helped her in the kitchen. He found recipes for her to try, and although he didn't like doing it, he carried out the garbage.

Loren, one of the residents, who had lived with Jerry for twenty years, asked repeatedly when Jerry was coming home. "He's already home," Mary told him quietly. "Jerry's gone home to heaven." The other two residents, Brad and Sean, struggled to grasp the fact that he was gone.

We held a simple graveside funeral for Jerry. Seventeen carloads of Jerry's friends came. There were former residents he had lived with, coworkers at the workshop and caregivers who spanned three decades.

The workshop supervisor, a man named Gary, talked warmly about Jerry's career. He seldom missed a day of work, and even after "retiring" a couple of years ago, he continued to go to the workshop, where he would spend the day reading magazines.

Jerry was buried in an old part of the city cemetery. Several magazines and toy cars were placed in the casket with him.

Mom and Dad have long since passed on, but I have to feel that they would have been surprised and pleased not only with Jerry's funeral but also with the way he had lived.

My brother died May 19, 2009.

THE BOAT

It seems strange that I would develop an intense love of boats and water. As a kid growing up in the North Woods of Wisconsin, I hated the water. It was always cold, even in July. Despite my father's coaxing at family outings at one lakeshore or another, I flatly refused to go into the water. As a result of this early paranoia, I didn't learn to swim until I was twelve years old, and that was only after we had lived for several years in the warmer climes of Missouri.

I never saw the ocean until I was an officer candidate at the US Naval Officer Candidate School in Newport, Rhode Island, in 1962. I was twenty-six years old.

Nobody attending OCS had much time for anything but study. The program was intense, and passing grades—essential to attaining a commission—were hard to come by. About a third of each class washed out before graduation.

One Saturday afternoon while taking a break from the books, I went for a walk and discovered the navy had a sailing school tucked into the shoreline near the Enlisted Men's Club. The school was open to all naval personnel and their dependents. Sailing instruction and use of the boats were free.

From that day on, every spare moment I could find I spent sailing. I learned later that the instruction and the boats at Newport were the same as those at the US Naval Academy in Annapolis, Maryland. An instructor sailed with me the first half-dozen times out. After that I was on my own.

There is no greater body of water for sailing than Narragansett Bay: always a good breeze, the channels well marked, and plenty of open water for a long reach.

When I was there, a dozen or more America's Cup yachts were training for the big race in September. The course we sailed out of the naval base paralleled the America's Cup course. I remember being on the water one bright Saturday afternoon and being sharply startled as one of these sleek vessels skimmed past me at hull speed, its rigging humming with energy.

The simple fact is I was hooked, probably from the first hour on the water. During my time in the navy I sailed in Hawaii, Japan, and the Philippines. Every time our ship came into port, I headed for the yacht basin.

It was no surprise years later that when a friend at work suggested a sailing vacation for us and our wives, I immediately signed on. By this time it had been decades since I had sailed, and he was just learning the ropes with his own brand new Catalina day sailor.

We planned to rent a forty-one-foot boat in Fort Lauderdale, Florida, and sail over to Bimini in the Bahamas, some fifty miles distant. Since neither of us had experience in offshore sailing, we both agreed that we should brush up on our nautical expertise before shoving off.

For the next couple of months we met after work several times a week to study navigation, rules of the road, basic seamanship, and boat handling. We even took a Power Squadron safety exam and proudly tucked our certificates into our wallets when we passed.

Despite our intensive study, we remained uncomfortable about heading into open water on our own. So we hired a licensed captain who had sailed to the island before to sail with us on the outbound trip. We would come back by ourselves. After all, as the captain said, the United States would be pretty hard to miss.

The trip was sheer poetry. We played tourist in Alice Town, North Bimini, for a day and then anchored at one of the cays, where we spent the rest of the week eating, sleeping, snorkeling, reading, and exploring the small island. When we sailed back into Fort Lauderdale at the end of the week, we were both committed to a sailor's life.

Two years later the four of us rented another boat, this time on the Gulf Coast, sailing during the day and tucking into comfortable anchorages at night. The trip was another sublime success, and it wasn't long before our discussions drifted to boat ownership. After a couple of seasons talking about it, we decided it was time to do it. We planned a series of trips to Florida to look at boats.

The boat we found was a tired forty-five-foot Columbia that had been across the ocean twice since its initial launch in 1973 and had been owned by several people. Once a proud queen of private yachting, by the time we found her, *Winsome* had seen better days and was sitting on dry land down in Key West. She had a sound hull and a strong engine, but just about everything else was in an advanced state of decay. She also had a very attractive price, which was fortunate since it would cost a small fortune to bring her back to seaworthy condition.

We bought the boat and spent most of the next year refitting her. With each weekend trip to Florida, she came a little closer to being the boat of our dreams. What happened during these months and over the next seven years is the subject of this next set of columns.

The Boat Begins

For a long time I've dreamed of going sailing, of pointing a boat toward the open sea and following a course to different lands. Others have done it and written about their adventures. I have devoured their words hungrily, half expecting them to fertilize and give life to my own dream.

And in a way they have. At least to the extent that the dream has remained alive, seeking opportunity. Until recently, however, it had come to nothing more than fanciful wishing. The demands of family, mortgage, and car payments deemed it thus. Besides, boats, especially the kind one goes to sea in, are expensive enough to remain beyond my reach.

But now a friend who has nurtured a similar dream has suggested that we look for a boat together. As a first step, we flew to Florida to see what might be available and feasible. We visited many marinas and poked about in dozens of boats. It is safe to say that variety in boats approaches the infinite, from in-your-face party vessels with ice makers and wet bars to spartan cruising hulls designed for serious voyages. My friend pointed out that some of the former resemble condominiums more than boats, like giant RVs with sails.

As exciting as it was to see marinas filled with beautiful boats, something else that I saw troubled me. At virtually every stop, the water placidly lapping the shores was filled with trash. Empty bottles, cans, Styrofoam cups, and plastic bags thrown into the sea by boaters crowded the shoreline. And since at several places marina employees were busily picking up this flotsam and jetsam, it was apparent that what we saw was only today's trash. Tomorrow another wave of waste would wash ashore.

It made me think of Sylvia Earle, a worldly marine biologist who has spent much of her career probing the depths of the ocean and pointing out the delicate ecosystems in the sea and their crucial relationship to life on land. All life depends on the ocean, she says, stressing the word "all." Anyone who thinks a discarded bottle or can doesn't matter should read her book, *Sea Change.*

Ms. Earle, whose lifelong love of the sea led her in 1970 to become one of the first aquanauts to live beneath the ocean for an extended period off the US Virgin Islands, points out that destruction of ocean ecosystems has come from many sources. For years the Soviet Union dumped nuclear waste from its military arsenal and atomic power plants into the ocean. Chemical fertilizers from American farms have drained into streams, rivers, and ultimately into the sea for years. These chemicals have created an overabundance of algae and deadly organisms, which have killed fish by the billions and caused serious illness in humans, she points out.

She thinks the world's fishing industry should think about scrapping its trawlers for fish farms, enclosed pens where seafood is grown like farm crops. Such managed facilities would provide an ongoing abundance of fish while protecting the sea from overfishing. Figures published in 1995 reveal that 22 percent of the world's popular fishing areas is already seriously overfished or completely depleted, and another 44 percent has reached the limit of exploitation.

Easy to say, but admittedly hard to do, particularly where money is at stake. The bluefin tuna, for example, is highly prized for its delicate flesh and has become so valuable that a single fish can bring thousands of dollars on the Japanese fish market. As a result, it has been heavily fished, and the western Atlantic today has but 10 percent of the number of bluefins it had in 1970.

But how could depletion of one species have any effect on something as vast as the ocean? The bluefin, Ms. Earle points out, is one of the most prolific egg layers in the sea. Hundreds of other species rely on bluefin eggs for food. Likewise, commercial fishermen don't limit their catches to marketable fish; they catch everything that comes into their nets, including seals, otters, and rare sea birds. As Ms. Earle points out in a recent magazine article, "something always lives downstream."

The biggest enemy, she says, is ignorance of our absolute dependence upon the sea. When this lack of knowledge is combined with greed, the destruction reaches overwhelming proportions. It was exactly this combination that diverted water from the Everglades several decades ago, practically killing the entire southern end of Florida. That mistake is now being expensively rectified in hopes the Everglades—which is actually a shallow river—will one day come back.

Meanwhile, there are thousands of ships on the sea. Many still dump their garbage indiscriminately overboard. One round-the-world sailor wrote that the Mediterranean Sea was like a giant garbage dump. American beaches have periodically been closed to swimming because garbage including dangerous medical waste dumped into the ocean, sometimes far away, has washed ashore.

I read a story some time ago about a group of divers who found themselves surrounded by porpoises. For an hour or more the friendly mammals cavorted and squeaked among the divers. Then one of them swam quickly away and returned with a plastic garbage bag, which it dropped in front of the divers. The entire group of porpoises then swam away.

I still plan to go sailing, the Lord be willing. But I plan to view it as a gift to be protected. The last thing I want is to dump something over the side and have some animal bring it back to me.

Describing Key West

Ever since My Friend the Boat Owner and I started going to Key West to work on a rather large and unbelievably complicated sailboat, people have been asking me what it's like in Key West. What's a boatyard like?

Hard questions to answer. I like what one of our astronauts said when asked what it was like being in space. "You can't describe it," he said. "You have to experience it for yourself."

Key West is a bit like that. It certainly has its share of space cadets. A longtime resident there considered the question and finally said, "It's as though the country was suddenly tipped upward, and all the characters slid down to Key West." Yeah, there are a lot of "interesting" people there.

Many may be homeless. They wear odd assortments of clothing and often look as though they could use a shower and a haircut. But then I noticed one such person sitting on the curb in Old Town the other evening. I thought he was waiting for a handout. After a few minutes he got up, got into a new car, and drove off. In Key West you never know. It's like Texas that way. A Texan once remarked that only the filthy rich can afford to dress like bums.

It's easy to sort out the tourists in Key West. Most of them are riding mopeds or the ubiquitous three-wheeled golf carts. They all wear shorts and sport shirts. The natives (called Conchs) usually wear sweaters or jackets and ride bicycles, many decorated with pieces of rope, glass bottles, and even live plants. Also, tourists are always in a hurry to get somewhere. Conchs have one speed for every occasion: slow.

A lot of Conchs jog. Early mornings and in the evenings you'll see them trotting along the waterfront. One character wears red shorts and a wide-brimmed red hat, and has flashing lights on his belt.

Key West also is like California, in that it's almost impossible to find a native-born Conch. They come there from every state in the union and virtually every country on the planet. Some have been around so long and under such diverse conditions they don't remember where they came from originally—like Frank, who lives under a boat in the boatyard. He has a job somewhere, but no one seems to know where. And no one knows exactly how long he has been living at the yard. The previous owner of the yard reportedly was a sucker for people with hard-luck stories. When he's in the yard, Frank tinkers on several boats he has accumulated over time. Some say he used to work on Ernest Hemingway's boat, *Pilar*. But nobody knows for sure. Before he leaves for work in the morning, he puts out a dish of water and food for the seagulls.

Some people in Key West live on houseboats, but they all seem to operate on some sort of plan. Frank and others like him appear to live by no plan at all. Some of these live on houseboats, too, but ones without pedigrees. Many are unpainted accumulations of nailed-together boards fitted to some sort of floating platform. Mostly they float, but every once in a while dawn finds a drenched Conch sitting on the shore gazing out to where his home sank during the night.

One of the scruffiest characters in the yard apparently lives in an old Volkswagen Microbus. I confess I had already dismissed him as a bum when I discovered that he's one of the finest master cabinetmakers in Key West. Somebody said he was in a bad marriage once and just doesn't feel comfortable among domestic trappings.

Then there is the one they call Wedge. No one seems to know his real name or where he came from. He rides a bicycle with a trailer attached. The trailer is filled with his tools. Wedge is considered one of the best fiberglass workers in the Keys. He lives under an overturned boat that was washed up by Hurricane George and never reclaimed by its owner. Wedge patched up the holes, cut a door in the side, and moved in.

There is John the sailmaker, who lives with his wife on a sailboat in the yard but hasn't sailed in ten years because he is too busy making sails for other people's boats. A lot of people live on their boats in the yard. One couple work as physical therapists at the local hospital and have spent the last three years restoring a fifty-foot sailboat. They say another two years and they will be ready to sail around the world.

Then there is the man from New Jersey who lives alone on his boat and never comes out except at night. He also never sails.

One of my favorite characters is Bob Heisey, a retired journalist who worked for the *Oakland (CA) Tribune* for fifteen years and then quit to go to Vietnam and work for an engineering company. Bob's boat has been tied up at the dock for seven years and he has been swearing each week that he is going to clean it up and go sailing. Of course, he's been saying that for seven years.

Bob's problem is he likes yard sales and other bargains. Every day he shows up with another armload of stuff. His boat looks like a floating flea market. I will admit to watching him throw several boxes of stuff away just the other day, however, so maybe he's serious this time.

There are a lot of characters like Frank, Bob, and the physical therapists. Some have boats; others don't. Some plan to sail away one day; others have no plans at all.

Sometimes maybe it's enough to just put out food and water for the seagulls.

The Boatyard

When most people think of boats, boatyards, and marinas, they generally envision gleaming fleets of shiny vessels bobbing joyfully on the water in long, neat rows. Scattered among these images are cocktail parties made up of small groups of utterly carefree people doing what they do best—looking utterly carefree.

Usually the sun is setting gloriously in the background and soft music is mysteriously coming from somewhere. If it's the tropics, throw in a palm tree. For Alaska, add a polar bear fishing for salmon. In the mountains, add a grizzly bear ransacking a campground. Whatever the setting, it is always idyllic.

Let me paint a slightly different picture of boats, boatyards, and marinas in Key West. Don't get me wrong; there are palm trees and sunsets aplenty here, along with numerous immaculate rows of shiny boats and literally hordes of carefree people.

But there is also Peninsular Marine, the boatyard on Stock Island, one bridge short of Key West. That's where My Friend the Boat Owner keeps his sailboat, and where I camp out when I am here.

Granted, there are some pretty neat boats here too, like the fifty-foot Hatteras in the last berth or that forty-five-foot Hylas yacht over there in the corner. And while our thirty-five-year-old Columbia definitely shows her age, she does so with dignity.

But most of the really classy "yawts" are next door at Oceanside Marina, a gated community of utterly carefree people who spend a lot of time perfecting their smiles, toasting with their margarita glasses, and trying to figure out where the heck that music is coming from.

Back to Peninsular Marine. There are two kinds of boats here—those in the water and those on dry land. In both categories there are also two kinds of boats. In the water are those that routinely leave the dock to go sailing or fishing, and those that are permanently tethered to the shore, that never go anywhere.

On dry land are the boats being fixed up so they can return to the water and those that are such permanent land dwellers they might as well have basements and tuck-under garages.

Some of the permanent land dwellers are homes for people who get up every morning and go to work. Few of them have any plans to return their vessels to the water. It is probable that most of them would sink if they did.

The people who own these boats look at them as affordable housing in a place where the average price of a house is $850,000 and going up daily, and where rent for an apartment exceeds $3,000 a month. Hey, in that environment paying several hundred a month for docking fees, fresh water, electricity, and bathroom privileges is a golden opportunity for sure, even if Home Sweet Home is a fifty-year-old fishing boat with a plywood spare room tacked onto the deck.

Some of the land-dwelling boats have been around so long that people no longer live in them. Their hulls are rotted, their decks falling apart. Their once graceful timbers are being eaten by termites, and day by day they slowly collapse. But, occasionally, even some of these are pressed into service with a couple of plastic tarps and a can of bug spray.

In the water it's a similar story. There are dismasted sailboats, engineless powerboats, stark and empty hulls, and a full spectrum of houseboats along with numerous floating platforms decked out with a remarkable assortment of topside shelters.

Several hurricanes ago, for example, one guy salvaged the entire sunroom from a fast-food restaurant. He lugged it back to the boatyard and mounted it on a raft. A couple of panes of glass had broken out, and these he covered with pieces of plywood.

Today his home bobs quietly next to the seawall. Every morning he and his wife get up and go to work. They don't look particularly carefree, and I have never heard any mysterious music coming from their part of the boatyard.

But I have the feeling they consider themselves fortunate.

Stock Island

Stock Island is a quaint little community in the Florida Keys where life is lived in the same honest fashion it was a century ago by hard-working fishermen, boatwrights, electricians, carpenters, and boat riggers. Many of them came from Cuba several generations ago and consider the United States in general and Stock Island in particular their home.

They pay taxes, send their children to school, vote in elections, and enjoy a simple, basic life. In many parts of the country theirs would be considered a hardscrabble existence. Fishing is a hard, uncertain life, and in recent years harsh regulations and a decline in marketable fish, shrimp, crabs, and lobsters has made it even more so.

There used to be a large number of fishing companies on Stock Island; today only a few remain. The boats go out every morning before daybreak, their diesel engines roaring impatiently as they head out into deep water, to catch fish or run their crab and lobster traps. All too often their expectations exceed reality, and they return at dusk with a meager catch, sometimes nothing at all. In the off-season, everyone turns to repairing gear or building new crab and lobster traps. They lose an average of 25 percent of their traps each season.

There are several family-owned grocery stores, boat chandlers, hardware stores. repair shops, and restaurants on the island. They, too, are owned and operated mostly by descendants of Cuban immigrants. Everyone knows everyone else.

Prices on the island are reasonable, and merchants seem obligated to help out any member of the community who is down on his luck by either extending credit or finding what he needs for less money. I asked the owner of the hardware store why his prices were so much lower than the big chain just a couple of miles distant.

"We are part of the community," he said matter-of-factly. "We are here to make a living serving that community. We are not here to get rich," he added. The same thing is apparently true for the small café across the street. Breakfast of eggs, bacon, and pancakes costs about three dollars.

A drive through Stock Island is by no means a luxury tour. Businesses operate out of ramshackle, unpainted buildings; rusting cars and boat trailers sit along the side of the streets; people live in small houses or in mobile homes that are usually in varying degrees of deterioration. There isn't enough money to make repairs.

In spite of the hardships, the residents of Stock Island are a warm and happy people. They regularly hold festivals, and on balmy weekends many fathers take the wife and kids out on the family fishing boat for a picnic on one of the area sandbars.

Unfortunately, Stock Island has one problem. It is but a literal stone's throw from Key West. And although Key West has a quaint history of its own, much of the evidence of it has given way to burgeoning numbers of pricey condominiums, expensive boutiques and restaurants, and, of course, the ubiquitous T-shirt shops.

The truth is, pretty much all the land on Key West has been used up. In the local government building, serious heads ponder the future of Stock Island. Stock Island has no T-shirt shops.

And even as they ponder, the developers have begun moving onto the island. Several acres that used to house twenty or thirty families and their tired mobile homes have been bulldozed clean, and a development of condos is rising to the sky. I don't know where the families who once lived there went. The flocks of fabled Key West chickens that frequented the place remain and wander around the construction equipment looking confused.

Rumors abound. There's talk of a giant visitor's center where tour buses would congregate and drop off passengers. All the Key West attractions would have kiosks at the new center.

Folks are also talking about a major hotel chain and ultra-swank marina for yachts. Developers have their eyes on both the local boatyard and the fishing ports.

Since money seems to have the loudest and most irrefutable voice, there is little doubt that all of these things will happen, probably sooner than later. And when they do, it will most assuredly spell the end of life as we know it on Stock Island. It is doubtful that a shaky fishing enterprise could stand up against wealthy developers for very long.

Change is inevitable, to be sure. But I'm not sure it always deserves to be called progress.

The downturn in the economy has brought much of the lofty planning on Stock Island to a premature halt. As half-started projects bleach unfinished in the tropical sun, the island slowly returns to a languid pace vaguely similar to its tempo of many years ago.

Working on the Boat

This time we are going to do it differently. Every time we've gone down to the boat in the past, we've said, "Hey, let's get the work done, and then we'll go sailing."

What was wrong with that was, we could never get the work done. This has to do with the nature of boats. And the nature of boats is that they are terrifyingly like houses. While you sleep, they fall apart.

Also like houses, the minute you start on a task (say, cleaning out the gutters), you notice something else that needs immediate attention (say, a loose shingle). On a house the loose shingle would lead to rotted wood in the roof, requiring major repair. Suddenly a two-hour job has expanded to fill two days.

On a boat it works this way. While polishing the deck stanchions, you notice that the bolts at the base of one of them are heavily rusted. So you drop the metal polish and break out the wire brush to clean them up. That's when you notice the fiberglass decking at the base of the stanchion is cracked and in need of repair. This means you now must remove the stanchion and repair the fiberglass underneath.

But because the bolts are rusty, they won't come loose. That's when you make your first trip to the marine store to buy some of that high-octane bolt-loosening spray.

While you're waiting for the spray to penetrate the rusty bolts, you notice that the fiberglass is cracked a lot further out from the stanchion than you originally thought. Your second trip to the marine store is to purchase a bigger fiberglass repair kit.

When you get back to the boat, you discover that the high-octane penetrating spray has had absolutely no effect on the rusty bolts. Zero. Zip. Nada. Your third trip to the marine store is for metal-cutting blades for your reciprocating saw so you can cut off the rusty bolts. Naturally, just as you get back to the boatyard you remember that you should also have bought replacement bolts while you were at the marine store.

While you are kicking yourself for this lapse of memory, you also accidentally kick your new fiberglass repair kit overboard. For the next few minutes you stand gazing helplessly at the water, wondering stupidly if you should dive down and try to retrieve the lost kit.

Somewhere in the middle of all this, you realize the diving masks and snorkels are locked in the dock locker, and the last time you looked for the key, you couldn't find it. Besides, the tide is going out, and by the time you could get into the water the fiberglass kit will have drifted halfway to the Dry Tortugas. Also, the morning is now gone and it's time for lunch.

While munching on your baloney sandwich, you observe that the stanchions still need polishing, the rusty bolts haven't budged, the fiberglass is still cracked, and you've just watched a fifty-dollar fiberglass kit sink into the abyss.

After lunch you spend the afternoon replacing the lost fiberglass kit, buying new bolts, sawing off the old ones, and cutting away the broken fiberglass in preparation for repair. You finish this scenario just before sunset, and as you are putting away your tools and loose gear for the night, you notice that the caulking around one of the hatches is coming loose. Habitually, you think, "Oh, easy job. I'll do that first thing in the morning."

All of your experience screams otherwise, of course, and you know intuitively that that small caulking job will once again point you down a path of endless work filled with rusty bolts, rotting wood, decaying caulk, and cracked fiberglass. In your heart you know it will never end. Yet you stride blithely toward the inevitable. The reason for this, I have concluded, is that because of the nature of boats, the men who sail them are gifted with an insane level of optimism.

So this time, we sail first. Well, right after I tighten the loose screws in the gangplank. Wouldn't want to slip while going aboard, would we? Besides, it's an easy job. Five minutes tops.

A New Gangplank

I keep forgetting how destructive the elements are in places like Key West. When you live in a place like Indiana where it's usually raining or snowing or getting ready to, it's easy to look at all the blue skies, turquoise water, and sunshine down here as loving, gentle, and benevolent.

Actually, it is brutal, abrasive, and unbelievably destructive. I got down here the other day after a yearlong absence. I was astonished at how some things had changed. Two years ago I fashioned a beam out of a large piece of solid oak to raise the dinghy on the back of the boat. I stained it, sealed it, and varnished it with exterior spar varnish. I figured it would last forever.

But in just a year the saltwater and sunshine rotted it completely. The wood had turned soft and gummy, and the varnish had scaled away and hung in festoons like scales on a dead fish.

Three years ago I built a gangplank to get from the dock to the boat. I made it out of half-inch plywood and two-by-fours. When it was finished, I sealed it, primed it, and gave it two coats of Sears Weatherbeater paint. That stuff is supposed to last twenty years.

Wherever two wood surfaces touched, it had rotted. I admit the paint protected the open surfaces, but the water got in everywhere else. At first I hoped to just put on a new deck. But when I tore the old one off, it became obvious that I had lost the battle.

I am now building an entirely new gangplank. This time I am building with pressure-treated lumber. As a matter of fact, in looking around I noticed everyone down here builds with pressure-treated lumber. Duh!

On the main drag headed down to Old Town, I noticed a series of houses that were built a year ago. They need repainting. In Old Town itself, however, the houses gleamed brightly. Most of these houses were built more than a hundred years ago out of a particular kind of pine that resists rot and turns harder with age.

A coat of paint on these houses lasts for years. Unfortunately, they don't build houses out that kind of wood now. It's too expensive. So they have to be repainted every year.

Other things in Key West are indestructible. The Raw Bar, Sloppy Joe's, and the Hog's Breath Saloon will last forever regardless of their paint jobs. Ditto the tattoo shops, the art galleries, and, of course, the famous Key West chickens. Every day I have to stop and let at least one wandering hen and her chicks scamper across the road.

And just about every day ends with a sunset so spectacular it takes your breath away. I never get tired of looking at it.

And the laid-back weirdness that has characterized Key West for the last century also holds fast. Old men with long beards and ornately decorated bicycles still cruise along the sidewalks. No one pays much attention. The homeless are hanging in there, too. Surprisingly, most of them have jobs. They just can't afford a place to live, so they camp out under the bridges.

And, of course, it is warm. This just naturally is attractive when the snow flies up north. So, in spite of its destructive side, you can't help loving the place.

The Other Side of Key West

"How lucky can you get," my neighbor exclaimed, shaking his head, "going to Key West and being on a boat. Imagine, being in Paradise with nothing to do but lie around all day and enjoy it."

Tropical breezes, crystal clear water, golden sunshine. Yeah, right. Oh, Key West is considered Paradise all right. You can even go to Margaritaville in Old Town and buy a T-shirt that proclaims "I had a Cheeseburger in Paradise."

Not to discredit Jimmy Buffett, but Key West has a distinctly "nonparadise" side at times that can make living in Fargo, North Dakota, a plausible alternative. To begin with, they seldom have hurricanes in Fargo. Nor do they have exceptionally high tides that bring tons of seaweed ashore to rot and stink. Nothing I can think of save the legendary mountain goat smells as bad as rotting seaweed. Tourists get a whiff of it and look at each other accusingly.

Hey, I have nothing against Fargo. I understand they have some very pretty buildings there, and their municipal snowplow fleet is second to none. I just have an aversion to living in a place where the most important holiday is the day in June when all the residents officially take off their long johns.

Key West, on the other hand, can be insufferably hot, especially in July and August, but then, so can Fargo. And Key West does have wonderfully cooling tropical breezes. Admittedly, they don't help much when the air-conditioning in your car breaks down, which it always does in July and August. But that happens in Fargo too, also in July and August.

The cruelest thing that happens in Key West, however, is it gets cold. No kidding. The first time I went there was in November two years ago. I had worn my leather flight jacket on the plane to ward off the fall chill when I left Indiana. I fully expected to throw it in the trunk of the car and forget it until the return flight. But that night a cold snap hit the island, and even wearing the jacket I was cold. Tourists in shorts and T-shirts proclaiming they had just had a cheeseburger in Paradise were downright miserable.

Last December, Key West had the coldest temperatures in eighty-six years, plunging into the lower forties at night and barely breaking through fifty degrees during the day. Tourists desperate for warmth and solace hastily departed for Fargo. The locals, the Conchs, sought warmth wherever they could find it and stripped the local stores of sweatshirts, T-shirts, blankets, and even throw rugs. And when the stores were empty, they offered outrageous prices for anything someone else was wearing. I am told a few actually left the island, with the pronouncement they were sick and tired of Paradise and were headed for Fargo.

It also rains in Paradise. When my wife and I departed for Key West two weeks ago, we anticipated a leisurely drive down to the Keys and then several days of swimming, boating, sunning, and just loafing in Paradise. It was beautiful all the way to Miami. The clouds rolled in a little south of Homestead, and the rain started when we hit Key Largo. It intensified at Marathon Key and became a virtual downpour by the time we reached Key West.

At the marina we slogged through the wet to unlock the boat and drag our stuff aboard. The problem with boats is that most of the openings for fresh air are traditionally in the roof, which means you can't have them open when it rains. And that means the heat and humidity build to sauna dimensions in something less than ten microseconds. But hey, our boat has air-conditioning, and when it's plugged into shore power at the dock, you can be as comfortable as if you were in your air-conditioned car.

Another problem that sometimes emerges in Key West is touchy electricity. Being surrounded by the sea, there is just naturally a lot of salt in the air. Salt tends to corrode all things, but it is particularly fond of electrical equipment. Naturally, when I switched on the boat's air-conditioning system, it didn't respond.

I knew what the problem was, of course. The electrical outlet on the pole on the dock had become corroded and needed to be cleaned. Simple solution, except for one thing—the rain.

I don't know about you, but I really don't like messing around with electrical wires while standing in pouring rain. So until it stopped raining, we would just have to drape protective covering over as many hatches as possible so we could open and get by the best we could. Besides, Key West is famous for its tropical breezes.

Key West is also famous for its mosquitoes. As soon as the hatches were open, they swarmed inside, presumably to get out of the rain too. Naturally, they stayed for dinner, and by morning my wife and I were lumpy with mosquito bites. Predictably, we were not in the cheeriest of moods either.

We spent the next three days sitting in the boat blotting leaks (would you believe, our boat leaks when it rains?), and reading every word in the Sunday *Miami Herald*, twice. Of course, when I drove my wife back to Fort Lauderdale to catch her return flight, the sun came out. Genteel soul that she is, she never said a word.

"Well," I said clumsily in an attempt to break the soggy silence, "this has been interesting."

"Sort of like spending the winter in Fargo," she volunteered.

Key West Chicken Roundup

One thing that's happening in Key West that probably isn't all that common in your neighborhood is the Great Chicken Roundup. Apparently, the popular multi-hued little birds, so much a part of local color, have caused headaches in high places recently and are thus being deported.

Most of them—so far about a thousand birds—have been sent to organizations and individuals in Orlando, Tampa, and Miami, presumably to become pets or show birds.

I know what you're thinking: why go to the trouble of shipping the birds off the Keys? Why not just capture the pesky fowl and have a giant barbecue?

Well, that is what makes Key West so fascinating. The chickens were originally brought to Key West by Bahamians who moved here to work in cigar factories or as divers. In some parts of the Caribbean—including the Bahamas—chickens have a couple of uses besides occupying the Sunday stew pot. One is the sport of cockfighting, a bloody ritual where two fighting roosters are pitted against each other in a pen, sort of like NFL football but without halftime ceremonies.

In cockfighting, at the end of the battle one chicken is victorious and the other humiliated—sort of like NFL football. The difference is that in most places cockfighting has been outlawed. That means you now have to ask a cabdriver where the fights are rather than look it up in the local paper.

The other purpose chickens in Caribbean latitudes serve is sort of religious. Let's just say the bird becomes a part of the ceremony, and, like cockfighting, it also tends to be, well, messy. Which brings us to the why of the Great Chicken Roundup in Key West. To stop both practices involving chickens, Key West lawmakers passed an ordinance making it a crime to kill a chicken.

The result of this charitable act was the immediate overpopulation of Key West chickens. When I first visited here a couple of years ago, you had to stop your car repeatedly to let hens with chicks cross the road. (You may be wondering just why Key West chickens cross the road. The answer is to get to the other side, just like everywhere else.)

Anyway, as the numbers increased, so did the complaints. Where Key West used to be a sleepy and isolated island between the Gulf of Mexico and the Atlantic Ocean, it has rapidly evolved into a tourist mecca and a retirement center for the extremely wealthy (real estate prices here are unbelievable). People who just shelled out three-quarters of a million dollars for a two-bedroom tract home tend to get testy when chickens poop on their sidewalks. Hence, the Great Chicken Roundup.

I don't know how many more of the birds are on the hit list, but the nightly raids continue in Old Town. Presumably, these birds also will be found homes in places such as Miami and Orlando. The local government fiercely denies any arrangement with Colonel Sanders.

This whole operation brings to light the folly of attempting to interfere in Mother Nature's plans. Often when we try to compensate for our excesses in one area, we wind up paying for them in another.

Canada geese, for example, protected by federal edict, have set up housekeeping at the edge of literally every body of water on the planet. Seriously, I have seen geese checking out puddles on the street after a heavy rain. In Australia someone imported rabbits years ago without realizing the animals had no natural enemies in the country. The result was they overpopulated until they became a menace of millions. Foxes finally were brought in to bring the population down. After all the rabbits were gone, naturally, the foxes started raiding henhouses.

I wonder if Key West Chicken Roundup officials know anyone Down Under.

Chicken Roundup, Chapter Two

Remember the Great Chicken Roundup in Key West a couple of years ago? Stand by for Roundup No. 2.

The last time I wrote about this issue I reported that the free-roaming chicken population in Key West had gotten out of hand and that approximately half of the estimated two thousand birds on the island were going to be trapped and deported to a retirement farm near Miami. There they would live out their lives in peace and quiet. Or so they said.

The project got national attention, and the official chicken catcher—a part-time barber and erstwhile illegal cockfight aficionado (presumably an expert in the art of catching chickens)—found himself on national news and even a couple of well-known talk shows. The city of Key West promised to pay twenty dollars for each captured chicken. The problem was that bands of chicken lovers kept sabotaging his traps. As a result very few birds were actually caught and deported.

The fat that fueled this fire apparently was the nebulous information provided about the birds' ultimate destination. When a film crew from the University of Florida checked it out, the only thing they found at the given address was a slaughterhouse.

Immediately the pro-chicken lobby accused city fathers of conspiring with Colonel Sanders. After that, the Chicken Roundup pretty much ground to a halt. Hooray!

The reason chickens are an issue in the first place in Key West is a law that prohibits killing the birds on the island. The reason for that dates back to various voodoo practices once engaged in by early members of the city's Jamaican contingent.

As a result, chickens have had free rein in Key West for umpteen years and long ago became accepted as part of the charming landscape. Tour buses routinely stop to allow a hen and chicks to cross the street. And just about everybody wakes up in the morning to the arrogant crowing of one or more Key West roosters. More than once church services at St. Mary Star of the Sea Catholic Church have been interrupted by a contingent of chickens walking down the aisle.

Two years later the bird population has swollen to unprecedented numbers. Admittedly, it's hard to count chickens on the loose, but conservative estimates put the chicken population at near three thousand birds and growing.

The push for control measures has been ignited once again, and the sense of urgency has mounted dramatically. There are a couple of reasons for this. One is the rapid gentrification of Key West. Street talk has it that the billionaires are now buying out the millionaires. People are moving in who are, to say the least, unaccustomed to having chickens using their sidewalks. "Jeeves, you will get rid of those horrid birds at once!"

The other reason is mounting concern over bird flu. "Whatever will we do if that horrible disease gets here?" That question from influential mouths has spurred the city council to action. Some members are in favor of rounding up all of the Key West chickens, lock, stock, and pinfeathers, and getting rid of them once and for all.

And while we are at it, they argue, what can we do about all those seagulls? And let's not forget all the other birds on the island, including the multitude of caged parrots—and the pigeons, ospreys, pelicans, and egrets.

Maybe Key West should become a bird-free zone, someone urged. To which another replied that it would be a big-budget item to post bird control people all around the island 24/7 to shoot or scare off all migrating species.

As silly as all this sounds, the best is yet to come. Some members of the city council are seriously considering a proposal to feed the chickens chicken feed laced with birth control drugs. That way, they argue, no new chickens would hatch and the ones already here would wander around until they died of old age. Of course, this launched another discussion about the life expectancy of chickens.

In all of this I have to wonder if anyone has considered simply repealing the law about killing chickens. Hey, my guess is one big barbecue, and the problem would be over.

Getting Things Done on the Boat

I'm taking a long hard look at the boatyard today because tomorrow I pack up and hit the road. It seems impossible that two months have oozed away since I first parked in front of the boat, my car loaded with tools and materials and my heart loaded with enthusiasm for a gazillion jobs that I would accomplish. Yep, there must be some mistake. I gotta be looking at the calendar wrong. Hey, the list of jobs is almost as long now as it was when I got here.

Well, not exactly. I got several of the most horrendous tasks done. Plus I did a lot of stuff that wasn't even on the list. You know, like when you decide to replace a burned-out lightbulb in the garage only to discover it wasn't the bulb after all, the light had shorted out because of a bad wire, and you wind up rewiring the entire garage. Yeah, boats are no different. Tighten a screw on a stanchion, investigate a frayed piece of lifeline, and wind up replacing the boat's entire lifeline.

So here's a final update on the boat, the boatyard, and Key West.

Since I got here, I discovered that the bowsprit, the spar on the front of the boat that is supposed to dole out the anchor and hold it firmly, was barely secured to the boat. One good tug and it would have pulled away, leaving boat adrift and anchor somewhere at the bottom of the sea. Hoped-for solution: attach existing bowsprit firmly to the boat. Actual solution: build an entire new bowsprit out of stainless steel and fasten it to the boat with heavy steel plates and bolts.

Another task was potentially a major problem but turned out to have a simple fix. By law, if you have a toilet on your boat you must have a holding tank that it flushes into. You can no longer discharge raw sewage into the ocean inside the three-mile limit.

When we first got the boat nearly two years ago, My Friend the Boat Owner and I installed a new holding tank, along with a hundred miles or so of new hoses and a shiny array of double-clamped new fittings. Perfect. Except that it stank. Every time you'd flush, the boat would fill with the most odiferous fumes imaginable. My job was to find and fix.

As you can imagine, we both felt a little stupid when I reported that the vent line had never been attached to the tank. As a result, the fumes, which were supposed to vent to the outside of the boat, spewed into the boat. Five minutes with a screwdriver fixed the problem.

Another job that someone else was supposed to do was install and varnish the beautiful holly-striped teak flooring throughout the boat. When I arrived, most of the flooring had been installed, but none of it had been finished. The cabinetmaker doing the job had suddenly taken another job in another part of the world and had vanished under cover of darkness.

Could we find another cabinetmaker? Sure, several actually. One of them said he could probably get to it sometime this fall. Meanwhile, every time I walked across the raw wood, it left tiny scars, blemishes on the expensive teak. My Friend the Boat Owner and I consulted.

"You can do cabinet work."

"I've never done flooring."

"You've worked with teak."

"Never with teak and holly."

"Close enough. You are perfectly qualified. Get to it." By default and by trial and error, I got to it. The flooring now glistens with varnish and wax. Most of the blemishes are gone.

During the past two months I also took the boat out eight times, accumulating sixty more hours of the two hundred fifty at-sea hours needed to qualify for my Coast Guard captain's license. I also ran aground once by following an out-of-date chart and had to be towed off in the middle of the night. I subsequently spent a sickening night anchored in twenty feet of churning water waiting for daylight. That, by the way, was my wife's introduction to sailing. Needless to say, she is not eager for a rematch.

I also managed to rescue someone who had left her grounded boat and gotten caught in a strong current at one of the uninhabited keys.

And I changed the oil in the boat's engine, no easy task that. Hey, you can't jack a seventeen-ton boat up the way you can a car. With a boat you dive headfirst into the bilge beneath the engine, find the illusive siphon line, and attach a hand pump to the end of it. Then one slow, agonizing thrust at a time, you suck the old oil out of the engine into empty jugs, which you somehow have to balance on your knee.

When the pump gurgles, that means the oil is out. Then you unscrew the old oil filter—again while standing on your head in the bilge—and that's when you discover there was still another couple of quarts of old oil remaining in the engine. That oil is now slopping back and forth in the bilge. After the new oil and filter have been installed, the final task is to shove thick cotton pads into the bilge to collect all the oil that leaked out. These and the jugs of old oil must then be carried to the Boatyard Recycling Center, which, as you might have guessed, is located at the opposite end of the yard, about five miles away. Naturally, having just emerged from an oily bilge, you will be dripping with enough oil to wonder if you shouldn't just leave your clothes at the recycling center also.

I say farewell for now to the boat, to the boatyard, and to the people who live and work there. Bob Heisey is no longer buying things from eBay. His boat is on dry land in the yard as he repaints the bottom, determined that, after eleven years, he is finally going to set sail to somewhere distant. Frank, who continues to put out food and water for the seagulls every morning, has moved from the dilapidated boat that he called home into another boat that he swears is only a few days away from being seaworthy. An elderly couple, Jack and Sue, have given up sailing after thirty years and have put their beloved wooden sailboat up for sale. They didn't want to, but repeated lapses of memory proved to be Alzheimer's for Sue, and the risks at sea are too great for someone who forgets things. They are coping, somehow. Jack bought a dog for Sue, hoping it might soften the onslaught of her disease. She walks the dog around the boatyard trying to remember its name.

I'll be back, probably in the fall. By that time the to-do list will have grown again.

The Bells are Tolling—Hurricane Katrina

The bells are tolling all along the Gulf Coast today, for the multitude who have died and for those who must now live in the shadow of incredible loss. I feel the need to say something about Hurricane Katrina and the unfathomable devastation she levied upon New Orleans and the Gulf Coast of Mississippi and Alabama. But honestly, I don't know what to say.

The bells toll, but what can anyone say about an act of nature so violent that entire towns quite literally vanish? Whose words could possibly relieve the pain of the tens of thousands of refugees whose homes were destroyed and may never be rebuilt? How do you get your mind around the total and absolute destruction of a city like New Orleans, the fabled birthplace of Dixieland Jazz and *A Streetcar Named Desire*?

The death toll will probably number in the thousands. The dead of New Orleans cannot even be buried in their own cemeteries, landmarks which quite possibly have disappeared. Many who perished may never be found.

The economic impact has only just begun. The flow of crude oil has been interrupted in the Gulf, and several major refineries are out of commission. Gas prices shot skyward immediately. We will pay higher prices at the pump for quite some time.

But New Orleans also had one of the largest ports of entry for grain and a host of other imports. No one knows when ships will be able to return to unload their cargoes. And no one can say when the trucks will be able to get in to load up and deliver goods across the nation.

The flow of prayer, sympathy, and help began immediately. Government agencies and volunteers from just about everywhere showed up at the water's edge and rolled up their sleeves. The crisis brought out the best in people. It also brought out the worst as gangs among New Orleans' poor laid siege to the flooded streets to rob and ransack.

We are certainly not strangers to unthinkable devastation. Visions of the World Trade Towers collapsing and burning barely four years ago still haunt me. More than three thousand died in that single act of terror. Many bodies were never found then either.

The difference is 9/11 was a calculated act of terror. The bells tolled, but we were able to vent our anger, our rage on those responsible. But who do we get angry with for Katrina? Who do we hunt down and punish? These are, indeed, "the times that try men's souls" and the times that test our faith.

No one can look at this as an act of God without asking why. Why would a loving God allow such death and destruction? Sadly, we look for answers that aren't to be found. And we pray that the same God who allowed the destruction will mollify its reach. We pray for the living and the dead without ever knowing either.

And as we pray and offer help in whatever form we can, we ache in our hearts and our souls writhe in agony with each toll of the bell. Why? Perhaps John Donne summed it up best in his popular *Seventeenth Century Meditation*:

"No man is an island, entire of itself. Each is a piece of the continent, a part of the main. If a clod be washed away by the sea, then England is the less, as much as if a promontory were, or if a manor of thy friend or of thine own were. Any man's death diminishes me, for I am involved in Mankind. Therefore, never send to know for whom the bell tolls; it tolls for thee."

Wilma!

It was a good plan. At least I thought it was. Go to Key West, spend a couple of weeks working on the boat, and then go sailing in those drop-dead-gorgeous waters for another week before returning home to the land of weather-most-dreary.

Since winter weather has always been the bane of my existence, and since Indiana is the undisputed capital of weather-most-dreary, I figured a little tropical sailing would put a smile on my face that wouldn't fade until at least the first ice storm. Unfortunately, I didn't count on Hurricane Wilma joining the mix.

The first part of the plan worked flawlessly. My Friend the Boat Owner and I got to Key West, hauled the boat out of the water, and tackled the task of repainting the bottom. We also did a few other dry-land jobs like removing the propeller and having it balanced, replacing a leaky thru-hull drain, and putting new packing in the stuffing box around the propeller shaft.

Every task went smoothly, too smoothly, really. It was eerie. And somehow we just knew it was too good to be true. Yep, that's when we first became aware of that tiny little tropical depression south of the Yucatan Peninsula. Within a day it went from tropical depression to a tropical storm with a name—Wilma!

Wilma! I immediately conjured up an image of Fred Flintstone being blown horizontally while holding onto a palm tree and yelling, "W-i-l-m-a!"

Within yet another day Wilma had gone from tropical storm to hurricane. And a day later she was pushing Category 5 and forecasters were calling her the worst storm ever in the Atlantic. And, by the way, she's going to head toward Florida, probably somewhere around Key West.

Step forward another day, and all visitors were ordered to leave the Keys. Hotels emptied out and the airport in Key West was packed with tourists trying to arrange hasty departures. Traffic on Highway 1 staggered northward.

All of a sudden Key West was a ghost town. And this on the eve of Fantasy Fest, the island's biggest event of the year. The Chamber of Commerce announced, grimly, that Key West was now losing $5 million a day.

And the local residents, already weary from Rita, Katrina, Dennis, Ophelia, and three others over the past year, began preparing for yet another hurricane. Everyone stocked up on canned goods and water and filled their cars with gasoline. And those who had taken the plywood off their windows after Rita grudgingly put it back up.

Then they waited for the order to evacuate. First it was Thursday, then Friday, and then as Wilma lingered dangerously over Cancun, Saturday or later. Not knowing was fraying everyone's nerves and grinding patience into dust.

Meanwhile our newly painted and ready-to-sail boat was sitting on dry land. What happened to go-back-in-the-water-and-spend-a-leisurely-week-sailing-and-relaxing? After seven eighteen-hour days getting the boat ready, we now had to secure her on dry land for what promised to be the worst hurricane in history.

Back to the hardware store we trudged to buy ropes and ratchet straps, the kind truckers use to secure heavy loads, and oh yeah, something called sand augers—three-foot-long steel screws that were developed to anchor mobile homes to the ground. I don't know about you, but I wouldn't want to live in a home that had to be anchored to the ground with straps.

The idea is you figure out where you want to tie down, and then you simply screw the auger into the ground and attach your ropes and ratchet straps. Not much to it really, except for one thing. Key West is one gigantic chunk of coral. The thing about coral is this: In the water it is relatively soft. But once it dries in the air it takes on properties that resemble granite or obsidian. You don't put anything into the ground here without first digging a hole with a jackhammer or a medium-size stick of dynamite.

Once we figured that out, we made another stop at the local rental center and rented a gas-powered posthole digger, dragged it back to the boatyard, and began boring holes into the coral.

Hours later the holes were dug, the augers were in place, and the boat was tightly strapped to the ground. Then we locked it up and headed north. We thought maybe if we hung out in Miami for a day or so, the hurricane would pass by and we could return to Key West and refloat the boat.

Regrettably, Wilma had other ideas. She spent a couple of days destroying Cancun and then inched into the Gulf of Mexico. By the time she turned and headed toward Florida, we were out of time. Our only choice was to go back home to the land of weather-most-dreary and plan our return at some future date.

Who knows, the boat might still be there.

Key West Recovers

On the surface it looks like business as usual on the streets of Key West. But there is a lot beneath the surface that says otherwise.

One clue is the whole place seems more open than it used to. You can't figure out why at first. Then it dawns on you: all the trees that grew at the water's edge are gone. All those mangroves that grew up next to the seawall were wiped away by Wilma. Many of the mangrove islands that dotted the harbors are history, too.

The next thing is a kind of austerity in the shops. Sure, the merchandise is there pretty much as it used to be. But something is missing. Then you realize that it's all new. The old stuff was wiped out in the storm surge that reached as high as six feet in some places.

The manager at the Ben Franklin crafts store on Roosevelt just north of Old Town said there were eighteen inches of water in the store during the storm. "There was nothing we could do about the merchandise," she said. "Everything on the lower shelves was destroyed."

Down on Caroline Street on the waterfront, where the giant schooner *Western Union* idles in her berth, a dress shop manager shrugs off the hurricane. "After going through four of them in one season, you learn to take it in stride," she said. "We have gotten real good at moving the merchandise in a hurry." She added that the storm brought two feet of water into her store.

It is virtually the same story with all the ground-level businesses in Old Town. The ones built on stilts, like the West Marine store, were for the most part spared. "The wind blew a little water in under the door," a West Marine employee said. "Other than that we were okay."

But in the northern half of the island along Roosevelt, where resort hotels mingle with motorcycle shops and restaurants, four months after Wilma inundated the island, nearly everybody is struggling to make a comeback. In the shopping center, both the Sears store and Kmart have been completely gutted and are being rebuilt. Moldering piles of ruined merchandise still sit in the parking lot waiting for refuse trucks to haul it away. Both stores are open, sort of. Sears is selling appliances and electronics out of a small space in the front of the store, while Kmart has turned its low-ceilinged storage room at the back of the store into an impromptu sales outlet. Portable cash registers sit on tables, and a smattering of merchandise—much of it shipped in for Christmas—is stacked unceremoniously throughout the cramped space.

Albertsons food store is open as though nothing had happened. But one woman who saw it during the storm said it took a major hit. "There were fish swimming in the aisles," she said.

The mountains of sand washed into the street from Smathers Beach on the Atlantic side have been sifted clean and put back at the water's edge. A half-dozen giant front-end loaders still sit at the edge of the street awaiting their next assignment.

Water-logged washers and dryers, refrigerators, and dishwashers are piled up along the streets like pods of beached white whales. Downed trees have been cut into manageable logs and await removal. Dozens of semi-size dump trailers line the streets as loaders fill them with the wreckage.

All the scooters in the rental places are new, as are the cars in the dealership lots. There were at least a dozen car carriers loaded with damaged vehicles, waiting for orders to move out. They will wind up at salvage yards where they will be crushed into metal cubes the size of hay bales. All titles for flood-damaged cars have been surrendered to FEMA. The agency says the vehicles will not be sold.

Pretty much everywhere things are being put back together. Tourists are drifting back, and restaurants and hotels are filling up. Some places were damaged beyond repair and will not reopen. That goes for the hundred-fifty-foot gambling boat that was picked up by the storm surge and carried a mile into shallow water, where it now sits hard aground in a foot of water. No one is quite sure what can be done with it, but it will probably be cut apart and sold for scrap.

And everywhere people are back at work. Some grow impatient waiting for insurance checks or for repairs to get under way. But they put on a brave face and go to work. Most of the people I talked to wouldn't dream of doing anything else.

"Hey, this is Key West," one merchant quipped. "We aren't allowed to quit. Besides," he added with a grin, "we gotta get things fixed up; we're only six months away from next year's hurricane season."

Garbage Truck at Fort Jefferson

It's unusual to hear a garbage truck backing up with its ding-ding-ding alarm at three o'clock in the morning. It's even more unusual when you're out in the ocean on a sailboat miles from shore.

But there it was, ding-ding-dinging as we were anchored in the harbor at Fort Jefferson in the Dry Tortugas, some eighty miles from Key West. For several minutes I lay in my bunk, dumbly trying to figure out what was going on. Then it dawned on me: it was Mazola the parrot.

When My Friend the Boat Owner and I decided to sail out to the famous but remote National Monument, we invited a friend who lives aboard a boat in Key West to go with us; at sea it always helps to have an extra hand aboard. And besides, he had been to the Dry Tortugas before, while neither of us had.

The only fly in the ointment was that he has this African gray parrot, and there was no one in the boatyard able to take care of her while we were gone. After a hasty conference, we decided to take the bird along.

Hey, pirates always had parrots that rode around on the captains' shoulders yelling such things as "Avast, ye swabs!" and "Pieces of eight!" Actually, I have it on good authority that the parrot did most of the talking since the captain's vocabulary was limited mostly to "Argh, matey, argh."

So that was settled. Mazola came aboard in her cage, and we cast off all lines for the fifteen-hour sail west. Throughout the day we were blessed with fair winds and a gentle sea. We anchored the first night at the halfway point, in the lee of the Marquesas Keys. We finished the trip the second day and arrived at Fort Jefferson harbor just before sundown.

Throughout the trip Mazola had been relatively quiet. From time to time a whistle or a squawk, but that was all.

336

What you need to know about Mazola is that she has a remarkable vocabulary even for an African gray, which are known for their word power. But the really special thing about this bird is she doesn't just say words, she imitates sounds. When she repeats something that someone has taught her, she says it in their voice. She also imitates cell phones, toilets flushing, police sirens, and even the scratchy static of police radio. And oh yeah, the ding-ding-ding of a garbage truck backing up. That's the one she likes to do at 3:00 a.m.

The Dry Tortugas have a colorful history. They were discovered by sixteenth century Spanish sailors, who used the islands as a landmark to avoid piling up on the reef while hauling gold, silver, and emeralds from South America back to Spain.

Even though the reef was clearly marked on navigation charts of the day, storms drove many ships aground, with disastrous loss of life and valuable cargo. Among these, of course, was the fabled *Atocha,* discovered in 1985 by salvor Mel Fisher.

A lighthouse was built in 1822 on Garden Key, the main island where Fort Jefferson stands. Unfortunately, it was too weak to be effective, so a second, taller, and brighter light was built on Loggerhead Key, three miles to the west. It still stands today, warning seagoing vessels of the dangerous shoals.

The Dry Tortugas were named both for the sea turtles that use the islands as a nesting ground and for the fact that there is no fresh water on the islands. During the early years, Fort Jefferson collected rainwater in cisterns. Today, water is brought in by ship.

During the Civil War, Fort Jefferson became a military outpost to protect the Gulf of Mexico from invasion by Confederate warships. At the end of the war, it became a military prison, confining mostly Union troops convicted of desertion or other crimes.

The most famous prisoner at Fort Jefferson was Dr. Samuel Mudd, who was sentenced to life in prison for giving aid and comfort to John Wilkes Booth after he assassinated President Abraham Lincoln. Soon after his arrival at the isolated outpost, the entire area was hit with a yellow fever epidemic that killed thousands in the Florida Keys and Caribbean islands. Dr. Mudd was credited with saving hundreds of lives during the outbreak. After an extensive review of his role in the death of the President, Dr. Mudd was pardoned by President Johnson in 1869. He returned to his home in Maryland, where he died in 1883 at the age of forty-nine.

The fort itself is an imposing structure, made entirely of bricks, millions of them, all imported by ship from the mainland. At various times in its history, ever more elaborate plans for defenses were unveiled for Fort Jefferson.

Invariably, however, funding was too slow or military needs changed so that many projects died before they were completed. For example, five mammoth arsenals were planned, but only one was completed. And it was never used.

In the late 1890s Fort Jefferson was used as a coaling station for warships during the Spanish-American War. It continued in that capacity until 1910, when a hurricane devastated the island. Damage was so severe that the US military decided to abandon the Dry Tortugas, leaving it uninhabited except for the lighthouse keeper and his staff.

The fort was reactivated briefly during World War I as a coastal watch point protecting the entrance to the Gulf of Mexico. After the military left the island, the National Park Service took possession and has maintained the area ever since. A marine research center operates on Loggerhead Key.

In the middle of all this history is an eerie connection with the outside world. Resting on the beach when we were there were three derelict boats. Two looked like century-old steel whaleboats in an atrocious state of repair; the third was obviously homemade from sheet aluminum stuffed with Styrofoam. On the stern was the lower unit of an outboard motor with a Briggs & Stratton lawn mower engine attached to the top.

All three boats got there at the hands of Cuban refugees so desperate to escape conditions in their homeland that they were willing to risk their lives in treacherous seas They're hauled off and destroyed, while the refugees are turned over to the Immigration and Naturalization Service [now Immigration and Customs Enforcement], where most are accepted as legitimate political refugees.

After two days at the fort, we hauled up anchor and headed back toward Key West. On the way out of the channel, the setting sun glinted sadly on the derelict Cuban boats. Shortly after we raised the sails, Mazola warned us with a series of loud dings that somewhere a garbage truck was backing up.

Rescue at Sea

Out beyond the reef that protects this tropical paradise lies a vast and uncaring ocean. A high-speed current races outward from the keys to the Dry Tortugas, and then southward toward the Yucatan Peninsula, more than a thousand miles away. At Boca Grande Key this current runs at eight knots, faster than a man can walk and much faster than anyone can swim. Lose a life jacket overboard and it will be a hundred miles away by morning. Gone forever.

Few people appreciate the strength of this current more than Sally Howard (not her real name), a Key West resident. It happened last week when a boat trip with friends turned sour and then very nearly became a tragedy. It came so close, so very close.

Just before dark as the tide was going out, their boat ran aground. For a while they tried to push the boat back into deeper water, but it was soon obvious they were there for the night, stuck until high tide returned. Darkness settled over the Keys and the sea as the current rushed relentlessly on.

What happened next is unclear. Perhaps there was an argument. It was a hot night and there was no wind. Frayed tempers erupt easily when you're miserable. To get away from the situation, Sally got out of the boat and started walking through the shallow water toward the shore; it would be better there. Besides, it was only a short distance, and the water was shallow. Or so she thought.

What she didn't know was that between the shallow water where the boat was aground and the shore was deep water—and the current. It happened so fast. Suddenly she was swimming hard, fighting against a current that threatened to sweep her out to sea. She could see the anchor light on the boat. It looked close. She thought she could make it. After all, she was a good swimmer, and she worked out every day.

After many long and agonizing minutes, she realized that the light on the boat was getting farther away; she was losing ground against the current. And she was getting tired. She struggled to keep afloat and not panic, and then she started yelling for help.

That was when I woke up. Our boat, quiet for the night, was anchored about a half mile from where Sally's boat was aground. The calls for help were further away still. I came out on deck and strained my ears to determine the direction of the calls.

"Help, someone. Please!"

Quickly, I gathered up life jackets, the portable VHF radio, and our powerful handheld spotlight, and started the outboard motor on the dingy. I left instructions with my daughter and granddaughter—visiting me in Key West for their first taste of sailing—to stand by the radio and to blink a flashlight from the stern of the boat, a homing beacon for my return trip.

The trip seemed to take forever. There was no moon; it was pitch black, the only sound the low rumble of my outboard motor and the gurgle of the current. And out there in the water, desperate cries for help.

By the time I reached her, she was obviously near exhaustion, no longer swimming, just fighting to stay afloat. I cut the engine and got her into the dingy, and then happily announced over the radio that I had found her and she was okay. I told my daughter and granddaughter to man the flashlight and to get some warm clothes ready. You can get hypothermia even in eighty-six-degree water.

Once on board our boat, my daughter and granddaughter took over and got our passenger toweled off and into dry clothes. They fixed her something to eat and made up a bunk for her in the main cabin of the boat. Within minutes she was asleep.

Morning dawned as most mornings do down here, with incredibly blue skies, rich turquoise water, and sand flashing golden yellow in the shallows along the shore. It was hard in the warmth of this new day to remember how desperate the night had been. Sometime during the pre-dawn darkness when high tide swept over the reef, the grounded boat had floated free.

After breakfast we hauled up our anchor and headed back to Key West. Sally, smiling now, came on deck wearing a pair of my granddaughter's shorts and a tank top.

"I really believe in miracles," she said, "big ones and little ones." How did she mean? I asked.

"The big one was being rescued," she said, meaning it. "The little one is being rescued by someone my size."

A Funeral at the Water's Edge

As far as I know, Ernesto Basulto never complained about anything. At least he never did in the years I knew him at the boatyard in Key West.

I don't know what his earlier credentials might have been when he was a young man growing up in Castro's Cuba, but at the boatyard Ernie was the handyman. He picked up litter and pulled weeds rain or shine, sometimes in grueling heat, eight hours a day Monday through Friday and four hours on Saturday.

He also cleaned the laundry room and the toilets every day. Sometimes on Mondays the latter was a grief-stricken job because there always seemed to be one or two thoughtless souls who took fiendish delight in plugging up the johns over the weekend with massive amounts of toilet paper and anything else they could find.

No one ever knew who they were, and we could only guess at their reasons for such senseless acts. We felt sorry for Ernie, but he just waded in with a shrug and that permanent grin on his face. He never complained, but you could tell he felt ashamed for the culprit.

"See, I can fix my problem," he once told me, with a sweeping gesture toward a restored restroom. "But I guess this man, he can't fix his."

Sometimes weekend visitors left heaps of trash from their parties strewn around the boatyard. Ernie cleaned it up and never complained. When the trash truck dropped bags of rotting garbage during pickup on Mondays, Ernie routinely swept up the mess and deposited it without complaint in the dumpster.

Once a year Ernie returned to Cuba to visit relatives and friends. He always said he'd had a nice visit but admitted that he was happy to be back in America, back at his job. I always got the feeling that life in Cuba had not been

341

pleasant for Ernie, that it contained memories he would just as soon forget. Still, I never heard him complain even about conditions in Cuba.

Ernie was also a gracious man, ready with a greeting for everyone he passed during his day in the boatyard. I would be away for six months at a time, yet the minute I pulled in to spend a few weeks working on our boat, Ernie would trot over to give me a solid hug and a sincere welcome. He made me feel like a long-lost brother.

A year ago when I was in Key West working on the boat, word came that Ernie was in the hospital. Doctors said he had suffered a minor stroke. A friend from a neighboring boat and I went to see him and wish him a speedy recovery. He was so pleased to see us he tried to get out of bed. Fortunately, a nurse rushed in to quell his overactive sense of hospitality. Still he smiled broadly, with no complaints. Two weeks later he was back at work.

This year when I arrived at the boatyard, Ernie once again greeted me, welcomed me, and asked about my family. My Spanish was much worse than his English, but I tried to ask about his family. "Everyone is good," he said.

For the next week or so it was business as usual, with Ernie bent to his tasks around the boatyard. He looked tired and seemed to take frequent rest breaks, but no complaints. Then one day he didn't show up for work. We heard later that he had died of complications from pneumonia. We never knew he was sick because he never complained.

On December 6, there was a short memorial service held at the water's edge in the boatyard. A couple dozen people stood there while Ernie's daughter and granddaughter offered a few words of prayer and recollection. During the night a cold front had moved in, and a vicious winter wind blew down the channel. Everyone was shivering and glad to get back to the protective cover of their boats.

I have no doubt that Ernie would not have complained.

One Final Trip to Key West

With the hint of snow flurries in the air, it seemed a perfect time to head for Key West and *Winsome*, the forty-five-foot sailboat I enjoy with My Friend the Boat Owner. For the past seven years he and I have made regular sojourns southward to the land of tropical breezes and turquoise water.

The difference this time is it will be our last trip to Key West. The reason is the boatyard where we have reefed our sails all this time has been sold. The buyer is one of those high-octane developers bent on changing lowly boatyards into luxury yacht marinas.

We were welcome to stay, of course—if we wanted to pony up four hundred thousand dollars to buy our slip. Trust me when I say turning the offer down wasn't a difficult decision. I figure if I have a problem with hard-dirt real estate costing six figures, I am never going to feel good about paying big bucks for a patch of open water. Besides, every time the tide comes in, it's different water.

When we first got there several years ago, the water was full of boats and the boatyard was a thriving concern. Boats came in from everywhere to haul out and make repairs. Several tourist boats including the popular schooner *Wolf* routinely drifted in for maintenance.

Stopping, too, were offshore cruising sailors en route to exotic ports of call from Nova Scotia to Rio and just about every island in between. And there were some boats that never left the land, derelicts mostly, cobbled together from whatever was at hand to provide home and hearth for people who needed a place to live while they held jobs in the expensive Lower Keys. One man actually lived under a tarp attached to the side of a boat so far gone that everyone except him knew it would never float again. Another lived for several years in the back of his repair van. He paid a modest rent to keep his van in the boatyard.

They are all gone now and so are most of the buildings they occupied. The sail loft, the diesel engine shop, the hull repair shop, and a scattering of other marine-related operations have closed down, moved on, their images blotted from the landscape. Some found other shorelines on which to set up shop for a while until the developers displace them again.

Where the boats used to rest on stanchions, dump trucks now deliver loads of crushed rock as a foundation for the pricey condominiums that will soon appear. Men walk around in hard hats, with rolled-up blueprints under their arms. Only three boats remain in the water, and they will be gone within the month.

As for *Winsome* and her crew, we are headed for the small town of Cocoa on the Atlantic coast near Cape Canaveral. There is a quiet marina there, along with some inviting shops and restaurants and a cadre of friendly people. From there we can sail the Intercoastal Waterway on lazy weekends or head for the open ocean just a few miles away. We are looking forward to this new adventure and anticipate making new friends.

Still, when the boat is safely moored in her new berth and we turn out the cabin lights after a full day of sailing, each of us, I am sure, before drifting into sleep will say a quiet but fond farewell to that rowdy and magical place that was Key West.

Farewell to Key West

Our last night in Key West was a little more sobering than we had expected. After all, My Friend the Boat Owner and I had been traipsing down to this rowdy town crammed between the Atlantic Ocean and the Gulf of Mexico for seven years, ever since we first found our forty-five-foot sailboat *Winsome*, looking abused and neglected in the boatyard, and fell in love with her.

In those early days we planned long weekends around the boat. We would fly down to Fort Lauderdale on Friday, rent a car, and drive those sluggish 163 miles to our nation's southernmost point for the sole purpose of bathing in our own sweat as we laboriously stripped her interior, scraped her hull, and rewired and re-plumbed her innards.

It was a proud day when we started her engine and nosed her into the channel for her first sea trial. Like doting parents, we noted every subtle inflection in her sails, every creak in her rigging, and every nuance in her attitude. We both agreed she must have felt liberated and redeemed, proud to be on the water again.

What followed was a parade of joyful years, outfitting, polishing, revising, and improving. One windy day we blew out the genoa, ripping it from top to bottom. We happily discovered that she sailed well on just her main and jib. We immediately began counting pennies toward the day we could buy a new giant headsail to replace the one we lost. We're not there yet, but we're closer.

I filled the interior with lush teak, mahogany, and holly, and built a handsome gangplank for getting on and off safely. We found leaks and plugged them, things that stopped working and replaced them, and drew sketches for improvements to make our vessel more beautiful, functional, and seaworthy.

Winsome in Key West became the place to be for holidays, family gatherings, and quiet retreats. I have written several dozen columns while sitting in the cockpit watching the sunset explode just beyond the reef. I have eaten breakfast at the Cuban café just up the street from the boatyard and returned to the ship in time to greet the morning sun with a second cup of coffee.

There were day sails to Sand Key, Drei Rocks, and Middle Sambo, and weekenders to Newfound Harbor and the Dry Tortugas. We have sailed in a hard wind that put the rail in the water and lolled helplessly on a windless sea that looked like a turquoise mirror. We have run aground and waited long uncomfortable hours for the towboat to pull us to safety.

But then the boatyard was sold and everyone started talking about leaving. By the time the bulldozers arrived to begin making changes, many were gone, and everyone who remained was busy packing.

During the last days the place crackled with a sense of urgency. People with boats in the yard were frantic in their efforts to complete repairs and get their vessels back into the water. Some with repairs too vast to complete in the diminishing time allowed wrestled with necessary losses, struggled with the inevitable, and ultimately became resigned to moving on, often leaving their boats and their dreams behind.

The sailmaker and his wife packed up their final load from the loft they had occupied for fourteen years and drove away toward an uncertain future. An hour later wreckers began dismantling the polished loft floor that had held so many sails in those fruitful years.

We decided it would be fitting to end our stay here with one last trip to Duval Street, that gaudy and irreverent center for Key West at night. We ambled into Margaritaville for one more Cheeseburger in Paradise. We were determined to really have a good time this final night in the Conch Republic.

Yet Jimmy Buffet's venue was nearly deserted, the streets outside strangely quiet and serene. During dinner we made a little small talk and listened to Jimmy belt out his memorable music. Mostly, though, we sat quietly, each of us lost in his own thoughts.

After leaving Duval Street for the last time, we returned our rental car to the airport and caught a cab back to the boatyard, where we would finish preparations for getting under way in the morning.

On the short drive to the boat we chatted with the cabdriver. He told us that this season's tourist business was the slowest he had seen in twenty years.

We bid our final farewell to Key West, October 27, 2006.

THIS AND THAT

I could find no other suitable home in this book for a few entries. They cover everything from my own day-to-day foibles to the predilection of lawn mowers to break down when you most need them. There are even a couple examples of governmental lunacy at its best. I added several columns devoted to a few of my military experiences at the end of this section.

My Most Embarrassing Moment

Hang onto your sunglasses, kids, the annual migration to Florida is about to begin. It's become a tradition at the outskirts of winter to ease south for a week in the sun to thaw brain and body, a temporary fix to see us through the final freeze and blizzard.

Tanning spas are already working overtime, grinding out bronze pelts that will be compatible with the Florida sun. Suntan lotions, ointments, and nostrums are disappearing off store shelves at record speed. Gals are checking out the newest swimsuits, and a lot of guys I know are bemoaning a winter of pizza and french fries that pumped excess blubber into their midsections.

The retired snowbirds left right after Christmas. They drove off in their motor homes and campers, staking out their square yard in the sun just before the January storm hit. The snowbirds will be starting their return about the time spring break launches several gazillion high school and college youngsters toward the sandy beaches of Daytona and Fort Lauderdale. The minivan crowd, meanwhile, will set their automatic pilots for Orlando and the yearly splurge with the kids at Mouse World.

I, too, look forward to a respite from the cold, but I always think of Florida with a twinge of anxiety. The reason why came back to haunt me the other day when I ran into one of my friends who had just gotten back from ten days in the Keys, golden brown and looking relaxed. I told him I envied him his healthy smile, and he immediately started smiling constantly just to irritate me. He paused to scratch his ankle. I could see his leg was covered with red welts.

"Fire ants," he said. "Ran into a nest of them on the golf course." I winced in sympathy as I recalled my introduction to fire ants. It was an event burned indelibly into my memory not only as one of the most painful experiences of my life but also one of the most embarrassing.

It was my first trip to Florida and, as it turned out, not a vacation. At the time I was working for an audiovisual production company, and we were hard at it putting together the images and sounds for an annual sales meeting for one of our clients.

The sales meeting was going to be at the Saddlebrook Resort just north of Tampa, a rambling conglomeration of golf courses, private condominiums, cottages, swimming pools, and the main resort lodge. Running among the fairways and along many of the quiet roads that ran through the resort were black water lagoons and canals populated by hundreds of alligators. They spent their days sleeping in the sunshine along the shores and floating like submerged logs just below the surface of the water.

I had never seen an alligator, and when I was given the assignment to photograph some local color for a closing slide show for our client, I set out to get some alligator shots. One black water canal ran next to the main road through the resort, and I remembered seeing several alligators snoozing along the banks when we arrived the day before. I looped my camera around my neck, slung the camera bag over one shoulder, and hotfooted it over to the canal. When I got to the place where I had seen the gators, I left the road and walked slowly and quietly up the bank to see if they were still there.

On tiptoe I proceeded till I could see over the top. There, not ten feet away, a giant bull alligator slept peaceably. Perfect. Slowly, I removed the lens cap from my camera and looked through the viewfinder. The bull slept on, giant teeth extending from the bottom of his huge jaw. I shuddered slightly as I brought the beast into focus. Suddenly I felt a sharp pain in my legs and, a moment later, in my thighs. It was a stinging worse than anything I had ever experienced. My legs were on fire. I looked down and saw that I was standing on top of an anthill. Thousands of red ants were swarming over my shoes and up my legs.

Quickly I began slapping and brushing the ants away and quickly realized that most of them had crawled inside my pants and were attacking bare flesh. In an instant I had unfastened my belt and pulled my pants down, slapping madly and sweating like a prizefighter. The ants continued biting, stinging. The pain was excruciating.

I've gone over it a hundred times, and I am convinced there is no way I could have prevented the alligator from waking up. The way I was flopping around just a few feet from his nose, I probably resembled some crippled animal, a made-to-order lunch. It was at that moment the alligator charged. I will never forget the look in his eyes. There is, I think, no greater malevolence than that borne in the eyes of a male alligator rudely awakened from his afternoon nap. Naturally, I was quickly distracted from my war against the ants.

Any survival instructor will tell you that given the temperament of the average alligator, the only acceptable course of action when confronted is to run. Lamentably, with my pants down around my ankles, running was out of the question. I tried, though; I really tried. Trust me when I say I commanded my feet to move, and they did the best they could. The result was a series of desperate rapid-fire hops. In retrospect, it is amazing how much ground I covered in that fashion, bouncing in long, looping arcs with my pants dangling like anchors at my feet, my camera and shoulder bag flopping up and down, pummeling me in the face.

I was never able to determine how long the tour bus had been sitting there with its load of retired ladies from a visiting flower club. Awareness came to me by degrees as I galumphed like an enraged kangaroo away from the alligator. At first I heard the bus driver's droning voice on the bus's sound system calling attention to various points of interest.

"And to the right is one of our fabled black water canals, home to some of our most entertaining residents, the alligators … " The voice stopped abruptly, and all that remained was stunned silence and the sudden intake of breath by thirty blue-haired women. The bus rolled on silently, and after a hundred yards or so, the driver continued, "The compound also boasts record numbers of white egrets and blue herons, which nest along the water's edge."

I remember little after that. At some point after I had made good my escape and finally brushed away the last of the carnivorous ants, I think I sat down and cried. Needless to say, when I returned to the lodge I kept a wary eye out for little old ladies.

That was long ago, of course, but I find it impossible to think about the joy of going to Florida without also thinking at least for a moment about the pain—and indignity—of my first visit.

Using the Blender

It's been a long time since I used a blender. So I guess it's not surprising that I forgot some of the rules. Rules like "never open the lid while the blender is operating" and "never—but never—stick a spoon or other object into the blender while it is operating."

Yeah, I know, common sense should have kicked in somewhere along the line. But I was so totally focused on making cilantro-herb mayonnaise for some of those delicious meals on the South Beach Diet that I didn't think.

I mean, I had to drive all over town to find fresh cilantro leaves in the first place. Then I had to chop them into pieces so I could measure a cup and a half of them—loosely packed. Then I had to spoon out an equal amount of low-fat mayonnaise and add fresh lime juice and a clove of garlic.

And when I put the whole shebang into the blender, I didn't realize until it was too late that I should have put the garlic and cilantro in first and plopped the gooey mayo on top. That way the blades could have gotten right to work chopping up the cilantro and garlic and slowly blending in the mayo.

Lamentably, I did it backward and dumped the cilantro on top of the mayo, so that when I turned on the blender, nothing happened. I mean the cilantro and the garlic clove just sat there on top while the blades whirled away underneath, blending and re-blending the already silky smooth mayo.

I admit this is the point where I should have stopped and rethought the whole thing. But, as I said, I was busy making cilantro-herb mayonnaise, and nobody stops for that.

In the interest of product safety, they ought to print warnings on the side of blenders, maybe in letters three inches high. Of course, I probably wouldn't have read them anyway, preoccupied as I was with my task.

In retrospect, it was easy to see my mistake. It was obvious that the cilantro leaves needed to be pushed down toward the bottom so the blades could blend them in with the mayo. No problem. Hey, I used to watch my mom mixing cake batter with her Mixmaster. She always used one of these rubber spatulas to push the batter down toward the business end of the beaters. And wasn't a blender, after all, just another type of Mixmaster? How hard could it be?

I probably even looked like I knew what I was doing when I pulled the lid off the top of the blender. I suppose I even exhibited a certain air of confidence when I stuck the rubber spatula into the mixture.

Things happened pretty fast after that. The blades, whirling at supersonic speed, hit the end of the spatula and pulled it out of my hand. I don't know how much time passed after that before I had the presence of mind to reach over and shut off the blender. It may have been only a couple of seconds, but it seemed much longer.

There should be another warning that comes with blenders, one that says you should never set them on a counter close to things like telephones, vases filled with dried flowers, or containers holding a multitude of kitchen utensils.

For the longest time I couldn't find the spatula. Finally I saw it sliding slowly down the wall. The blender had thrown it there, and the mayo made it stick. And the mayonnaise, now partially blended with cilantro leaves, hung in festoons pretty much everywhere. It looked as if a cement mixer had exploded. On one cabinet door whole cilantro leaves were firmly affixed to the wood, like the craft project of a three-year-old. On the other side of the sink, mayo oozed down the front of the phone, filling in the space between the buttons. Have you ever tried to clean mayonnaise off of dried flowers? Fortunately, our sink has one of those high-pressure spray hoses; maybe they'll look okay once they dry.

I finally found the garlic clove, stuck inside a wire whisk in the utensil pot. Naturally, everything had to be scrubbed and hosed down.

It was after I had cleaned up the walls, the cabinets, and all the objects along the firing trajectory of the blender that I discovered the rest of the mixture on the refrigerator across the room. And oh yeah, the floor looked pretty blotchy, too. It turns out that my dog Brutie likes cilantro-herb mayonnaise, so by the time I got the fridge cleaned up, the floor looked pretty good.

It is an ill wind, indeed, that blows no good, and during this trying time I learned a few things about mayonnaise that I hadn't known before. First of all, it is impossible to pick up. Even with paper towels or wet dishcloths, it stubbornly refuses to leave the surface on which it is sitting. It smears, however, and spreads better than any paint I ever saw. And once it dries, it is totally impossible to remove.

When things calmed down, I started over and made a new batch of cilantro-herb mayonnaise. Of course, this time I put the cilantro leaves and garlic into the blender first.

By the time I finished, I had forgotten the excitement of my first effort. It all came flooding back, though, when I looked into a mirror and saw that my complexion had taken on a strange greenish cast, accented by a cilantro leaf in the middle of my forehead.

Looking for Grodies

It's spring, and yard sales are popping up like mushrooms. It's always that way—first comes spring cleaning and then the sale.

We used to make the rounds every spring, stopping in this neighborhood and that, sifting through the boxes and stacks of goodies in driveways around town. I was never sure what we were looking for. Inspiration, perhaps. It was sort of like looking through a home-and-garden magazine.

"We could use this by the front porch," my wife would say, picking up some functionless item. We'd look at the thing and try to kick-start the creative process.

"Maybe with a flowerpot on either side," I'd shrug. We'd look at the price tag. A dollar. We'd buy it and load it into the car, hoping that the seeds of genius might sprout later.

Most of the things we buy at yard and garage sales are what an old friend of mine used to call "grodies." A grodie is anything that is interesting to look at and might be used for home decoration. We've collected a lot of grodies over the years, everything from old wrought-iron gates to antique newel posts. We've bought vinegar jugs and odd flowerpots. Once I bought a flywheel from an old tractor and tried to make it look at home in the flower bed. We spent a couple of seasons looking at it hopefully and then retired it to the garage.

I remember picking up an old map case one year, putting it in a corner of the family room and filling it with weeds. Somehow it didn't look quite right, so we added some artificial flowers. That wasn't right either, so we replaced the weeds with a different kind of floral arrangement. Nope. We tried a half-dozen other things and finally realized the problem was the map case. It was just plain ugly and couldn't be made attractive with anything.

I don't know why people in this country are so obsessed with *things*. The truth is, few of them really enrich our lives very much. We gather them anyway. My wife and I used to pile into the car on Sunday afternoons to make the rounds. Grodie hunting, we called it. Around dusk we'd return, unload, and spend the evening admiring our treasures.

Some of these items fit into the decor immediately and became part of the landscape, such as the vase that seemed to have been created for one corner of our living room. Many of the items, however, lose much of their glitter by the time we get them home. We struggle to make them fit in somewhere. Sometimes we're successful.

Often, however, the items go to the garage for later discernment. We look at them a few times over the course of the summer, a last effort to make the grodies work in the yard or on the porch. Finally, in the spring we drag them out and line them up on the driveway. Then we put out a yard sale sign and wait for customers. Sometimes I eavesdrop as potential customers examine the merchandise.

"Wouldn't this work on the front porch?" she'll ask.

"Maybe with a flowerpot on either side," he'll say, scratching his head. "Hey, it's only a dollar."

Moving Pianos

A friend from another state was visiting recently and went into shock at the high cost of automobile licenses in Indiana. I quickly pointed out that as bad as it may be today, it was worse up till last year, when the government greatly reduced license fees.

Besides, I said, we don't have personal-property taxes. He nodded and agreed that personal-property taxes in his state remained contentious. I used to live there, so I know what he means. As a matter of fact, one particularly troublesome property-tax issue remains unresolved years after the fact.

Every two years in the farm community where I lived over thirty years ago, the county assessor would bring his clipboard to every house in the area and count possessions—particularly luxury items, such as pianos and antiques—that were highly taxable.

Everyone in the community agreed the tax was inequitable and stupid. Even the assessor admittedly didn't look too hard to find things hidden behind a curtain or temporarily moved to the barn for repair.

Two brothers owning separate farms in the area, however, presented the assessor with an irresistible challenge. It seems the brothers' grandmother had considerable wealth, including two antique grand pianos reputed to be worth several hundred thousand dollars each.

When the grandmother died, the boys inherited the pianos. When the assessor heard the news, he gathered up his clipboard and went to see the brothers. As it turned out, the pianos hadn't been shipped from the old woman's home in Michigan yet. The assessor allowed that he couldn't accurately assess the value of these fine instruments without seeing them, and he told the brothers to let him know the minute they arrived.

When the assessor left, the brothers went into a huddle. They hadn't thought about having to pay property taxes every two years on their inheritance. They kicked themselves for bragging at the local feed store about their good fortune. They particularly regretted telling everyone how valuable the pianos were.

Of course, as long as the pianos hadn't been delivered, they were safe. That's when they figured out their strategy. When the pianos arrived, the brothers built wooden platforms for each piano to sit on. Then they attached heavy rollers on the bottoms, making the platforms movable. They moved the pianos into their parlors and proceeded to enjoy their inheritance for a full year and eleven months.

The plan was simple. When it was time for the assessor to pay his next visit with his clipboard, the brothers would hook a large farm wagon behind a tractor, put a loading ramp in place, and roll the first piano onto the wagon. Then they would drive to the other brother's house and load the second piano.

Since the county assessor was nothing if not organized, he unwittingly cooperated with the brothers' conspiracy by announcing ahead of time the date and hour he would be at each brother's house. The piano wagon would be at the other brother's home while the assessor was on the premises.

He always asked about the pianos, of course, and was always told they hadn't been shipped down from Michigan yet. The assessor never questioned this in spite of having personally attended several Fourth of July parties at both brothers' homes where the central focus had been musical entertainment emanating from a piano on a raised platform.

The boys' plan was beautiful and probably could have worked flawlessly into the next millennium had it not been for a young sheriff's deputy by the name of Hansen. Deputy Hansen was new to the job and eager to prove his mettle. It was with this attitude he was driving the road between the two brothers' farms when he met one of the brothers driving a tractor pulling a loaded wagon.

As the wagon passed, Deputy Hansen noticed what looked like a piano leg under the tarpaulin covering the wagon. He decided to take a look. He turned on his flashing red light, got out of his car, and walked over to the wagon. He pulled back the canvas and revealed not just one piano, but two. The deputy shook his head woefully, which made the brother on the tractor nervous. "What is the problem?" he wanted to know.

The problem, Deputy Hansen pointed out with some pride since he had just covered this on his final exams at deputy training, was that unlicensed farm vehicles were restricted to hauling farm materials. If they were used for any other purpose, such vehicles had to have commercial license plates. Unless the brother could convince the deputy that the two pianos were in fact rare fertilizer spreaders, the load would have to taken into custody until fines were paid and licenses were bought.

The brother watched helplessly as the wagonload of pianos was towed away for safekeeping in the county highway department garage. For several days the brothers whispered between themselves and shook their heads. To pay the fine and the license fees would involve admitting that their grandmother's pianos had finally arrived from Michigan. The resulting property taxes would be an unbearable burden. The brothers decided to do nothing.

For the next several years, the farm wagon sat covered with a tarp in the garage. But every summer on the Fourth of July the tarps were removed, the doors were opened, and the entire town was invited to a special holiday celebration featuring spirited musical selections played on twin grand pianos.

Blowtorches and Cows

I was listening to Garrison Keillor talk about the Chatterbox Cafe the other day. He allowed as how in the wintertime the Chatterbox became the heartbeat of Lake Wobegon, the place where the soul of the community whiled away the harsh winter days, nurturing itself from within.

People would come to the cafe with no special purpose, he said. Rather, they would come and sit at a table, drink coffee, and sooner or later, purpose would come to them. Maybe someone would tell a story, and that would remind someone else of another story, and that, in turn, might remind someone else of a story he could tell.

A community is made up of stories, Keillor said. And telling one at the Chatterbox Cafe was an important form of community service, especially in the wintertime.

Having lived a few years in rural Minnesota, I suspect that Garrison Keillor speaks the truth. In the community where I lived at the time, the local cafe was called Edna's. But everyone referred to it as the New York Times. It was where people went to get the news.

The area was largely a farming community, a fertile contributor to the Valley of the Jolly Green Giant. And when the harvest was over and the ground was frozen solid, there was precious little to do but gather at Edna's and tell stories.

And if it is true that telling stories contributes to the community, there is little doubt that Lars Johnson, a local farmer, would be considered a living philanthropist. We heard Lars' story one morning when he came limping into Edna's with his face bruised and his arm in a cast.

It seems the night before had been particularly cold, and his twenty young beef cattle had huddled tightly together in one corner of the shelter to keep warm. As they relieved themselves during the night, the liquid froze around their hooves, freezing them solidly to the ground.

"By morning not a damned one of them could move an inch," Lars moaned. "It posed a real dilemma. I couldn't figure how to get 'em loose."

"I suppose you could have left them 'til spring thaw," a neighbor chortled.

"At least you'd know exactly where they were," another added with a snort. Laughter swept the tables like a warm breeze.

"Well," the perplexed farmer continued, "I thought about that. Trouble was, the only way to get to the feed trough was to walk across their backs. Keeping your balance on the backs of twenty cows while carrying buckets of feed seemed a little precarious.

"Besides," he continued, "they weren't all facing the feed trough. And only about three of them could get to the water. Nope, we just had to break them loose."

By this time every table in the cafe was filled. The distraught man's neighbors all sat there, quietly reflecting on his situation, waiting for him to continue.

"I first thought about pouring hot water over them," Lars mused thoughtfully. "But at thirty below, I realized they'd just get wet and freeze.

"That's when I remembered the blowtorch," he said. For several moments after that he just sat quietly, sort of rocking back and forth as though recalling some tragic event.

"I've made some mistakes in my life," Lars said at last, "but I have to admit this idea was particularly ill-conceived."

Apparently Lars had lit the blowtorch and had crawled on his hands and knees underneath the animals when he realized the whole idea was flawed. This had to do with the nature of cows. It seems that if you're a cow and somebody builds a fire under your belly, you just naturally tend to get a little nervous.

Near as Lars could figure out, he had started melting the ice around one set of hooves when their owner, sensing that something was amiss, shuddered, bellowed, and gave a mighty lunge, breaking loose from the ice. Of course this startled poor Lars, who sat bolt upright under the next cow in line, his blowtorch pointed straight up toward the animal's underbelly.

Needless to say, this cow didn't have much trouble breaking loose from the ice either. In seconds, all the cows were lunging against their captivity, and Lars was scrambling around underneath trying to escape while inadvertently assaulting first one and then another with the blowtorch.

"Apparently, all but three broke loose in the next thirty seconds," Lars said painfully. "Then things went black."

Lars' wife found him when he didn't come in for breakfast. He had a broken arm and bruises on his chest and face, and he had set his own pants on fire with the blowtorch, inflicting second-degree burns to delicate parts of his anatomy.

She later freed the remaining cows with a bucket of salt. And the next week Lars sold all the animals to a beef producer in the next county, vowing to concentrate on growing sweet corn from then on.

Lawn Mower Racing

There was an article in the paper the other day about lawn mower racing. I didn't know they still did that.

And I never realized it went beyond the small community in Minnesota where I lived before I got tired of winter and headed south. Obviously, I didn't move quite far enough south.

Not only did lawn mower racing spread, but apparently it also went into hyperdrive. The mowers these guys are riding top out at speeds in excess of 65 mph. No one in our neighborhood ever got more than 35 mph out of his souped-up Sears 8 hp Lawn and Garden Master.

I know what you're thinking: why would anyone race lawn mowers in the first place? I can't testify to the new generation of mower racers, but in our subarctic village in central Minnesota there is a phenomenon called "winter-most-dreary." This is the part of winter that comes after the early part of the season, you know, the part when snow is pretty and fun, has passed and what's left is like the frozen salt mines of Siberia.

By this time the guys are sick and tired of repairing their snowmobiles—you never ride snowmobiles; you just endlessly repair them—and they haven't yet recovered from the latest round of polka parties. At this point they are desperate for some new pursuit that will keep them from going berserk, ripping out the walls, and converting the house into a paintball course as the latest blizzard roars across the tundra outside.

The answer: soup up the lawn mower. The idea would come to virtually every man in the community at precisely the same moment.

"You know what, dear," each would say, getting up from his chair in front of the television and wading through knee-deep beer cans, "I think I'll get a jump on spring and tune up the lawn mower."

Out in the garage, serious alchemy ensued. There were kits you could buy at the motorcycle and hotrod shops that turned docile 8 hp Briggs & Stratton engines into fire-breathing torqued-up monsters. And every guy had his own formula for tuning the engine and mixing the gas with a variety of highly volatile chemicals guaranteed to leave a fifty-foot scorched path in his wake.

After the initial rebuilding phase, everybody proceeded to the testing phase. Up and down the street guys would rev up their engines and make short test runs up and down their driveways. And, naturally, everyone popped wheelies. It was not uncommon to drive down the street and see four or five mowers rearing up and growling like angry pit bulls.

By the time the snow finally melted, sometime between Memorial Day and the Fourth of July—I'm kidding; the snow was almost always gone by Memorial Day—all the guys would drive their impatient steeds over to the small industrial park that bordered our neighborhood. There was no organized race schedule. If it was Saturday, you just showed up, ready to strut your stuff.

Some of the guys used to get to the track late because they had to mow their lawns before they could drop the mower deck and use the machine for the serious purpose for which it was built. Actually, it was pretty exciting to watch the lawn mowing process, too. At 30 mph it was possible to cut a two-acre lawn in just under fifteen minutes and throw grass clippings a quarter mile down the road.

On the track, great expectations often dissolved into a blown head gasket or a fouled carburetor. Usually about half the mowers stalled somewhere in the middle of the circular race course, which wound around two auto parts warehouses. And just as often, the winner was having so much fun that he kept on running long after the race was over. Only the enticement of cold beer and ham sandwiches eventually lured him off the track.

There were no trophies or prize money for these races, just the satisfaction that you'd found yet another way to waste money and have a good time doing it. After the race, everybody limped back to his garage and spent the ensuing week rebuilding, repairing, and re-strategizing for the following Saturday.

I never raced my mower, at least not officially. And my lawn mower today is a quiet and sedate Snapper rear-engine job that doesn't even have a removable mower deck. It does a wonderful job of cutting grass, and that's all.

Still, it does have a five-speed transmission, and sometimes when I look down a long stretch of lawn, I can't resist revving up the engine to full bore, snapping it into high gear, and popping the clutch.

Farm Sculpture

The most stubborn people on the planet may be Minnesota farmers. They also may be the greatest gamblers.

I was reminded of this the other day while driving through farm country here in central Indiana. Out in the middle of a cornfield, harvested and cleared except for three rows of corn, stood a combine. Its wheels were buried to the axles in mud.

The reason this reminded me of Minnesota was because this is pretty common fare along Minnesota's farm roads. Take a drive through the snowy winter landscape in Minnesota's farm region and you will inevitably come across the occasional combine sitting in a partially harvested field, cold and quiet, drifted over with snow.

Why this happens has to do with the nature of corn and, of course, the nature of Minnesota weather. When corn ripens in the summer, the ears are heavy with moisture. This is good because moisture makes the ears big and plump, which makes the farmer the envy of his neighbors. It is bad because moisture-laden corn will rot, which makes the farmer the laughingstock of his neighbors.

The good news is that after the corn reaches maturity, the leaves wither and die back and the ears begin to dry naturally. Leave a field of corn standing long enough and it will dry completely so it can sit in bins throughout the winter without rotting. Hooray!

A pretty easy plan, really. After the corn ripens and the leaves die back, all you have to do is wait until it is dry enough, and then crank up the combine and harvest it. Simple, no? Unfortunately, that doesn't take into account Minnesota's weather, which at its best can be perverse.

This is why virtually every Minnesota corn farmer has a doodad called a batch dryer. It's sort of like a clothes dryer. You dump in moisture-laden corn, turn it on, and a combination of heat and circulating air dries it out. For years, farmers almost always harvested their corn when the weather was good and then used their batch dryers to remove the moisture.

Then came the energy crunch of the 1970s, and the cost of operating a batch dryer tripled overnight. Lamentably, this happened at the same time the price of grain plummeted. The reason was political: the United States refused to sell grain to the Soviet Union and they, in turn, refused to sell us oil, with the result that we had a shortage of fuel and glut of unsold grain at the same time.

This was when Minnesota farmers started playing Russian roulette with the weather and their corn crops. Around the first of November you'd see the farmers walking along their fields, testing an ear here, an ear there, shaking their heads and muttering to themselves. Later at the coffee shop you'd hear them talking.

"My guess is the weather's gonna hold for at least another week to ten days," says one, sipping his coffee thoughtfully.

"Yep," says another. "That'll give you another couple points. You probably won't have to dry at all."

"Hell, Lars," offers a third, "you could probably sell your batch dryer no more than you use it these days."

"Then you could put the money into a snowplow and hook it to the front of your combine," someone else chuckles. "Or maybe a tow truck." Everybody laughs, even Lars, who peeks out the window to assure that the weather is still holding.

A lot of corn farmers got into the habit of waiting out the weather back then, and they just continued the practice. Inevitably, there comes a time when their luck runs out and they are forced to abandon their combines until spring. Mostly they don't like to admit it, however, and likely insist it was all part of their overall farm plan.

"I figure fuel prices will be down by spring and it won't cost as much to drive it out of there," says one with a straight face.

"You know," another muses, "I've always had a problem with drifting snow at that spot. Had to work all winter to clear the road beyond. I figure the combine will make a perfect windbreak." Everybody nods and tries not to laugh.

Throughout the winter the farmers gather at the coffee shop and joke about the odd pieces of "field sculpture" in nearby fields. About the first of March, however, interest wanes, and they start speculating on whose tractor will get stuck in the mud come spring when they try to pull their combines out.

And who said farming wasn't a serious business?

Winter Storms Didn't Bother Stepin Fetchit

Winter storms worry me. I don't get terrified or go screaming into the night when snow is forecast, but I fret and stew in the same way my old dog Moosey used to when we'd run the vacuum cleaner.

Whenever my wife or I would pull out the Hoover, old Moosey would open her eyes with a start and stiffen as if she'd just been threatened with a bath. Then she would lie there with a glazed look while the vacuum was running. She never took her eyes off the machine, and she never relaxed until it was turned off and put away. Then she'd close her eyes, utter a deep whimpering sigh, and go back to sleep.

That's how I feel about winter storms. I guess I came by this concern honestly. When I was in the first grade, we spent the winter in a one-room log cabin owned by the US Forest Service. The cabin was deep in the woods, and when we got snowed in for several days, we had to rely on Dad's hunting skills to eat. At first I thought it was pretty cool, all that snow to play in. Then I got hungry, and the seeds of fear sprouted deep inside as we waited till dark for Dad to come back with a snowshoe rabbit for dinner. All that night in my sleep I kept wondering what would have happened if Dad hadn't gotten the rabbit.

I don't worry about going hungry anymore, but when I go the store and find the shelves swept clean on the eve of an impending storm, I get a sudden urge to buy big boxes of cookies and lots of milk—sort of a childhood flashback, I suppose.

Although we lived for several more years in Wisconsin and had lots of snow and even a storm or two, mostly it was time spent building snowmen, snowshoeing in the woods, and sledding pell-mell down Suicide Hill behind the grade school. My mother worried about winter, too, but mostly she worried about Suicide Hill.

It wasn't until the winter of 1978 that my fear of winter storms blossomed into full-blown paranoia. That winter was bad everywhere, but it was especially vicious in the Valley of the Jolly Green Giant, where I lived on a farmstead fifteen miles from the nearest town.

It started with a blizzard on Thanksgiving Day. After that we never saw the ground until May. I had to plow the driveway at 5:00 a.m. each day in order to get my car out to go to work. Several times I also had to plow as much as a half mile of the county road as well. In the evening I sometimes had to park a mile away and slog through waist-deep drifts to the house to get the tractor and plow my way home for the night.

All the vehicles had block heaters, and we had to plug them in whenever they weren't being used in order to make sure they would start again when we needed them. The temperature got down to twenty-five below around Christmas and stayed there for forty-five days. The water pipes froze even with heat tapes and the faucets turned on. Frost formed on the inside walls of that century-old farmhouse, and we spent days huddled around a wood-burning stove wondering if we would survive. At night we slept fitfully beneath featherbeds, worrying about the storm knocking out the power lines.

When that cold cycle broke and the temperature soared to a balmy fifteen degrees one day, everyone in that farm community turned out to play softball in the snow. By then our brains had frozen, and any observer would have testified that we were completely nuts. Before the next winter hit, I had packed up and moved away, determined to live where they had never seen a snow shovel.

One of the most memorable winter storms came one January night in Sioux Falls, South Dakota. I was working for The Associated Press at the time, and for a week most of our top stories had been about the weather. Cattle were freezing in the Badlands, ranchers were trying to get horses into barns, and all along I-35 semi trucks were stalled, the fuel in their fuel tanks turned to jelly in the subzero temperatures.

Although it wasn't an assignment, I had decided to write a short feature story about an entertainer scheduled to appear that night in a small bar called the Pomp Room. I seldom took much interest in the entertainment in Sioux Falls, for the simple reason that most of the time there wasn't any. Oh, there were the usual local rock bands, and sometimes a small bluegrass group came in from Rapid City. But the headliner at the Pomp Room that blustery winter night was an old black movie actor by the name of Stepin Fetchit.

I could hardly believe my eyes when I saw the tired old ad in the local newspaper. Stepin Fetchit had been a co-star with Shirley Temple in several of her movies and a regular on *The Little Rascals* along with Buckwheat, Spanky, and the silly dog with the ring around his eye. I had seen him dozens of times in these films, playing the role of Lightning, a slow-moving, slow-talking "Gentleman of Color." But instead of going on to bigger things in a modern world, he had packed up his world as it had been in the twenties and thirties and taken it on the road, doing one-night stands in small-town pubs for subsistence-level paychecks.

The day Stepin Fetchit was to arrive, it began snowing around mid-morning. By noon you couldn't see the streets, and cars slogged along at a snail-like pace, sliding and slipping in the mounting snow. By evening the plows were out in full force, and it continued to snow. About an hour before showtime, I eased into the Pomp Room to make sure I got a good seat. The regulars were all there, of course, but then they'd be there even if the jukebox was broken. And there were a handful of special customers, many of them black, sitting at tables in front of the small, dark stage. Stepin Fetchit was nowhere to be seen. The manager of the Pomp Room was plainly nervous; the storm promised to be a bad one.

About five minutes before showtime, a tall, incredibly thin man pushed his way through the front door carrying a battered briefcase and a broken umbrella. He had a stocking cap on his head, and a pair of glasses—broken and repaired with adhesive tape—rode down on his nose. Snow clung to the bottoms of his trousers, and he wore a pair of thin-soled street shoes caked with snow.

"Where's th' stage?" he wheezed softly. "Ah'm Stepin Fetchit." The manager jerked his thumb toward the rear of the bar. "Mah car got stuck," he drawled, taking off his stocking cap and wiping his face with it. "Ah had to hike the las' couple miles. Y'all came to see mah show," he continued, opening his briefcase and taking out a faded pair of white gloves and a collapsible top hat. "Jes' give me a couple minutes here, and y'all gonna see a show."

Three minutes later he clicked on the microphone and began a two-hour stand-up routine that came partly out of his childhood in rural Mississippi, partly out of his glory days in the movies, and partly from the emerging Civil Rights movement. It was both funny and moving with pathos. He did a race reconciliation bit with a white glove and a black glove. It was startling and ahead of its time.

He did several bits from his Shirley Temple movies, tired and covered with the dust of forgotten time, lost in the past. He talked about being a star and going back to his home neighborhood in Mississippi. "I visited one family," he said, "so poor they only had five pork chops to feed seven people. Course, I enjoyed the three I had." Sometimes he was fresh and funny.

Throughout the show, people wandered in, and after about an hour the place was packed. For the first time the manager, who obviously had to pay the talent whether anyone showed up or not, smiled.

After the show, several of us volunteered to help him dig out his car. We found it—a twelve-year-old pink Cadillac convertible—three miles from town, half buried in the snow. After we pushed him out of the snowdrift, he waved his thanks through the open window and skidded the rest of the way into town. At the good hotel they told him there were no vacancies. He spent the night in the other hotel, down by the penitentiary, where a lot of Indian women stayed when they came in from the reservation to visit their sons and husbands at the prison. Most of them, of course, had never heard of Stepin Fetchit, but they probably would have identified with the lonely way he lived.

It was nearly midnight and still snowing when I got back to the AP office. I wrote my story and went out to the parking lot to dig out my own car. The next morning the storm was worse, and I seriously considered staying home. Then I remembered the night before, when a man walked three miles in a blizzard to put on a show for a handful of customers in a small-town bar. I went to work. I got stuck a block from the office and had to walk. It didn't bother me.

I Thought I Hated Winter

For the longest time I've thought I really hated winter. How many times have I sat shivering in my car, waiting for the heater to kick in and the ice on the windshield to melt?

What about all the times I've slogged across the parking lot through ankle-deep slush and spent the next two hours trying to thaw out my feet and calm my chattering teeth?

Sure, I've got overshoes—somewhere. The same goes for gloves and mufflers. Somewhere in the hall closet are all those things that would protect me against the ravages of winter. The problem is I have lived my entire adult life in total denial about the concept of winter. It was, I knew, a horrific lie, a conspiracy matching the Great Communist Threat of the 1950s or the sinister warblings of The World Is Flat Society, which squared off against Christopher Columbus more than five hundred years ago.

For years I refused to wear a hat. The Conspiracy of Winter would get no concessions from me. Then I moved to Minnesota, where January temperatures can dip to fifty below. Frostbite, I learned, is no laughing matter. Ears are particularly sensitive. I not only put on a hat but also pulled a stocking cap down over my ears, wrapped a heavy scarf around my head, and pulled taut the drawstring on the hood of a quilted parka. With sweatshirts and heavy sweaters under the parka, I looked like a Manchurian border guard, an upholstered hand grenade.

I bought heavy wool socks—the kind with the red ring at the top—and a pair of insulated leather boots. The literature that came with the boots guaranteed waterproof warmth in eighty-below temperatures. I've often wondered how many people there are who would willingly go where it can get that cold. Unless the world is totally insane, this boot company should sell no more than two pairs of these boots every ten years.

Then, one February day, I was standing on the frozen shore of Lake Calhoun in downtown Minneapolis, watching a bunch of dogsled mushers trying vainly to get their dogs to come out from the protective warmth of their burrows in the drifted snow.

It was something of an epiphany. It was thirty below, and the dogs were smart enough to know it was too damned cold to be galloping across the permafrost. Days later, I packed my belongings into my car, strapped a snow shovel across the hood, and headed south. I figured I'd keep driving until someone asked me what the contraption on my hood was. There I'd settle.

I made it as far as Indianapolis. Here, I was assured, winter was more a whisper than a shout. And often one could mow the lawn as late as Thanksgiving, rake leaves into December, and sometimes spend Christmas in shirtsleeves barbecuing in the backyard. That was more like it. And, with a few exceptions over the past fifteen years, the assurances have proved valid.

Then came Christmas 1995. Snow pelted down in arctic fury and by Christmas Eve it was wing deep to a tall penguin. I looked in vain for my long-neglected snow shovel and had to spend several coffee breaks trying to remember how to shovel snow from the sidewalk.

Christmas morning we dug out one of the cars and headed across town to a daughter's house where most of my wife's considerable family would gather around a well-stocked dinner table and an equally endowed Christmas tree. As we pulled into the driveway, I saw them—sleds. There were four or five of them poised at the crest of the steep hill in the backyard. And there were grandchildren waiting as I emerged from the car.

"Hey, Grandpa, c'mon and ride the sled," one yelled, and they all joined the chorus.

"Not me," I shot back. "Looks like fun, though," I added, wistfully pausing at the top of the hill. A steady line of kids trudged up the hill, dragging their sleds. At the top, one after the other, they plopped onto the sleds and launched themselves toward the white abyss below.

"C'mon, Grandpa. Try it," something with a pink face urged, pushing a sled into my hands.

"Well, maybe just once," I agreed. They say a drowning man's entire life flashes before him. The same is true for an old poop who rockets down a snowy hill after five decades of assorted stodginess. Suddenly I was nine years old again and committing my trusted Flexible Flyer to another shot down Suicide Hill.

Suicide Hill was a quarter-mile section of street in the city park of Hayward, Wisconsin. The Park Department's garage and supply building was at the bottom. The street served no other purpose, and in the winter it was never used. The Park Department closed it off for sledding when it snowed.

There was a bump halfway down Suicide Hill, and when the packed snow was really glassed up, you could hit it at warp speed and literally go airborne for several seconds. The trick, of course, was to stay in the saddle once you returned to earth. This was not always easy, and sometimes even veterans of fifty or more downhill missions would lose it, fly through space, and skin up their faces in the snow. The other obstacle, of course, was the garage at the bottom of the hill. Once you survived the trip down, you had to twist sideways and skid to a stop before hitting the building. More than one miscalculating daredevil limped home those days with a goose egg on his noggin.

Back to Christmas present. At the bottom of the hill I stood up in wonder. I'd made it all the way down. Not bad, I thought, as I trudged back to the top. Then I went back down again. Yahoo!

"My turn, Grandpa," a young voice complained.

"Not yet it isn't," I said. "It's still my turn. Besides," I added, launching off the hilltop again, "I've got a lot of catching up to do."

Today, of course, my butt aches and my face is chapped. But I finally realize I never really hated winter. I had just stopped having fun.

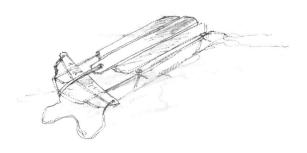

Considering the Horse

Consider the lowly horse, or more precisely, a horse's beam as viewed from behind. I was surprised to learn that the width of a horse's patootie is a universal standard unit of measure. Moreover, it dates back some two thousand years and has dictated just about every step of progress since, including our space program.

Here's the way it works. Start with the standard railroad track gauge in the United States, a precise four feet eight and a half inches from track to track. That's the measurement used because that's what they used in jolly old England. And, of course, American railroads were built by English expatriates who came over here to vacation in the New World, lost all of their tea things in transit, and decided to do something constructive while waiting for them to show up.

It seems that when the English started building their own railroads, they just used the same track width they had used previously with their horse-drawn trams. And everyone knows the trams were built to the same specifications applied to earlier wagons.

The wagon makers had no choice, it seems, because four feet eight and a half inches was the width between wagon wheel ruts in all English roads. Any other width would have resulted in broken wheels. Of course, these roads, along with most of the long-distance roads across Europe, were originally built by Imperial Rome in the days of the Caesars and their mighty legions.

Apparently, those old Romans were pretty good road builders because their roads continued to be used even after Nero burned the place down to his own musical accompaniment. Most of them, it seems, were built of stone paving blocks.

The ruts in those ancient roads were made by Roman war chariots. Anyone who has seen Ben Hur, of course, knows that those chariots were built exactly wide enough to accommodate the rear end of two horses. That way, any passageway the horses could get through, the chariot could follow. This was important, I'm told, for running down enemies in their chariots, or running away if the enemy was bigger and meaner.

Now, as to our space program. The next time you see one of the space shuttles sitting on the launch pad at Cape Canaveral, take a close look at the two solid rocket boosters strapped to the sides of the shuttle.

These booster rockets are made by a company called Thiokol at its factory in Utah. Once finished, they have to be shipped to the launch site in Florida. The engineers developing the space shuttle program originally designed the booster rockets to be bigger and fatter than they are. They had to be slimmed down, however, because the rockets are shipped by rail and somewhere between Salt Lake City and Cocoa Beach, the train has to go through a tunnel in the mountains.

The railroad tunnel, as it happens, is only slightly wider than the railroad track, which, of course, is about the same width as two horse butts. So in the final analysis, specifications for the world's most advanced space technology were determined more than two thousand years ago by the width of a horse's fanny.

Lost Soybean Project

"I'm from the government, and I'm here to help." Probably no statement strikes greater fear into the hearts of men than these nine words. It is usually heard just before a bad situation gets worse and a difficult one becomes impossible.

Don't get me wrong; in many respects our government is the greatest in the world. Anyone who doubts this simply needs to pick up the morning paper and see what horrors have befallen other countries, big and small.

The goodness of our way of government comes from our Constitution, which was probably divinely inspired. The ills, on the other hand, spring from the interpretation of this august document by men who obviously are not.

Most often things go awry when the government decides to go into business, either to cement economic alliances or to wield political clout. History offers a full menu of both.

Years ago someone discovered that soybeans are an almost perfect food. Not only are they an incredible source of protein, but they also are flexible enough to be shaped into an imitation of many other foods—from hamburger to milk. Moreover, they will grow almost anywhere, and because they are legumes, they build up poor soil in the process. Soybeans, in short, can feed a starving world.

This revelation led a consortium of soybean growers in the United States to offer impoverished Latin American countries assistance in producing soybeans. For several years, the US farmers met with their Latin counterparts to work out the details. An elaborate, workable plan unfolded that would enable these blighted countries to stop hunger and build a prosperous agricultural economy.

Then our government stepped in and announced it would take over and work out the final details. And it did, but not with the farmers. Instead, our bureaucrats set out to strike deals with the heads of state of these Latin countries. The reason: political influence. The result: soybean production in these countries became a bargaining chip with strings attached. In the end thousands remained hungry. The last I heard, these aging negotiations were still droning on with no end in sight.

In another case, tractors were reportedly sent to a Third World country to boost farm production while our government negotiated the sale of the gasoline to operate them with the country's military dictator. Unconfirmed reports indicated that the fuel was sold and the profits went into the dictator's personal bank account while the tractors sat idle.

Millions of dollars in aid intended for the Vietnamese people went instead to corrupt politicians in that beleaguered country during the Vietnam War. Other goof-ups in aid probably were simple but stupid administrative errors. People shook their heads when CARE packages of ping-pong balls and toothpaste reportedly showed up on the shores of starving countries.

Now our government is back in business, and this time the victim is the American farmer. The culprit is genetically engineered seeds that grow sterile crops. The process, which alters the genetic code of a plant so the second generation of seed won't germinate, was developed to prevent the unauthorized planting of seeds saved from the previous year's crop.

Originally, the idea was to control tobacco growing and keep farmers from illegally planting more tobacco plants than they were allocated. The concept has since taken a more sinister tone. The author again is government involvement far beyond what the framers of the Constitution had in mind. Here is what has happened.

In 1986 the government enacted the Federal Technology Transfer Act, a law that allows private corporations to fund government research. The resulting technology is then held jointly by the government and the sponsoring corporation. In other words, corporations can now use your tax dollars to fund research that will build profits for themselves.

In the matter of seed technology, according to *Small Farm Today* magazine and its publisher, Ron Macher, a corporation by the name of Delta and Pine Land Corp. entered into a deal with the USDA to develop the genetically altered seeds. The patent for this technology, called "terminator seeds," is jointly held by Delta and Pine and the USDA. The government has granted Delta and Pine the exclusive right to license the process to others.

The technology is already in place with tobacco and cotton, and major seed companies now are at work developing "terminator" seeds for soybeans, sorghum, wheat, and rice. These companies try to allay fears by pointing out that farmers will not be forced to buy terminator seeds. They will be able to continue the longstanding farm practice of saving seeds from each year's crop to plant the following year's crop. Currently, as much as 30 percent of our nation's soybean crops are planted with farmer-saved seeds. Most wheat farmers in the United States rely on farmer-saved seed and return to the seed market only every four or five years.

The problem with this, according to Macher, is that if a farmer plants terminator seeds, his fields might possibly pollinate his neighbor's nonterminator fields, rendering that crop sterile as well. Unfortunately, the unsuspecting neighbor won't know about it until he plants the following year and nothing comes up.

I say look on the bright side. If that happens and suddenly half our farmers go broke, within a short time a fleet of station wagons will show up at the farmers' front doors, and the drivers will step out and announce with a broad smile:

"I'm from the government, and I'm here to help."

Beware of Promises Too Good to Be True

It all started with the traveling medicine show, usually a truck pulling a trailer. It lumbered into the outskirts of town and set up at the edge of an open field, where there was plenty of parking (and a clean route out of town). Within a couple of hours handbills would show up in store windows and on the windshields of cars.

"Huge Medicine Show. See Amazing Cures. Guaranteed Results. Suffer No More!"

By evening a crowd began to gather. No one really believed Dr. Good's Amazing Snake Oil Elixir would do the things the handbills claimed, and everyone swore they were only going to see the acrobats. The handbill also promised an "Amazing Show of Acrobatic Skill by the Top Acrobats from Barnum & Bailey." There was also a snake charmer and a man who had been cured of the incurable when the finest doctors in the world had given up—cured, of course, by Dr. Good's Amazing Snake Oil Elixir.

No one believed the claims, not for a minute, not even about the acrobats. But they went anyway. And within minutes after the pearly words of Dr. Edgerton Good began wafting through the crowd like fog on a warm summer night, people found themselves nodding their heads a little, tapping their feet to the beat. "Maybe," they said. "Possibly. Well…it might be true."

Truth is most folks weren't thinking about their aches and pains at all when they lined up for Dr. Good's Medicine Show. But somewhere between the acrobat and the snake charmer, people began rubbing their shoulders, wincing from headaches, and favoring a weakened knee.

When Dr. Good offered a limited supply of his Amazing Snake Oil Elixir for the sacrificial price of only five dollars a bottle, people just naturally reached for their wallets.

By dawn the next day, the field at the edge of town was vacant once more. Dr. Good and his entourage were approaching the outskirts of some other town, handbills at the ready, and a hundred or more local residents were nursing a strange hangover and swearing they'd never be taken in again.

Of course they would be taken in again, probably by the next smooth-talking con artist to slither into town and make impossible promises. It's human nature, I think, to want to believe that a bottle of water, alcohol, and artificial flavoring can, indeed, cure baldness, cancer, and plantar warts. One hundred fifty years ago, tens of thousands of hopeful citizens sold everything they owned in the belief that they would strike it rich in the gold fields of the Yukon. When drought choked Oklahoma a half century ago, thousands of sharecroppers piled their belongings into worn-out trucks and set out to claim untold riches picking fruit and vegetables in the fertile valleys of California.

As far as I know, there aren't any medicine shows around anymore. Dr. Good works part-time at McDonald's, and the only snake charmer I know is studying reptiles at the university. Few patent medicines make it past Food and Drug Administration scrutiny these days, and those that do make claims so general as to quell the hopes of even the most ardent optimists.

Yet for those who want to believe in untold riches and amazing cures, there is junk mail. On any given day your mailbox may yield a booklet promising that you can "beat the seven biggest threats to your health after age fifty" or guaranteeing the opportunity of a lifetime by going into business for yourself.

With no minimum investment, no credit check, and little more than five hours' work a week, you can make $150,000 in your first year.

One I especially like promises that by sending out a simple one-page letter, I will receive a check for $500. Moreover, I am guaranteed to receive a check for $500 every time I mail this wonderful letter. All I need to start raking in this boundless wealth is to send in the coupon with $14.95 plus five dollars for shipping and handling. If I don't get a check for $500, the offer continues, I will get a full refund. Absolutely no risk.

I am told this offer captures hundreds of believers, who shell out $14.95 plus shipping and handling every day. So, too, do the mailers that promise you can get rich in the $120 billion laundry industry. Imagine that—there is money to be made in dirty socks after all. There are literally dozens of such offers in the mail every day. They all promise huge markets, gigantic profits, minimum effort, and absolutely no competition.

Do we believe it? You bet your bottle of Dr. Good's Amazing Snake Oil Elixir we do.

Cemetery of the Innocent—1995

I was in Cape Girardeau, Missouri, some time ago and a friend told me about a special cemetery. He thought I might be interested in seeing it.

While I've never visited Flanders Field—the national cemetery in Belgium immortalized in the poem about the World War I dead buried there—I can imagine what it must be like: endless rows of white crosses, flowers and grass blowing in the wind; a voiceless pathos that decries the tragedy of war.

It must be like this place just off the interstate highway at the southern edge of this Missouri river town. At Flanders Field, I suppose one might walk among the crosses speculating about those buried there, the young Americans whose lives were ended prematurely by a war of someone else's making.

This one might have been a mighty general had he lived. Another, a famous doctor. Yet another, a missionary ministering to the sick and dying. All had hopes, dreams, and futures that were instantly lost to a bullet or an exploding bomb.

I thought of this while walking among the crosses in Cape Girardeau. They stretched out across the field, more than ten thousand of them. Each was exactly like the others: four feet high, painted white, posted in a straight line. Some were decorated with wreaths. Others had vases of cut flowers at the base.

As I walked that solemn place, I thought about the future these dead might have had. One might have been a doctor; another, a scientist. One might have developed a cure for cancer, another might have become president of the United States or a justice of the Supreme Court. There might have been poets and teachers among them. Certainly there would have been husbands and wives, fathers and mothers, neighbors and friends.

At the front of the cemetery is a row of larger crosses bearing black ribbons. These crosses tell us how many have died. In 1973 they numbered

615,834. A year later, 763,476. The next year the number was 854,853, and the year after that it was 988,267. By 1977 the death toll had climbed to 1,079,430, and it has been over 1.5 million each year ever since.

All of this killing began in 1973, the year the Supreme Court decided, in *Roe v. Wade*, that it was okay for a woman to have an abortion. The count goes only through 1995, when the grand total of abortions reached 45 million—nearly eight times the number killed in the Nazi Holocaust.

The name of this place is on a sign in one corner: Cemetery of the Innocent. Its creator is a man named Drury of Cape Girardeau, well known for a chain of hotels bearing his name. I don't know where he got the idea, but the numbers stagger the imagination. Another sign proclaims that abortion kills 4,400 unborn children each day.

The quiet despair of the poem "In Flanders Fields" did little to stem the slaughter of war, and it is unlikely that Mr. Drury's sober testimony will stop the flow of death in America. Few listened when Mother Teresa lamented the selfishness of a nation that would kill its own children. And even the president of the United States has approved legislation that would allow fetal tissue from abortions to be used in research.

Yet I contend that it is impossible to walk among these crosses or even to drive by and catch a glimpse of them in the rearview mirror without hearing the voiceless cry of 45 million lost children.

Goodbye to Tavern on the Green

In case you missed it, New York City's fabled Tavern on the Green has shut its doors. A week from now most of the furnishings in the decades-old Central Park restaurant will go on the auction block to settle some $8 million in debts.

Baccarat and Waterford chandeliers and a host of other glitzy Old World accessories installed years ago by Warner LeRoy—whose family has leased the Tavern from the city since 1973—will be removed from the premises forever.

The restaurant has been a popular tourist attraction since 1934, when it was built on a sheepfold at the edge of Central Park's Sheep Meadow. In its heyday it served as many as seven hundred thousand meals a year and brought in more than $36 million in revenue.

Of the tens of thousands of patrons who gathered there over the years for lunch or dinner, I may be the only one with the distinction of having slept in the Tavern. That was twenty years ago.

At the time, I was working for an audiovisual production company documenting a team effort between Navistar (International Trucks) and Cummins Engine Co., Inc. The two had joined forces in a bold effort to set a new fuel economy standard for big-rig trucks. To prove the new engine's fuel efficiency, the companies did a cross-country run from California to New York.

Our film crew recorded every mile of the weeklong trip and then assembled a full-blown dog and pony show to present the results to Wall Street bankers and investors. The presentation was scheduled for high noon in the largest banquet room in the Tavern on the Green. My job was to go in the day before to set up the room for the big show.

I did say high noon in a room that had two floor-to-ceiling glass walls. It was beyond a doubt the worst possible place to show a daytime movie. When I saw the huge expanse of glass, I immediately called my boss and described the problem. Couldn't we reschedule the presentation for someplace else? One of the major hotels in Manhattan, for instance.

"Sorry," he said. Apparently, the client had eaten lunch at the Tavern once, loved it, and decided that was where he wanted to make the presentation. It was not negotiable.

I hung up the phone and wondered how on earth I was going to cover a hundred acres of glass to keep out the midday light.

The solution I hit on involved a shipping-supply company in New Jersey, a hardware store in Lower East Manhattan, and three taxicabs. I needed five giant rolls of corrugated packing material, a dozen rolls of duct tape, a tape measure, a utility knife with extra blades, and a twenty-foot stepladder. "No problem," said the manager at Ajax Shipping Supplies in New Jersey. They could deliver the corrugated cardboard no sooner than Friday afternoon. It was Tuesday, and the presentation was Wednesday.

"Hey, I don't own the truck," he said. "You want the order or not?"

"Sure," I said. "I'll arrange my own truck."

"Well, okay, but I close at six." It was 3:30 p.m.

The New York City Yellow Pages was slightly smaller than an average floor safe and listed an estimated ten thousand delivery companies. I called twenty companies before I realized same-day delivery was a concept that had not yet reached the Big Apple. Moreover, licensing is a very tightly controlled process in New York, and a company licensed to deliver in Queens was not necessarily licensed to deliver in Manhattan.

It was the same with all the other boroughs, and none of them wanted to drive to New Jersey. And the companies in New Jersey weren't sure they could find New York City. In desperation I called a cab company and explained the problem.

Two cabs hotfooted it over to the Jersey side of the river while a third headed for the hardware store. As luck would have it, the Tavern had a stepladder I could use. At least the cabdriver wouldn't have to figure out how to strap one on the top of his cab.

I don't remember what everything cost, but I do recall doling out one hundred dollars in tips to cranky cabdrivers. All three drivers left shaking their heads and thinking I was nuts.

With my supplies delivered to the sunshine room, I got to work. Slowly, I measured strips of cardboard and painstakingly cut and fitted them to the inside of enormous plates of glass, securing them with duct tape.

By eight o'clock in the evening, I was half done and decided to take a break for dinner. Eating in the Tavern itself was out of the question. I didn't have a reservation, and patrons were lined up four deep waiting for tables.

Besides, three hours of working with dirty cardboard had given me a grimy look that would rival any panhandler on the street.

I did the only thing I could do: I grabbed a cab and went to McDonald's, where I ordered a Big Mac, fries, and a shake and then took the cab back to Tavern on the Green. Now there were four cabdrivers in New York who thought I was nuts.

About ten o'clock the restaurant crew delivered the tables, chairs, the sound system, and some extra tables for our equipment that we would need for our lunch presentation the next day. At midnight all the glass was covered, and I had a roll and a half of corrugated material left over, plus two rolls of duct tape. An hour later someone from the restaurant came in to tell me they were closing and I would have to sign out with the security guard when I left.

I finished setting up shortly after 3:00 a.m. and set out to find the security guard so I could go back to my hotel for a few hours of sleep. If you've never been to the Tavern, you need to understand that it is a rambling assortment of dining rooms connected to a common kitchen and pantry area.

The guard was nowhere to be found, and—after a half hour of searching—I decided to simply sack out on the floor where I had been working. As I covered myself with a strip of leftover corrugated material and commandeered a bag of tablecloths for a pillow, it dawned on me that there probably were no cabs available at that hour in the park anyway. And I had been warned that walking in Central Park after dark was like sending out a written invitation to muggers who prowled around in the dark.

I slept—sort of—and was already up and thinking about breakfast when the cleanup crew for the restaurant arrived. They briefly poked their noses into my now darkened room, shook their heads, and left. One of them muttered something about out-of-towners being nuts. I looked around at the cardboard walls and had to agree.

The presentation went off without a hitch. While another member of our audiovisual team packed up the equipment, I stripped from the windows all the cardboard I had so painstakingly installed. We took the extra rolls of duct tape with us, but left the extra cardboard behind.

The Tavern may reopen later next year under new management after extensive remodeling, but it might not be called Tavern on the Green. Although the city owns the building, the LeRoy family lays claim to the name. A federal judge will decide the issue later this month.

I hope to visit New York again one day and maybe check out the restaurant. I would enjoy telling whoever was around, "I covered all these windows with cardboard once. Then I slept in that corner."

They would probably just shake their heads and think I was nuts.

This column ran January 10, 2010. On May 21, New York City Mayor Michael Bloomberg announced that, for now, Tavern on the Green would become a visitor's center with a snack bar.

Navy Destroyer

The other day I ran into someone who was in the navy with me. We weren't buddies. Actually, we didn't even know each other. We just served in the same squadron of Pacific Fleet destroyers.

Our home port was San Diego, but soon after I reported on board, the entire squadron sailed over to Japan for an eight-month Western Pacific cruise. On the trip over, we escorted the aircraft carrier USS *Ranger*. That was both good news and bad news.

The good news was that every day a selection of officers and enlisted men from all the escort ships got transferred to the *Ranger* to spend the day seeing how an aircraft carrier operated. And, of course, an equal number of men from the carrier spent the day riding the destroyers.

For the destroyer guys it was great. An aircraft carrier is more like an industrial city than a naval ship, and even in rough seas movement is barely perceptible. The food is great, and you can pop into the wardroom anytime day or night for something to eat. There were more than a thousand men on board the *Ranger* during our cruise. They included two admirals and a large contingent of other high-ranking officers. Bottom-of-the-ladder junior officers like me could spend days never even being noticed. I felt like Ensign Pulver in the play *Mr. Roberts*.

Meanwhile on the destroyers, the visitors from the carrier spent the day one on one with the captain or the executive officer getting a short but intensive course in anti-submarine warfare and high-speed carrier escorting.

This brings us to the bad news. When aircraft carriers launch airplanes, they turn into the wind and crank up as much speed as necessary to assure they have enough wind going over the deck to get the planes into the air before they reach the end of the flight deck. Somebody figured out that if a jet fighter needs one hundred fifty knots to fly and the catapult will provide the first one hundred, the additional fifty must come from wind across the deck. This means if the wind at sea is twenty knots, the carrier will put the pedal to the metal and plunge through the sea at thirty knots.

The destroyers, of course, have to keep up. That's what escorts do. When a destroyer careens through the ocean at thirty knots, it goes under more waves than it goes over. Is it a rough ride? Let's just say a bucking destroyer was the inspiration for the mechanical bull. We felt sorry for the carrier guys on board, very sorry.

In spite of the rough ride, the lack of air-conditioning, and the endless equipment failures, we all loved our ship. Ours was a World War II–vintage Fletcher-class destroyer built in 1943 and a decorated veteran of the Pacific. In 1944 a Kamikaze pilot flew his fighter into the bridge of the ship, killing the captain and nine other crew members. In spite of extensive damage, the ship managed to steam back to port for repairs. In three weeks she was back at sea. A row of painted battle ribbons on her new bridge testified to her heroic past.

During the eight months I was on board, we steamed up and down the Formosa Strait listening to radio transmissions by the Chinese just a few miles away. We had little black boxes installed on the ship, and special guys came aboard to operate them. Black boxes and the guys who operate them make me nervous. I think everybody was nervous during those patrols. We knew what our orders were if we were confronted by Chinese vessels.

After eight months we returned to San Diego, and I packed up my family for another assignment in another part of the world. I never thought much about the ship after that. Now, sitting and talking with someone who was there brought back the memories. We laughed about the poor sick carrier guys trying to survive a day of destroyer duty. We smiled when we talked about liberty in Hong Kong. We didn't say much about the black boxes. We just nodded quickly and moved on to another subject.

He stayed with his ship for another six months after I left. He said that a year later all the old destroyers in the squadron were decommissioned. They brought in cranes and took the guns off. Then for a long time they sat in deathly silence in the mothball fleet at the far end of San Diego Naval Base. The last time he was back in San Diego they were gone. He heard they'd been cut up for scrap.

Sometime after writing this column I learned that my old ship was hauled out to sea and used for target practice by navy fighter planes. A witness said she stubbornly remained afloat for several hours while taking wave after wave of rocket and machine gun fire. Then, without fanfare, she filled with water and slipped silently beneath the surface to the hero's grave she had so valiantly earned.

Patrolling in Taiwan

In the early summer of 1962, I was in the navy serving as a communications officer aboard a World War II–vintage destroyer in the Western Pacific. Our job during deployment was to cruise up and down the Formosa Strait, a few miles off the coast of China, and monitor Chinese radio transmissions.

To help us do our job, we had a special "black box" installed aboard the ship and a couple of "ditty boppers"—special-assignment communications specialists—assigned to ride with us and monitor the black box. These guys never smiled, seldom spoke, and never socialized with the rest of the wardroom officers.

There were four ships in our squadron and two squadrons on patrol. Every ship had black boxes and ditty boppers on board.

Operating and navigating the ship, however, was the responsibility of the ship's crew. Navigation was especially important because in 1962 the Chinese were, by and large, an unfriendly group, and while we were monitoring them, they were monitoring us. And they had a fleet of heavily armed patrol boats at the ready in case we strayed into territorial waters. For that reason, accurate navigation was critical.

The ships in our squadron, fortunately, had highly qualified navigators on board who had received special training for navigating the Chinese coast before we left our home port of San Diego. The other squadron's navigators didn't all receive the special training and had to rely on general navigation skills along with radar images of the coast.

Navigators on board navy vessels are usually enlisted quartermasters. They are highly intelligent and heavily trained in the physics of celestial navigation and the trigonometry of coastal navigation.

It worked this way in the Formosa Strait. Every fifteen minutes someone in the combat information center of the ship would look at the radar screen and mark the ship's position on a chart. Once during each four-hour watch, the quartermaster would take a celestial reading of three or four stars using a sextant.

The accuracy of celestial navigation depends on the stars that are visible and their positions in the sky. The closer to the horizon they are, the more accurate the positioning. The best positions are usually determined just before sunrise and right after sunset; middle-of-the-night stars tend to be unreliable. These are some of the concepts our quartermasters learned in the special training they received before we left for the Orient.

We had just come off patrol and were looking forward to some R & R in the Taiwanese city of Kaoshiung when we got an emergency message that one of the ships from the other squadron had run aground off the Chinese coast.

What happened was this: because their quartermaster had not received the special coastal training, he relied almost entirely on radar positioning. Unfortunately, along that part of the coast is a range of mountains ten miles inland that closely follows the contour of the coastline. Yep, the quartermaster read the mountains as being the coastline and the ship wandered ten miles into shallow water and grounded on the reef.

Immediately, all ships from both squadrons were deployed to the grounding site, along with several fleet tugs. Fortunately, the US Navy was able to pull the disabled vessel off the reef and back into international waters before the Chinese were able to respond. Whew! Unfortunately, that ship's captain retired from service right after a lengthy and undoubtedly painful inquiry. The rest of us redoubled our vigilance, and all quartermasters were enrolled in special Chinese coastal training after that.

This scenario couldn't happen today, largely because of the lifelong efforts of a man named Ivan A. Getting. Dr. Getting died recently after a lifetime of scientific military achievement. The pinnacle of his success is the Global Positioning System (GPS)—a system implemented only after more than thirty years of developing and combining satellite and timekeeping technology, along with fierce battles with both the Pentagon and Congress.

Today, a network of twenty-four satellites with atomic clocks accurate to one-billionth of a second (that's one second every million years) sends signals back to earth, where GPS receivers translate the signals into positions accurate within one hundred feet.

This means that ships at sea, aircraft in the air, and cars on the road can now determine exactly where they are and precisely how to get where they want to go. In a car it is as simple as finding the closest Italian restaurant or gas station; for an airplane with engine trouble, the closest airport; and for a guy like me, who sails small boats in deep water, the ability to set a course to a harbor entrance when it is socked in by fog.

For navy ships, it means no more running aground. And their quartermasters can trade their bulky sextants for GPS receivers that they can slip into their shirt pockets.

Well done, Dr. Getting. The world is a better place because of your efforts.

Dr. Ivan A. Getting died November 11, 2003; this column was written the following January.

Ditty Boppers at Kunia

I was making a copy of an audiocassette the other day, and it reminded me of my small role in Project Mercury—America's early program of manned space flights.

My cassette player/recorder makes copies of tapes at twice normal speed. They call the process High Speed Dubbing, and when you're recording, the tape you're copying squeals across the speakers in what sound technicians call Mickey Mousing. The tape being copied was a person talking. At high speed it sounded like Alvin the Chipmunk reading the Declaration of Independence.

At the time the Mercury flights were holding the world spellbound during the 1960s, I was in the US Navy assigned to Fourteenth Naval District headquarters in Pearl Harbor. One of my dubious assignments was as a member of the Project Mercury Tracking Task Force.

The Task Force was made up of a hundred or more officers and enlisted men from all branches of the military, including the US Coast Guard. Whenever one of the Mercury missions blasted off from Cape Canaveral, members of the Task Force packed their bags, kissed their wives and kids goodbye, and headed for a place called Kunia—an underground command post hidden beneath the ubiquitous sugarcane fields a few miles from CinPac Headquarters on Oahu. Once inside its highly secured confines, no one left until splashdown and the mission was complete.

Kunia probably originated during the worrisome early days of World War II when we really thought the Japanese might indeed invade Hawaii. Once it was established, of course, nobody was willing to shut it down—even though it wasn't needed. To emphasize the point, budgets for manning and equipping the place must have grown exponentially. By the time I first saw the place, it had state-of-the-art everything.

There was a command center with banks of the newest gee-whiz communications equipment that theoretically could communicate with anyone anywhere in the universe. There was a dining hall that served up three meals a day and round-the-clock snacks, a recreation area, and comfortable living quarters. A mission at Kunia was not a mission of deprivation—except for daylight. Whenever we had a power failure, we were plunged into absolute blackness.

I was never quite sure what our mission was during the Mercury flights. In spite of our latest-word technology and bee's-knees state of readiness, we were unable to do anything. When I was there, it was used mainly for training exercises. We could not communicate by radio with the space capsule, with Houston, or, apparently, with anyone else including Pearl Harbor. It seems the only link we actually had with the outside world was the telephone. We did, however, receive tracking reports from the space capsule during the periodic intervals when it was flying directly over Hawaii—in high-speed Morse code.

Originally, I was assigned to the Task Force because I had been trained as a cryptographic officer. I suppose that meant if anything happened to the mission and someone thought it was important to tell us about it in code, I could decode it. Presumably, I would then get on the phone and tell the rest of the world.

My real job, however, was to produce a news report every time the capsule roared by. Among other niceties, Kunia had a fully equipped and manned television studio. My task was to take the position and activity reports that came to us in high-speed code and put together a fifteen-minute television show. I was never sure what the purpose was since my only audience were the other members of the Task Force.

As a journalist, I'd had some experience with television. I knew from nothing about Morse code. To accomplish this part of the task, I was teamed with two Air Force "ditty boppers." That's what the military called Morse code specialists. Twice a day, these guys would sit at the control panel, don earphones, and listen to ten minutes of screaming code. At a pen-scorching pace, they wrote down everything they heard. After the capsule had winged its way out of range, they would compare notes. Often they disagreed, and they always argued—in Morse code.

"Dit-dah-dit," one would claim. Dah-dit-dah-dit," the other would counter, shaking his head. "Dah-ditty-dit-dah-dit," the first would reply.

It was geeky to the max. And it wasn't just official conversations that went like this either. These guys were so imbued in their trade they carried on routine conversations in code.

"Dit-dit-dah-ditty-dah-dah-dit?"

"Dah-dah-dit-dit."

They couldn't help it. They were trained that way. Once the military found out they were adept at code, they isolated them. The only people they saw day or night for umpteen weeks of training were other ditty boppers. They were actually penalized for uttering words instead of code.

"After a couple of months," one of them told me, "you're brain-dead, and code is the only thing you remember." "Ditty-dit-dah-dit," the other agreed with a nod.

Newport Revisited

Now I know what the old-timers in Key West mean when they say things "aren't the same." My wife and I spent last week in Newport, Rhode Island. It was there back in 1962 that I trudged through the US Naval Officer Candidate School.

OCs, as we were called back then, spent virtually every waking moment studying the complex subjects of naval engineering, seamanship, and navigation. If you didn't study, you didn't graduate, and that meant you didn't get those coveted gold bars to pin on your collar.

But on weekends, if we didn't have to stay on the base to walk off penalties incurred through infractions of navy rules, we sought solace from the drudgery in the streets of downtown Newport. One place in particular several of my buddies and I visited as often as possible was called Oyster Bay—a steamy hole-in-the-wall on Long Wharf.

Oyster Bay was owned and operated by a Greek family of lobster fishermen. Mama manned the kitchen, Papa handled the bar, and the sons, uncles, and cousins brought the boat in every day about noon loaded with live lobsters. The Grecos, as they were called, had a soft spot for OCs. They gave us special prices on rum and coke, clams on the half shell, and when it was dinnertime, they made us go across the wharf to pick out our own lobsters.

When the uncles saw us coming toward the boat, they would open a wooden lobster trap and dump a half-dozen infuriated crustaceans onto the wharf with the admonition, "Catch 'em quick." Then, as we scrambled to glom onto our lobsters without being scissored by one of those angry claws, they would howl with laughter.

Once we had our quarries in hand, we would deliver them to Mama, who dumped them into a steaming pot and then called to Papa to serve up another round of rum and coke. Then, giddy from rum and that strange spontaneous fellowship with strangers, we would sit at the table by the window and savor the most delicious seafood God ever created.

Later, after steaming cups of black coffee to counter the effects of the rum, we would pay the bill and head back to our textbooks. More than once the Grecos forgot to charge us for the lobsters. Papa always called a cab for us before we left. In those days Long Wharf was a seamy collection of waterfront dives that catered mostly to the hard-working, hard-drinking fishermen who were the backbone of the Newport fishing industry. Brawls were commonplace, and I don't remember a time when there wasn't at least one police car on the scene. I think Papa wanted us safe so we would be back the following week.

Naturally, I was eager to show my wife the area during our visit to Newport—from a safe distance, of course. Imagine my surprise to learn that it had all changed. Not only was Oyster Bay—and all the other waterfront bars—gone, so were the grimy and weathered lobster boats. The wharf itself had been paved in fashionable brick and lined with trendy shops and upscale restaurants. Bobbing in the water where the lobster boats once tied up were freshly painted tour boats. Even the smells of fish and seaweed were diminished by an overactive dedication to cleanliness.

All of this came naturally, of course, since, like Key West, Newport had relied heavily on the military to sustain its economy. When the military was severely downsized in the 1980s, both cities turned to tourism to make up their losses.

The good news is that many of the old waterfront buildings that were empty and decaying when I was an OC had been revitalized and turned into homes for shops, bed-and-breakfast inns, and museums dedicated to preserving the heritage of this remarkable area.

One such place is the International Yacht Restoration School, a hands-on institution dedicated to preserving old wooden boats. This includes the once-magnificent 190-foot schooner *Coronet*, currently being rebuilt from the keel up by students at the school.

The ferry that used to go across the bay to Jamestown is gone too, long ago replaced by a marvelous two-mile-long bridge. I still remember the thrill of riding the ferry in close quarters with a half-dozen twelve-meter yachts tuning up for the America's Cup race.

The America's Cup trophy, ensconced for more than 130 years at the New York Yacht Club in Newport, was finally wrested away by Australia in 1983. The year I was there as an OC, America won an unexciting race through the tepid efforts of a boat named *Waverly*.

Later, Newport became the staging area each fall for hundreds of offshore cruising sailors who annually spend the winter months in tropical waters.

Moreover, boat manufacturers show off their newest sailboats at Newport each year.

Of course, the incredible mansions of Newport remain a powerful attraction. It is astonishing to see the ghosts of opulence and decadence still flaunting their influence in the decorous halls of these mighty buildings. We took a bus tour, and our guide pointed out some of the excesses these super-rich Americans practiced. The wife of one, for example, spent several million dollars having a major chunk of a seaside bluff removed so she could see the water from her bedroom.

And so, Newport, like Key West, has been gentrified. Everything has a fresh coat of paint now, and the essence of how it used to be is hard to find. All in all, this is a good thing, though. For without change, places like Newport would have slipped into obscurity and decay.

Things aren't the same, but if you look hard enough, the past can still be found, including the rum-tainted ghosts of Oyster Bay.

Remembering Pearl Harbor

Pearl Harbor has been much on my mind lately. For one thing, December 7 fell on a Sunday this year (1997). I don't remember the last time that happened, and usually I've simply taken a moment from a normal weekday to offer a silent toast to those who were there when World War II started.

But this year it was Sunday, just as it was in 1941. There's a special kind of stillness that pervades Sundays that isn't present in other days. The wind is gentler and clocks seem to measure time with greater deliberation, as though they will be held accountable later for every tick and tock. That's how it was in 1941, and that's how it was this year.

December 7, 1941: Sunday dinner was over, the leftover pieces of chicken gathered for later appetites, and Mom had helped me lace up my boots so I could go outside and play with the dog in the thick blanket of new snow that had fallen the night before.

She may have called to me, but all I remember is suddenly looking up from my snowy environment and seeing my mother standing at the back step, the door open behind her. There was something about the way she looked, the way she stood there, that told me something had happened. I got up and shook off the snow and walked toward my mother. I remember the silence ringing in my ears.

Inside, Dad was huddled next to the radio. Newscaster Cedric Adams was saying that Pearl Harbor had been bombed and that America was at war. We listened and sat quietly for a long time. It was difficult to put it together, to figure out what it meant, and to know what would happen next. I remember crying in bed that night.

Fast-forward to the early 1960s. As a junior naval officer, I was assigned to the Fourteenth Naval District headquarters in Pearl Harbor. One of my responsibilities was boat tours to the USS *Arizona* Memorial.

We scheduled six tours in the mornings and six in the afternoon. The boats used for the tours were outfitted with a large map of Pearl Harbor. The crew of each boat was hand-picked and carefully trained. The tour was without frills, sobering.

The narrator explained the chronology of the Japanese attack, pointing out on the map where the different waves of planes came from. They described the weather—seventy degrees and sunny. The tour boat inched across the harbor, past Ford Island, where scars of the attack remain to this day, and then down battleship row, where each giant ship was tethered.

At the end of battleship row stands the USS *Arizona* Memorial. It is stark white and spans the width of the battleship it honors. The memorial does not touch the ship, and the ship has never been decommissioned. The flag flies every day from the *Arizona*'s sunken bridge.

At the end of the memorial, inscribed on the wall, is a roster of the men who died aboard the *Arizona* when a Japanese bomb touched off the ship's forward munitions magazine. The huge battleship sank in less than ten minutes. Nearly one thousand of those aboard remain entombed in the ruined ship's murky interior.

As I said, the tour boat crews were well trained. But every once in a while I'd go along on a tour just to make sure. When the tour ended at the memorial and everyone got back onto the boat to return to shore, there were invariably a few moist eyes.

Four years after Pearl Harbor this tragic war ended and the Japanese surrendered aboard another American battleship, the USS *Missouri*. Plans have recently been disclosed to move the *Missouri* from its current decommissioned port of Bremerton, Washington, to Pearl Harbor and park it next door to the USS *Arizona* Memorial.

There is a lot of controversy, of course. Opponents say the huge ship and its thousands of visitors each day would overshadow the somber atmosphere that has always been present at the memorial. Those in favor say it is a perfect addition, adding closure to the war next to its beginning.

It does make sense, of course. But it depends on how the *Missouri* is treated. If it is presented reverently as an extension of the memorial, it can help teach children the horrors of war for generations to come. I think the US Navy could make it happen. The US Park Service operates the memorial now, and they are among those expressing concern about the USS *Missouri* becoming little more than a boisterous tourist trap selling souvenir T-shirts on the quarterdeck.

It doesn't have to be that way. The two ships could work together in peacetime as they did in war. But for the *Arizona* and *Missouri* to continue the lesson that was taught in this place, there must be a moment for every visitor to be unexpectedly touched by the incredible silence that has remained here since that quiet Sunday years ago.

In 1998 the Missouri *was brought to Pearl Harbor, where she sits in harmony with the USS* Arizona Memorial. *By all accounts both memorials have maintained the air of dignity and respect due vessels so steeped in history.*

FINAL THOUGHTS

Since the inspiration for this book was born with the very first column I wrote for the Zionsville newspaper, it seems fitting that its conclusion might best be summed up by my final contribution, which appeared in the April 28, 2010, edition.

Your Columnist Bids Farewell

Over the past sixteen years, I have written over eight hundred columns under the heading "I Was Just Thinking." By conservative estimate that amounts to more than a million words—something shy of the complete works of Tolstoy, I believe.

I certainly cannot compare my writing to that of Tolstoy or any other literary great. But I can say in all honesty that each word I have written has come from the heart. Each week I have latched onto a thought or idea and struggled with it—sometimes for hours—to turn it into something that would amuse, enlighten, or convince.

Moreover, I have written my columns with you in mind. I have wanted to tell you what I really thought about things.

And I would like to believe that from time to time, in some small measure over the years, I have succeeded. I hope that some of you were able to travel back in time with me as I visited the dark ages of my youth and explore again the simple joys of growing up in a different time.

Do you remember old Miss Hansen, who always promised to take her ancient Essex out for a Sunday drive "one of these days" but never did? Did you share my absolute joy in blowing things up with firecrackers when I was twelve years old?

Perhaps some of you agonized with me over my own missteps and foibles as I stretched a three-month building program into one that took more than eight years: the never-to-be-completed addition to our house. Maybe you sympathized as I helplessly matched wits with a dog more headstrong than I.

I hope you enjoyed meeting the people I wrote about: some good, some bad, all unforgettable. I'd like to think that you shared my tears when I wrote about the tragic death of our granddaughter and the untimely loss of dear friends.

Did you get the whiff of salt air as I walked through the steamy streets of Key West? Did you feel the pathos that stabbed my heart as I watched the forlorn and forgotten homeless men and women of that town pitch their meager tents beneath the bridges?

What about the boatyard? Do you remember the man who lived in a derelict boat and put out bread and fresh water every morning for the seagulls? And how many columns did I write about the endless and seemingly impossible task of restoring our sailboat to seaworthy condition? I can still smell the rank and pungent odor of varnish. Can you?

I hope you got as big a laugh as I did when I discovered that it is not a good idea to turn a blender on without the lid. Permanent stains still mark the wall from that day.

There were a lot of days, times, and events in the space of sixteen years and eight hundred columns. It was my intent to share as many of them with you as I could.

While this is my final column for these pages, I have no plans to stop writing. I still have much to see, to feel, and to live, and I intend to put as much of it down on paper as God grants me wits to achieve.

So, until we find the means to connect once more, I simply say farewell, and thank you from the bottom of my heart.

THE END

Degler continues to write at warddegler.wordpress.com.
Visit his web page: www.warddegler.com
And see Facebook.com/ward.degler

CPSIA information can be obtained at www.ICGtesting.com
Printed in the USA
235939LV00002B/1/P